Street Names of Sheffield

Streets of Sheffield

First published in 2001

ISBN: 1 85048 025 7

191 Upper Allen Street, Sheffield S3 7GW

This book is dedicated with love to my wife, May Harvey, who lived with it being written for a long time and was an enormous help in getting it finished.

Marcus Walk, photographed from Neville Street in 1959

STREET NAMES OF SHEFFIELD

Exchange Street, looking towards Waingate, in the 1950s

Peter Harvey

Sheaf Publishing • Sheffield

Contents

Ecclesall Road in July 1953

Introduction

ONE Sheffield street is named – indirectly – after a Chippawa Indian chief; another is named after a Roman foot soldier; a third has the same name as the Italian goddess of fruit and gardens; a fourth gets its name from the Zulu word meaning hill of doves, and yet another is named after an English bowman at the Battle of Crecy. One of the best-known streets in the east end was named after a man who helped to organise the first Oxford and Cambridge boat race in 1829, and rowed in it, at stroke, for Oxford. A street at Hillsborough is named after a former England cricket captain. Nearby is a street that appears to have been named after a dog.

There are streets in the city named after a tree that was struck by lightning, a valley in Norway, a village in New York State, USA, and the mountain from which Moses viewed the promised land. Whatever else might be said of them, Sheffield street names do not lack variety.

The biggest single influence on them has been the Howard family, Dukes of Norfolk. The names of more than 300 Sheffield streets can be traced to the family in one way or another. Successive Dukes and their agents have plundered the Norfolk lineage for the names of streets built on land owned by the family in Sheffield. They have used their ranks (Duke, Duchess, Earl, Countess, etc), their titles (Norfolk, Arundel, Surrey, Fitzalan, Maltravers, Clun, etc), their own names (Howard, Bernard, Charles, etc.), their wives' names (Minna, Strutt, Herries), their sisters' names, their ancestors' names, the names of village and towns in Norfolk, Suffolk, Surrey, Shropshire and Scotland in which they had some interest, the names of their estates elsewhere in the country, and even, in one case, the name of a school that one of the Dukes attended. Looking through the Howard ancestry in one of the peerage reference books is like looking at a street map of Sheffield. Familiar names crop up every two or three lines.

Several Sheffield street names (Bannham, Roundel, Fellbrigg, Wreakin, for example) are wrongly spelt, and have been from the day they were first introduced, Others were deliberately simplified. Botsford, for example, is a simplified version of Bottesford. Babur seems to be an easier-to-cope with form of Babergh.

Several streets were named after men who were upright, respectable businessmen at the time, but later in life strayed off the straight and narrow. One disappeared owing quite a large sum of money. The street names were kept, perhaps because it was too much bother to change them. In recent years the City Council has had a rule that streets must not be named after anyone who is still alive. This reduces the risk of honouring someone who turns out to be a rogue in later years.

Nearly 500 Sheffield streets have had more than one name. Some have had three different names. Some were changed because their names were cumbersome. They had prefixes like Lower, Upper, North, South, East or West. But in most cases renaming was necessary because names were duplicated.

At various times, for example, there were six different High Streets in the city, six Chapel Streets, ten Back Lanes, four Duke Streets, eight School Lanes, six Victoria Roads, four Wilson Roads, five Carr Lanes, and three Thomas Streets, all three of them in the same postal district. This state of affairs came about partly because Sheffield grew from the amalgamation of six separate townships, and as it grew absorbed several villages. The townships and villages often had their own High Street, Chapel Street, School Lane – names that already existed in the town centre. It was also partly due to the haphazard way in which streets were named before street naming became a local authority responsibility.

The Town Council did not take control of streets until September 1864. Before that, several separate and independent highways boards were responsible for the town's streets. Three years later, in December 1867. the council authorised the Chief Constable 'to number the houses and name the streets in the borough'. Most streets were already named, of course, but the council resolution dumped the job of sorting out all the duplication, and naming all new streets, in the lap of the Chief Constable. Although the council set up an Improvement and Highways Committee for the first time in 1864 (and appointed a Borough Surveyor at the same time), street naming continued to be a Watch Committee responsibility up to 1st April 1924, when it passed to the Highways Committee.

There were four large bouts of renaming: in 1872, when more than fifty streets were given new names, 1886 (more than seventy new names), 1903 (about seventy), and 1923 (more than seventy). It is impossible to be exact about totals because it is clear from examining council minutes that some changes were approved but did not take place.

The Town Council, later the City Council, has often been bitterly criticised by newspaper writers and local historians for being too ready to change names 'in the cause of so-called progress'. In fact, the opposite is true. On many occasions the council resisted change until it became unavoidable. In the late 1860s, for example, the council was under pressure to make changes – from local shops, the fire brigade, and the postal authorities, all of whom had suffered inconvenience and extra work because of duplicated street names. And yet it took the best part of ten years before changes were made. Council reluctance is easy to understand. People do not like having their own particular street name changed. Regardless of whether or not they like the name, they are used to it. They want to keep it. Changes always produce resentment.

In an effort to stifle discontent, the council deliberately tried to make the changes as slight as possible. One Chapel Street was renamed Capel Street, another Chatham Street, and a third, Chapman Street. One Green Street was renamed Greenhow Street, another Greenock Street. A High Street became Highton Street, Plum Street became Plumpton Street, Rose Street became Roselle Street, and so on. Wherever possible the first two, three, or four letters of the old name were retained in the new one. Although this probably worked in reducing local

Seen here in the days of horse trams, Montgomery Road, Nether Edge, was named after the poet, journalist and hymn writer, James Montgomery.

The corner of London Road and Boston Street as it was just before the Lansdowne Cinema was built. Boston Street was originally called George Street.

resentment, it tended to produce names which no longer had any local meaning.

Another aspect of the four large renaming programmes was that the person or people landed with the job evidently had some trouble thinking up so many new names at once. Council policy has always been to favour names that have some significance to the area in which streets are built. Even with the normal flow of a few new streets every month this can be difficult, but with seventy new names to be conjured up all at once, it would have taken weeks, perhaps months, of research to think up locally relevant names. There is an easier way of doing it: to look through a gazetteer of Britain and pick out names of places that have not already been used for local street names. This is what seems to have been done. Of the seventy or so new names in 1886, more than fifty were the names of places elsewhere in Britain. Convenient as this might have been for the person responsible for thinking up the new names, once again it produced names without any local meaning.

There is another quick and easy way to name streets: to name them in groups with a common theme, trees for example, flowers, poets. artists, or places in the Lake District. All cities do this. A group of streets in Leicester is named after varieties of nuts, the best known of which is Filbert Street, site of Leicester City FC's ground. A group of streets at Nottingham is named after members of England's successful 1966 World Cup football team. Sheffield has groups named after flowers, forests, dales, vales, trees, battles, places in the Lake District, and even, in one case, famous Rugby football grounds. Where the theme formula is used there is sometimes a reason for the choice of theme, but more often than not the choice is random and again, has no local significance.

There does not have to be a meaning or story behind a street name, of course. The only absolute requirement is that it should identify the street, ie, it should be different from all the other street names in the same locality. It does not even have to be a name. In 1949 there was a suggestion that the City Council should adopt the United States system and start numbering streets rather than naming them. The proposal was rejected. If it had been approved, Sheffield might by now have had its Fifth Avenue or 42nd Street.

The majority of people like their street names to have a story behind them. Most Sheffield street names do have a story, but finding it is not always easy. Nobody has ever kept a list of why streets were given their names. Council minutes list new names from the 1860s up to modern times, but looking through more than 120 years of council minutes I did not find a single case where the thinking behind the name was explained. What usually happens is that the name is explained by the person who has researched it when it comes before a council sub-committee for approval. It may be explained again when it goes to full committee. But the explanation is never given in the council's printed minutes.

The explanations in this book were arrived at mostly by guesswork and deduction. But the guesses were made only after a great deal of research into who owned the land on which a street was built, who built it, when it was built, what the field on which it was built was called, if it was built by a firm, who the directors of the firm were, if it was built by a land society, who the officials of the society were, family trees of owners and builders, historical associations, and so on. Many of the explanations were first published as part of a long-running daily newspaper series called What's in a name?

The series started in the *Morning Telegraph* in 1980 and continued till the *Telegraph* closed in 1985, when it transferred to *The Star* where it ran till 1989. The research, therefore, took the best part of ten years. It involved examining maps, field books, documents, obituaries, local histories, family histories, old newspapers, council minutes (Sheffield and others, because some of the present Sheffield streets were originally in neighbouring areas, such as Rotherham, Chesterfield and Wortley rural districts, and were named by them); it involved writing to firms and libraries in other parts of the country, acquiring documents relating to the formation of local property companies and tramping round graveyards. To help in tracing some of the people who were involved in building and naming streets I took a sabbatical in 1984 and compiled a list of people whose obituaries appeared in local newspapers between 1850 and 1975.

Some of the paragraphs that appeared in the What's in a Name? series have been expanded for this book to give fuller information; others have been corrected in the light of later information; where appropriate, cross references have been added. I have deliberately limited the scope of the book to streets that were within the city boundary in 1974, before widespread local government reorganisation. In other words, Mosborough is included, Ecclesfield, Bradfield, Oughtibridge and Stocksbridge are not. This keeps it more manageable. In addition to which, street names in the areas added to Sheffield in 1974 are rooted in a local history which had little or nothing to do with the city. The same is true of some of the streets in the Beighton-Mosborough area, but by now they are outnumbered by the new streets built since that area was absorbed, and named by Sheffield City Council.

One curiosity occurs in the street names of Frecheville, which was part of the Mosborough boundary extension. In the years before Sheffield took it over many of the Frecheville streets were named after places in Derbyshire. This was mainly because the streets were built by Charles Boot (who thought up the name Frecheville), and many of them were named after places near his home, Thornbridge Hall, Great Longstone. However, even in those days Sheffield had its eyes on Frecheville for a possible take-over, and giving the streets Peak District names did tend to emphasise the fact that they were in Derbyshire. Since Sheffield took them over it is noticeable that some of the new streets have been named after places in Yorkshire.

Not all streets are called streets. Some are avenues, closes, crescents and so on. I have listed at the back of this book all the different alternatives that have been used in Sheffield. In some cases one name has been applied to a large group of streets. There are ten streets with the name Binsted, for example, ten more with the name Jaunty and ten called Firshill. This can result in confusion, and the City Council now tries to avoid giving the same name to any more than four or five streets.

In the course of researching existing street names I came across several names that were approved but not used, either because the streets were not built, or because somebody changed his mind about the name. Among them were Luanard Road, Co-operative Street, Kangaroo Street, Great Central Street, Oddment Place, Rigma Hill, Volksrust Road, Betsy Street and Dingle Road. In the 1920s there was a suggestion that a street off Ridgeway Road should be named Plimsoll Crescent, to mark Sir Samuel Plimsoll's links with Sheffield but it remained no more than a suggestion.

Some Sheffield street names are ancient, or are taken from ancient place names. Where this is the case I have relied mainly on explanations given in the relevant volumes of the English Place-Name Society's series, *The Place-Names of the West Riding of Yorkshire* and *The Place-Names of Derbyshire*. Where other, varying explanations have been published I have tried to quote them. A fact that emerges from some of these old names is that modern pronunciations of some place names that are thought to be slang, or mis-pronunciation, are sometimes surprisingly near to the ancient spelling, and presumably, to the ancient pronunciation. Greenhill, for instance, used to be spelt Grenill, which is exactly how locals sometimes pronounce it today. Stannington was spelt Stanyton in the fourteenth century and it is still sometimes pronounced that way today. Shirecliffe can be still heard as *Shercliff*, the way it was spelt 400 years ago.

There are bound to be mistakes in this book, or explanations with which people disagree. This is inevitable. There is, as I explained earlier, no convenient, authoritative source of street name explanations. I have tried to compile one. But at least two-thirds of the explanations given here are deductions, and I confidently expect that I have deduced wrongly in places. I can only hope that the errors are few.

My thanks to the staff of Sheffield Central Library Local History Department for tolerating me and helping on many occasions; to Derbyshire Library Services, Hillingdon Borough Libraries, Wakefield District Council Libraries, Cumbria County Library, Northamptonshire County Libraries, Bedfordshire County Record Office, the Public Record Office at Kew, Mike Haverty of Sheffield Highways Department, George Parkes, formerly of Sheffield Highways Department, J.H. Duffield, of Millom, Cumbria and many individuals who have given me information or advice; to R.J. Wiseman for use of photographs, and to various editors of *The Star* and the *Morning Telegraph*, for allowing me to reproduce material first published in their newspapers.

Peter Harvey
October 2001

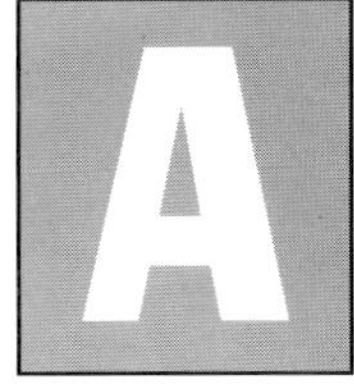

Abbey Brook Close, Court, Drive, Gardens, 8

were built on a site bounded on one side by a stream called the Abbey Brook.

Abbey Crescent, Croft, Grange, 7

side streets off Abbey Lane, from which they were named.

Abbeydale Park Crescent, Rise, 17

from a house built in 1860, first called Abbeydale Villa, then Abbeydale Park. It was the home of John Roberts, silversmith and benefactor (he paid for the building of St John's Church, Abbeydale). Later his business partner (and former apprentice), Ebenezer Hall, lived in the house. Mr Hall died in 1911.

Abbeydale Road, 7

runs along the dale in which Beauchief Abbey was built. The road used to be longer than it is now. In 1894, to avoid the possibility of house numbers on the road going over 1,000 (they were already in the 900s), the stretch from Millhouses post office to Totley Brook was renamed Abbeydale Road South.

Abbeydale Road South, 7 and 17

see Abbeydale Road.

Abbeyfield Road, 4

from the house, first called Pitsmoor Abbey (although it had no apparent religious significance), later called Abbeyfield, built in the 1790s by William Pass, coal owner, and later the home for many years of Bernard Wake, well-known solicitor. The house was bought by the Corporation in 1909 and for a time was an annexe to Firth Park Grammar School. The grounds became Abbeyfield Park.

Abbey Lane, 7, 8 and 11

from Beauchief Abbey, founded about 1176 by Robert Fitz-Ranulph. Sir William Dugdale, the seventeenth century scholar and antiquarian, said Fitz-Ranulph was one of the four knights who murdered Thomas à Beckett, Archbishop of Canterbury, and that he founded Beauchief as an act of expiation for his part in the crime. Later historians have insisted that Fitz-Ranulph had nothing to do with the murder. Innocent or guilty, Fitz-Ranulph certainly dedicated the abbey to St Thomas the Martyr. It was dissolved about 1536 and a smaller chapel was built on the site in 1670.

Abbey View Drive, Road, 8

sites look across to Beauchief Abbey.

Aberdeen Lane, Street, 3

after George Hamilton Gordon, Earl of Aberdeen, who was Foreign Minister from 1828 to 1830 and again from 1841 to 1846, and Prime Minister from 1852 to 1855. He died in 1860. Aberdeen Street was demolished in the redevelopment of Broomhall area.

Abinger Street, 9

probably from the village of Abinger Hammer, near Dorking, Surrey.

Abney Close, Drive, Road, 14

from an old house on Gleadless Road called Abney House, probably named after the hamlet of Abney, two miles from Hathersage.

Abbeyfield House, Pitsmoor, with its famous old sundial clearly visible on the frontage. See Abbeyfield Road.

Abney Street, 1

was originally called West John Street. It was changed in 1890 as part of a programme to lose cumbersome names which had the prefixes north, south, east and west. The new name was from the Peak District hamlet of Abney.

Acacia Road, 5

one of a group of streets named after flowers and shrubs, and referred to as the Flowers Estate (along with Bluebell, Clematis, Cowslip, Daffodil, Foxglove, Heather, Honeysuckle, Hyacinth, Jessamine, Lilac and Primrose). The first batch of names was approved in December 1904. Two names approved, but not used, were Anemone and Harebell.

Ackworth Drive, 9

from a link with Earl Fitzwilliam who was lord of the manor of Tinsley and a substantial landowner there. One of the Earl's ancestors, the second Marquis of Rockingham, married a daughter of the Bright family and inherited the Brights' Badsworth estate in West Yorkshire. The villages of High Ackworth and Low Ackworth were part of the estate.

Acorn Drive, Hill, Way, 6

Acorn Hill is mentioned as a location in a document dated 1777. Acorn Drive and Way were named much later. The name simply indicates that there were oak trees in the area.

Acorn Street, 3

from the old *Acorn Inn*, now demolished, at 288-292, Shalesmoor. The lease of the inn dated back to July 1819 when the area around it was open land. From the 1860s to the 1890s it was kept by the Thompson family, notably Charles Thompson.

Acres Hill Lane, Road, 9

from an old field name. Acres Hill was a three and a half-acre field belonging to the poor of Darnall. It is mentioned in Harrison's survey of 1637.

Acton Place, 6

after Lord Acton (1834-1902) historian and Liberal MP who received his peerage around the time that the street was built in the early 1870s.

Adastral Avenue, 12

was built close to RAF Norton and took its name from the Royal Air Force motto *Per Ardua Ad Astra* meaning 'Through Difficulties to the Stars'. The RAF station closed in January 1965.

Addison Road, 5
uncertain. Possibly something to do with Christopher Addison, former resident surgeon at the Royal Hospital, Sheffield, who went into politics, became resident of the Local Government Board, and in 1919, the country's first Minister of Health. He was made a Baron in 1937, a Viscount in 1945.

Addy Close, Drive, Street, 6
Addy Street was built first, and was originally called Addey Street. It was built on land owned by two brothers, members of the Addey family of Cudworth, who came to Sheffield in the late eighteenth century, set up in business as tanners and did rather well for themselves. It remained Addey Street until April 1915 when the Watch Committee decided for some unknown reason that it should be changed to Addy Street.

Adelaide Road, 7
probably after Queen Adelaide, wife of King William IV. She was born in 1792, married William in 1818, when he was Duke of Clarence, and was Queen – although not a popular one – for seven years. She died in 1849.

Adelphi Street, 6
was first called Queen Street. It was changed in 1872 to avoid confusion with Queen Street in the town centre. The new name seems to have been purely fanciful. The Adelphi district of London, developed by the Adam brothers, was named from the Greek word *adelphos*, meaning brother. The area became very fashionable and so did the name. It was used for streets, theatres, public houses and cinemas all over the country.

Adkins Drive, Road, 5
not known; approved February 1937.

Adlington Crescent, Road, 5
after William Adlington, Elizabethan scholar best remembered for his translation of *The Golden Ass of Apuleius*, published in 1566.

Adrian Crescent, 5
not known; name approved March 1938. Adrian was the name of the only Englishman ever to have been Pope – Adrian IV. It may have been named in honour of him.

Adsetts Street, 4
was built in the 1860s by Sheffield and Grimesthorpe Freehold Land Society and named after the society's president, George Adsetts, who lived at that time at Brightside and was a land agent with offices in Change Alley. He was also a director of the Borough Benefit Building Society.

Agden Road, 7
probably from the area of Loxley Valley called Agden, site of one of Sheffield's reservoirs.

Ainsley Road, 10
after William Ainsley who was given planning permission to build 22 houses in the new road in 1899. Mr Ainsley, who lived in Burgoyne Road, and later in Whitehouse Lane, was a building inspector.

Ainsty Road, 7
from the area of land near York called The Ainsty which includes twenty villages between the Ouse, the Wharf and the Nidd. It was acquired by York Corporation by royal grant in the thirteenth century and held by the city up to 1836. A local hunt was called the York and Ainsty.

Airedale Road, 6
was first called Argyle Road. It was changed in 1904 when the Wadsley area came into Sheffield (where there was another Argyle Road). There was no particular reason for the new name. Airedale, the valley through which the River Aire flows, stretches from Malham Cove to Leeds.

Aisthorpe Road, 8
from the village of Aisthorpe, six miles north of Lincoln; one of a small group of Woodseats streets named after places in Lincolnshire (along with Broxholme, Hackthorne and Nettleham).

Aizlewood Road, 8
was part of a development carried out by Sheffield Brick Company who had kilns nearby and owned a large area of land off Abbeydale Road. It was named after the chairman of the company, Councillor John Aizlewood. Nearby streets were also named after people connected with the brick company (see Corrie, Dalton, Hale, Holdsworth, Marples, Sellers and Storm).

Akley Bank Close, 17
Akley Bank and Akley Wood were recorded at Totley in the sixteenth century. The name comes from the old English word *ac*, meaning oak. Akley means oak field.

Albanus Croft, Ridge, 6
Albanus was a foot soldier who served in Britain during the Roman occupation but he was not a Roman. He belonged to the Sunuci tribe. His name is mentioned on a copper military diploma dated AD 124 which was discovered by a ploughman at Stannington in 1761. The diploma records that Emperor Hadrian had granted the honour of Roman citizenship to the son of Albanus.

Albany Road, 7
most Albany Roads, Streets etc are named after Queen Victoria's son, Leopold, who was created Duke of Albany in 1881 (Albany being the old name for the part of Scotland north of the Forth and the Clyde). But this road was built much earlier, in 1867. It may be named after Albany, the state capital of New York, USA. George Wostenholm, on whose land it was built, had a great admiration for the state, visited it several times and named his Sheffield home Kenwood, after a village on Oneida Lake, NY.

Albert Road, 8
after Prince Albert (1819-1861), husband of Queen Victoria and Prince Consort, who died of typhoid fever. The Albert Medal, the Albert Hall, and Albert Roads and Streets throughout the country were named after him.

Albert Road, 12
uncertain; possibly also after Prince Albert, as above.

Albert Terrace Road, 6
after Prince Albert, as above. The road was built in 1851 on land belonging to the Royal Infirmary and let by the Infirmary at threepence or fourpence per square yard.

Albion Row, Street, 6
Albion was a very popular patriotic street name in the nineteenth century. There were seventeen different Albion Streets in London at one time. It is an old name for Britain. One story is that it was a name bestowed by the Romans when they saw the white cliffs of Dover, *albus* being the Latin word for white.

Alcester Road, 7
after the Warwickshire market town of Alcester, fifteen miles from Warwick.

Aldam Close, Croft, Road, Way, 17
after William Aldam Milner, magistrate and landowner, who lived at Totley Hall up to his death in the 1930s. Aldam Road was built first. It could not be called Milner Road because there was already a Milner Road at Attercliffe named many years earlier after a member of the same family.

Aldene Avenue, Glade, Road, 6
after Aldene, one of the Saxon landowners who held several manors around Ecclesfield including Onesacre and Ughill. Under William the Conqueror, Aldene's lands passed to Roger de Busli, lord of the manor of Hallam.

Alder Lane, 9
one of a group of streets named after trees (along with Chestnut, Larch, Maple and Willow) forming the Triangle Estate. The co-developer of the estate in the 1930s lived at a farm near Huddersfield called Triangle Farm.

Alderney Road, 2
one of four streets built in 1877 for Sheffield and South Yorkshire Building Society and all named after Channel Islands (along with Guernsey, Jersey and Sark).

Alders Green, 6
not known; presumably there were alder trees in the area.

Alderson Place, Road; Alderson Road North, 2
from the Alderson family who owned property in the Highfield area in the nineteenth century. The house called Highfield was inherited in the 1830s by the Rev Jonathan Alderson, Rector of Harthill, and his wife, but they never lived in it. They also owned Highfield Terrace. The property stayed in the family until 1879 when it was sold.

Aldfield Way, 5
from a field name. Ald means old – old field.

Aldine Court, 1
appropriately, for a site where printing has gone on for more than 150 years, Aldine comes from the name of a famous printer, Aldus Manutius (1450-1515), who started a printing press in Venice, was the inventor of italic type, and issued a set of books known as the Aldine editions. Originally called Trippet's Yard (the family owned property in it). the court was renamed by Joseph Pearce, printer, bookseller and founder of the *Sheffield Daily Telegraph*. His father, also called Joseph, lived in a house called Aldine Cottage, in Victoria Road (see also Caxton).

Aldred Road, 10
after Dr John C. Aldred, medical officer and public vaccinator for Nether Hallam district in the 1880s. The road was named around the time he retired in 1887.

Alexandra Road, 2
after Queen Alexandra (1844-1925), wife of King Edward VII. She was born in Copenhagen and the day she landed in England – June 26th – became known as Alexandra Day on which flowers were sold in aid of hospitals.

Alfred Road, 9
was built in the 1860s for Henry Wilson of the well-known snuff manufacturing family. Mr Wilson, a Church Burgess and philanthropist, died in 1880. He named the road after his son, Alfred Wilson who, like his father, was a generous benefactor. Alfred Wilson died in 1890 at the age of 51.

Algar Close, Crescent, Drive, Place, Road, 2
were built on the Duke of Norfolk's land and named after Sir Algar Henry Stafford Howard, of Thornbury Castle, Gloucestershire, nephew of the twelfth Duke. Sir Algar held office in the College of Arms for many years.

Alison Crescent, 2
not known; the name was approved in May 1924.

Allenby Drive, 8
after Field Marshal Sir Edmund Allenby, first Viscount Allenby, distinguished soldier and High Commissioner for Egypt from 1919 to 1925. The drive was named four weeks after his death in May 1936.

Allende Way, 9
after Dr Salvador Allende, former president of Chile, who was assassinated. The name was suggested by members of the Chilean community in Sheffield and the street was officially named in September 1982.

Allen Road, 19
not known.

Allen Street, 3
was first called Allen's Lane, from Allen's Farm which stood nearby in the early nineteenth century. What was believed to be the old farm well was discovered during building work in 1937. The farm, near the end of what later became Radford Street, was named after a former owner.

Allerton Road, 9
from the hamlet of Allerton Mauleverer, near Boroughbridge (see Staniforth Road).

Alliance Street, 4
not known.

Alma Street, 3
from the Battle of Alma, fought between the British and French on one side and the Russians on the other, near the River Alma in the Crimea in 1854. After heavy fighting the allies finally took the heights above the river and the Russians withdrew.

Alms Hill Crescent, Drive, Glade, Road, 11
some accounts say that it ought to be Holms Hill, from the old word meaning marshy land, but in fact there was an alms house nearby. It is shown on the 1778 enclosures map.

Alney Place, 6
was first called Carr Place (from Birley Carr). It was renamed in 1924 after Alney Island, Gloucestershire. Welney Place (previously Ward Place) was renamed at the same time.

Alnwick Drive, Road, 12
Alnwick Road was built in the 1870s by Hollinsend Freehold Land Society and was originally called Albert Road. To avoid confusion with Albert Road, Heeley, it was renamed in 1924 after Alnwick, the Northumberland market town. Alnwick drive was built later.

Alpine Road, 6
from its steepness. There was another Alpine Road (also steep) at Heeley (see Skelton Road).

Alport Avenue, Drive, Grove, Place, Road, 12

from the village and dale called Alport, near Youlgreave, Derbyshire; one of a group of Frecheville streets with Derbyshire names.

Alsing Road, 9

after Gustave Valentine Alsing, who masterminded the building of the nearby Blackburn Meadows sewage works. He came to Sheffield in 1883, designed the works, superintended the building, and stayed on as engineer to the Sewerage and Rivers Department. He resigned in 1891 and went to Glasgow to build a large new works there.

Alsop Lane, 1

from Alsop Farm which is mentioned in Harrison's survey of 1637. The land attached to the farm stretched from what is now The Moor to the River Sheaf. It was built on by the Duke of Norfolk in the early 1800s.

Alton Close, 11

from Alton Towers, former home of the Earl of Shrewsbury; one of a group of streets named after stately homes (along with Harewood, Holkham, Petworth, Wentworth and Woburn).

Amberley Road, Street, 9

probably from the village of Amberley, Sussex, four miles north of the Duke of Norfolk's family seat at Arundel. The 15th Duke owned Amberley.

Ambleside Close, 19

from the place called Ambleside, near Windermere; one of a group of streets named after locations in the Lake District (along with Borrowdale, Ennerdale, Ullswater and Wasdale).

Amos Road, 9

probably after Amos Moss who was involved in several freehold land and building societies in the mid-19th century. He was a law clerk and lived at Sheaf Gardens.

Andover Drive, Street, 3

were built on the Duke of Norfolk's land and named from a title held by the Duke's family. The fourth Duke's son, Lord Thomas Howard, Earl of Suffolk, was created Viscount Andover in 1622.

Andrew Lane, Street, 3

Andrew Street was originally known as Andrews Street and was named after a former tenant of the land, John Champion Andrews. He is shown on a 1790 Fairbank map as tenant of a plot on what was then the Duke of Norfolk's nursery gardens.

Angel Street in the 1930s. Many of the buildings seen here were destroyed or badly damaged in the blitz of 1940.

Andwell Lane, 10

formerly called Andrew Lane after a local resident, Philip Andrew, of Green House Farm. It was changed to avoid confusion with Andrew Lane, 3. The new name was an effort to change the old one as little as possible.

Angel Street, 3

from the *Angel Inn* which was for many years one of the town's foremost inns. There is a reference to it in the Burgery accounts for January 1682. In its heyday it was an important coaching inn. In the early twentieth century it became a temperance house, and it remained until the Second World War when it was completely destroyed by enemy bombing.

Angerford Avenue, 8

is a mystery. It was approved in 1908 with two other new streets, Paythorne Avenue and Winterburn Avenue. Paythorne and Winterburn are both villages in Ribblesdale. If the theme applied to all three names, Angerford ought to be a village in Ribblesdale as well, but if it is I can't find it.

Paythorne Avenue became part of Warminster Road in 1935, and Winterburn Avenue seems not to have been built.

Angus Square, Terrace, 11

after Joseph Angus, of Washington Road, who was well-known as a Wesleyan preacher for 50 years. He and his son, Joseph junior, owned property in the area, including twenty houses on the north side of the square and ten on the south. Mr Angus died in 1873. His son died in 1878.

Anlaby Street, 6

from the place called Anlaby, four miles west of Hull; one of a group of five streets all named after places in Yorkshire and – as an added novelty – laid out alphabetically (along with Brough, Cottam, Driffield and Eden).

Annesley Close, Road, 8

after a member of the Strelley family of Beauchief, lords of the manor of Ecclesall. Strelley Pegge married Elizabeth Annesley, of Ballyshannon, in the seventeenth century. The name cropped up again in the nineteenth century with another member of the family, Edward Annesley Pegge-Burnell.

Ann's Road, Ann's Road North, 2

from the name of an old well in the area. It was common practice to name wells after saints, especially St Ann. (Rotherham, Buxton and Nottingham all had a St Ann's Well). Nearby Well Road and Wellhead Road were named from the same source.

Ansell Road, 11
not known; approved, April 1926.

Anson Street, 2
probably after William Anson, builder and bricklayer in Duke Street around 1900.

Antrim Avenue, 10
was built in 1908 and originally called Richmond Avenue, from two houses in nearby Park Lane called Richmond Villas. It was renamed in 1905 and there seems to have been no strong local reason for the new name. Antrim is a town and a county in Northern Ireland.

Anvil Close, 6
was built near the site of an old blacksmith's shop.

Applegarth Close, Drive, 12
after a pioneer Sheffield trade unionist, Robert Applegarth, secretary of the Carpenters' and Joiners' Union, and member of the executive of the Association of Organised Trades of Sheffield and Neighbourhood when it was first formed in 1859. The association later became Sheffield Trades Council.

Apple Street, 3
came about through a crafty bit of renaming. It was originally called Orchard Street, because there was an orchard nearby. In the 1870s, when there were four different Orchard Streets in Sheffield, three were renamed, this one by word association.

Arbourthorne Road, 2
Harrison's survey of Sheffield, made in 1637, mentions an area called Arbor Thorne Hurst, within Sheffield Park. It means bower, or shelter, formed by trees.

Archdale Place, Road, 2
from an old Eckington field name, Archdale Croft, recorded in a document of 1717; one of many Manor estate streets with names taken from the history of Eckington area.

Archer Gate, 6
not known.

Archer Lane, 7
from an old farm called Archer House, once owned by the Younge family, and thought to have been named after a former owner. Mary Walton says in her *History of the Parish of St Peter, Abbeydale,* that there was an Archer family living in the area in the early seventeenth century. The farm was demolished to make way for the building of Edgedale Road.

Archer Lane, from Brincliffe Edge, as it was around 1905. The fields in the background are now covered with housing.

Archer Road, 8
from an old field name, Archer Field, recorded in the sixteenth century and still in use as a field name on a Fairbank map of 1828. Up to 1906, the stretch from Abbeydale Road to Millhouses railway station was known as Station Road.

Archibald Road, 7
uncertain; the road was built on what used to be part of the Sheldon family's land at Nether Edge. It may have been named after George Archibald Wilson, architect, who was one of the beneficiaries of the Sheldon estate, just as Sandford Grove Road was named after another beneficiary, solicitor Henry Barlow Sandford.

Ardmore Street, 9
was built by the Shirland Freehold Land Society in 1867 and was originally called Bates Street, after a man who was involved with the society. It was renamed in 1872 from a place called Ardmore in Scotland, although which one is not certain. There are three Ardmores in Scotland.

Ardsley Close, Drive, Grove, 19
from the district of Ardsley, three miles east of Barnsley town centre.

Argyle Close, Road, 8
seems to be an Anglicised version of Argyll; one of several Heeley streets named after members of the Royal Family. John Douglas Sutherland Campbell, ninth Duke of Argyll, Governor General of Canada from 1878 to 1883, married Princess Louise, daughter of Queen Victoria.

Arkle Road, 9
from a Yorkshire river, the Arkle Beck, which runs through Arkengarthdale and joins the River Swale near Reeth, west of Richmond (see Staniforth Road).

Arley Street, 2
was originally called Cross George Street. It was changed in 1890. There seems to have been no special reason for the new name. There are two places

called Arley, one in Cheshire, the other in Warwickshire.

Armley Road, 9
was first called Albert Road. It was renamed in 1886 and there was no local reason for the name Armley, a district of Leeds best known for its prison.

Arms Park Drive, 19
from Cardiff Arms Park, the well-known rugby stadium; one of a group of streets built by William Drabble and Sons Ltd – a strong rugby family – all named with a rugby theme (along with Auckland, Dunedin, Murrayfield, Stonegravels and Twickenham).

Armstead Road, 19
was built in the 1870s by the Provident Freehold Land Society and named after the society's guarantor, John Armstead, stock and share broker in Paradise Square, Sheffield. There was also an Armstead Road at Attercliffe named after him. Mr Armstead was involved in a number of freehold land societies but in the 1880s ran into financial difficulties.

Armthorpe Road, 11
from Armthorpe, a suburb of Doncaster.

Arnold Avenue, 12
not known.

Arnold Street, 6
was originally called Primrose Hill. It was changed in 1886 and renamed after the Arnold district of Nottingham.

Arnside Road, Terrace, 8
from the small town of Arnside which overlooks the Morecambe Bay; two of a group of streets built in 1897 on land owned by John Firth, all named from locations in the Lake District (along with Buttermere, Crummock, Coniston, Grasmere, Keswick, Langdale, Rydal, Thirlmere, Troutbeck and Windermere).

Arran Road, 10
from the Isle of Arran, Scotland; one of a group of Crookes streets given Scottish names (along with Bute, Elgin, Forres, Nairn and Roslin).

Arras Street, 9
was originally called Berlin Street. It was changed during the First World War at a time when German names were very unpopular. The new name, Arras, is from the French city which was the site of a major battle in 1917.

Arthington Street, 8
was built on land attached to the old Meersbrook Tannery Co Ltd, and named after Robert Arthington whose trustees gave the tannery company a £10,000 mortgage in 1903. It was not a good investment. The tannery went bankrupt in 1908.

Artisan Place, View, 8
in the mid-nineteenth century great store was set by the freehold land societies on building small houses for artisans, or skilled workers, to buy. In 1848 the *Sheffield and Rotherham Independent* said of one land society: 'By this means, in a few years, we might see the most sober and industrious of our artisans put themselves in the possession of the freehold franchise', referring to the fact that at that time only freeholders could vote at elections.

Arundel Gate, Lane, Street, 1
from the family seat of the Duke of Norfolk, Arundel Castle, Sussex, which was first built in the tenth century, was destroyed in the English Civil War, and restored in the eighteenth century as a baronial style residence surrounded by about 1,000 acres of land.

Ascot Street, 2
was first called Union Street. To avoid confusion with the much grander Union Street in the town centre, it was renamed in 1886 after the famous horse racing centre in Berkshire. The new name had some local relevance. The street was on the Duke of Norfolk's land and the Duke was the monarch's representative at Ascot.

Ashberry Gardens, Road 6
after Philip Ashberry, founder of an electro-plate and Britannia metal works in Bowling Green Street and former town councillor for St Philip's ward. Mr Ashberry lived in Springvale Road. He died in 1881. Property in Ashberry Road (no longer listed), Horam, Chatwin and Bannon Streets was built by his executors after his death.

Ashbourne Grove, Road, 13
from the Derbyshire town of Ashbourne; one of a group of streets given Derbyshire names.

Ashbury Drive, 8
after Joseph Ashbury, sometimes spelt Ashberry, who lived at Hemsworth-Backmoor. He died in 1810.

Ashdell; Ashdell Lane, Road, 10
from the house called Ashdell, sometimes called Ashdell Grange, which was built in the early 1800s and stood in about 7,000 square yards of land, part of which, according to an 1864 auction advertisement, was 'a dell laid out under the personal superintendence of Sir Joseph Paxton, planted with the rarest shrubs and trees'.

Ashdown Gardens, 19
from the Ashdown Forest, East Sussex, once thickly wooded, now mainly heath; one of a group of streets named after British forests (along with Charnwood, Delamere, Epping, Grizedale, Pembrey, Radnor, Stainmore and Waltham).

Asher Road, 7
not known; built in the 1890s.

Ashfield Close, Drive, 12
probably from an old field name. A house nearby called Ashleigh (leigh, ley and lee are all old words for field) was the home of George Holmes in the early 1900s.

Ashford Road, 11
was originally called Clifford Road. It was changed in 1886 because there was another Clifford Road not far away. There seems to have been no strong local reason for the new name. Ashford is a village in the Peak District.

Ashfurlong Close, Drive, Road, 17
from an old field name. Fields called Great Ashfurlong and Little Ashfurlong are mentioned in the 1809 Dore Enclosure awards.

Ashgate Close, Lane, Road, 10
a variation on the ash theme adopted in so many house names in the Broomhill area, among them Ashdell, Ash Mount, Ashcroft, Ash Grove and Ash Rise. There must have been lots of ash trees in the area.

Ash Grove, 10
from the house called Ash Grove built in 1869 by George Neill in Clarkehouse Road. He built the house to live in but a year later offered it for sale with 'eight lofty bedrooms and dressing rooms' and extensive grounds.

Ashland Road, Nether Edge, in winter. There are no leaves on the trees and the girls on the other side of the street have their mufflers on.

Ash House Lane, 17
formerly called Workhouse Lane. It was renamed from the building called Ash House, home in the early 1900s of George Edward Webster, solicitor, and in the 1920s of Reginald Webster, solicitor and secretary of Sheffield Masonic Hall Ltd. In later years it became an old people's home.

Ashland Road, 7
from the ash theme which occurs in several house names in the area – Ashfield House, Ash Cottage, and one called Ashland.

Ashpool Close, 13
from a pond which used to be a feature of Woodhouse village. It was near the Wesleyan chapel and it was filled in about 1889.

Ash Street, 6
no special reason; it was built as one of a pair of tree names with Lime Street.

Ash Street, 19
one of a group of Mosborough streets named after trees (along with Elm, Oak and Sycamore).

Ashurst Close, Drive, Place, Road, 6
from the Hampshire village of Ashurst; built at the same time as the nearby Marchwood streets which were named after another Hampshire village. Ashurst and Marchwood are both near Southampton.

Ashwell Road, 13
was originally called Ashgrove Road but after Woodhouse came into Sheffield in 1921 it was changed to avoid confusion with Ash Grove, 10. The new name was an effort to stay as near as possible to the old one. Ashwell is the name of two villages, one in Hertfordshire, the other Rutland.

Askern Street, 9
was originally called Water Street. It was changed in 1886 and renamed from the village of Askern, near Doncaster.

Asline Road, 2
from the name of a well-known Sheffield family. Sarah Asline was the second wife of Joseph Ward and stepmother of Samuel Broomhead Ward, who lived at the house nearby called Mount Pleasant. One of their children was Thomas Asline Ward, Master Cutler in 1816, Town Trustee, magistrate and diarist.

Asquith Road, 9
was first called Albert Road, after Prince Albert, Queen Victoria's husband, but there were so many Albert Roads that several had to be renamed. This was renamed in 1903 after Herbert Henry Asquith, Home Secretary from 1892 to 1895, Chancellor of the Exchequer 1905 to 1908, and Prime Minister 1908 to 1916. He later became Earl of Oxford and Asquith.

Aster Close, 19
one of a group of streets named after flowers (along with Daisy, Jasmine, Lilac, Primrose, Rose and Violet).

Aston Street, 2
was built on the Duke of Norfolk's land and named after Walter, Lord Aston Forfar, who married, in 1698, Mary Howard, descendant of Henry, sixth Duke of Norfolk.

Athelstan Road, 13
after Athelstan (895-940), son of Edward the Elder, and grandson of Alfred the Great, who was King of England for fifteen years. When the street was first built in 1935 (by J.F. Bullen, of Gleadless) the name was spelt Athelstun.

Athersley Gardens, 19
from the district of Athersley, Barnsley; one of a group of Mosborough streets given South Yorkshire place names.

Atherton Close, Road, 2
were built on the Duke of Norfolk's land and named from the fact that one of the Duke's ancestors, Thomas Howard, a colonel in the Royal Army, was killed at Atherton Moor.

Athol Road, 8
uncertain; approved 1897. If it was named after the Duke of Atholl it lost its last letter somewhere.

Atkin Place, 2
possibly after Edwin Atkin (he appears as Edward Atkin in one directory), bank clerk, who lived in nearby Highfield Terrace in the 1840s and 1850s.

Atlantic Crescent, Drive, Road, Walk, Way, 8
commemorate the exploits of three brothers, members of the Kirke family of Greenhill Hall, who left Sheffield, crossed the Atlantic, and led an expedition that captured Quebec from the French in 1629. Two of them, David and Lewis, were knighted.

Atlas Street, 4
from the nearby Atlas Works. John (later Sir John) Brown originally had works in Furnival Street which he called Atlas Works. In the 1850s Queens Works, Savile Street, came up for sale, Brown bought them and renamed them Atlas Works because, he said, the name

Attercliffe Road was extra busy when this photgraph was taken in the 1930s. Watched by a large crowd, part of a procession holds up normal traffic. The float is advertising Wheatsheaf Shoes.

had brought him good fortune. In 1859 he bought ten acres on the other side of the Sheffield-Leeds railway line to extend the works which eventually covered more than 100 acres.

Attercliffe Common, Road, 9

Attercliffe is recorded in the Domesday Book as Ateclive. Language experts disagree about its meaning. One theory is that it comes from an Old Norse personal name and means the cliff of Attir, or Attir's Cliff. The more widely accepted explanation is that it means the place at the cliff, the cliff in question being the rising ground on the east side of the River Don. Attercliffe Common was a large area of open land between the modern road called Attercliffe Common and Tinsley Park Road, and stretching from Coleridge Road to beyond Broughton Lane. Up to the nineteenth century Enclosure Act it was common land. After enclosure it was given to private owners, forty-four acres of it to the Duke of Norfolk.

Auckland Avenue, 6

was named at the request of Bradfield Parish Council after Austin Auckland, clerk to the parish council from 1950 till his death in 1969 (see also Austin Close and Court).

Auckland Drive, Rise, Way, 19

from Auckland, New Zealand, because of its rugby football connections (see Arms Park Drive).

Audrey Road, 13

obviously named after a person called Audrey, but I don't know who. The name was approved in February 1934. At a guess I would say it was named after a female relative of the builder.

Aughton Close, Crescent, Drive, 13

from the village of Aughton, four miles from Rotherham.

Aukley Road, 8

looks suspiciously like a wrong spelling of Auckley, the village near Doncaster. Several streets nearby have Yorkshire place names.

Austin Close, Court, 6

after Austin Auckland, former clerk to Bradfield parish council (see Auckland Avenue).

Avenue Court, 10

from nearby Riverdale Avenue.

Avenue Road, 7

like nearby Crescent Road, is simply a device to avoid thinking up a proper name.

The Avenue, 9

another device to avoid searching around for a proper name.

Avisford Drive, Road, 5

from Avisford House School, near Binsted, Sussex. The sixteenth Duke of Norfolk was a pupil there for a time.

Avondale Road, 6

one of a pair with nearby Clarence Road. Prince Albert Victor, eldest son of King Edward VII, was created Duke of Clarence and Avondale in May 1890. He died suddenly from pneumonia in 1892 at the age of twenty-eight and on his death the title became extinct (see also May Road).

Aylesbury Crescent, 9

from the agricultural area called the Vale of Aylesbury, Buckinghamshire; one of a group of streets named after English vales (along with Evesham and Taunton).

Aylward Close, Road, 2

were built on the Duke of Norfolk's land and named after a woman in the Duke's family history. Henry Charles Howard, of Greystoke, Cumberland, grandson of the Earl of Arundel, was married in 1730 to Mary Aylward.

Aysgarth Road, 6

was built by Birley Carr Freehold Land Society and was first called Cross Street. After the area came into Sheffield (where there were two other Cross Streets) the Highways Committee decided in 1926 to rename this one Parson Cross Street. Residents did not like the new name and wrote to the committee with their own suggestions. Aysgarth was the idea of Mr and Mrs Hobson who had just done a motor bike tour of the Yorkshire Dales during which they visited Aysgarth Falls. Because the residents listed their suggestions alphabetically, Aysgarth was top of the list, and the Highways Committee accepted it.

Babington Crescent, 2
after Anthony Babington, a Derbyshire youth who came to Sheffield as page to Mary Queen of Scots during her imprisonment in the town in the sixteenth century. He was devoted to her and in 1586 formed a plot to free her. Spies told the authorities what he was up to and Babington and his fellow plotters were arrested and hanged.

Babur Road, 4
was built in 1901 on the Duke of Norfolk's land and seems to have been named phonetically after the ancient hundred of Babergh in Suffolk, a county in which the Duke's family owned large areas of land. Babergh was mentioned in the Domesday Book and the name is still used today for an administrative district of Suffolk.

Backfields, 1
from an old field name. On the 1771 Fairbank map there are no buildings beyond Coalpit Lane (now called Cambridge Street) and the large area of land there is marked Back Fields.

Back Lane, 10
Back Lane used to be a very common name for small, off-the-beaten-track lanes in all areas. Many of them, including one at Stumperlowe, one at Norwood and one at Meadowhall Road, have been renamed, but there are still 14 of them listed in South Yorkshire.

Backmoor Crescent, Road, 8
Backmoor was an area of common land at Norton before the Enclosure Act of 1803. It is shown, as 'Back Moor', on a seventeenth century map.

Bacon Lane, 9
G.R. Vine, in his booklets, *The Story of Old Attercliffe,* says it was originally called Beighton Lane, possibly after Richard Beighton, who lived nearby in the seventeenth century. There was also a family called Beighton living in Attercliffe in the sixteenth century. Repeated use seems to have worn Beighton to Bacon.

Badger Close, Drive, Place, Rise, Road, 13
not known; names approved July 1963. There may have been badgers in the area before the streets were built. There don't appear to have been any people called Badger living in the area.

Up to 1886, Bagshot Street, Sharrow Vale was called School Lane. This was the schoolhouse from which it took its name.

Badger Lane, 1
after John Badger, joiner, who had two workshops in the early 1800s, one in Portobello Street, the other near Pond Street. The one at Portobello was known as Badger's Yard and this lane took its name from the yard.

Bagley Road, 4
from the old Bagley Lane which appears in Harrison's survey of 1637 three times and is spelt differently each time – Bagaley Lane, Baggalye Lane and Bagalie Lane. Whatever the correct spelling, it is believed to come from the name of a former resident of the area.

Bagshaw Road 12
after James Bagshaw, engraver, who lived in the area for about forty years.

Bagshot Street, 11
was originally called School Lane, from the nearby Sharrow Moor School. The name was changed (to the disgust of local residents) in 1886, along with three other streets of the same name. Bagshot, the name of a place in Surrey, was a random choice.

Baildon Street, 9
from the place called Baildon near Bradford; one of several Attercliffe streets named after places in Yorkshire.

Bailey Lane, Street, 1
from an old area of meadowland known as Bailey's fields. The fields are shown on a 1771 Fairbank map with a note across them saying: 'Intended street to be called Bailey Street'.

Bakers Hill, 1
from the public bakehouse which stood in the Ponds area in the seventeenth century for the use of everybody in the town. A man called Moseley had the lease of the bakehouse in 1624 at a rent of £20 a year. The name may simply mean the hill where the baker worked, or it might be a local corruption of the word bakehouse – 'Bake-uss Hill'

Bakers Lane, 1
not known.

Baker Street, 9
not known; name approved in 1889 for the Sheffield Union Banking Company, which later became part of the Midland Bank.

Balaclava Lane, Road, 6
were built soon after the famous Crimean War military action at Balaclava during which the Light Brigade made its epic and costly charge. Of about 670 men involved in the charge nearly half were lost.

Bala Street, 1
was first called West John Lane. It was renamed in 1890, after the market town of Bala, Gwynedd, on Bala Lake, which is the largest natural lake in Wales.

Baldwin Street, 9
probably after William Baldwin who was a joiner and builder at the time the street was built in the 1860s, first in partnership as Baldwin and Carlisle, later on his own account.

Balfour Road, 9
after Arthur James (later Lord) Balfour, who was First Lord of the Treasury and leader of the Unionist Party in the House of Commons at the time this road was built in 1900. (The Prime Minster, Lord Salisbury, was in the House of Lords). In 1902 Balfour became PM himself. He visited Sheffield six times, including once in 1892 when he was howled down in Paradise Square, and once in 1896 as chief guest at the Cutlers' Feast.

Ballifield Avenue, Close, Crescent, Drive, Place, Rise, Road, Way, 13
from Ballifield Hall which was built and lived in by the Stacey family whose pedigree can be traced back to 1593. In the 1860s the hall was bought and rebuilt by Peter Cadman. In recent years it has been a Family and Community Services Department home. The name Ballifield, recorded as Balifield in a charter dated 1277, is of doubtful origin. Language experts say it may come from an Old Norse word meaning a dwelling, or farm (the likeliest explanation), or from the Middle English word baili, meaning a steward.

Ball Lane, 1
from a public house called *The Ball*. There was a public house of this name on Carver Street for more than 100 years, although not always at the same address. In the 1830s it was at number fifty-five. From the 1860s onwards it was at number eighty-six and this lane was built alongside it.

Ball Road, 6
after James Ball, provision dealer in Langsett Road, who lived in Rippon Road. He owned land and houses in Rippon Road, Wood Road and Ball Road.

Ball Street, 3
from a public house called *The Ball* on Green Lane which was kept in the 1820s by Joseph Bray. At that time there were no fewer than 18 taverns, inns or public houses in Sheffield called *The Ball*.

Balmain Drive, Road, 6
although I have not been able to confirm it, I am convinced that Balmain, like the names of several neighbouring roads, is a link with Sir John Fowler, the eminent engineer and builder of the Forth Bridge, who lived at Wadsley Hall. Balmain is an area in Sydney, New South Wales. Fowler had several connections with New South Wales. He superintended the building of the state railways. His sister, Elizabeth, lived in New South Wales and was married to the head of the state railways. His brother, Charles, also lived there.

Balm Green, 1
there is some doubt about this name but the most favoured theory is that it comes from the Latin word *balneum*, meaning bath. A document of 1333 refers to the area as the Balne. Certainly this part of the town centre was well-known for its water supply, from the early days of springs up to the pool, named after Mr Barker, which was filled in around 1793. The name Balme Green was in use by 1609.

Balmoral Court, 11
from the Royal residence of Balmoral in Aberdeenshire, which was bought by Prince Albert in 1848.

Balmoral Road, 13
was built in the 1890s on land that was once church-owned, and was first called Belmoor Road. When Woodhouse became part of Sheffield in 1920 it was changed because it duplicated Belmoor Road, 9. The new name, chosen for its similarity to the old one, comes from the same source as Balmoral Court, 11.

Baltic Road, Way, 9
from a nearby house which was called Baltic House (because Vickers George Beardshaw, of the Baltic Steel Works, lived there). Earlier, the house was also known as Beardshaw's House, Shirland House and Shirland Cottage (as which it also gave its name to Shirland Lane). The old Baltic Lane, now no longer listed, was originally called Bradford's Court, after William Bradford (1754-1828) who owned six houses, a shop and a garden in the lane.

Bamforth Street, 6
from the Bamforth family, owners of High House, Owlerton, from the time of George Bamforth, born 1601, until well into the eighteenth century.

Bangor Street, 10
was originally called Henry Street, after Henry Watson, son of John Watson, of Shirecliffe Hall, the owner of Broomhall Park in the early 1800s. It was renamed in 1886 to avoid confusion with another Henry Street. There was no special reason for the new name. Bangor is a city in north Wales. (Nearby William Street was named after another of Watson's sons).

Bank Close, 7
from nearby Machon Bank.

Bankfield Lane, Road, 6
from two old field names. Near Bank Field and Far Bank Field, totalling a little over six acres, were offered for sale in 1843 described as being 'eligibly situated for the erection of cottage houses or other dwellings'. The name indicates that there was a bank or hillside in or near the fields.

Bank House Road, 6
from the house called Bank House, at the corner of Heavygate Road and Fir Street. In the 1880s it was the home of George W. Ashberry, of Philip Ashberry and Sons, silver and electro- plate manufacturers. It had a large greenhouse, a twenty-four foot vinery and a peach house.

Bank Street, 1
was built in 1791 through land owned by Shores, the banking family. At first the intention was to call it Shore Street but for some reason this was changed and it was named instead after the family business.

Bank Terrace, 10
from its position on the hillside.

Bankwood Close, Road, 14
from a nearby wood. In the early 1880s when it was in an area of land owned by Robert Robinson Brownell, it was known as Bank Plantation.

Banner Court, Banner Cross Drive, Rd, 11
the origin of the name Banner Cross is doubtful. Apparently there was the base of an old stone cross in the area in the late eighteenth century, but the Banner element of the name is a mystery. S.O. Addy, the local historian, offered two possibilities: that it came from an old Norse word referring to

prayer – the cross where prayers were said; or that it came from an old German word meaning boundary – the boundary cross.

Bannerdale Close, Road, View, 11
are in the dale below Banner Cross.

Bannham Road, 9
is wrongly spelt and has been for many years. It ought to be Banham, from the village of Banham, near Diss, Norfolk. It was built on the Duke of Norfolk's land along with Elmham Road and Shelfanger Road – all three named after Norfolk villages. Shelfanger Road was later renamed Logan Road. When the names were approved by the Highways Committee in 1901, the minutes recorded this one as Banham Road, but an extra letter crept in somewhere.

Bannon Street, 6
not known. It was one of several streets built in 1881 for the executors of Philip Ashberry. Three of the other streets were given names from the Ashberry family, and this too may be a family name (see Ashberry Gardens).

Barber Crescent, Place, Road, 10
after the Barber family who were well-known farmers and landowners in the Crookes area for many years. William Barber, cattle dealer at the farmstead known as Barber Nook (from which the nearby road, The Nook, gets its name) died in 1840. Building in all three roads was approved in 1869 for William Barber's executors.

Bard Court, Street, 2
Bard Street was first called High Street. It was changed in 1872 to avoid confusion with High Street in the town centre. The name Bard is a mystery. It might be a belated tribute to Shakespeare best known of bards. In 1864, a few years before the renaming, the Shakespeare tercentenary was celebrated, but Sheffield Town Council decided after several debates to do nothing to mark the event. Bard Street, on the Duke of Norfolk's land, may have been a late effort to retrieve the situation, but this is no more than a guess.

Bardwell Road, 3
after Thomas Newman Bardwell, auctioneer and general agent in Haymarket, who lived at Woodside. Another Bardwell Road, at Wincobank, was named after his son, Frederick, who paid for the building of Wincobank Church, but the Wincobank road was later renamed Barrow Road.

Barholm Road, 10
after Barholm Castle, Dumfries and Galloway, now a ruin, but once a stronghold of the McCulloch family. Nearby Cardoness Road is named after Cardoness Castle, Dumfries and Galloway, another McCulloch family fortress.

Barkby Road, 9
after Joseph Barkby, of Cricket Road, who was a member of the committee of the Second Meadowhall Freehold Land Society, which developed about thirty three acres of Lower Wincobank in the 1870s, including this road.

Barker's Place, 6
not known.

Barkers Pool, 1
after a man called Barker, who made a pool for the storage of drinking water in the 15th century. The pool remained until 1793 when it was condemned as a nuisance and filled in. A pump built nearby by the Town Trustees in 1825 remained until 1876. Unknown to most people, the section from Leopold Street to Pool Square was officially part of Fargate up to 1963.

Barker's Road, 7
after Thomas Rawson Barker (1813-1873), magistrate, director of several companies. He was mayor in 1848 and Chairman of Ecclesall Guardians. He lived nearby.

Barlby Grove, 12
after the place called Barlby, near Selby, one group of streets given Humberside place names.

Barking Street, 9
was first called Thomas Street, after Thomas Marrian, for whom it was built in 1876. It was renamed, because two other streets had the same name, in 1886. There was no special reason for the name. Barking is a town in Essex.

Barleywood Road, 9
from an old field name. When Attercliffe church cemetery became full in the late 1870s, a new burial ground had to be found. Most of Barley Wood Field and part of Tinsley Wood were bought and laid out as the new Tinsley Park cemetery.

Barlow Drive, Road, 6
Barlow Road was built by the New Woodland View Freehold Land Society in the 1870s and named after the secretary of the society, John Barlow, brickmaker and contractor, of Summerfield Street. Barlow Drive was built later (see Butler Road).

Barmouth Road, 7
from the resort called Barmouth in Gwynedd; one of a group of streets approved for R. Styring in 1896 and all named after places ending in 'mouth' (along with Falmouth, Lynmouth, and Plymouth).

Some streets have straightforward directional names – from the places people arrive at if they travel along them. Bawtry Road, at Tinsley, is one. It was originally part of the old turnpike road from Sheffield to Tickhill and Bawtry.

Barnadiston Road, 9
was built on land owned by Lt-Col Wilfrid Stanyforth JP (1861-1939) of Kirk Hammerton Hall, near York, and named after his wife, Mary Evelyn Barnadiston, daughter of Admiral Thomas Barnadiston (see Staniforth Road).

Barncliffe Close, Crescent, Drive, Glen, Road, 10
from old field names. Two fields on a seventeen-acre farmstead in the area, owned in the 1850s by Edmund Wilson, were called the Far Barn Cliffe and the Near Barn Cliffe, possibly a corruption of barren cliff. A house nearby, built about 1860, was also called Barncliffe.

Barnes Court, 2
was built on the site of a group of old properties called Barnes Square. In the 1850s there were three people called Barnes living and working in or near the square, Alexander, Christopher and Matthew. The name almost certainly came from one or all of them.

Barnes Place, 6
after the Barnes family, John in the 1850s, Mary in the 1870s, grocers, provision dealers and beer retailers, whose shop was on the corner of Barnes Place and Infirmary Road.

Barnet Avenue, Road, 11
the name of Barnet Road was approved in January 1927, but it seems not to have any particular local significance. Barnet is a place in north London.

Barnfield Avenue, Close, Drive, Road, 10
from an old field name. Barne Field, just over three acres of arable land, is listed in Harrison's survey of 1637 as being among lands held by George Morrey. It was a fairly common field name indicating a field with a barn in or near it.

Barnsdale Avenue, 19
from the area called Barnsdale in Yorkshire.

Barnsley Road, 4 and 5
a directional name. When the Sheffield end of it was built in 1837 (to avoid the steep climb up Pye Bank) it was first called the New Barnsley Road.

Baron Street, 1
was built in 1879 on the Duke of Norfolk's land and named, like Duke Street and Earl Street, after a rank of peerage held by the Duke and his ancestors. At various times the Dukes of Norfolk have held several baronies, notably those of Clun, Oswaldestre and Mowbray.

Barrack Lane, 6
is on or near the site of the old barracks which served Sheffield till the more imposing Langsett Road barracks were completed in 1850.

Barretta Street, 4
after Andrew Barretta, grocer and beer retailer, who had a shop on the corner of this street and Page Hall Road in the 1880s.

Barrie Crescent, Drive, Road, 5
after Sir James Matthew Barrie (1860-1937), dramatist, novelist and essayist, author of *Quality Street, The Admirable Crichton*, and creator of Peter Pan.

Barrow Road, 9
was originally called Bardwell Road after Frederick Bardwell, benefactor of Wincobank Church. There was another Bardwell Road (named after his father) so this one was renamed in 1886, for no special reason, after the west coast town and seaport of Barrow.

Bartle Avenue, Drive, Road, Way, 12
not known; there are two hamlets in Lancashire called Higher Bartle and Lower Bartle but it may have nothing whatever to do with them.

Bartlett Close, 6
after the Bartletts, James and William, who were farmers at nearby Nethergate Farm, Stannington, from the 1890s till the 1950s.

Bartlett Road, 5
after William Henry Bartlett (1809-1854), artist and author of travel books about English cities, Switzerland, the USA and Canada, which are now highly prized by collectors. He also edited Sharpe's *London Magazine* for three years.

Barton Road, 8
after Jabez Barton, who was an optician in Charles Street in the 1850s. For many years up to his death in the 1890s, he had a small optical instrument factory at sixty-six and sixty-eight Thirlwell Road. Barton Road, first called Thirlwell Mount, was renamed around the time of his death.

Basegreen Avenue, Close, Crescent, Drive, Place, Road, Way, 12
from an area of common land called Base Green, which is mentioned in a survey made in 1650. By the nineteenth century the green had become part of the land attached to Charnock Hall Farm, and at nineteen acres was the farm's biggest field.

Basford Close, Drive, Place, Street, 9
Basford Street, built first, was originally called Freedom Hill, but there were similar names elsewhere in the town and it was renamed in 1886. Basford, a random choice for the new name, is an area of Nottingham, where it is pronounced Base-ford, not Bass-ford.

Baslow Road, 17
a directional name; it was developed as part of the Baslow turnpike road in 1813-14 and the Town Trust gave £200 towards its cost. Toll bars were abolished on the road in 1880.

Bassett Lane, 10
from the old names of four fields at Fulwood. The fields, part of Yarncliffe Farm, were called Far, Middle, Upper and Lower Bassett, and the farm was sometimes called Bassett Farm.

Bassett Place, Road, 2
after George Bassett, founder of the world famous liquorice allsorts and confectionery firm, who was a Conservative town councillor for the Park ward from 1851 to 1854 and again from 1871 to 1873, when he was made an alderman. He was Mayor in 1876 when the American General Ulysses S. Grant visited Sheffield and stayed at the Bassett home in Endcliffe Crescent. Mr Bassett died in 1886 at the age of sixty-eight.

Bassledene Road, 2
not known; the name was approved, one of a batch of new streets on the Manor estate, in May 1924.

Bastock Road, 6
uncertain; it first appeared in the street directory in 1905. The only person called Bastock listed in the directory at that time was Harry Bastock, shopkeeper, of Charles Street. It may,or may

not, have had something to do with him.

Batemoor Close, Drive, Place, Road, Walk, 8

the area around is recorded as Bate More in a document dated 1581, and as Bates Moor in 1683. It means the moor belonging to, or used by, someone called Bate or Bates. There are records of a man called Roger Bate living in the area in the fourteenth century.

Bates Street, 10

after Henry Brian Bates, surveyor, who was linked with John Townend, land and property agent, in house building in this area in the 1860s. They lived locally in houses they had built themselves, Mr Bates in Townend Street, Mr Townend in Bates Street.

Bath Street, 1

after the Marquis of Bath, Lord Lieutenant of Ireland from 1765 to 1768, and later Secretary of State. The street was built around the time of his death in 1826.

Bathfield Place, 3

no longer listed. The name comes from an old field, Bathfield Close, described in a sale notice of 1852 as being two acres three roods five perches in size, in use as gardens, but 'most eligibly situated for building purposes'. The field probably had a spring-fed bath in it as water supply.

Batley Street, 5

was originally called Brook Lane (because there was a stream nearby). The name was changed in 1886 and the new name, from the Yorkshire town of Batley, had no special significance.

Batt Street, 8

is a link with the Wake family. Bernard Wake (1820-1891) solicitor, churchman, businessman and benefactor, was advisor to several property developments and owned land in various parts of the town. One of his four daughters, Isabel, married a surgeon, C. Dorrington Batt, of Witney, Oxfordshire. Batt Street, and the parallel Witney Street, built in the 1880s, were named from him.

Batworth Drive, Road, 5

not known, names approved 1956.

Part of Beaver Hill Road, Handsworth, looking towards Woodhouse, in days when a photographer could stand in the road to take his photograph without risking life and limb.

Bawtry Gate, Road, 9

Bawtry Road, built first, is a directional name. It was part of the route of the turnpike road from Sheffield to Bawtry and Tickhill, built in the 1760s.

Baxter Close, Drive, Road, 6

Baxter Road, built first, was originally called Back Lane but there were so many Back Lanes that several had to be renamed. The new name of this one, approved in 1924, came from the Baxter family who farmed in the area.

Baysdale Croft, 19

one of a group of streets named with a dale theme (along with Cragdale, Kildale, Mossdale and Stonesdale).

Bazley Road, 2

was built on the Duke of Norfolk's land and named from someone in his family. Ruth Evelyn Howard, daughter of Sir Edward Howard, was married in 1903 to Gardner Sebastian Bazley, son of Thomas Bazley, of Hatherop Castle, Gloucestershire.

Beacon Close, Croft, Road, Way, 9

from a beacon that stood on Wincobank Hill, one of a national network of beacons used for signalling. The story is that in 1805, when Britain was threatened from invasion by the French, the man on duty at Wincobank mistook a distant field of burning stubble for the invasion signal and caused alarm by lighting his beacon.

Beall Street, 9

no longer listed; named after G. Beall, who built more than fifty houses in the street in the 1890s.

Beauchief Abbey Lane, 8

leads to Beauchief Abbey.

Beauchief Court, Drive, Rise, 8 and 17

the name Beauchief has the same origin as Beachy Head in Sussex. It comes from the French (despite its un-French local pronunciation) Beau Chef, meaning beautiful headland.

Beaufort Road, 10

from the Dukedom of Beaufort. Several of the rows of houses in Whitham Road had names taken from the peerage.

Beaumont Avenue, Close, Crescent, Road, Way, 2

from the name of a distant ancestor of the Duke of Norfolk, Henry de Beaumont, who was given lands and summoned to Parliament in 1309 as a baron.

Beaver Avenue, Close, Drive, Beaver Hill Road, 13

Beaver Hill Road was first called Carr Lane. It was changed after Handsworth and Woodhouse came into Sheffield in 1920. The name Beaver Hill comes from an old field. A survey of the area made in 1802 mentions a field called Beaver Hill, nearly four acres, owned by Ann Stacye's trustees. The adjacent field, owned by John Shirt, was called Weaver Hill. Beaver Avenue, Close and Drive were built much later.

Beck Close, Road, 5
first there was a small lane called Brook Lane, named after the nearby Hartley Brook. Its name was changed in 1924 to Beck Lane, beck being another name for brook. Beck Road took its name from the lane, and Beck Close was built later.

Becket Avenue, Crescent, Road, 8
from the fact that Beauchief Abbey, nearby, was dedicated to Thomas à Becket, St Thomas of Canterbury,who was murdered in 1170.

Beckford Lane, 5
was originally called Back Lane. It was changed to avoid confusion with other Back Lanes in 1924. The first intention was to call it Backford Lane. Beckford could be a mistake or it could be from the fact that Thomas, second Earl of Effingham, who lived at nearby Thundercliffe, married in 1744, Elizabeth, daughter of Peter Beckford, Speaker of the Jamaican house of Assembly.

Beckton Avenue, Court, 19
from the thirteenth century spelling of the name Beighton, sometimes also spelt Becthon, meaning the farm or settlement by a bend in the river, the river in question being the Rother.

Bedale Road, 8
after the north Yorkshire market town of Bedale, which also gave its name to a famous hunt. By accident or design, several streets in the Abbeydale Road area were named after places associated with hunts.

Bedford Street, 6
was built on land owned by the Royal Infirmary and named after John Bedford, of John Bedford and Sons, who was a member of the Infirmary board for nearly fifty years.

Bee Street, 9
no longer listed. It was built by the Sheffield, Attercliffe and Carbrook Freehold Land Society in the 1850s and probably named after an official of the society. The likeliest candidate is John Bee, clerk, of Blast Lane wharf.

Beeches Avenue, Drive, 2
built in an area known for its beech trees for many years. A nearby house, owned by John Yeomans, merchant, in the 1850s, was called Beech Hill.

Beeches Grove, 19
there were beech trees on the site when it was developed.

Beech Hill Road, 10
from the beech trees in the area. A house nearby, built in the 1850s, was called Beech House.

Beechwood Road, 6
one of several streets built by Hillsborough Freehold Land Society, and yet another variation on the beech theme.

Beehive Road, 10
was built in the 1890s for Warrington Slater, partner in Slater Brothers, cutlery manufacturers, who lived in Crookesmoor Road. He named it after his firm's Rockingham Street premises, Beehive Works (see Warrington Road).

Beeley Street, 2
after George Beeley, official of several building and land societies, associate of George Wostenholm, of Kenwood, and substantial property owner. He owned houses all around the Cemetery Road area.

Beeley Wood Lane, Road, 6
from the nearby wood called Beeley Wood, the name of which goes back to the fourteenth century when it was called Byllauwode. Later it appears on maps and in documents as Billey Wood. It is thought to come from the old English personal name Billa – the wood belonging to Billa.

Beet Street, 3
from the Beet family, Jonathan Beet and his sons, who made table knives, forks, penknives, etc, at their works in Broad Lane. In the 1840s, they invested in housing, some of it built on land belonging to the Church Burgesses, and some of it built in the street.

Beeton Road, 8
not known; there was a house called Beeton Villa on nearby Meersbrook Park Road, and it may have had something to do with that.

Beighton Road, 12; Beighton Road 13
both are directional names. They lead towards Beighton.

Beighton Street, 9
was originally called Arthur Street after Prince Arthur, Duke of Connaught, one of Queen Victoria's sons. It was renamed in 1903 from the village of Beighton.

Beldon Close, Place, Road 2
after Joseph Beldon, partner in the firm of Roberts, Eyre, Beldon and Co. silver platers, together with Samuel Roberts, who lived at nearby Park Grange (and later became Sir Samuel). As well as their business interests, the Beldon and Roberts families were linked by marriage.

Belgrave Road, 10; Belgrave Square 2
Belgrave and Grosvenor were street names made fashionable in London, where the Grosvenor family developed land they owned and called part of it Belgrave Square – after the family estate at Belgrave in Leicestershire. The area around it became known as Belgravia. Another part of the London development was called Grosvenor Square, from the family name. Both names were copied in other cities.

Bellefield Street, 3
from a house called Bellefield House, built by Samuel Saynor, originally for use as an inn, but by the early nineteenth century used by the Fawcett sisters as a girls' boarding and day school. Later, in the 1840s, the school was run by Mrs Grindrod and her daughters.

Bellhagg Road, 6
there was a Bell Haggs Farm in the 1700s. S.O. Addy says hagg means a common or pasturage, and bell is a corruption of bale.

Bellhouse Road, 5
was called Pismire Hill until August 1902 when the City Council was urged by a group of residents (one in particular) to change its name because it was not in good taste. One councillor said there was nothing wrong with Pismire, which was an old word meaning ant hill. Another councillor said the name was 'not pleasant' and told how one local woman avoided using the word by referring to the hill as 'Primrose Hill'. At first the council refused to make any

change, but after a residents' protest meeting, the name was changed to Bellhouse Road, from five cottages in the area called the Bell Houses.

Bell Square, 1
is listed in the 1823 directory as Bell's Square, so it was probably named after someone called Bell. The three people listed as living in the square in 1823 include Mrs Sarah Bell. It may have been named after her, or her husband.

Belmonte Gardens, 2
was built in the grounds of a group of old houses called Belmonte, which dated back to the early nineteenth century. The 1856 directory lists eleven people living at Belmonte, among them Joseph Parkin, file manufacturer, Joseph Lockwood, of Lockwood Brothers, and the Rev Robert Henry Deane.

Belmoor Road, 9
not known.

Belper Road, 7
was first called Fern Road. It was changed in 1886 to avoid confusion with another road of the same name. The new name, a random choice, was from the town of Belper, eight miles from Derby.

Belsize Road, 10
when the Town Trust decided to build houses on the Machon House Farm land in 1913, the Corporation approved the plans but stipulated that the words Machon House should not be used in any of the street names to avoid confusion with the Machon Bank area of Nether Edge. In May 1914 the Town Trust decided that the roads on their new estate should be named Sefton Road, Clarendon Road, and Carr Bank Road. At some later date the name Belsize Road was substituted for Carr Bank Road. There appears to have been no strong local reasons for any of the names, all aristocratic, and all (appropriately for what was planned as a garden suburb) the names of well-known parks.

Ben Close, Lane, 10
probably named after someone called Ben, but similar names elsewhere in the country are said to have evolved from the old word bense, meaning cow stall.

Bennett Street, 2
not known; built about 1870, first as a short street between London Road and Hill Street, and later extended. It was almost certainly named from someone called Bennett but there were several people of this name in the area in the nineteenth century, including George Bennett, 'gentleman', at Highfield, and John Bennett, table knife cutler at Broomfield.

Bents Green Road with the old-style 1930s street lights and a motor bike and sidecar parked with its front wheel against the kerb to make sure it doesn't run away. It was probably the photographer's bike.

Benson Road, 2
after Alderman Joseph Benson, auctioneer in the Park district, magistrate, Park representative on the City Council, and Lord Mayor in 1925. He was also chairman of Sheffield United Harriers and president of the Exchange Cricket Club. He died in 1928.

Bentley Road, 6
not known; the road was built about 1900. There was an accountant and estate agent called Bentley in Sheffield at that time. It may have had something to do with him.

Bents Close, 11; Bents Crescent, Drive, 11; Bents Green Avenue, Place Road, 11; Bents Road, 11 and 17, Bents View, 11; Benty Lane, 10
all are named from bent grass, a coarse, rough type of moorland grass with broad leaves. The name occurs often as a field name, Bents Field, Hilltop, is mentioned in a land sale of 1848. Bents Green, being originally on the edge of moorland, would be a likely place for such grass.

Berkley Road, Street, 9
the street was approved – as Berkeley Street – in 1867 for Thomas Steade, the builder. If the land belonged to the Duke of Norfolk (which is possible) it may come from his ancestry. Katherine, daughter of Henry Howard, Earl of Surrey, married Lord Berkeley, Lord Lieutenant of Gloucester, in 1554.

Bernard Gardens, Road, Street, 2 and 4
after Bernard Edward, the twelfth Duke of Norfolk, owner of large areas of land in and around Sheffield. He sold some of his land to the town for improvements, built the Corn Exchange, gave the site of St John's Church, Park, and opened Norfolk Park to the public. He died in 1842.

Berners Close, Drive, Place, Road, 2
was built on the Duke of Norfolk's land and named from the fact that one of his ancestors, Catherine, daughter of the first Duke of Norfolk, married John Bouchier, Lord Berners, in the fifteenth century.

Bernshall Crescent, 5
Bernshall is the old spelling of Barnes Hall, the nearby house that was the home of the Smith family for many years.

Berresford Road, 11
after Admiral Charles Williams de la Poer Berresford, commander at the bombardment of Alexandria in 1882, and member of Wolseley's Nile expedition of 1884-85; one of a group of three streets named after prominent Victorian military men.

Bertha Street, 6
no longer listed; built around 1903 and

obviously named after a person called Bertha, but which Bertha is a mystery.

Bessemer Place, Road, 9
after Sir Henry Bessemer (1813-1898), prolific inventor and, notably from Sheffield's point of view, the man who discovered a cheaper and more efficient way of making steel. He had his own firm in Carlisle Street East.

Bessingby Road, 6
after the village of Bessingby, near Bridlington; one of three streets named after villages in the old East Riding (along with Carnaby and Speeton).

Bethel Walk, 1
was first called Chapel Walk, but this duplicated the better known Chapel Walk off Fargate. It was renamed from the building it ran alongside, the Bethel Sunday School, which was established in 1853 on Coalpit Lane (now Cambridge Street) and closed in 1936.

Beulah Road, 6
was first called Beverley Road, after the Yorkshire market town. It was renamed in December 1903. The second name is a mystery. There are two villages called Beulah in Wales, but it could just as easily be from some other source.

Bevercotes Road, 5
after the Nottinghamshire village of Bevercotes.

Beverleys Road, 8
after Councillor George Henry Beverley, who was widely respected in Woodseats, Norton Lees and Heeley – where he had a butcher's shop. In 1883, when times were bad, he gave 100 gallons of soup to needy people and helped to cart coal to them. He was a councillor from 1904 till his death in 1908. The road is opposite the church where he worshipped and was churchwarden.

Beverley Street, 9
was first called Frederick Street, but there were two other streets with the same name and this one was renamed in 1886 after the market town of Beverley, eight miles from Hull.

Bevis Row, 2
from the old Bevis Street, now demolished. The street stood on the Duke of Norfolk's land and was named after Bevis, the legendary strong man of Arundel, the Duke's Sussex estate. Bevis is reputed to have flung an axe from the top of a tower to mark the spot where he should be buried in Arundel park. The story is that the axe fell half a mile away and that is indeed where he was buried. The tower at Arundel is still called Bevis Tower.

Bickerton Road, 6
not known; there is a Bickerton in the Duke of Norfolk's lineage, Jane Bickerton, who was mistress, and later wife, of the sixth Duke in the seventeenth century, but it may have nothing to do with her.

Bignor Place, Road, 6
from the Sussex village of Bignor, which is near, but not actually part of, the Duke of Norfolk's estate at Arundel.

Bigod Street, 2
no longer listed; it was built on the Duke of Norfolk's land and named after his distant ancestors, the Bigod family, who owned large estates in Suffolk and Norfolk. Hugh Bigod was made Earl of Norfolk in the twelfth century.

Bilston Street, 6
was first called Alflat Street, after a builder called William Alflat. It was renamed in 1886, for no special reason after the Staffordshire market town of Bilston, three miles from Wolverhampton.

Bilton Road, 9
after a district of Harrogate called Bilton; one of the Staniforth family street names (see Staniforth Road).

Binfield Road, 8
after Binfield Bird, engineer, surveyor, valuer and director of Jabez Balfour's ill-fated Lands Allotment Company which built the Meersbrook Park estate. When Balfour's financial empire crashed in the 1890s, he fled to South America, but was arrested and brought back to England, where he was sentenced to 14 years' imprisonment for fraud. At his trial, in 1895, Bird's valuations of the Meersbrook estate were disputed. There were two valuations and one was suspiciously higher than the other. After the crash, the Meersbrook Park estate was sold at auction, in May 1894, for £28,410.

Binge Lane, 1
no longer listed; named after John Binge, pawnbroker, who lived at the corner of Broad Lane and Bailey Lane in the 1840s. His house backed on to Binge Lane. His son, John Binge jr, is described in directories as a professor of music.

Bingham Court, 10;
Bingham Park Crescent, Road, 11
from nearby Bingham Park which was named after the man who gave it to the city, Sir John Bingham (1839-1915), head of the firm of Walker and Hall, Master Cutler in 1881 and 1884, town councillor, magistrate and benefactor.

Bingham Road, 8
after James Bingham, of Linley, Linacre and Bingham, steel and file manufacturers, at Cobnar Works, Woodseats and Clough Works, Sheffield, in the 1880s. Mr Bingham lived at Woodseats.

Bingley Lane, 6
is mentioned in Harrison's survey of 1637, but is even older than that. It appears in documents of the 1500s, and, like nearby Bingley Farm, sometimes called Byngley, or Binley House, is thought to have been named from a local person called Bingley.

Binsted Avenue, Close, Crescent, Croft, Drive, Gardens, Glade, Grove, Road, Way ,5
from a small village called Binsted near the Duke of Norfolk's estate at Arundel, Sussex. There are ten streets in a group all carrying the name. Since they were named the Corporation has adopted a policy of trying not to give the same name to groups of more than three or four streets.

Birch Farm Avenue, 8
from the old Birch House Farm at Little Norton. There is a sketch by Charles Ashmore showing how the farm used to look in Harold Armitage's book *Chantrey Land*. When the farm became vacant in 1892 it had forty-two acres of land. It was thought to date back to the seventeenth century.

Birchitt Close, Place, Road, 17
the name Birchitt is recorded as Bircheheued in a document written in 1260. There were various spelling changes over the years, Birchehead, Byrchet, etc. It means birch-covered headland.

Birch Road, 9
after Mrs Eliza Harriet Birch, who had a shop on Staniforth Road and owned

Birklands, a house just off the main road at Handsworth, was demolished in 1946, but its name was used for three new streets built nearby. During the Second World War the house was used by the Home Guard. The brick wall in front of one of the downstairs windows was built to reduce blast damage from bombs.

the ground rents of factories, shops, and houses in Birch Road, Trent Street, Faraday Road and elsewhere. Harriet Road, off Birch Road, was also named after her. The ground rents were sold in 1927 after her death.

Birchvale Road, 12
from the Derbyshire village of Birch Vale, near Hayfield; one of many Frecheville Streets with Derbyshire names (see Thornbridge).

Birchwood Close, Croft, Gardens, Grove, Rise, View, Way, 19
from a nearby wood which is shown as Birk Wood, meaning Birch Wood, on a 1773 Fairbank map.

Birdwell Road, 4
was built on Earl Fitzwilliam's land and named after the village of Birdwell, near Barnsley. The Earl owned land at Birdwell.

Birkendale, Birkendale Road, View, 6
Birkendale was the old name of the valley between Walkley and Upperthorpe. It means the valley of birch trees. When the roads were first built in 1900 (during the Boer War) the idea was to name them after places in South Africa that were in the news at that time. It was agreed they should be called Spion Road, Modder Road and Plato Road. Owners and occupiers objected to these names and the Watch Committee changed them, Spion Road became Birkendale Road, Modder Road became Birkendale, and Plato Road became Birkendale View.

Birklands Avenue, Close, Drive, 13
after a large house called Birklands, built about 1900, the home of William Atkinson, chairman of Fisher Son and Sibray Ltd, the seed and nursery firm which had extensive nurseries in Handsworth area. The house, set back from Handsworth Road, was demolished in 1946.

Birks Avenue, 13
after a family prominent in the Woodhouse area for more than 300 years. John Birks was a freeholder in the village in 1657, Samuel was an overseer in 1676, Joshua a churchwarden in 1701, Peter a churchwarden in 1759, and later members of the family were well-known farmers and landowners.

Birks Green, 10
no longer listed. It means Birch Green, so presumably there were birch trees in the area.

Birley Lane, 12; Birley Moor Avenue, Close, Crescent, Drive, Place, Road, Way, 12
the name Birley, recorded in the thirteenth century as Byrley, comes from the old words byre, meaning cowshed, and leah, meaning a field or forest clearing.Birley Moor was a large area of common land.

Birley Rise, Crescent, Road, 6
from Birley Edge, recorded in thirteenth century documents, and having the same meaning and origin as Birley Lane etc, above.

Birley Spa Lane, Walk, 12
there was a spa nearby. The Duke of Portland stayed there for a week in 1843, taking hot baths every day. In later years it was the custom among local people to visit the spa at the start of the season, on Easter Monday, when there were games, dancing (to Woodhouse Prize Band), swing boats and teas. In recent years the spa buildings have been owned by the Recreation Department.

Birley Street, 3
no longer listed; it was built on land owned by Birley's Charity, founded in the eighteenth century by William Birley.

Birley Vale Avenue, Close, 12
the vale, or valley, near Birley Moor (above).

Bishop Hill, 13
Ernest Atkin says in his history of the Woodhouse area that the name is a very old one but that its origin is uncertain. It probably came from the name of a person who lived nearby.

Bishops Close, 8; Bishopscourt Road, 8
from the nearby Bishop's House, built in the sixteenth century, altered many times since, and now a museum. It was so named because of its links with the Blythe family, two of whom, John and Geoffrey, became Bishops. At least, that is the story. Certainly the two men became Bishops, but some authorities doubt their connections with the house.

Bishopholme Close, Road, 5
from the old house first called Norwood Hall, but changed to Bishopholme when Dr Leonard Burrows, first Bishop of Sheffield, bought it as his residence in 1914. Later bishops lived elsewhere. The house was taken over by Sheffield Corporation and after several years of neglect was controversially demolished in June 1976.

Bishop Street, 3
after Samuel Bishop, edge tool manufacturer, whose works were on Young Street in the 1830s. By the 1850s, the works were being run by Elizabeth Bishop and her son, James.

Blackmoor Crescent, Road, 17 Blacka Moor View 17
from the area of moorland known as Blacka Moor, meaning simply black moor. Councillor J.G. Graves, the Sheffield benefactor, gave 450 acres of the moor to the city in 1933.

Blackberry Flats, 19
from an old Mosborough field name. Several of the local fields were called flatts (because they were more or less level) and this particular field, part of the Mosborough Hall estate, was known for its blackberries.

Blackbrook Avenue, Drive, Road, 10
from the local stream, the Black Brook which runs from Hallamshire golf course, under Manchester Road, and into the Rivelin. It was a fairly common descriptive stream name. There are several Black Brooks in Yorkshire. Another runs into the Ewden Beck at Bradfield.

Blackburne Street, 6
after C.G.C.M.I. Blackburne, who owned land in the Hillsborough area in the early 1900s.

Blackdown Avenue, Close, 19
from the Blackdown Hills which run along the borders of Somerset and Devon; one of a small group of streets named after hills (along with Cleeve Hill, Pentland and Purbeck).

Blackmore Street, 4
was built on the Duke of Norfolk's land and seems to be a corruption of a title held for many years by the Duke's family, the ancient English barony, Strange of Blackmere. Most of the family's titles have been used in local street names.

Blackstock Close, Crescent, Drive, Road, 14
from an old Norton Field name, Black Stocks. The name appears on a map of the area made in 1808. Stock, or stocks, come from an old English word, *stocc*, meaning land with tree stumps left standing.

Black Swan Walk, 1
from the old hotel, the *Black Swan*, which stood at 5 Fargate, up to the 1880s when it was demolished for street widening.

Blagden Street, 2
after William Blagden, lime burner at Park Kilns in the 1820s, who is listed in later directories as lime burner and boat builder at the canal basin, and later still as a boat owner.

Blair Athol Road, 11
comes from the somewhat convoluted history of Banner Cross Hall. John Bright, of a well-known Sheffield family, owned the hall in the eighteenth century. Bright's grand-daughter married Lord John Murray, an army general, and son of the Duke of Atholl. Their daughter married General William Foxlowe, who later assumed his wife's name – Murray – and had Banner Cross Hall rebuilt. In 1811, the Murray estates were divided up, and Banner Cross passed to another branch of the family, the Bagshawes, of Ford Hall, Derbyshire. It was during the ownership of a descendant of this branch of the family, W.H. Greaves-Bagshawe, that the land around Banner Cross Hall was developed for housing in the 1890s. Mr Greaves-Bagshawe was said to have a more illustrious pedigree than any other commoner in England, with family lines going back to King Edward I. He named most of the streets on the Banner Cross development from his family history, notably his links with the Dukedom of Atholl. Blair Athol is a village in Perthshire very near to the Duke of Atholl's family seat, Blair Castle.

Blake Grove Road, 6
is another variation on the Blake family's connection with Upperthorpe (see Blake Street).

Blakeney Road, 10
after John Edward Blakeney (1824-1895), vicar of St Paul's Church from 1860 to 1877, vicar of Sheffield from 1877 to 1895, first Archdeacon of Sheffield (from 1884 to 1895), a man who loved Sheffield and, by all accounts, was loved by the people of Sheffield. He was said to be genial, kindly, broad-minded and large-hearted.

Blake Street, 6
after Thomas Blake, JP, typefounder, of the firm of Stephenson, Blake and Co, and director of the Manchester, Sheffield and Lincolnshire Railway. He owned land and property in and around Blake Street.

Bland Lane, 6
from an old field name. Bland Field was one of several fields and areas of woodland offered for sale along with the *Robin Hood and Little John Inn* in the 1850s. Thomas Bagshaw was tenant of the field at that time.

Bland Street, 4
was built by Sheffield and Grimesthorpe Freehold Land Society around 1860 and named after John Bland, who kept the *Brunswick Hotel* in Old Haymarket and was on the committee of the freehold land society.

Blast Lane, 2
from a coke-fired blast furnace used for smelting iron built in nearby Effingham Street by a man called Booth in 1786.

Blaxton Close, 19
from the Yorkshire village of Blaxton, five miles north of Bawtry; one of a group of streets given Yorkshire place names.

Blayton Road, 4
was approved in 1898 and built on the Duke of Norfolk's land, with two other roads, Sturton and Kirton. The names appear to have been chosen primarily for the fact that they all ended in the same three letters. Three roads built

later followed the same pattern: Gayton, Pexton and Skipton.

Blenheim Gardens, 11
was built in the grounds of what was first a private house called Blenheim, built 1920, and home in the 1930s of Edward Boot, of the building firm. The house was converted into a private nursing home in the 1970s.

Blonk Street, 1
from the name of a firm of scissorsmiths, Blonk and Co, headed by Benjamin Blonk, and based on the bank of the River Don in the early nineteenth century. The works had a wheel known as the Blonk Wheel.

Bloor Street, 6
no longer listed; it was named after Henry Bloor, who was the vestry clerk, highway clerk, registrar of births and deaths, and poor rate collector for Nether Hallam township in the nineteenth century. It was said that 'his tall, erect form and austere, blanched expression awe the ordinary civilian'. Mr Bloor lived in York Place, off Whitehouse Lane.

Blossom Crescent, 12
a name suggested by the developer who planned to carry out an extensive tree-planting scheme in the area.

Bluebell Road, 5
a group name on the theme of flowers (see Acacia).

Blue Boy Street, 3
was built about 1830 and named after a nearby tavern called the *Blue Boy*. The tavern was named from the uniform jacket worn by pupils at the Bluecoat School.

Blyde Road, 5
after James Blyde, manufacturer, of Hallcarr Works, who lived at Pitsmoor and owned property in Barnsley Road. He later sold up and left Sheffield for Birmingham, where he died in 1888.

Bochum Parkway, 8
was first called Norton Parkway; it was renamed in 1982 after Sheffield's twin city in Germany. Bochum, population nearly 300,000, is an industrial town in the Ruhr district producing steel, iron, coal and textiles. One of its ring roads is called Sheffield Ring.

When this photograph was taken in 1915 the area round Bocking Lane was still undeveloped countryside.

Bocking Close, Lane, Rise, 8
from an old field name. Bocking Fields, Beauchief, once belonged to the parish of Norton. They were offered for sale in September 1873 as 'well adapted for a land society to build on'. The name is believed to come from a person called Bocking, or Bockin, possibly Will Bockin who is listed in the Norton Hearth Tax Assessment for 1670.

Boden Lane, 1
not known; probably from a person called Boden. The 1841 directory lists five different Bodens living or working in the town centre.

Boden Place, 9
from a family called Boden, sometimes spelt Bowden, who owned property in the Place, and in nearby Mandeville Street. Thomas Boden, toll collector at Darnall toll bar in the 1850s, may have belonged to this family.

Bodmin Street, 9
was first called Orchard Street, because there was an orchard nearby. It was changed in 1886 to avoid confusion with Orchard Street, 1. There was no special reason for the new name. Bodmin is a Cornish market town.

Boland Road, 8
after Father Robertus Boland, who was a monk at Beauchief Abbey in the fifteenth century. His name is on a list of monks made in 1478 and reproduced in Samuel Pegge's *Historical Account of Beauchief Abbey*.

Bold Street, 9
not known; approved in 1867 for Thomas Steade, the builder.

Bole Hill Lane, 10; Bole Hill Road, 6
bole hills were places where lead was smelted. High ground, as at Crookes, was chosen deliberately so that winds would help the fires to burn well. There was another bole hill at Graves Park.

Bolsover Road, 5
was first called Dixon Lane. It was changed in 1906, The new name came from a house called Bolsover, or Boulsover, Cottage, which was probably named after a former owner. Eastwood, in his *History of Ecclesfield*, says George Boulsover, son of Samuel Boulsover de Brushes, was baptised in 1714, so it could have been someone from this family.

Bolsover Street, 3
is a link with the Mitchell family who owned land and property in the area (see Mitchell Street). Joseph Mitchell's second wife, Mary, whom he married in 1760, was a daughter of Thomas Bolsover, of Whiteley Woods.

Bolton Street, 3
was first called Petre Street. It was changed in 1886 to avoid confusion with Petre Street, 4. There was no special reason for the new name, from the well-known town in Lancashire.

Bonville Gardens, 3
from the earlier Bonville Street,

approved in 1877 for William Fox Tibbitts, but why he chose this particular name is not known.

Booker Road, 8
Booker was a well-known name in Norton and Woodseats area for many years. In the mid-1800s Richard Booker farmed at Carrfield and Robert Booker at Lees Hall. George Booker was a surgeon at Woodseats in the 1870s, and public vaccinator and Medical Officer for the Derbyshire district of Eccesall Union. Henry Booker was a town councillor and Ecclesall Guardian. It was almost certainly named after one of them, but I don't know which.

Booth Close, Croft, 19
from a man called Booth who was a trustee of the turnpike road at Mosborough in 1743.

Bootle Street, 9
was first called School Hill, because there was a school nearby. The new name, chosen in 1886, was a random choice, from Bootle, the town near Liverpool.

Borough Road, 6
was originally called Back Lane and was on the Sheffield boundary. It was renamed in 1900 when, under boundary extensions, it became part of the borough.

Borrowdale Avenue, Close, Drive, Road, 19
group name on a Lake District theme (See Ambleside).

Boston Street, 2
was first called George Street, then New George Street. It was changed again in 1890 and named after the town and port on the River Witham.

Bosville Road,10
not known.

Bosworth Street, 10
after the Battle of Bosworth which took place on 22nd August 1485, fought between Richard III and Henry, Earl of Richmond, near the Leicestershire town of Market Bosworth. It was the thirteenth and final battle in the Wars of the Roses and it resulted in the death of Richard III. One of a group of streets named after famous British battles (along with Flodden, Marston, and Newbury).

Botanical Road, 11
from the nearby Botanical Gardens. Sheffield Botanical and Horticultural Society, formed in 1833, bought land for the gardens, then ran into financial difficulties. A second society, formed in 1838, operated the gardens till 1898. The Town Trust then took them over till December 1951, when control passed to the Corporation. The road was built in the 1890s.

Botham Street, 4
was built by Sheffield and Grimesthorpe Freehold Land Society in the 1860s and named after W. Botham of Old Haymarket, who was a member of the committee of the land society.

Botsford Street, 3
is a simplified spelling of the name Bottesford, a village in Leicestershire. Like Rutland Road and other neighbouring streets, it comes from a link with the Duke of Rutland's lineage. In 1835 the Duke was given the title Baron Bottesford of Bottesford.

Boundary Road, 2
probably from the fact that it was the boundary of the Arbourthorne estate development. It doesn't seem to have been the boundary of anything else.

Bourne Road, 5
from the legend of Hereward the Wake. Bourne Abbey was founded by Hugh de Wake who claimed to be a descendant of Hereward.

Bowden Wood Avenue, Close, Crescent, Drive, Place, Road, 9
from Bowden Houstead wood which is recorded in the fourteenth century as Baldwynhoustead, meaning the homestead belonging to Baldwyn. The corporation bought the 100-acre wood from the Duke of Norfolk for £6,000 in 1914.

Bowdon Street, 1
from the Bowdon family who owned land off The Moor up to the nineteenth century. James Bowdon, of Little Sheffield Moor, was given land under the Ecclesall Enclosure Awards of 1788.

Bowen Street, 9
after Charles Synge Christopher Bowen, later Lord Bowen, eminent barrister, who was a judge from 1879 and a Lord of Appeal from 1893 till his death a year later. It was one of a group of streets built for William Wake, the Sheffield solicitor, and named after famous legal men.

Bower Road, 10
was built in the late 1860s and named after Samuel Saville Bower, who owned property at Crookes and in the city centre. He died about 1909.

Bower Spring, 3
from a family called Bower who owned land in the area. One of them, Robert Bower, is mentioned in Harrison's survey of 1673. The spring was a stream that passed through Bower land.

Bower Street, 3
from W. Bower, who built a silk mill near the street in 1758. He may have belonged to the same family from which Bower Spring (above) was named. The silk mill had a chequered history (see Cotton Mill Street).

Bowfield Road, 5
not known; approved February 1920. It may be from a field name. Bow Field is a fairly common name indicating a field shaped like a bow.

Bowler Street, 2
no longer listed; it was named after John and William Bowler who lived at Heeley Green from the 1840s to the 1870s. They were in business as horn pressers and turners, umbrella and parasol horn hook manufacturers.

Bowling Green Street, 3
there was a bowling green nearby in the early 1800s. It was on West Bar, roughly where the Ebenezer chapel was later built, and it was kept by a man called John Hinchcliffe who ran a nearby public house.

Bowman Close, Drive, 12
not known.

Bowness Road, 6
from the village of Bowness on Lake Windermere in the Lake District.

Bowood Road, 11
not known; plans were approved in 1893 for Harry Kitchin, cutlery manufacturer at Soho works, who lived at Clifford, Psalter Lane. There are villages called North Bowood and South Bowood in Dorest.

Bowshaw Avenue, Close, View, 8
from the nearby Bowshaw Farm. The name Bowshaw appears on a Fairbank map of 1795 and means a bow-shaped woodland.

Boyce Street, 6
not known; built 1892-93.

Boyland Street, 3
appears first in the 1865 directory as Boyland's Street which suggests that it was named after someone named Boyland. The only person of this name listed is Joseph Boyland, coal dealer and beerhouse keeper in White Croft, so he might be the one.

Boynton Crescent, Road, 5
from the Humberside village of Boynton, three miles west of Bridlington.

Brackenfield Grove, 12
after the hamlet called Brackenfield, five miles east of Matlock (see Thornbridge).

Bracken Road, 5
from the old name Bracken Hill, presumably so-called because there was bracken growing on it.

Brackley Street, 3
from a title held by a member of the Duke of Norfolk's family. The Earl of Ellesmere, brother of Sophia, Duchess of Norfolk, also held the title of Viscount Brackley of Brackley, Northamptonshire. Ellesmere Road was named after the same man.

Bradbury Street, 8
after Arthur Bradbury for whom property was built on the street in 1894.

Bradfield Road, 6
a directional name for the old road from Owlerton to Bradfield, which is recorded as Bradesfield in the twelfth century. The village name means a broad stretch of open countryside.

Bradford Street, 9
after George Bradford (1787-1861) who had a large farm in the Attercliffe area. According to G.R. Vine, in his *Story of Old Attercliffe*, Bradford's Farm 'consisted of nearly the whole of Attercliffe Common and a quantity of land towards Tinsley'.

Bradley Street, 10
after John Rose Bradley, horn, haft and scale presser in West Street, who lived at Spring Hill and owned property in the Crookes area. Later, he moved to live in School Road.

Bradway Close, Drive, Road, 17
from the area called Bradway which is recorded in various spellings back to 1260. Language experts say it comes from the old words *brad weg*, meaning a broad road.

Bradway Grange Road, 17
from the house called Bradway Grange, home in the early 1990s of Tedbar Tinker, 'engineer, surveyor, farmer, brick and tile manufacturer, and quarry owner' of Twentywell Stone and Brick Works.

Bradwell Lane, 1
after Edward Bradwell, flax dresser, who owned land in the area – adjacent to Thomas Holy's land – in the early 1800s. His land is shown on a Fairbank map of 1801.

Bradwell Street, 2
was built around 1886 and named after the Derbyshire village of Bradwell.

Braemore Road, 6
from a link with Sir John Fowler, engineer of the Forth Bridge, who lived at Wadsley Hall. Sir John later lived at Braemore, Ross-shire, Scotland, where he owned about 47,000 acres of land.

Brailsford Avenue, Road, 5
after William Brailsford, who died in 1784 and left a sum of money known as Brailsford's Dole to help the poor in Ecclesfield parish. He also left money for schools at Thorpe Hesley and Kimberworth, his birthplace.

Bramall Lane, 2
was originally called White House Lane, from the white house on it. There were two other White House Lanes and this one was renamed after the man who lived in the house for a time, Daniel Brammall, who owned a file factory nearby. Over the years one of the m's in his name has been dropped from the street name.

Bramber Place, Street, 3
no longer listed; they were built on the Duke of Norfolk's land and named after the village of Bramber near the Duke's stately home at Arundel, Sussex.

Bramham Road, 9
after the village of Bramham, four miles south of Wetherby. The name is a link with the Staniforth family on whose land the road was built (see Staniforth Road).

Bramley Avenue, Drive, Lane, 13
Bramley is recorded as a Handsworth place name in the twelfth century. It means the clearing in the broom.

Bramley Close, 19
from an old field name recorded in the Mosborough area in 1798. The meaning is the same as Bramley Avenue, above.

Bramley Hall Road, 13
from the hall built in the seventeenth century on the site of a much older house that was originally the home of a man called Hugh de Bramley.

Bramley Park Road, 13
refers to the land surrounding Bramley Hall, above. When the hall was offered for sale in 1868 it had 155 acres of land attached to it.

Brampton Court, 19
from the village of Brampton, near Wombwell; one of a group of Mosborough Streets given South Yorkshire place names.

Bramshill Close, Court, 19
from the Bramshill Forest, Hampshire; one of a group of streets named after

First it was called White House Lane, after this house; then it was renamed Bramall Lane, after the man who lived in the white house.

forests (along with Collingbourne, Hursley, Inglewood and Milburn).

Bramwell Gardens, Street, 3
the street was built in the early 1860s for John Henry Bramwell, who was a file manufacturer in Milton Lane and lived in Lower Hanover Street. Bramwell Gardens took their name from the old street.

Bramwith Road, 11
after the South Yorkshire villages of South Bramwith and Kirk Bramwith.

Brandon Street, 3
was first called School Lane (because there was a school on it) but there were four School Lanes and three had to be renamed. This one, renamed in 1886, took its name from a market town in Suffolk.

Brandreth Close, Road, 6
Brandreth Road was named after the man for whom it was built, the Rev Benjamin Brandreth Slater, the first vicar of St Bartholmew's Church, Langett Road, from 1880 till his death in 1904. He lived at a house called Brandreth House.

Bransby Street, 6
not known; it was built in the 1890s. There is a hamlet called Bransby in Lincolnshire.

Brathay Close, Road, 4
after the River Brathay which rises in Wrynose Pass, Cumbria, and flows into Lake Windermere; one of a group of Streets with Cumbrian names (along with Hawkshead, Rothay, Skelwith and Wansfell).

Bray Street, 9
not known; it was built in 1896 for Col E.W. Stanyforth. Most of the streets built for him were given family names, or Yorkshire names associated with the family, but this one I can't explain (see Staniforth Road).

Brecon Close, 19
after the Brecon area of Wales.

Brentwood Avenue, Road, 11
Brentwood Road was first called Stanwood Road. It was changed in November 1906. There seems to have been no particular reason for the new name. Brentwood is a town in Essex.

Bressingham Close, Road, 4
were built on the Duke of Norfolk's land and named after the Norfolk village of Bressingham, near Diss.

Brett Street, 9
no longer listed; named after Sir William Baliol Brett, later Viscount Esher (1815-1899), Solicitor General in 1868, High Court Judge, Master of the Rolls, 1883-97; one of a group of streets named after prominent legal men (together with Chelmsford, Jessel, Palmer, Roundel, Selborne, Westbury).

Bretton Grove, 12
after the Derbyshire area of Bretton, near Great Hucklow (see Thornbridge).

Briarfield Avenue, Crescent Road, 12
from an old Gleadless field name. Briar Field, or Briar Ley, is mentioned in many old documents. A cottage nearby also took the name Briar Ley. It was the home in the 1870s of William Richardson, Sheffield cutlery manufacturer.

Briar Road, 7
from the tangly shrubs on or near here.

Brickhouse Lane, 17
the first brick house built in Sheffield (in Pepper Alley) is said to have been built about 1696, but brick houses were still unusual for many years after that date. There was one near this lane, as shown on an 1801 Derbyshire map by J. Cary.

Brick Street, 10
as Brickhouse Lane, above, indicating the early use of brick as a building material.

Bridby Street, 13
not known; originally called Walker Street. Renamed 1924.

Bridgehouses, 3
the area was known as Bridgehouses in 1366, 400 years before there was a bridge there, when the only means of crossing the river was a ford, and some years later, stepping stones. The bridge was not built till 1770. The houses took their name from another, much older, bridge down river, Lady's Bridge.

Bridge Street, 3
was formerly called Under-the-Water, for reasons that are not hard to guess. Its modern name came from nearby Lady's Bridge, named after a small chapel dedicated to Our Lady which once stood nearby.

Bridle Stile,
Bridle Stile Avenue, Close, 19
stile in this sense means a path or narrow lane, from the Old English word *stig*. Bridle stile, or bridle sty, meaning bridle path, used to be common in Yorkshire and north Derbyshire.

Bridport Road, 9
has had three different names. It started as Albert Road, then in 1886 it became Bawtry Road. It was changed again in 1907 (to avoid confusion with another Bawtry Road). There was no special reason for the third name. Bridport is a town in Dorest.

Brier Close, 19, Brier Street, 6
like Briar Road, 7, there were tangly shrubs in the area.

Brightmore Drive, 3
after Elizabeth Brightmore, daughter and heiress of William Brightmore, merchant, who married Samuel Mitchell, merchant, town trustee, and owner of land in this area (and the man after whom nearby Mitchell Street was named).

Brighton Terrace Road, 10
from a group of houses called Brighton Terrace. Brighton was much favoured as a Victorian house name. There was another Brighton Terrace at Pitsmoor, and some Brighton Villas on Brunswick Road.

Brightside Lane, 9
S.O. Addy, the local historian, thought the name Brightside simply meant fields on a south facing slope, the fields that would get most sunlight. The more widely accepted explanation is the one given by the earlier historian, Joseph Hunter, who said the name was originally Brekesherth, from a man called Brik who had a hearth, or smithy in the area. The theory is that people found Brekesherth difficult to write and say, and over the years it was changed to Brigsid, and then Brightside.

Bright Street, 9
from the Bright family who owned Carbrook Hall in the seventeenth century. One of the family, Col John Bright, served with Cromwell's army and was made governor of Sheffield Castle when the royalists surrendered in 1644.

Brimmesfield Close, Drive, Road, 2
were built on the Duke of Norfolk's land and named from one of the old titles held by the Duke's family, the barony of Giffard of Brimmesfield, which fell into disuse in 1777.

Brincliffe Crescent, Gardens, Hill; Brincliffe Edge Close, Road, 11
the spelling has changed several times over the centuries, but Brincliffe is thought to come from the old words *brende*, meaning a place cleared by burning, and *clif*, meaning steep hill.

Brindley Close, Crescent, 8
from the Brindley family, former owners of the house nearby, through the grounds of which the streets were built.

Brinkburn Close, Court, Drive; Brinkburn Vale Road, 17
from the old house called Brinkburn Chase, nearby, which was demolished about 1938.

Brinsworth Street, 9
from the village of Brinsworth; one of several streets named after villages near Rotherham (along with Treeton and Whiston Streets).

Bristol Road, 11
was approved in 1875 and built for Brocco Bank Freehold Land Society. The name is a mystery unless it came about by thought association with another of the society's roads, Dover Road. If so, it was illogical because Dover Road was named after a man, not a port.

Britannia Road, 9
seems to be a patriotic name, rather than any link with Britannia metal, which was the reason for the name of a group of houses elsewhere in the city.

Britnall Street, 9
not known; the only name anything like it I have been able to find crops up in directories of the 1840s and 1850s, that of Mrs Sarah Bretnall, of the *White Hart Inn*, Attercliffe.

Brittain Street, 1
after Samuel Swann Brittain who owned land and property in the street. He died in 1873.

Broadcroft Close, 19
from the old field name, Broade Croft, recorded in 1617.

Broad Elms Close, Lane, 11
Broad Elms Lane was originally called Broad Oaks Lane. It was changed in 1903. There were elms in the area. An old sketch in Sheffield Central Library of Alms Hill Farm shows 'one of the large elm trees in the lane on the right'.

Broadfield Road, 8
after the house called Broadfield which had a plantation and several fields and stood roughly where Saxon Road was later built. In the early seventeenth century it was the only building in the area. It was successively home to several families, the Flathers, Shores and Gillotts among them, and it was demolished in the 1870s.

Broadfield Park Avenue, 8
no longer listed; it was first called Broadfield Park Square. The 'park ' was the area of land around the house called Broadfield, above.

Broadlands Avenue, Rise, 19
from a place called Broadlands in West Yorkshire. The name was suggested by the developer, who came from West Yorkshire.

Broad Lane, 1
from its width. Before the building of West Street and Glossop Road, about 1820, Broad Lane was the main route west out of town. Every Holy Thursday a feast was held on the lane with gingerbread stalls, puppet shows, pony races, etc.

Broadley Road, 13
uncertain; the name was approved in August 1932 and sounds like an old field name. Broad Ley means the same as Broad Field.

Broad Oaks, 9
was built across some allotments called Broad Oaks Gardens, presumably because there were oak trees on or near the site.

Broad Street, 2
because of its width, as with Broad Lane, above.

Brocco Bank, 11, Brocco Lane, Street, 3
there are two theories. One is that there were badgers (old British name, *brokkos*) in the area; the other, more likely, explanation is that brocco was the name for a hilly, uncultivated piece of common land, from the old word, *brocca*, meaning spiky grass. Either way, the name has been in use for a long time. Harrison's survey of 1637 mentions Brockes Lane, Brockoe Hill, Brockow Common and Brockow Lane.

Brocklehurst Avenue, 8
was named in 1934 after Ernest Brocklehurst who was a dairy farmer in the area before it was built on. Mr Brocklehurst later joined his brother in the motor trade, where he became much better known.

Brompton Road, 9
was originally called Don Road, after the river. To avoid confusion with another Don Road, it was renamed in 1886 after the Brompton area of London.

Bromwich Road, 8
was first called Broomfield Road, from an old Woodseats field name. To avoid duplication, it was renamed in 1903 after the Little Bromwich-West Bromwich area of the midlands.

Brook Drive, Hill, Lane, 3
from a brook which is shown, but not named, on early maps, and has since disappeared under building development. Brookhill Lane is mentioned, as Brokhill Lane, in a document of 1609.

Brookfield Road, 7
probably from a field name. There was a small brook in the area which ran down to the River Sheaf.

Brookhouse Hill, 10
from a house built near a stream. Brookehouse is mentioned at Fulwood in a document of 1613.

Brooklands Avenue, Crescent, Drive, 10
the avenue and crescent were built in 1915 on land owned by Shelley Barker, solicitor, and the name was a variation on nearby Brookhouse Hill.

Brook Lane, 12
from the nearby Ochre Dike.

Brooklyn Place, Road, 8
after an old house at Heeley called Brooklyn Mount. In 1857, it was the home of Joseph Johnson, maker of 'the improved water filterer, dealer in glass, china and earthenware, French moderator lamps, and fine coloza oil for same', whose business premises were in Fargate.

Brook Road, 8
from the nearby Meers Brook.

Brookside Close, 12
from the nearby Ochre Dike.

Brookside Lane, 6
from the nearby Storrs Brook.

Brook Terrace, 4
no longer listed; from the nearby stream, the Bagley Dike.

Broom Close, 2
from an old field name, Broom Close.

Broomfield Road, 10
from an old field name, Broom Field.

Broomgrove Crescent, Lane, Road, 10
from the house called Broom Grove, home for many years of the Branson family, the well-known solicitors. Thomas Branson, who was also vice consul for the United States, lived there in the 1840s and 1850s, and his descendants continued to live in the house up to the twentieth century.

Broomhall Place, Road, 10; Broomhall Street, 3
from the house, Broom Hall, thought to have been built by the Wickersley family and mentioned in a will of 1506. Up to the 1820s it had 100 acres of land around it. Rebuilt and changed many times, it was later the home of the Swyfts, and the Jessops. The vicar of Sheffield, the Rev James Wilkinson, lived there from 1754 till 1805.

Broomspring Lane, 10
in this case, the spring was a wood. Broomhall Spring consisted of a grove of oak trees in the area of what is now Wilkinson Street. It was chopped down about 1795.

Broom Street, 10
a variation on the broom theme of Broomhall.

Broomwood Close, Gardens, 19
from an old Beighton field name which was in use in 1796.

Brotherton Street, 3
was built on the Duke of Norfolk's land and named from his family history. Thomas of Brotherton (1300-1388) younger son of Edward I, was created Earl of Norfolk in 1312. He had no sons, so when he died his daughter became Countess of Norfolk in her own right.

Brough Street, 6
no longer listed; named after the area called Brough on Humberside (see Anlaby).

Broughton Lane, 9
the popular explanation is that the lane was named after Spence Broughton, the highwayman, the last person to be gibbeted in Sheffield. Broughton was hanged at York on 14 April 1792 for robbing the post at Attercliffe. His body was brought back to Sheffield and hung in chains on Attercliffe Common. It is said that the whitened remains of his bones were not removed for thirty-five years.

I hesitate to undermine a good story, but I have my doubts. The first use of the name Broughton I have been able to trace was in the 1860s, when that area started to be called Broughton Park. I suspect that the Duke of Norfolk, who was awarded land at Attercliffe under the enclosures, had a hand in this name. If so, it is hardly likely that Spence Broughton was its inspiration. The Duke of Norfolk did not make a habit of naming bits of his land after highwaymen. He usually chose names from his own family history, and it just so happens that the name Broughton crops up in his family history. Lord William Howard, first Lord Howard of Effingham. was married to Katherine Broughton, sister and co-heir of John Broughton. Several streets in the east end of Sheffield (and more at Rotherham) were named after the Effingham Howards, including, of course, Effingham Street.

Broughton Road, 6
was built by the Burrowlee Freehold Land Society and named after a house nearby called Broughton Villa, owned in the 1860s by Joseph Deakin, Britannia Metal manufacturer, who had works in Spring Street.

Brow Crescent, 19
from a geographical feature at Mosborough, a ridge known for many years as The Brow.

Brownell Street, 3
from a well-known Sheffield family who owned land in the area for many years. John and George Brownell were working land nearby at the time of Harrison's survey in 1637. Peter Brownell (1762-1828) was Master Cutler in 1807 and served for many years on the Town Trust, latterly as Town Collector.

Brown Hills Lane, 10
a descriptive name. Brown Hills are shown on the 1841 map, although the name is probably much older than that.

Browning Close, Drive, Road, 6
after Robert Browning (1812-1889), the English poet; one of a group of streets named after famous literary figures.

Brown Lane, Street, 1
probably after Ralph Brown, who is listed in the 1821 directory as victualler at the *Rose and Crown*, Paternoster Row, and seems to have owned property in the area.

Broxholme Road, 8
after the village of Broxholme, six miles from Lincoln (see Aisthorpe).

Bruce Road, 11
not known; one of five roads approved in 1897 for Messrs Neill and Hickmott (see Neill Road and Hickmott Road).

Brunswick Road, 3
was first called Tomcross Lane. It was renamed about 1860, and the reasons for the new name are unclear.

Brunswick Street, 10
like the parallel Hanover Street, was named after the royal house of Hanover which ruled England from 1714 to 1837. Brunswick was the second capital city of Hanover and King George III's sister married Charles William, Duke of Brunswick.

Brushfield Grove, 12
after the place called Brushfield, one mile from Taddington, Derbyshire (see Thornbridge).

Brunswick Street, at its junction with Collegiate Crescent. The house on the left was one of the gate houses to what was then the private estate of Broom Hall. One of the estate gateposts can be seen on the extreme left of the picture.

Bubwith Road, 9

after the village of Bubwith on Humberside.

Buchanan Crescent, Drive, Road, 5

after Robert Williams Buchanan (1814-1901) who wrote several volumes of poems and a series of novels including the *Shadow of the Sword*; one of a group of streets named after literary figures.

Buckenham Drive, Street, 4

was built on the Duke of Norfolk's land and named from his family history. Margaret, daughter of Sir John Howard, married, in the fourteenth century, Constantine Clifton, of Buckenham Castle, Norfolk.

Buckwood View, 14

from the nearby wood called Buck Wood. According to Melvyn and Joan Jones in their booklet, *Sheffield's Historic Woodlands Past and Present*, the sixteen-acre wood was called Berrystorth for hundreds of years and did not become Buck Wood till very late in the nineteenth century.

Bullen Road, 6

after Frank Thomas Bullen (1857-1915) writer of sea stories. After three years as an errand boy and street arab, he went to sea as a cabin boy at the age of twelve. His best known book, *The Cruise of the Cachelot* was inspired by his own experiences on a whaler of that name. He wrote thirty-six books in seventeen years.

Bungay Row, 2

from the earlier Bungay Street, now demolished. The name comes from the town called Bungay in Suffolk. The Bigods, ancestors of the Dukes of Norfolk, lived at Bungay Castle, and one of them was said to haunt the ruins in later years. Most of the town was destroyed by fire in 1688. Its name is thought to come from Bon Gue, meaning good ford.

Bunting Close, Nook, 8

after a man called Bunting who lived in the area, probably Joseph Bunting, farmer, yeoman and bowling green proprietor, who lived at Norton in the mid-nineteenth century.

Burbage Grove, 12

from the area called Burbage in Derbyshire (see Thornbridge).

Burcot Road, 8

was built by Jabez Balfour's notorious Lands Allotment Company (see Binfield) and named after Balfour's thirty-five acre country seat at Burcot, south Oxfordshire.

Burgess Road, 9

was built in the 1880s on land at Attercliffe owned by the Church Burgesses.

Burgess Street, 1

dates from 1738, and like Burgess Road, above, was named from the fact that it was built on land owned by the Church Burgesses. In 1738 the Burgesses leased 588 square yards of land between the present-day Pinstone Street and Cambridge Street, and the new Burgess Street was built soon after.

Burgoyne Road, 6

from the Burgoyne family who were lords of the manor of Owlerton from the late eighteenth century, when Catherine Burton, lady of the manor, married Sir Roger Montagu Burgoyne, of Sutton Park, Bedfordshire. Lady Burgoyne gave the manor to her second son, Montagu George Burgoyne, in 1853.

Burlington Close, Glen, Grove, Road, 17; Burlington Court, Street, 6

from the title Earl of Burlington, which is held by the Duke of Devonshire. The title was first given to a member of the Cavendish family in 1831 and since 1858, has been held by successive Dukes. The name crops up in Dore street names because the Dukes were lords of the manor of Dore and owned land there. It seems to have cropped up at Upperthorpe as one of several streets with names copied from London streets (see Oxford Street).

Burnaby Court, Crescent, Green, Street, Walk, 6

Burnaby Street, the first of the group to be built, was originally called Cromwell Street North. It was renamed in 1887 after Frederick Gustavus Burnaby, soldier and traveller, who crossed the Channel by balloon in 1882, served with Gordon in the Sudan, rode on horseback across the Steppes (about which he wrote a famous book), and was killed by arabs at Abu Kiea, on his way to join Sir Herbert Stewart's Nile expedition.

A group of streets at Crookes were all given Scottish names – Arran Road, Elgin Street, Forres Road, Nairn Street, Roslin Road and this one, Bute Street, seen in Edwardian days with some of its younger residents.

Burnell Road, 6

after Burnell Cottage Farm which was part of the Hillsborough Hall estate. When the estate was sold by the Dixon family in 1890, the Corporation bought most of it to make Hillsborough Park. A small area where the farm had been was developed by the Burrowlee Land Society and this was one of the society's roads.

Burngreave Bank, Road, Street, 3

Burngreave, recorded as Byrongreve in 1440, and Burngrave in 1694, was the name of a wood. The name means Byron's wood.

Burngrove Place, 3

from a house called Burngrove, which was probably named as a variation on the locality, Burngreave.

Burnside Avenue, 8

the name was suggested by the developer, George Hall, in 1903. What he had in mind is not known, but there are eight different villages called Burnside in Scotland, all of them near streams. He may have chosen the name because of the street's nearness to the Meers Brook.

Burns Road, 6

was first called Montgomery Road, after the poet, journalist and hymn writer, James Montgomery. It was renamed to avoid confusion with Montgomery Road, 7, and the new name, from Robert Burns, was the substitution of one Scots-born poet for another.

Burnt Stones Close, Drive, Grove, 10

from an area of land called Burnestone which is mentioned in Harrison's survey of 1637. The name may come from the fact that the land was cleared by burning.

Burnt Tree Lane, 3

in R.E. Leader's *Reminiscences of Old Sheffield*, Samuel Everard, an old resident, says that in his childhood there stood in the lane 'an oak tree which, during a severe thunderstorm, was struck and scathed by lightning'. Hence the name.

Burrowlee Road, 6

the name Burrow Lee is recorded in the seventeenth century, and means town field. In some documents it is spelt Borough Lee. The Creswick family, lords of the manor of Owlerton lived there.

Burrows Drive, 5

after the first Bishop of Sheffield, Dr Leonard Hedley Burrows, who was enthroned in 1914 and retired in 1939. The drive was built on the site of his old home, Bishopsholme, formerly called Norwood Hall.

Burton Road, 3

not known; built about 1870.

Burton Street, 6

after the Burton family, who succeeded the Bamforths as lords of the manors of Wadsley and Owlerton. William Burton (1704-1764) of Royds Mill, Attercliffe, married Margaret Bamforth and the lordships passed to their three sons, John, William and Michael.

Bury Street, 3

was first called Malton Street. It was renamed in 1886 after the town in Lancashire.

Bushey Wood Road, 17

from the name of a nearby wood. The wood, covering one and a quarter acres, was given to the old Norton Rural Council by Edward Sampson for use as a public park. The wood name explains itself.

Busk Knoll, Meadow, Park, 5

from an old field name. Harrison's survey of 1637 mentions 'a close of arrable called Buske Croft upon Norwood Greene'. Busk is the old word for bush.

Butchill Avenue, 5

the only explanation I can think of is that it is a corruption, or simplification, of the name of an old field at Ecclesfield – Butcher's Bill. Butcher's Bill Field, just over an acre in size, was part of Wheel Farm.

Bute Street, 10

from the island of Bute, off the coast of Argyllshire; a group name (see Arran).

Butler Road, 6

was built by the New Woodland View Freehold Land Society in the 1870s and named after an official of the society, Charles Butler, ivory carver and pearl cutter, whose works were in Tudor Street.

Buttermere Road, 7

after the lake and village in the Lake District; a group name (see Arnside).

Butterwaite Crescent, Road, 5

Butterwaite, formerly an outlying hamlet, with a population of 102 in 1861, gave its name to a hall, a wheel, a farm, and these two streets. The name is said to mean a clearing with rich pasture.

Campo Lane, at the back of Sheffield Cathedral, is shown on early maps as Camper Lane.

Button Hill, 11
is believed to come from the name of somebody who lived in the area, but whoever he was, or they were, it is a long time ago, because Buttonhill is mentioned in a will made in 1558 and listed in the *Index of Wills* at York Registry.

Butts Hill, 17
S.O. Addy, in his *Glossary of Sheffield words*, says butts, sometimes called gores, were short pieces of ploughed land in the corners of irregularly-shaped fields. In other words, they abutted on to the main field. The name was sometimes used as a field name. There is a Goosebutt Street at Rawmarsh which has the same origin.

Byron Road, 7
was built in 1864 and named after Lord Byron, the poet (1788-1824).

Byron Road, 19
has a link with Byron Road, 7. It was built in the 1870s by the Provident Freehold Land Society. The president of the land society, Benjamin Staniforth lived in Byron Road, Nether Edge.

C

Cadman Court, Street, 19
after the Cadman family who were well-known farmers at Mosborough in the nineteenth century. George Cadman is listed in the 1850s as farmer, maltster and sickle manufacturer, and he was followed by Ann, Charles and Eleanor Cadman.

Cadman Lane, 1
only part of it remains. Before the Town Hall extensions were built it joined Norfolk Street and it was named after the firm of Peter Cadman and Sons, merchants, table knife and saw manufacturers in Norfolk Street.

Cadman Road, 12
from Cadman Wood which is shown on a 1773 Fairbank map of Intake. The wood is thought to have been named after a local man, possibly Nicholas Cadman who is mentioned in the 1543 Subsidy Rolls as living in the area.

Cadman Street, 4
after Charles Cadman who established Canal Street Works in nearby Blast Lane in 1751. He lived at Pitsmoor.

Cairns Road, 10
was built for the solicitors Henry and Alfred Maxfield and named after an ancestor of theirs, Hugh Cairns, later Lord Cairns (1819-1885), who was Lord Chancellor briefly in 1868, and again from 1874 to 1880. The Maxfields must have been very proud of him. They named their offices, in Church Street, Cairns Chambers, and placed his statue on the frontage. It is still there today (see Cairns Road, 19, below).

Cairns Road, 19
by the 1920s, Cairns Chambers, Church Street (see above) were the offices of Sheffield Coal Company Ltd, and when the company built this road for their miners at Beighton, they named it after their offices.

Calder Way, 5
from the River Calder which rises near Todmorden and flows into the Aire at Castleford.

Callow Drive, Mount, Place, Road, 14
from the place called Callow, near Hathersage; four of a group of streets named after places around Hathersage.

Calvert Road, 9
was built in 1869 by the Greenland Freehold Land Society and named after an official of the society, William Calvert, bank clerk, who was also president and trustee of the Second Attercliffe and Darnall Society.

Cambourne Close, Road, 6
Cambourne Road was originally called Crescent Road because of its shape. After it came into Sheffield in 1921 it was changed to avoid confusion with Crescent Road, 7, and renamed after the market town of Cambourne in Cornwall.

Cambridge Road, 8
one of a group of royalty-related names at Heeley (Alexandra, Denmark, Albert, etc). The title Duke of Cambridge has been held by several members of the royal family since 1706.

Cambridge Street, 1
was first called Coalpit Lane. It was renamed to mark the laying of the foundation stone of the Crimea Monument at Moorhead by the Duke of Cambridge on 21st October 1857. The Duke, who was Commander in Chief of the army, died in 1904. The monument was moved to the Botanical Gardens in 1959.

Camdale Rise, View, 12
one of a group of streets named after dales (along with Ribblesdale and Teesdale).

Cammell Road, 5
after Charles Cammell (1810-1879) who was born at Hull, came to Sheffield as a young commercial traveller, and built up a giant steelworks. After his firm linked with Laird Brothers early in the twentieth century the name became associated with shipbuilding.

Camm Street, 6
was named after a man called W.H. Camm, but there were two: William Henry Camm, of Camm and Corbridge, accountants, land and estate agents, and debt collectors; and W.H. Camm, hammer manufacturer in School Croft, who was also a small landowner and lived in Martin Street. I am not sure which of them the street was named after but I would guess at the accountant-estate agent.

Campbell Road, 9
was named in 1899 along with Melville and Ravensworth Roads. The only common theme seems to be that all three are the names of ancient castles. Castle Campbell in Dollar Glen, Scotland, was built in the fifteenth century by the Earl of Argyll.

Camping Lane, 8
from two old field names, Upper Camp Field and Lower Camp Field, which S.O. Addy says were also known as the Camping Fields. Like Campo Lane, below, the name seems to mean fields where football was played. Fields where sports were played, particularly football, are often referred to in old documents as the campo, or camping, land.

Campo Lane, 1
is shown on the 1736 Gosling map as Camper Lane (see Camping Lane, above) and the theory is that it led to the field where football was played, possibly in the open space where Paradise Square was later built.

Campsall Drive, 10
from the village of Campsall, seven miles from Doncaster.

Canada Street, 4
no longer listed; it was named from the fact that the seventh Earl Fitzwilliam was born in 1872 at de Meuron City, near Fort William, Canada. The Earl, who was Lord Mayor of Sheffield in 1909, took his Canadian birthplace as one of his names – William Charles de Meuron Wentworth-Fitzwillam.

Canal Street, 4
from its nearness to the Sheffield and South Yorkshire Canal.

Candow Street, 9
was built in 1867 for the Shirland Land Society and was first called Beeley Street, after an official of the society. It was changed in 1870 and the new name came from Walter John Candow, property speculator, estate agent, brickmaker, and president of several local building societies, who eventually overreached himself and left town mysteriously with debts of £6,000. The three-storey houses he built on Abbeydale Road were known for some time as Candow's Folly because everybody thought they would be difficult to rent.

Canning Street, 1
after George Canning (1770-1827), barrister and statesman, Foreign Secretary 1822-27 and Prime Minster in 1827, but only for four months. His health broke down under the strain.

Cannock Street, 6
was approved in 1898 for G.W. Hawksley and was first called Charles William Street, after one of Mr Hawksley's sons. It was renamed in 1908 after the Cannock area of Staffordshire. (See Cheadle Street.)

Cannon Hall Road, 5
from the house called Cannon Hall. It was owned in the mid-nineteenth century by Edward Smith, of William and Edward Smith, ironmasters in the Wicker. Mr Smith lived at Firvale but not at Cannon Hall, which he leased out. When the hall was offered to let in 1846 it had three acres of ground with it, three rooms on the ground floor and four main bedrooms. How it got its name is not known.

Canny Street, 9
no longer listed; named after John Canny and Co, builders and contractors in Alfred Road in the early 1900s.

Canterbury Avenue, Crescent, Drive, 10
Canterbury Avenue was first called School Lane from the nearby church school. It was renamed in 1903 (because there were several other School Lanes) from the city and ecclesiastical capital in Kent.

Canterbury Road, 8
not known; possibly a thought association name with nearby Kent Road.

Capel Street, 6
came about through a cunning bit of renaming. It was first called Chapel Street from the Methodist New Connexion Chapel at its corner with Penistone Road. To avoid confusion with other Chapel Streets it was changed in the early 1870s by simply dropping one letter and producing the Middle English and Welsh word for chapel.

Carbrook Street, 9
from the area known as Carbrook, which means the stream running through a marsh.

Cardiff Street, 9
was first called Queen Street. It was renamed in 1886 to avoid confusion with Queen Street in the town centre. There was no special reason for the new name, from the capital of Wales.

Cardoness Drive, Road, 10
from Cardoness Castle, Scotland (see Barholm).

Carfield Avenue, Lane, Place, 8
from the sixteenth century farm called Carfield, or Carr Field, meaning marshy land. In the 1860s the farm had twenty-five acres of land.

Carlby Road, 6
was first called Carr Road. It was changed in 1903 and the new name was simply an effort to keep a similar sound to the old one. Carlby is a village on the Lincs-Leicestershire border.

Carley Drive, 19
not known.

Carlin Street, 13
was originally called Chapel Street because there was a chapel on it. It was renamed when Normanton Springs came into Sheffield, after the Yorkshire village of Carlin How, near Saltburn.

Carlisle Road, Street, Street East, 4
after Charles Edward, great grandson of the fourth Duke of Norfolk, who was created Earl of Carlisle in 1661.

Carlton Close, 19
from an old sickle-grinding wheel known as Carlton Wheel which stood nearby. It worked up to the 1930s. The wheel may have been named after Thomas Carlton who was a cutler in the area in the seventeenth century.

Carlton Road, 6
Carlton was a popular Victorian street and house name, mainly because of its aristocratic associations. Carlton House, London, was the home of the Prince of Wales up to 1827. London also had the Carlton Club and Carlton Gardens. In Sheffield there was a Carlton Place, several Carlton Cottages and any number of Carlton Villas.

Carltonville Road, 9
not known; built in the late 1890s. It may have been just a variation on Carlton (above).

Carnaby Road, 6
from the village of Carnaby, three miles from Bridlington; one of three streets (Bessingby and Speeton the others) named after villages in the old East Riding.

Carnarvon Street, 6
one of three streets built in 1879 for John Yeomans, Town Clerk, who owned land in the Infirmary Road area. The other two were Cleveland Street and Westmoreland Street. The names seem to have been random selections probably for their up-market sound, from British Dukedoms and Earldoms.

Carpenter Croft, Gardens, Mount, 12
after Edward Carpenter, pioneer Socialist writer, philosopher and reformer who lived at Millthorpe, near Sheffield, from 1879 till 1922.

Carr Bank Close, Drive, Lane, 11
from an old field name, Carr Bank, which is shown on the 1840 map but is probably much older than that. Carr indicates that there was wet or marshy land nearby.

Carrfield Court, Drive, Road, Street, 8
have the same origin as Carfield. For some reason, the four streets on the city side of the Meers Brook were spelt Carrfield, and the three on the other side of the brook were spelt Carfield.

Carr Forge Close, Lane, Mount, Place, Road, Terrace, View, Walk, 12
from the old Carr Forge, which stood on the Shire Brook, in the valley between Hackenthorpe and Woodhouse. Believed to have been set up in Tudor times as a cutler's wheel, it later changed to making scythes.

Carrill Drive, Road, 6
not known; the name was approved in 1938. The other street names approved at the same committee meeting (Browning, Cowper, Keats, etc) were from famous literary figures. Unless it is a mistake for Carroll, as in Lewis Carroll, creator of *Alice in Wonderland*, or John Caryll, author of *Sir Solomon Single*, this one does not fit the pattern.

Carrington Road, 11
from the village of Carrington, three miles from Coningsby, Lincs; one of a group of streets developed by the Otter family of Ranby Hall, Wragby, and named after places in Lincolnshire near the family seat (see Louth, Ranby, Stainton, and Wragby).

Carr Lane, 1
after John and Riley Carr, merchants and manufacturers of saws, files machine knives, etc, whose works, known as Bailey Lane Works, stood at the corner of Bailey Lane and Carr Lane in the mid-nineteenth century.

Carr Road, 6
was built by the Whitehouse Lane Freehold Land Society and named after the secretary of the society, Walter Crabtree Carr, sharebroker and accountant, who lived in Hoole Street, and had offices in Queen Street. The society was wound up in 1873.

Carrville Drive, Road; Carrville Road West, 6
Carrville Road was originally called Carr Road, a shortened form of Birley Carr Road. When the Birley Carr area came into Sheffield, it was changed to avoid confusion with another Carr Road by simply adding ville to the end of it. The other roads, built later, took their names from it.

Carrwell Lane, 6
not known; presumably there was a well nearby.

Carsick Grove; Carsick Hill Crescent, Drive, Road, Way, Carsick View Road, 10
from the area called Carre Sick, meaning a marshy area with a stream running through it, sick being the old word for a stream or ditch. Carsick Hill Drive was first called Burlington Road. It was changed in February 1967 to avoid confusion with Burlington Road, 17.

Carson Mount, 12
from a nearby well called Carson Mount Well.

Carson Road, 10
after William Carson who was a joiner and builder in St Mary's Road in the 1870s, and later at Attercliffe. His home was in Greenhow Street, Walkley and he built quite a lot of houses in the Walkley and Crookes areas.

Carterhall Lane, Road, 12
from the old Carter Hall Farm, recorded as Curtare Hall in 1625, and thought to have been named after a former owner.

Carter Knowle Avenue, Road, 11

Carter comes from the name of a family who lived in the area in the twelfth century and knowle, or knoll, as it is spelt in old documents, is a grassy hill. The 1788 enclosures set aside two acres for a burial ground for Ecclesall at Carter-knoll.

Carter Lodge Avenue, Drive, Place, Rise, Walk, 12

from Carter Lodge Farm which stood on Spa Lane, Hackenthorpe, before the area was developed. The farm, thought to have been named after Jonathan Carter who lived there in the early eighteenth century, was demolished in 1954.

Carter Place, Road, 8

Carter Road was built in the 1870s by the Heeley Central Freehold Land Society, and named after somebody connected with the society, possibly Charles Carter who was a well-known auger manufacturer at Woodseats around that time.

Cartmell Crescent, Road, 8

seems to be a mis-spelling of the village of Cartmel, Cumbria. Nearby Ulverston Road is named after a town in Cumbria. The extra final letter is a mystery.

Car Vale Drive, View, 13

from the nearby stream, the Car Brook.

Carver Lane, Street, 1

Carver Street, a name decided by the commissioners under the Ecclesall Enclosure Act in 1779, comes from an old field name, Carver Fields. The street led to the fields.

Carwood Close, Green, Grove, Lane, Road, Way, 4

from the Hallcarr Wood which was quite a large area of woodland up to the middle of the nineteenth century.

Cary Road, 2

from Henry Cary, Lord Hunsdon, a cousin of Queen Elizabeth I, by whom he was made lord of the manor of Eckington. The lordship continued in the Cary family until the time of Cromwell. Cary Road at Eckington is named from the same source.

Castlebeck Avenue, Court, Croft, 2

Lower Manor was renamed Castlebeck in 1983. The name is a variation on the theme of Manor Castle.

Castledine Croft, Gardens, 9

after the Rev Edwin Castledine, first vicar of St Margaret's Church, Brightside, from 1918-1920. The church was formed out of the older St Thomas's, Brightside, and became the centre of a separate parish in 1918.

Castlegate, 3

was built in the early 1930s and the original intention was to call it River Don Street (which is what it was called in the planning stage). Castlegate, from its nearness to the site of the old Sheffield Castle, was thought (correctly) to be a better name.

Castle Green, 3, Castle Square, 1, Castle Street, 3

from Sheffield Castle, which occupied about four acres between Dixon Lane, Waingate and the Rivers Don and Sheaf. The exact date of building is not known but it was there in the thirteenth century. It was demolished in 1648 after being captured by Parliamentary forces in the Civil War. Castle Green was named from the open area in front of the castle, and Castlefold from the old sheep pens.

Castle Row; Castlerow Close, Drive, 17

from a group of cottages called Castle Row, which were named after the *Castle Inn*. The inn was built in 1866 primarily for navvies working on Bradway tunnel, one of four new beerhouses built for them at Bradway between 1864 and 1868.

Castlewood Crescent, Drive, Road, 10

was named after the fictional Castlewood family (Sir Francis Edward Castlewood and his descendants) in two novels by William Makepeace Thackeray called *Henry Esmond* and *The Virginians*. In June 1907, the Watch Committee agreed on three names for new roads off Crimicar Lane, all from characters in Thackeray novels, Castlewood Road, Esmond Road (from *Henry Esmond*) and Newcome Road (from *The Newcomes*). Only Castlewood has survived.

Castor Road, 9

a link with Earl Fitzwilliam who owned large areas of land in Northamptonshire. The Fitzwilliams had a home at Castor, a Northants village on the bank of the River Nene, and at least one Earl was born there.

Catch Bar Lane, 6

a catch bar was a small toll bar intended to prevent travellers from slipping down a side route to avoid paying at the main bar. The catch bar near this lane was to stop people coming into Sheffield from branching off down to Penistone Road and dodging the Barracks toll bar.

Catcliffe Road, 9

a name given by the Enclosure Commissioners in 1811 as part of the Darnall enclosures. It leads to the old footpath across Tinsley Park to the village of Catcliffe.

Catherine Road, 4, Catherine Street, 3

were built on the Duke of Norfolk's land and named after a lady in the Duke's ancestry. There have been several Catherines in the family, but the most famous was the ill-fated Catherine Howard, grand-daughter of the first Duke, and fifth wife of King Henry VIII. She was beheaded in 1542.

Cat Lane, 2

S.O. Addy, in his *Sheffield Glossary*, suggested that the name came, like that of a field at Dore called Cat Croft, from the Swedish word *kaette*, meaning a fold for lambs.

Catley Road, 9

uncertain; may be from the fact that it follows the ancient track from Darnall to Catcliffe, which was sometimes pronounced Catley.

Cattall Street, 9

was built on Staniforth family land and named after the village of Cattall, on the River Nidd, halfway between York and Harrogate (see Staniforth Road).

Causeway Gardens, Glade, Causeway Head Road, The Causeway, 17

the area called Causeway Head at Dore is referred to as Cawse Head in a document dated 1772. Cawse, still occasionally used as a dialect word in Sheffield, means raised path.

Cave Street, 9
after Sir Lewis William Cave (1832-1897), former Recorder of Lincoln, and High Court judge from 1881 onwards; one of a group of streets named after prominent nineteenth century legal men.

Cavendish Avenue, 6
uncertain; probably no more than an aristocratic name (see below).

Cavendish Avenue, 17
from the family name of the Dukes of Devonshire who were lords of the manor of Dore and owned large areas of land there. The early ancestors of the family came from Cavendish in Suffolk.

Cavendish Road, 11
from one of the Duke of Devonshire's ancestors, probably Spencer Compton Cavendish, a Liberal MP for more than thirty years, who held several Government posts during the nineteenth century. He became the eighth Duke in 1891.

Cavendish Street, 3
after Lord John Cavendish, who was Chancellor of the Exchequer in 1782-83; one of a group of streets named after prominent eighteenth century politicians.

Cavill Road, 8
was first called Victoria Road. It changed when Meersbrook and Norton Lees became part of Sheffield in 1900. The new name came from a well-known local family, the Cavills, who built houses in the street. Walter Cavill, grocer, had a shop at the corner of the road. Mount View Methodist Church was started in a room over the shop, which was destroyed by bombing in 1940.

Cawdor Road, 2
was built on the Duke of Norfolk's land and named from the fact that a member of the Duke's family, Sir Edward Stafford Howard, of Thornbury Castle, Gloucestershire, married, in 1876, Lady Rachel Campbell, daughter of the second Earl Cawdor.

Cawston Road, 4
from the Norfolk village of Cawston (see Blayton).

Cawthorne Close, Grove, 8
not known; Cawthorne Grove first appears in the 1933 directory. Since several nearby streets were given Yorkshire names, this one may be from the village of Cawthorne, near Barnsley.

Caxton Lane, Road, 10
from the name of a house in Ashdell Road. The house was the home in the mid-nineteenth century of Joseph Pearce jr, bookseller, printer and founder of the *Sheffield Daily Telegraph*. He named it after the famous English printer, William Caxton. Caxton Road was built alongside the house.

Cecil Road, 7; Cecil Square, 2
Joseph Cecil inherited the house called Priory Grange at Sharrow in 1799 and although he never lived in it – he lived at Dronfield – his family owned the land at Sharrow until the 1880s, when it was sold for the building of Sharrow Lane School, two churches and housing.

Celandine Court, Gardens, 17
after the celandine, a yellow-flowered plant; the streets were given a floral name because they were built on the site of a former nursery garden.

Cemetery Avenue, Road, 11
from the nearby General Cemetery, which opened in 1836 on a six-acre site. It was extended to fifteen acres in 1848 and Cemetery Road was built at about the same time, replacing a narrow lane called Mackenzie Walk (named after the Rev Alexander Mackenzie, curate of St Paul's Church from 1778 to 1816, who lived at Sharrow Head).

Century Street, 9
was built in 1901, the first year of the twentieth century. It appears first in the 1902 directory, with two shopkeepers listed as living on it.

Chadwick Road, 13
not known; the name was approved in August 1931 as part of the Woodthorpe Estate. It could be something to do with the firm of Chadwick and Sons, Victoria Street, who worked regularly for the Corporation.

Challoner Green, Way, 19
after John Challoner who was allocated a piece of land on Mosborough Green at the time of the land enclosures in 1795.

Chambers Lane, 4
is mentioned in Harrison's survey of 1637 as Chamber Lane and thought to have been named after a local resident.

Champion Close, Road, 5
not known; Champion Road was approved in August 1931.

Chancel Row, 2
from the older Chancel Street, so named because it was built at the Chancel end of St John's Church, Park.

Chancet Wood Close, Drive, Rise, Road, View, 8
from the nearby wood which was recorded in 1586 as Johnsett Wood, meaning John's dwelling in the wood. The name changed later to Chauncet and then to Chancet. When it was sold in 1850, the wood was twenty-one acres in size.

Chandos Street, 10
uncertain; possibly from Sir John Chandos, the Derbyshire-born soldier who fought at Cambrai, Crecy and Poitiers and was one of the founders of the Order of the Garter.

Change Alley, 1
no longer listed; named from the fact that horses were changed there in days when the old *King's Head Hotel* was a coaching inn. In the 1780s, York waggons left the *King's Head* every Monday and Friday.

Channing Gardens, Street, 6
was built in the 1850s and named after the same man that Channing Hall, Surrey Street, was named after, William Ellery Channing, American author and Congregational minister.

Chantrey Road, 8
after Francis Legatt Chantrey (1781-1841), who was born in humble circumstances at Norton and became an internationally renowned artist and sculptor. He was knighted in 1835.

Chapel Close, Terrace, 10
from the nearby Ranmoor Methodist Church which was built in 1870 on the site of an earlier chapel.

Chapel Lane, 9
led to the old Attercliffe Wesleyan Chapel.

Chapel Lane, 17
from the nearby Totley Methodist Chapel, built in 1848.

Chapel Street, 13
at one time it had three chapels on it, Primitive Methodist, New Connexion Methodist and Congregational.

Chapel Street, 19
previously called Market Street; it was renamed after the Methodist Church which was built on land nearby in 1830.

Chapel Walk, 1
Gosling's 1736 map calls it Tuckers Alley. By the 1771 Fairbank map it had become Chapel Walk, from Nether Chapel, which was built in 1726. Another chapel was built on the other side of the walk in 1780, the Methodist Chapel which was eventually replaced by the Victoria Hall.

Chapelwood Road, 9
from a nearby wood which was named after the family who owned it. One old map shows the wood, and land near it, owned by Thomas Chapell.

Chapman Street, 9
was originally called Chapel Street because it ran alongside the Primitive Methodist Chapel in Barrow Road. It was renamed in 1903, and the main reason for the new name was its similarity to the old one.

Charles Ashmore Road, 8
was first called Ashmore Road. It was renamed in 1926. Charles Ashmore was an artist who came to Sheffield from Birmingham and settled at Norton. He was a noted water colourist, member of both the Surrey and Heeley art clubs, and he did the illustrations for the book *Chantrey Land*, by Harold Armitage, which was published in 1910.

Charles Lane, Street, 1
after Charles, tenth Duke of Norfolk (1720-1786). It was while he was Duke, and lord of the manor, that the area between The Moor and Pond Street was developed, which is why so many of the streets in that area are named from the Norfolk ancestry.

Charlotte Lane, 1
after Princess Charlotte, only child of King George IV, who was born in 1796, married Leopold of Saxe-Coburg in 1816 and died in 1817 in childbirth. The lane was built off Charlotte Street and took the same name, but Charlotte Street was later renamed Mappin Street.

Charlotte Road in more sedate times; one of many street names connected with the Duke of Norfolk.

Charlotte Road, 1 and 2
was built on the Duke of Norfolk's land and named after Charlotte Sophia Leveson-Gower, daughter of George Granville, first Duke of Sutherland, who married Henry Charles Howard (later thirteenth Duke of Norfolk) in 1814.

Charnley Avenue, Close, Drive, Rise, 11
after the Rev Henry Charnley, who was curate of Ecclesall in the 1690s. His name appears on a list of early incumbents on an oak tablet in the north transept of Ecclesall church.

Charnock Avenue, Crescent, Drive, Grove; Charnock Dale Road; Charnock Hall Road; Charnock View Road; Charnock Wood Road, 12
the name is mentioned in sixteenth century documents as Sharnock Hall, but its origin is uncertain. It may have been imported in some way from Lancashire, where there is a place called Charnock.

Charnwood Court, 19
after the Charnwood Forest, Leicestershire; one of a group (see Ashdown).

Charter Row, Square, 1
commemorate the charter granted to the inhabitants of Sheffield by Thomas, third Lord Furnival, in 1297, which gave the town its first step towards local government. The original intention was to call the square Grosvenor Square, from the nearby hotel, but there was already a Grosvenor Square in the city – a small street off London Road – so it became Charter Square instead.

Chase Road, 6
from the large area of land nearby called Loxley Chase. A chase was usually privately-owned open land where game was bred and hunted.

The Chase, 10
a fanciful name with no special significance.

Chatfield Road, 10
after Edward Chatfield (1802-1839), a painter who exhibited at the Royal Academy from 1827 till his death; one of a group of roads built for James Duffield, of Wilson Cammell's works, Dronfield, who was an art collector (see also Crosby, Fraser, Kennedy and Linscott).

Chatham Street, 3
was originally called Chapel Street because there was a chapel nearby. It was renamed in 1886 after Chatham, the seaport and market town in Kent, to keep it similar to the old name.

Chatsworth Court, 11; Chatsworth Park Avenue, Drive, Grove, Rise, Road, 12; Chatsworth Road, 17
from the Duke of Devonshire's stately home in Derbyshire. The name comes from the Old English *Ceatt's Worth*, meaning the enclosure belonging to Ceatt.

Chatterton Street, 2

no longer listed; named after Benjamin Chatterton, who represented Park ward on the town council from 1868 to 1880, owned property, and as a young man, played cricket for Sheffield Wednesday. He died in 1902.

Chatwin Street, 6

no longer listed; origin of name not known. The street was one of several approved in 1881 for the executors of Phillip Ashberry (see Ashberry Road).

Chaucer Close, Road, 5

after Geoffrey Chaucer (died 1400) poet, and author of *The Canterbury Tales*. Group name.

Cheadle Street, 6

was originally called Frederick George Street, after Frederick George Hawksley, son of G.W. Hawksley, for whom the street was built in 1898. It was renamed in 1908, after the Staffordshire town of Cheadle, eight miles from Stoke (see Cannock Street).

Chelmsford Street, 9

no longer listed; named after Frederick Thesiger, first Baron Chelmsford (1794-1878), who was Lord Chancellor in 1858-59 and again from 1866 to 1868 (see Brett).

Chelsea Court, Rise, Road, 11

Chelsea Road, built first, was originally called Palmerston Road, after the famous statesman. It was renamed in 1886 (because there was another Palmerston Road). The new name, of an area in London, seems to have been an arbitrary choice.

Chemical Yard, 17;

from the old Totley Chemical Works, operated in the mid-nineteenth century by Tinker and Siddall, manufacturing chemists, later by Thomas Kilner, 'manufacturer of pyroligineous acid, naphtha, charcoal, etc.' In the early 1900s, after the factory had closed, Mr Kilner's daughter, Elizabeth, was still living at Chemical Yard.

Cheney Row, 1

after Edward Cheney, who bought surplus land in the area after St Paul's Church had been built. St Paul's stood on the site of the present Peace Gardens. Mr Cheney, member of a well-known Sheffield family, was the grandfather of Dr Hugh Cheney, one of the first surgeons at the (Royal) Infirmary.

Cherry Bank Road, 8

was originally called Cherry Tree Road, from a local field called Cherry Tree Field. It was changed in 1903 to avoid confusion with Cherry Tree Road, 11.

Cherry Street, Cherry Street South, 2

from a house in Clough Bank called Cherry Mount. In the 1850s, when the house was surrounded by open land, it was the home of Alfred Green, edge tool, knife, file and instrument maker, whose works were in Pond Street.

Cherry Tree Close, Court, Dell, Drive, Road, 11

from the old Cherry Tree farm believed to be early seventeenth century, and demolished about 1906. Cherry Tree Road was originally called Cherry Tree Hill.

Cheshunt Road, 6

no longer listed; it was originally called Rossall Road (presumably from Rossall Point, near Fleetwood, Lancashire). It was renamed in 1907, for no special reason after the Hertfordshire town of Cheshunt.

Chessel Close, 8

not known; approved, June 1935.

Chesterfield Road, Chesterfield Road South, 8

directional names. Up to the end of the eighteenth century the main road to Chesterfield was up Derbyshire Lane, through what is now Graves Park, and Coal Aston. The route through Woodseats was approved in 1795.

Chester Lane, Street, 1

Chester Street was built for the Church Burgesses in the 1830s and named after the city of Chester, but I don't know why. Dee Street was built at the same time.

Chesterwood Drive, 10

not known; approved May 1964. There is a hamlet called Chesterwood in Northumbria.

Chestnut Avenue, 9

group name on a tree theme (see Alder Lane).

Chestnut Avenue, 19

as above, a group name on the theme of trees (along with Elm, Lime, Oak, Poplar and Sycamore).

Chichester Road, 10

was one of two roads built in the 1890s for Alfred Hoole, and named after the city of Chichester in Sussex. The other road was named Colchester Road.

Chiltern Road, 6

one of six roads built for Sheffield Land and Mortgage Corporation Ltd, in 1907 and first called Chilton Road, probably after a person called Chilton. It was renamed in December 1925, after the Chiltern Hills. A month later, nearby Evandale Road was renamed Cotswold, after the Cotswold Hills.

Chinley Street, 9

was built on land owned by the Staniforth family and named after the place called Chinley, near Chapel-en-le-Frith.

Chippingham Place, Street, 9

from the house called Chippingham House, which was built about 1850 and for a time was the home of John Eadon, of Moses Eadon and Sons. The man who owned, and probably built, the house was John Shortridge, the well-known civil engineer, and the name may have been a variation on the name of Shortridge's own house at the other side of town, Chipping House (see below).

Chippinghouse Road, 7 and 8

John Shortridge, a civil engineer from Cumberland, built a home for himself at Broadfield, and called it Chipping House. A letter writer to the *Sheffield Telegraph* suggested in 1955 that the name came about because the house was built of chippings left over from the Wicker Arches (which Shortridge, as engineer of the Sheffield to Manchester railway, had built). In fact it was a more romantic reason. In 1826, Shortridge married Ellen Leach, who lived in the parish of Chipping, Lancashire. The house was demolished in the 1890s.

Chorley Avenue, Drive, Place, Road, 10

Chorley Road was first called Church Lane, from the nearby Fulwood Church. It was renamed after the Lancashire town of Chorley in 1886. The other three streets were built later.

The statue of Lord Cairns stands in a niche on the frontage of a building in Church Street. The building itself, and two Sheffield streets – one at Crookes, the other at Beighton – were also named after Lord Cairns.

Christ Church Road, 3
from the parish church of Pitsmoor which was built at a cost of £2,311 in the 1840s and consecrated in 1850. Most of the cost was raised by public subscription.

Churchdale Road, 12
after Churchdale Hall, which is near Thornbridge Hall, Derbyshire (see Thornbridge).

Churchill Road, 10
after Lord Randolph Churchill, Victorian politician, son of the seventh Duke of Marlborough, Conservative MP for Woodstock, and Chancellor of the Exchequer in the 1880s. He visited Sheffield in 1885. The road was built around the time of his death in 1895.

Church Lane, 9
from Christ Church, Attercliffe, which was consecrated in 1826, and was destroyed by bombing during the Second World War.

Church Lane, 12
seems odd, being so far from Hackenthorpe church, but it was named from the old mission church which served Hackenthorpe before Christ Church was built and dedicated in 1899. The old church later became a grocery shop, then a button factory, but the lane kept its name.

Church Lane, 13
from St James' Church, Woodhouse, which opened in February 1878.

Church Lane, 13
although it is not listed in most commercial directories, the lane at the side of St Mary's Church, Handsworth, is known as Church Lane.

Church Lane,17
from Christ Church, Dore, which was built in 1828.

Church Lane, 19
from Beighton parish church, originally dedicated to St Radegund, but at some time re-dedicated to St Mary the Virgin.

Church Street, 1
Formerly known as Church Lane, it was widened, at the expense of the parish churchyard, in 1785, 1866 and 1890. There has been a church in the area since the twelfth century, for many years the parish church, in modern times, the Anglican Cathedral.

Church Street, 6
from Christ Church, Stannington, which was built in 1830.

Church View, 13
from St James' Church, Woodside.

Cinderhill Lane, 8
Cinderhill is a common English name usually connected with the cinders left by the smelting process. It often occurs near bole hills, as in this case.

The Circle, 2
exactly what it is.

City Road, 2 and 12
was first called Intake Road. It was changed, at the request of residents, in 1898, five years after Sheffield became a city.

Clarefield Road, 9
not known; it was approved in 1898 for G. Talbot.

Claremont Crescent, Place, 10
from a house on Glossop Road called Claremont Villa. In the 1840s, it was a school run by the Misses Lewis. Claremont was a popular house and street name in the early 1800s because of the large house called Claremont built near Esher, Surrey, by Sir John Vanburgh. It was the home for a time of Princess Charlotte.

Clarence Lane, Street, 3
after the Duke of Clarence, Lord High Admiral of England, who became King William IV in 1830. He visited Sheffield in November 1806.

Clarence Lane, 6
after Prince Albert, eldest son of Edward VII, who was created Duke of Clarence and Avondale (hence nearby Avondale Road) in May 1890. He died suddenly from pneumonia in 1892 at the age of twenty-eight, and the title became extinct (see May Road).

Clarendon Drive, Road, 10
see Belsize Road.

Clarke Dell, Drive, 10
variations on nearby Clarkehouse Road. Clarke Dell was first called Clarke Grove. Clarke Drive was Leven Road till 1948.

Clarkegrove Road, 10
from the house called Clarke Grove, built by John Smith Hawksworth, of Howard and Hawksworth, silversmiths. It had two acres of grounds and was said to have been built 'regardless of expense'.

Clarkehouse Road, 10
from the house called Clarke House. In the late 1800s, it was the home of

William Fawcett, silver plate manufacturer, of Dixon and Sons. In the 1930s it became a preparatory school.

Clarke Square, 2
after Reuben Clarke, builder and contractor, who had premises in the street (it is not a true square) in the 1870s.

Clarke Street, 10
after John Clarke, joiner and builder, who lived in Chester Street in the mid-nineteenth century and was involved in building work on the Broom Hall Estate when it was developed by John Watson.

Clarkson Street, 10
possibly after Thomas Clarkson (1760-1846) the English anti-slavery campaigner. There was a strong movement for the abolition of slavery in Sheffield.

Claro Road, 9
no longer listed; built on Staniforth family land and named after Claro Hill, near the Great North Road, which gave its name to the ancient wapentake of Claro, stretching from Craven in the west, to the River Ouse in the east (see Staniforth Road).

Clay Lane, 1
not known.

Clay Street, 9
approved 1867 for Henry Wilson, landowner; reason for name uncertain. It could be named after a person but in the absence of a likely candidate, it seems more likely it was named from the state of the local soil.

Clayton Crescent, Hollow, 19
one of a group of four Mosborough street names taken from local landowners listed on eighteenth century property rolls (along with Galley, Harwood and Raseby).

Clayton Terrace, 3
no longer listed; probably named after Richard Clayton, builder and joiner at Neepsend in the mid-nineteenth century.

Claywheels Lane, 6
from the nearby works known as the Clay Wheels, set up by the Clay family of Bridgehouses, who were well-known in Sheffield in the eighteenth and nineteenth centuries. The works had one of the last forges in the Sheffield area to use water-powered hammers.

Church Street in Edwardian times. The café on the right, at the corner of St. James Row, 'Ye Mecca Café', is advertising: 'Smoke Room and Lounge; Billiards; Pool.' Next door to the café is 'The Irish Linen Depot'. An open topped tram is on its way down the street, and a carriage, with top-hatted driver, is overtaking a milk cart on the left.

Claywood Drive, Road, 2
from the old Clay Wood, named, like the Clay Wheels, above, after the Clay family of Bridgehouses.

Cleeve Hill Gardens, 19
after Cleeve Hill, at 1,000 feet, the highest point in the Cotswolds, well-known beauty spot and site of an ancient camp; one of a group of streets named after hills.

Clematis Road, 5
group name – flowers (see Acacia).

Clementson Road, 10
after the Rev Constantine Clementson, vicar of Crookes from 1882 till his death in 1901. He aroused some controversy over his high church views, but was well liked by local people who referred to him affectionately as the Bishop of Crookes.

Clement Street, 9
not known; approved 1898-99 for Frederick Uttley Laycock, the solicitor.

Clevedon Street, 9
no longer listed; it was originally called Clifton Street, but as there was another Clifton Street it was renamed Cleveland Street in 1872. There was another Cleveland Street, so it was renamed again as Clevedon Street. Both the new names were an effort to retain some similarity to the previous names. Clevedon is a town on the Severn estuary.

Cleveland Square, 9
no longer listed; named from one of the ancestors of Earl Fitzwilliam, who owned land at Darnall. Sir Thomas Wentworth (1591-1667) fourth Baron Wentworth, was also the first Earl of Cleveland, a title given to him in 1626.

Cliffe Farm Drive, 11
after the nearby Cliffe House Farm, on Cow Lane.

Cliffefield Road, 8
from a house called Cliffe Field, for many years the home of the Ryalls family. It was demolished about 1896. The house probably took its name from a local field. Cliffe refers to the nearby steep hill. Lister Road (probably named after John Lister, a local landowner) became part of Cliffefield Road in 1926.

Cliffe House Road, 5
from a house called Cliffe House, built about 1808 by a member of the Booth family and demolished in 1930 for the building of Elm Lane Fire Station.

Cliffe Road, 6
from the nearby steep hillside. There was also a Cliffe Wood nearby.

Cliffe View Road, 8
a variation on Cliffefield (above).

Clifford Road, 11
after the house called Clifford, built on a site which is now the corner of Psalter Lane and Bagshot Street by Thomas Wilson, of the well-known Wilson family of Sharrow, in 1800. It was demolished early this century.

Clifton Avenue, Crescent, Lane, 9
from the house called Clifton House, built near the entrance to Bowden Housteads Wood about 1860 by George Fisher, one of the partners in the Handsworth nursery firm, Fisher, Holmes and Co, later Fisher, Son and Sibray. After Fisher died in 1874, it became the home of John Craven, railway wagon builder.

Clifton Street, 9
not known; built in the 1860s for Henry Newbold, it was first called Clifton Road.

Clinton Lane, Place, 10
after Sir Henry Clinton (1771-1829), soldier, and a senior officer at Waterloo.

Clipstone Gardens, Road, 9
from the village of Clipstone, Nottinghamshire.

Clixby Road, 9
from the village of Clixby between Scunthorpe and Grimsby.

Cloonmore Croft, Drive, 8
built 1938, as part of the Norton House Estate by M.J. Gleeson Ltd, and named after the house called Cloonmore, in Meadowhead. It was the home of the head of the firm, Michael Joseph Gleeson.

Clough Bank, Road, 2
from a mill called Clough Mill, which stood in the area. Joseph Hunter said a clough was a floodgate where water was artificially dammed. S.O. Addy said a clough was a small, narrow glen or ravine. In view of the mill, Hunter's explanation seems to fit better in this case. The 1832 map shows a group of buildings called The Banks near Clough Mill.

Clough Lane, 10
see Clough Bank, above. In this case, Addy's explanation seems more fitting. There is a Clough Hollow and a Clough plantation nearby.

Club Garden Road, 11
was built on the site of a five-acre field used as gardens in the early nineteenth century and known as Fifty Gardens Field. It was used by members of a local club and its name was changed later to Club Gardens Field.

Club Mill Road, 6
is the relic of a bold early experiment in co-operation. In 1795, members of forty-three Sheffield sick clubs banded together to build a corn mill with the object of providing reasonably-priced corn and meal for their members. The club mill was built, operated for some years, then ran into money troubles. It was sold to a private buyer in 1811.

Club Street, 11
as Club Gardens Road, above.

Clumber Road, 10
was built on land owned by Dan Coupe (see Coupe Road). Mr Coupe was born near Clumber, Nottinghamshire.

Clun Road, Street, 4
were built on the Duke of Norfolk's land and named from a title held by the Duke, Baron Clun, one of three titles annexed to the Earldom of Arundel in the seventeenth century. Clun is a small market town in Shropshire, where the Duke owned land.

Clyde Place, 3
no longer listed; named from Samuel Osborn's old works at Brookhill called Clyde Works. Mr Osborn is said to have named the works in gratitude for the help he received from friends in Scotland when he started in business. The firm later moved to The Wicker.

Clyde Road, 8
not known; built in 1880 and first called Clyde Terrace. The land was owned by the Midland Railway.

Coalbrook Avenue, Crescent, Grove, Road, 13
from the old Coalbrook Farm at Woodhouse Mill. The 1841 directory lists it as Colebrook Lodge, so the origin of the name is probably the same as the Derbyshire village of that name, the old words *cald broc*, meaning cold stream. The old Coalbrook Crescent was known to locals as 'Canary Island', supposedly because of the number of canaries kept by residents.

Coalpit Lane, 6
was first called Water Lane. It was changed in 1904. Dr H. Kirk-Smith says in his *History of Wadsley* that the new name came from the fact that there was a pit shaft within a few yards of the roadside.

Coates Street, 2
not known; built on the Duke of Norfolk's land in the 1890s.

Cobden Place, Terrace Cobden View Road,10
after Richard Cobden (1804-1865) reformer, MP for the West Riding from 1847-57, later MP for Rochdale, and champion of the nineteenth century freehold land societies, who was much admired in the Sheffield area. When he visited the town in 1850, a public breakfast was given in his honour at the Cutlers' Hall.

Cobnar Avenue, Drive, Gardens, Road, 8
from the nearby Cobnar Wood. According to some sources, cob was the old name for top – the cob of the hill – and Cobnar Wood was the wood on top of a hill. Cobnar Road was originally Bole Hill Lane. It was renamed in 1903.

Cockayne Place, 8
after William Cockayne, senior partner in the Angel Street firm of T.B. and W. Cockayne, who lived at Lees House, Norton Lees, served on Norton Parish Council, Derbyshire County Council and Ecclesall Board of Guardians, and was a JP for Derbyshire. He died in 1898.

Cockshutt Avenue, Drive, Road, 8
from Cockshutts Farm, which, in early times belonged to Beauchief Abbey. A cockshut was a large net suspended between two poles, used to trap woodcocks.

Coisley Hill, Road, 13
from an old field name. Coisley Hill was a four-acre close adjoining a small stream. S.O. Addy thought the name came from an Old Icelandic word *Kjos*, meaning a deep,or hollow, place.

Coit Lane, 11
was originally Kote Lane, which is how it appears in a fourteenth century document. Local pronunciation turned kote, the old word for cottage or hut, into coit. It means cottage lane.

Colby Place, 6
after the village of Colby, two miles from Port Erin, in the Isle of Man; one of three neighbouring streets given the names of locations in the Isle of Man (along with Laxey and Onchan).

Colchester Road, 10
after the Essex town of Colchester (see Chichester).

Coldwell Lane, 10
is mentioned in an eighteenth century document. There was a well nearby.

Coleford Road, 9
was first called Copster Road. It was renamed in 1908 after a place called Coleford. There are three Colefords, one each in Devon, Gloucestershire and Somerset.

Coleridge Gardens, Road, 9
Coleridge Road was first called Pothouse Lane (because there was a casting pot maker on it). It was renamed in 1887 after the Hon Bernard Coleridge, MP for Attercliffe 1885-1894, later, as Lord Coleridge, a High Court judge 1907-1923.

Colister Drive, Gardens, 9
not known.

College Street, 10
from Wesley College, built 1838, originally with the idea of offering university-type education. In 1906 the college was combined with the Royal Grammar School and enlarged to become King Edward VII School.

Collegiate Crescent, 10
from the Sheffield Collegiate School which opened in 1836. The school became the Sheffield Royal Grammar School in 1885 and in 1906 amalgamated with Wesley College to form King Edward VII School. The old Royal Grammar School building then became the home of the Teachers' Training College.

Colley Avenue, Crescent, Drive, Road, 5
from the ancient manor of Cowley which is mentioned in documents of the twelfth century and in later documents appears as Colley. The manor was linked with Sheffield when it was bought by the Earl of Shrewsbury in the seventeenth century.

Colliers Close,13
from the Woodhouse area's association with coal mining. (There used to be a Colliers Row in the Park district of Sheffield).

Colliery Road, 4
from the old Brightside Colliery which closed in the 1880s when the coal ran out. The proprietors, John Denton and Co, offered the colliery plant for sale at an auction in 1887.

Collin Avenue, 6
from a village called Collin, near Dumfries, where Sir John Fowler, of Wadsley Hall, owned land (see Braemore).

Collingbourne Avenue, Drive, 19
from Collingbourne Forest, Wiltshire; one of a group of streets named after forests (see Bramshill).

Collinson Road, 5
formerly called Hukin Lane. It was renamed in 1938, after Thomas Collinson (1826-1897) who, for more than forty years was assistant overseer, collector of poor rate, clerk to the Highways Board, and to the Burial Board, for Brightside township. He lived in a house nearby called The Elms, and later at The Beeches, Bolsover Hill.

Colver Road, 2
built 1874-75, and probably named after Thomas Colver, of Colver Brothers, steel, file and saw manufacturers, who lived at nearby Chipping House at the time.

Colwall Street, 9
was first called Chapel Street (from the nearby Methodist New Connexion Chapel built about 1836) and was renamed in 1924 after the village of Colwall in Herefordshire.

Commercial Street, 1
from the *Commercial Inn* which stood at the head of Haymarket, facing down towards Waingate. Like the *Angel*, it was a well-known coaching inn. When it was sold at auction in 1866 it fetched £3,950, at that time the highest price ever paid for property in Sheffield.

Common Lane, 11
from Whiteley Wood Common which covered twenty-eight acres before the enclosures of the 1790s.

Commonside, 10
was alongside an area of common land.

Compton Street, 6
formerly Sycamore Street; renamed 1886. Reason for new name not known.

Conalan Avenue, 17
was built on land owned by Thomas Tedbar Osborne, farmer, of Bradway Road. The name Conalan was concocted from the names of Mr Osborne's daughter Constance, and his son, Alan.

Looking towards Commercial Street, around 1905.

Concord Road, 5
from Concord Park, the name of which was chosen by the man who presented it to the city, Alderman J.G. Graves. At the official opening of the park on 4th September 1930 he suggested the name Concord because he said it represented national and international aspirations.

Conduit Lane, Road, 10
from the Crookes conduit, 5,800 yards long, which was built about 1853. Town water came from Loxley Valley reservoirs, through the Ughill tunnel to Rivelin Valley, then through the Crookes conduit to the Godfrey service reservoir at Crookesmoor. It went out of service in 1935.

Congress Street, 1
was built alongside S. and C. Wardlow's Portobello Steel Works and named after another works the firm owned, the Congress Works, Oughtibridge.

Coningsby Road, 5
after the Lincolnshire village of Coningsby, between Sleaford and Horncastle.

Coniston Terrace, Road, 8
after the lake, village and peak called Coniston in the Lake District (see Arnside).

Constable Close, Drive, Place, Road, Way, 14
after John Constable (1776-1837) the famous English painter; one of a group of streets named after artists (along with Gibbons, Landseer, Leighton, Morland, Orpen, Raeburn and Sandby).

Convent Place, Walk, 3
from the Convent of Notre Dame in Cavendish Street. The Institute of the Sisters of Notre Dame started work in Sheffield in 1855 from Holy Green House on The Moor and moved to the Cavendish convent in 1862.

Conway Street, 3
from a group of houses built on Upper Hanover Street in the early 1800s and given the name Conway Place. Conway Street was built alongside the houses in the 1850s, and took its name from them. The houses were probably named after the North Wales beauty spot.

Coo Hill, 13
comes from the Old English word *cu*, meaning cow, ie Cow Hill.

Cook Street, 3
no longer listed; named after John Dawson Cook, city councillor 1918-26, president of the Master Builders' Association in 1905, and of the Builders' Exchange Club for a time. He built houses at Heeley, Meersbrook and Neepsend.

Cookson Close, Road, 5
were named in February 1937 at the same meeting as Barrie Road and seem to have been named after one of the chief characters in one of J.M. Barrie's best known books, Cookson the pirate in *Peter Pan*.

Cooks Road, 19
after a former Beighton property owner, Henry Cook, who died in the 1920s. He owned property in this road, West Street, Portland Road, Orchard Lane and at Woodhouse.

Cooks Wood Road, 3
from a nearby wood, Cooks Wood, once extensive, now virtually gone, and thought to have been named after a person called Cook. The wood is mentioned in Harrison's survey of 1637.

Coombe Place, Road, 10
after the Rev Charles George Coombe, vicar of Crookes from 1855 till he moved to St Paul's, Worthing, in 1882. When he left Sheffield he was presented with a purse of 325 guineas. He died at Worthing in 1902.

Cooper Place, 9
after John Cooper, earthenware manufacturer, with premises in Darnall Road, who was secretary of the Albert Freehold Land Society which built Cooper Place and nearby streets (see Frederick, Whitby and Nightingale).

Copley Street, 8;
after Frederick Charles Copley, 'hairdresser, pyrotechnist, and dealer in fishing tackle' who had shops in The Moor and Carver Street. He owned houses in Copley Street and Saxon Road which were auctioned in 1892 after his death.

Copper Street, 3
is shown on the 1771 Fairbank map and the assumption is that there was a copper works of some kind in or near the street.

Coppice Lane, 6;
Coppice Road, View, 10
from the nearby Coppice Wood, formerly owned by the Duke of Norfolk, who gave part of it for the building of King Edward VII Hospital. In Harrison's survey of 1637, it is mentioned as 'ye coppy'. A coppice is a thicket or wood of small growth. Coppice View was first called Stephen Road. It was renamed in 1932.

Coppin Square, 5
from an old field name which appears in the Ecclesfield Court Rolls of 1523 as Copinglands, two acres in size. An 1869 newspaper advertisement refers to two acres at Ecclesfield called Upper Copying Lands. Language experts are undecided on its origin. They say it either comes from an old word meaning lopped trees, or from another old word meaning summit, or peak.

Corby Road, 4
from a link with Earl Fitzwilliam, who owned land in the Corby area of Northamptonshire.

Corby Street, 4
was built on land owned by the Duke of Norfolk, a branch of whose family have lived at Corby Castle, Cumberland, for many years. The Corby Castle estate was acquired from the Dacre family by the fourth Duke of Norfolk in the sixteenth century.

Corker Bottoms Lane, 2
there is a reference to Corker Hill, near Manor Park, on Fairbank maps made between 1760 and 1762. Corker Bottoms were presumably below the hill. It is thought that the name Corker was that of a local person.

Corker Road, 12
after George Corker, 'the grand old man of Gleadless', lifelong member of Gleadless Congregational Church (deacon and choirmaster for thirty-nine years), member of Handsworth urban council for sixteen years (chairman for two), JP, Guardian, and school board member, Mr Corker, who lived in Seagrave Road, was also the first alderman to be elected for Handsworth ward on the City Council. He died, aged seventy-four, in 1923.

Corn Hill, 3
in the 1700s there was a windmill nearby, on the hill above Broad Street.

Cornish Street, 6
tricky. There is a Cornish Works on the street. There was a *Cornish Inn*. The street seems to have existed long before the works. The inn is not shown in the 1821 directory, but is shown in the 1837 directory, when Mary Green was victualler. I suspect the street was named from the inn.

Corporation Street, 3
was Sheffield Corporation's first big new street, built under the Bridges and Streets Act of 1853, ten years after the Corporation was established.

Corrie Street, 8
no longer listed; it was built by Sheffield Brick Company Ltd., and named after two men who were prominent shareholders in the company, J. Brown Corrie, of Adelaide Road, Nether Edge, and John Baxter Corrie, plumber of Wilkinson Street (see Aizlewood).

Cortworth Road, 11
was built on Earl Fitzwilliam's land and named after Cortworth, an area on the Earl's Wentworth's estate (along with Harley, Haugh and Hoober).

Corwen Place, 13
from the Welsh village of Corwen, west of Llangollen.

Cossey Road, 4
was built on the Duke of Norfolk's land and named after a small village four miles from Norwich, Costessey, pronounced locally 'Cossey'. It used to be the country seat of Lord Stafford, a distant relation of the Duke.

Cotleigh Avenue, Close, Crescent, Drive, Gardens, Place, Road, Way, 12
from an old field name. Cotley Fields are mentioned in old documents and were still known by the same name (although the spelling had changed) in the early 1900s. There was also a Cotley Hill. The fields were built on in the 1950s.

Cotswold Road, 6
was first called Evandale Road. It was renamed in 1926 (to avoid confusion with nearby Avondale Road) from the Cotswold Hills.

Cottage Lane, 11
after Whiteley Wood Cottage.

Cottingham Street, 9
I suspect this is a mistake. The surrounding streets (Brett, Chelmsford, Jessel, etc) were all named after prominent nineteenth-century lawyers, several of whom were Lords Chancellor. For this one to fit the pattern it should be Cottenham – after Sir Charles Christopher Pepys (1781-1851) first Earl of Cottenham, who was Lord Chancellor from 1836 to 1841 and again 1846-50.

Cotton Mill Row, Walk, 3
there was a cotton mill in the area. In 1829 it became a workhouse, which it remained till 1880 when Firvale Workhouse was built.

Cotton Street, 3
from the old cotton mill (above).

Coulston Lane, Street, 3
from an old field name. The field, Coulston Croft, is mentioned in Harrison's survey of 1673. In other documents it appears as Colson, Colston, and even Goldstone. Whatever the spelling, it is believed to have been named after a person, probably someone connected with Joseph Coulson who occupied the land in the 1700s.

Countess Road, 1
just as Earl Street commemorates the Earl of Arundel and Surrey, a title held by the Dukes of Norfolk (and the oldest title of its kind), Countess Road is named after the Countess of Arundel and Surrey.

Coupe Road, 3
after Councillor Dan Coupe, who was born in Nottinghamshire, came to Sheffield penniless about 1850, and for the first three nights slept in a hayloft. He became a carter and eventually built up his business to the point where he had eighty horses. He invested heavily in property and became the largest owner of what was known as 'cottage property' in town. Somebody estimated that if he had sold all his houses in the 1870s they would have fetched £150,000. He said it would be more like £200,000 to £250,000. He claimed he paid more rates than any other man in town. It was said he had an income of £10,000 a year.

In later years, with depression, his property declined in value, and many of his houses were left without tenants. Councillor Coupe, described as 'a rough diamond', represented Brightside on the Town Council from 1867 till his death in 1883 at the age of fifty-two.

Coventry Road, 9
was first called Cemetery Road (because it led to Darnall Cemetery). It was changed in 1886 to avoid confusion with Cemetery Road, 11. The new name was chosen for its similarity to the old one.

Coverdale Road, 7
from a Yorkshire dale called Coverdale, north west of Masham; one of a group of streets off Carter Knowle Road named after dales (along with Dovedale, Fossdale and Swaledale).

Cow Lane, 11 (Greystones);
Cow Lane, 11 (Parkhead);
Cow Lane, 19
were all near farms and used by cows at some time.

Cowley Gardens, 19
after John Cowley, who was sicklesmith, wheelwright and blacksmith at Mosborough at the end of the eighteenth century and the beginning of the nineteenth.

Cowlishaw Road, 11
built through land belonging to Y.T. Cowlishaw, cutler.

Cowper Avenue, Crescent, Drive, 6
after William Cowper (1731-1800) English poet; one of a group of streets named after literary figures.

Cowslip Road, 5
group name – flowers (see Acacia).

Cox Place, Road, 5
not known; Cox Road is listed first among the smaller streets in the directory of 1930.

Crabtree Avenue, Close, Crescent, Drive, Lane, Place, Road, 5
the name Crabtree is documented in 1699 and Crabtree Hill is mentioned in a document of 1817. It is thought to mean that there were crab apple trees in the vicinity.

Cradock Road, 2
was built on the Duke of Norfolk's land and named from the fact that Charlotte Frances Howard, a relative of the Duke, was married in 1855 to Sir J.W. Cradock Hartopp (whose name was also used for the Hartopp streets).

Cragdale Grove, 19
one of a group of streets named on the dale theme. Cragdale is in North Yorkshire.

Cranford Court, Drive, 19
after a place called Cranford in South Yorkshire; one of a group of streets with South Yorkshire names.

Cranworth Place, Road, 3
built on the Duke of Norfolk's land and named after the village of Cranworth in Norfolk.

Craven Close, 9
from the older Cravens Road, no longer listed, which was named after Alfred Craven, one of three brothers who set up the well-known Darnall firm, Cravens Ltd, in 1866. He was a member of the Board of Guardians, treasurer of Darnall School and a churchwarden at the parish church.

Craven Street, 3
not known; built 1860, dedicated 1869.

Crawford Road, 8
not known; built 1903-04.

Crawshaw Avenue, Grove, 8
after Frank Crawshaw, estate agent, who bought the Beauchief Abbey estate in 1923. He served on Norton parish council and Sheffield City Council, presented the abbey and its grounds to the city, sold some of the land to make the nearby golf course, and developed some for housing. He died in 1943.

Cream Street, 2
there was a dairy business on the corner of the street in the early years of this century, and this may have been the inspiration of the street name. It could not have been called Milk Street because there was already a Milk Street in the city centre. But this is only a guess.

Crescent Road, 7
it is crescent shaped.

The Crescent, 17
mysterious. It isn't crescent shaped.

Creswell Road, 9
possibly from the Derbyshire village of Creswell; built in the 1890s.

Crest Road, 5
from its hilly position.

Crestwood Court, Gardens, 5
a variation on Crest, above.

Creswick Avenue, Lane, Creswick Greave Close, 5
the name Creswick, or Creswyk, was known in the area as early as the fourteenth century. S.O. Addy says it comes from the old words *cres*, meaning twig, and *wic*, meaning dwelling – a house made of wattle or twigs. Eastwood, in his *History of the Parish of Ecclesfield*, and most other languages experts, have a different explanation. They say it means a place where cress was grown.

Creswick Street, Way, 6
after Thomas Creswick who was lord of the manor of Owlerton and was responsible for the building of Owlerton Hall about 1534. His family were prominent in the area till the 1680s and owned quite a lot of land.

Cricket Inn Crescent, Gardens, Road, 2
Darnall cricket ground, which was nationally known in its time, was opened in 1822 by Mr Steer, who is described in the 1825 Sheffield directory as 'victualler, Cricket House, Manor Hill'. The house, later called the *Cricket Inn*, gave these streets their names.

Crimicar Avenue, Close, Drive, Lane, 10
there is mention in Harrison's survey of 1637 of Crimeker Land and Crimeker Meadow (held at that time by William Archdale). S.O. Addy first thought the name came from the old Icelandic word *Krim*, meaning grime – ie black acre – then decided it more probably meant crooked acre, from the Middle English *crumb*, or *croum*. Either way, it was originally a field name.

Crispin Close, Drive, Gardens, Road, 12
after the Rev Crispin Gretton Holt, the first pastor of Gleadless Independent Chapel. He became pastor in 1893, remained till 1915, retired through ill health, and died in 1918.

Croft Lane, 11
from an old field name, Whirlow Croft, which was used in the name of Whirlow Croft Farm. The lane led to the farm.

Crofton Avenue, 6
from the village of Crofton, near Wakefield. It was built on Burgoyne family land. The Burgoynes had interests in the Wakefield area.

Croft Road, 6
from an old farm nearby called Croft Farm.

Croft Road, 12
from an old field name. An area nearby was known as The Crofts.

Cromford Street, 2
from the Derbyshire village of Cromford; named at the same time as Rowsley Street, which was also given a Derbyshire name.

Cromwell Street, 6
was built by the Municipal Freehold Land Society in the 1850s and named after Oliver Cromwell (1599-1658), Lord Protector of England from 1653 till his death.

Crookes, Crookes Road, 10
Crookes was spelt Crokis, or Crokys in the thirteenth century and appears in later documents as Crokes and Crowkes, before becoming Crookes in the sixteenth century. Language experts say it comes from the old Norse word *Krokr*, meaning a nook or corner of land. There was a farm in the area (and there is still a street) called The Nook.

Crookesmoor Road, 6 and 10
Crookesmoor was a large area of open moorland stretching from Western Bank to Broomhill and Fulwood Road. From 1711 to 1781 it was the site of the old Crookesmoor racecourse. It was developed for building in the early and middle nineteenth century.

Crookes Valley Road, 10
in 1881 a petition signed by 3,115 Crookes ratepayers asked for a new road to replace the old steep and inconvenient road that went down into the valley bottom. Three plans were considered: improvements to the old road; an iron bridge across the valley; or

a new road on an embankment. The embankment plan was chosen and more than 200,000 cubic feet of material was tipped to form the embankment. Throughout the planning stages it was called the Great Dam Road, from the nearby reservoir called the Great Dam, but some people thought this sounded like bad language, so it was changed to Crookes Valley Road.

Crosby Road, 8

after William Crosby (1830-1910) Sunderland-born oil and watercolour artist who exhibited at the Royal Academy from 1859 to 1873 (see Chatfield).

Cross;

where the word Cross is used as a prefix (such as Cross Allen Street, Cross Bedford Street etc) the origin of the name is given under the street crossed, that is, Allen Street or Bedford Street.

Cross Drive, Street, 13

from the old Woodhouse village cross, erected by Joshua Littlewood in 1775 on the site of an earlier cross. A bit was added to the top in 1820 and the whole thing was renovated in 1897 and again in 1950.

Crossland Drive, Place, 12

after the Rev Cyril Thomas Crossland, vicar of Christ Church, Gleadless, from 1887 till his death in 1923.

Cross Lane, 10; Cross Lane, 17

like several other lanes of the same name now either changed, or cleared, the explanation is that they cross from one larger road to another. The one at Dore crosses from Causeway Head Road to Hathersage Road, and the one at Crookes from Lydgate Lane to Mulehouse Road.

Two streets, Cross Drive and Cross Street, were named from the old village cross at Woodhouse, pictured here in 1907.

Cross Park Road, 8

crosses Meersbrook Park Road.

The Crossways, 2

where a number of roads cross.

Crowder Avenue, Close, Crescent, Road, 5

from Crowder House, one of the oldest homesteads in the area. Farmed for many years by the Wilkinson family, it was later converted into a private house by Bernard Wake, the Sheffield solicitor and it was cleared in the 1930s to make way for new council housing. Crowder Road was originally called Crowther Lane.

Crowland Road, 5

after the famous abbey in Lincolnshire called Crowland, or Croyland, which features prominently in Charles Kingsley's novel, *Hereward the Wake* (see Bourne Road and Hereward Road).

Crown Place, 2

possibly from the older Crown Alley, shown in early nineteenth century directories, which in turn was probably named from a public house in Duke Street called the *Crown Inn*.

Crookes, during the 1950s. Possibly early on a summer Sunday morning.

Crowther Place, 7

after Alderman William Crowther, president of the Mount Pleasant Land Society which was formed in 1867 to develop the land around Mount Pleasant, Highfield.

Croydon Street, 11

was originally called Frederick Street. It was changed in 1886 because there were other Frederick Streets, and renamed, for no special reason, after the town of Croydon, Surrey.

Cruise Road, 11

after Martin Cruise, builder, who lived in Bradley Street up to his death in 1910. He owned property in Ecclesall Road, Walkley, Greystones, and other

Road, Walkley, Greystones, and other parts of the city, some of which he had built himself. He also owned property around this road, including four shops in Oakbrook Road and a house in Hangingwater Road.

Crummock Road, 7
after the two-and-a-half-mile long lake called Crummock in the English Lake District (see Arnside).

Crumpsall Road, 5
not known; possibly from the Crumpsall district of Manchester, though why it should be, I can't imagine.

Cullabine Road, 2
from the firm of John Cullabine and Co, plumbers and gas fitters, who worked for the Corporation for many years, particularly in the supply of copper gas lamps, reflectors and fittings.

Cumberland Street, Way, 1
was laid out (with Hereford Street) in 1788 by the Enclosure Commissioners, and probably named, like several other nearby streets, from a link with Earl Fitzwilliam's family, one of whom was married in 1611 to Lady Margaret Clifford, daughter of the Earl of Cumberland.

Cundy Street, 6
after Thomas Cundy, farmer and quarry owner on Whitehouse Lane in the first half of the nineteenth century. The street was built through his land.

Cupola, 3
in *An Early Description of the Town of Sheffield, wrote in the year 1832*, by Joseph Woolhouse, which was reprinted by the Hunter Archaeological Society in the 1920s, Mr Woolhouse says there used to be a cupola (he calls it cupalo) at the top of the street. A cupola was a vertical furnace similar in principle to a blast furnace.

Curlew Ridge, 2
one of a group of streets named after birds (along with Heron Mount, Kestrel Green, Magpie Grove, Osprey Gardens, Partridge View, Plover Court, Quail Rise, Starling Mead, Swift Way, and Wren Bank).

Cuthbert Bank Road, Cuthbert Road, 6
a field called Cuthbert Bank was owned at the time of the 1805 enclosures by Catherine Cope and William Bamforth. The name may come from a man who is mentioned three times in Harrison's survey of 1637, but his name is spelt differently each time – Thomas Cutbert, Cutbird, or Cuttburd.

Cutlers Walk, 2
could have been almost anywhere in Sheffield. It seems sad in a way that one of the city's proudest trades should be commemorated in such an insignificant thoroughfare.

Cutts Terrace, 8
after George Cutts, of George Cutts and Sons, electro-plate and Britannia metal manufacturers, of Broad Street, Park. Mr Cutts lived in Glen Road, Nether Edge, owned land on Broadfield Park Road, on which eleven houses were built, and houses in this terrace. He was a trustee of Broadfield Park Freehold Land Society which built in the area.

Cyclops Street, 4
from the old Cyclops Works set up by Charles Cammell in 1845.

Cypress Avenue, 8
was the name suggested by the developers who preserved a large cypress tree on the site when they built the houses in 1975. The City Council accepted the suggestion.

Cyprus Road, 8
not known; built around 1903-04.

Cyprus Terrace, 6
was built soon after the island of Cyprus, previously a Turkish possession, came under British rule in 1878.

Cyril Street, 6
no longer listed; origin of name not known. It was obviously named after a person called Cyril, possibly someone in the Woollen family, who owned property nearby.

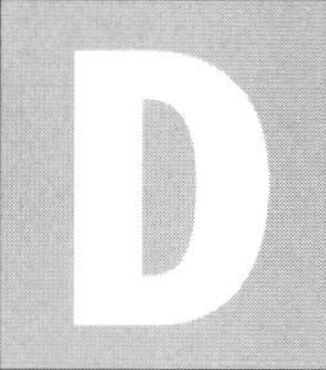

Dacre Street, Row, 2
the street (no longer listed) was built on the Duke of Norfolk's land and named from a slightly complicated series of marriages in the Duke's family in the sixteenth century. Philip, Earl of Arundel, and his half brothers, Thomas, Earl of Suffolk, and Lord William Howard, married three sisters, Anne, Marie and Elizabeth Dacre, co-heiresses of their brother, Lord Dacre of Gillesand. The girls' widowed mother married the boys' father, the fourth Duke of Norfolk, and thus became step-mother to her own sons-in-law. One way and another, the Dacre estates in Yorkshire and Cumberland passed to the Howards.

Daffodil Road, 5
group name – flowers (see Acacia).

Dagnam Close, Crescent, Drive, Place, Road, 2
were built on the Duke of Norfolk's land; named from the fact that Henry Howard, of Corby Castle, Cumberland, an ancestor of the Duke, married Catherine Mary, daughter of Sir Richard Neave, of Dagnam Park, Essex, in 1793.

Daisy Bank, Walk, 3
daisies grew there. Daisy Bank was a common field and place name. There were at least four other places called Daisy Bank in the West Riding.

Daisy Walk, 19
group name – flowers (see Aster).

The Dale, 8
descriptive name for the large bowl between the hills in which Woodseats developed. The name goes back at least 400 years. Entries in Norton parish registers for the late sixteenth century show people living at 'Woodsette-dale'. There was also a Dale Farm, now demolished.

Daleview Road, 8
looks across to The Dale, above. Up to 1927 it was called Folds Place.

Dalewood Avenue, Drive, Road, 8
The Dalewood development was built in the 1920s and 1930s on land that was formerly part of Folds Farm. The name was a concoction from Abbeydale and local woodlands.

Dalmore Road, 7
after a place called Dalmore in Scotland. There are three, one on Lewis in the Western Isles, two in Ross and Cromerty.

Dalton Court, 8
from the earlier Dalton Street (no longer listed) which was named after Frederick G. Dalton, of Clarendon Villa, Ecclesall Road, who was a shareholder in Sheffield Brick Company Ltd, which built the street (see Aizlewood).

Damer Street, 10
uncertain; it was built in the 1860s and first called Albert Street. To avoid confusion with other Albert Streets it was renamed in 1872, possibly after Anne Seymour Damer, the noted sculptress.

Danebrook Close, Court, Drive; Danewood Avenue, Croft, Gardens, Grove, 2
in 1982 the Highways Committee decided to rename areas in what was formerly Lower Manor, after the ancient races in British history, in this case, the Danes.

Dane Street, 9
not known.

Daniel Hill, Daniel Hill Court, Street, Terrace, Walk, 6
Daniel Hill is an ancient name mentioned, as Daniell Hill, in Harrison's survey of 1637. It is thought to come from the name of a local resident. S.O. Addy, the historian, guessed that the resident was Francis Danyell, whose name appears in a rental made in 1624, and he is as likely to be right as anybody.

Dara Street, 9
was originally called Duke Street, after the landowner, the Duke of Norfolk. It was renamed in 1903 along with two other Wincobank streets that were given Scottish names. For this to fit in with the Scottish theme, it ought to be Darra Street, after the place called Darra in the Grampian region. I think that is what was intended.

Daresbury Close, Drive, Place, Road, View, 2
were built on the Duke of Norfolk's land and named from the fact that one of the Duke's ancestors, Margaret, daughter of Sir Robert Howard, married Thomas Danyell, of Daresbury, Cheshire.

Darnall Road is the only road in the City which is crossed by a canal. The depth of the stonework above the arch gives the game away. The view from the aqueduct is inset.

Darfield Avenue, Close, 19
after the place called Darfield, near Barnsley; one of a group of Mosborough streets given South Yorkshire names.

Darley Grove, 6
from the Darley Dale area of Derbyshire; one of a group of Stannington streets given the names of places around Matlock (see Matlock).

Darnall Drive, Road, 9
the name Darnall is an old one which has been spelt several different ways since the thirteenth century – Darnehale, Darnale, Darnell, Darnoll, etc. It comes from the old words meaning secluded nook of land.

Dart Square, 3
was originally called West Grove Square, after a house in Winter Street called West Grove. The name was thought too cumbersome and it was renamed in 1890 after the River Dart in Devonshire.

Darwin Close, Lane, 10
from the Darwin family who held large areas of land nearby in the seventeenth century. At the time of Harrison's survey in 1637, James Darwin of Storth Farm, had more than sixty acres, and Thomas Darwin had thirty-eight.

Darwin Road, 6
uncertain; possibly after Charles Darwin, the scientist. The road was built in the 1890s, not long after his death.

David Close, 13
one of a group of streets named after members of the Watson family – George Watson Builders Ltd – who owned the land and built the houses (along with Hannah Road, June Road, Rodger Road and Sylvia Close).

David Lane, 10
after David Woodhouse, one of a family of well-known farmers in the district in the eighteenth and nineteenth centuries. The Enclosure Commissioners tried to call it Mill Road but local people ignored this name.

Davy Lane, 11
no longer listed; named after William Davy (1821-1902), scale cutter, who owned land and property in the lane and in nearby Harrow Street. He sold some of his land to the Corporation in 1901 for the widening of Ecclesall Road.

Dawlands Close, Drive, 2
from the names of two fields near Eckington, Daw Lands, and Near Daw Lands, which were owned by Thomas Hounsfield at the time of the 1795 land enclosures; one of a number of Manor Estate streets given names from the history of Eckington Manor.

Deakins Walk, 10
after Isaac Deakin, who was a grocer on Fulwood Road in the 1850s and 1860s. The walk was not officially named till later in the century. When Mr Deakin's property was advertised for sale in 1870, the walk was described as 'an occupation road', that is, a private road.

Deane Field View, 19
after a former landowner, a man called Deane, who owned a field called Honey Hole at the time of the land enclosures. The field was near the site of this development.

Deanhead Court, Drive, 19
after the place called Dean Head, two miles from Penistone; one of a group of Mosborough streets given South Yorkshire names.

Dearne Court, Street, 9
after the River Dearne which starts near Hoylandswaine, wends its way round Barnsley, and joins the Don east of Mexborough.

Deep Lane, 5
straightforward descriptive name.

Deerlands Avenue, Close, Mount, 5
Deerlands was the name of a small group of seventeenth century cottages. Like nearby Doe Royd, the name dates back to the time when deer roamed in the area.

Deer Park Close, Place, Road, View, Way, 6
from a sixty-two acre area of land near Rivelin Firth which is recorded in Harrison's survey of Sheffield, 1637, as being 'reserved for ye deare'. At that time, Sheffield area had a large deer population. Harrison estimated that there were 1,000 in Sheffield Park alone.

Delamere Close, Grove, 19
from the Delamere Forest, Cheshire; one of a group of streets named after forests (see Ashdown).

Delf Street, 2
formerly known as Delph Street. Both words mean the same thing: a quarry. There was one nearby.

Delph House Road, 10
as above, delph comes from a nearby quarry, and the delph house was the house attached to it.

Delves Avenue, Close, Drive, Place, Road, Terrace, 12
delves are places where the land has been dug, by quarrying, or mining. In this case the name referred to two fields, Over Delves and Nether Delves, which had been dug for coal. They were later built on.

Den Bank Avenue, Close, Crescent, Drive, 10
Den Bank is mentioned in Harrison's survey, 1637, as Deane Bank. At that time it was part of Rivelin Common. The name probably comes from a person called Deane.

Denby Street, 2
was originally called New Thomas Street. It was changed in 1890 and named, for no particular reason, after the village of Denby, near Barnsley.

Dene Lane, 1
not known; before 1872 it was called Blagden Street.

Denham Road, 11
from the village of Denham, Buckinghamshire. The road was built on land belonging to the Wilson family. Louisa Ellen Wilson and her sister, Elizabeth Harriet Wilson, inherited the land. Louisa married the Rev Albert Augustus Harland, once a curate at Ecclesall, later vicar of Harefield, Middlesex, for fifty years. When the family land was developed, one of the roads was named Harefield, and several of the others, including this one, were named after villages near Harefield (see also Fulmer, Pinner, Walton).

Denholme Close, 3
from the old Denholme Street, no longer listed, which was originally called Edward Street (after someone in the Duke of Norfolk's lineage). It was renamed in 1872, after the village of Denholme, south of Keighley.

Denmark Road, 2
from Queen Alexandra, wife of King Edward VII. Before their marriage in 1863, she was Princess Alexandra of Denmark, daughter of King Christian IX of Denmark.

Denson Close, 2
after the Rev Henry Denson Jones, chaplain of the General Infirmary, who was the first vicar of Christ Church, Heeley, from 1846 to 1888. During his time Heeley grew from a small rural village to a suburb of 16,000 people.

Dent Lane, 12
from the Dent Main Colliery Co Ltd, which had its headquarters on the lane from the 1920s up to the nationalisation of the coal industry in 1947.

Denton Road, 8
no longer listed; was built on land belonging to the Firth family, and probably named after the village of Denton, near Ilkley. Many of the roads on Firth land were given Yorkshire place names.

Derby Place, Street, Terrace, 2
Derby Street was first called Upper Myrtle Road. It was changed in 1890 and named after the city of Derby. Derby Place was built later.

Derbyshire Lane, 8
a directional name. It is recorded in seventeenth century documents, and at that time it was itself in Derbyshire. It did not become part of Sheffield (and of Yorkshire) till the boundary extension of 1900.

Derriman Avenue, Close, Drive, Glen, Grove, 11
not known; first name (Derriman Drive) approved June 1964.

Derwent Row, Street, 2
after Derwent Hall, Derbyshire, the remains of which are now submerged beneath the waters of Derwent Reservoir. The hall was owned by the Duke of Norfolk's family and was for some years the home of Viscount Fitzalan (Lord Edmund Talbot), third son of the fourteenth Duke.

Deveron Road, 19
Deveron is the name of a river in the Grampian region of Scotland, which flows into Banff Bay. How it comes to be applied to this road is a mystery, unless the developer was a keen fisherman.

Devon Road, 4
presumably named after the county, but I do not know why.

Devonshire Close, Court, Drive, Glen, Grove, Road; Devonshire Terrace Road, 17
after the Dukes of Devonshire, who were lords of the manor of Dore for many years. The first Duke bought the manor from the Pegge family in 1705.

Devonshire Street, 3; Devonshire Lane, 1
after William, the fourth Duke of Devonshire, who was Prime Minister for eight months, from November 1756

to July 1757; one of several streets in the area named after prime ministers.

Dewar Drive, 7
not known; plans for the drive were approved in 1934 along with the plans for Stowe Avenue and Rex Avenue.

Dial House Road, 6
from Dial House, once a private house, later a club, so named because over the door was a sundial with the inscription: 'Of shade and sunshine for each hour, see here a measure made. Then wonder not if life consists of sunshine and of shade'.

Dial Way, 5
probably because it forms a circle.

Dickey Lane, 6
the word dick used to mean ditch, and there was a field near this lane called Dick Field – the field with a ditch. The lane took its name from the field.

Dickinson Road, 5
after Gilbert Dickinson (sometimes spelt Dickenson, or Dickonson), who was steward to the Earl of Shrewsbury in the sixteenth century. He was a feoffee of Ecclesfield, and lived at Barnes Hall for a time.

Dieroff Street, 9
no longer listed; named after Frederick Dieroff, who lived in Chippingham Street in the 1870s and built houses in the area.

Dinnington Road, 8
from the place called Dinnington in South Yorkshire; one of a group of streets given Yorkshire place names.

Ditchingham Street, 4
was built on the Duke of Norfolk's land and named after the village of Ditchingham, two miles from Bungay, Norfolk, where the Duke had interests.

Division Lane, Street, 1
Division Street began as a very small street in the late 1700s. R.E. Leader said that by 1808, it was still 'in embryo'. It was so named because it divided the angle between the routes out of town to the south and the west.

Dixon Lane, 1
is one of the oldest street names in the city. It can be traced back to the seventeenth century. Almost certainly the name comes from the surname of an ancient resident, but nobody knows who he was.

Dixon Road, 6
after the Dixon family, of the well-known cutlery firm, James Dixon and Sons. The Dixons lived for some years at Hillsborough Hall, which was later a branch library. When part of their land was developed, the streets were mostly given family names (see Dorothy, Garry, Lennox, Shepperson, Warner, Willis, Wynyard).

Division Street has changed more than most other streets in the centre of Sheffield. The inset photographs show the Central Fire Station and the Graves (later Transport Department, even later Miners' Union) building long before both became bar-cafés.

Dixon Street, 6
from the same family as Dixon Road, above. The family works were on nearby Cornish Place. Land and houses near the works were sold by auction after the death of Henry Isaac Dixon in 1912.

Dobbin Hill, 11
the name is recorded in 1771, but language experts disagree about its origin. One theory is that it comes from a person's name; another is that it indicates a 'dob' or dip in the ground.

Dobcroft Avenue, Close, Road, 7 and 11
believed to come from an old field name, Dobb Croft, the field with a dip in it (see Dobbin Hill).

Doctor Lane, 9
after Joseph Turner, eminent medical man who left Attercliffe last century, went to France, the USA, and the West Indies where he suffered a severe attack of sunstroke. On his return to Attercliffe, he lived in a cottage at the corner of the lane.

Dodd Street, 6
not known; the street was approved, with six others, in 1898 for the trustees of M.G. Burgoyne.

Dodson Drive, 13
started out as Howard Road (after the Howards, Dukes of Norfolk, lords of the manor of Handsworth). In 1923 it was changed to Hall Road West (the first idea, to rename it Viceroy Road, was scrapped). It was changed again in 1961, and renamed after the Dodson family, Edward (died 1867), and later Jane, and John Richard, who farmed at Handsworth Hall for more than 60 years.

Doe Royd Crescent, Drive, Lane, 5
Doe Royd was the name of two old farmsteads in the area which dated back to the seventeenth century and were presumably named from the fact that there were deer in the area.

Dominoe Grove, 12
from a character known as 'Dominoe Joe', who led a miners' protest march from Hollinsend to Woodhouse in 1893 after colliery owners at Birley Vale and Woodhouse reduced miners' wages. Full wages were ultimately restored.

Don Avenue, 6
after the Don Brick Company Ltd, of Don Brickworks, Middlewood Road, who built the avenue, in 1910.

Doncaster Street, 3
after Daniel Doncaster, founder of the famous steel firm. When he first set up business in Copper Street, he lived in a house in Allen Street. Doncaster Street, and his works, were built in the grounds of his house.

Donetsk Way, 12
after Sheffield's twin city in Russia, Donetsk, population 950,000, 335km south-east of Kharkov, in the Ukraine. When it was founded in the 1860s it was called Yuzovka. From 1924 it was known as Stalino. It was renamed Donetsk in 1961.

Donnington Road, 2
is wrongly spelt. It should be Donington. It was built on the Duke of Norfolk's land and named from the fact that Henry, the fifteenth Duke, married Lady Flora Paulyna Hetty Barbara Abney Hastings, elder daughter of the first Baron Donington, in 1877. Up to 1902 it was called Plain Street.

Donovan Close, Road, 5
after Edward Donovan, naturalist, illustrator and prolific author, whose works included a ten-volume *Natural History of British Birds*, ten volumes about British insects, five volumes of British fishes, five volumes on British shells, and three volumes about British quadrupeds. His best work is thought to be his three-volume *General Illustrations of Entomology*.

Don Place, Road, 9
from the nearby River Don, the name of which comes from the old Celtic word, *dana*, meaning water.

Dore Hall Croft, 17
from the old mansion called Dore Hall which stood near Vicarage Lane and was once the home of the Barker family. The hall was removed in the nineteenth century and the last part to disappear was the kitchen, in 1840.

Dore Road, 17
a directional name; Dore was spelt Dor in the year 942 and it had various other spellings over the years. It means a narrow pass.

Dorking Street, 4
was built on the Duke of Norfolk's land and named from the fact that one of the Duke's ancestors, Bernard, son of Henry Frederick, Earl of Arundel, married Catherine Lichford of Dorking in 1672 (see also Lichford Road).

Dorothy Road, 6
after a member of the Dixon family (see Dixon Road). One of James Willis Dixon's children, Gladys, married Reginald Thorpe Wilson, of Bolsterstone. Dorothy, born 1901, was their daughter.

Dorset Street, 10
an early nineteenth century name from the Dukedom of Dorset, a title held by the Sackville family up to 1843.

Douglas Road, 3
was originally called Norfolk Road North (after the Duke of Norfolk). It was renamed in 1872 from the nearby Douglas beerhouse.

Douse Croft Lane, 10
is recorded in a fifteenth century document. According to language experts, it comes from the Middle English words *dey-hus*, meaning dairy – dairy croft.

Dovedale Road, 7
one of a group of roads named after dales.

Dovercourt Road, 2
was built on the Duke of Norfolk's land and named after the district of Dovercourt in Essex. The Duke was lord of the manor of Dovercourt.

Dover Gardens, Street, 3
not known; Dover Street was approved in 1875 for William Fox Tibbits, solicitor.

Dover Road, 11
built in the 1870s by Brocco Bank Freehold Land Society and named after Frederick William Dover, president and co-trustee of the Society.

Downgate Drive, 4
was built on the site of a former steelworks and named from a term used in the steel industry. A down gate is a tube within a core, which allows the free flow of molten metal in the casting process.

Downham Road, 5
after a place called Downham, but which? There are Downhams in Cambridgeshire, Essex and Lancashire, a Downham district of Lewisham, and a Downham Market in Norfolk. The Norfolk one seems most likely.

Downing Lane, 3
probably after William Downing, estate agent, who lived in Watery Street up to his death in 1897.

Downing Road, 8
after Edward V. Downing, who lived at The Manor, Greenhill, in the 1920s and 1930s.

Drakehouse Lane, 19
from the nearby building called Drake House. There were Drakes living at Beighton in the sixteenth century. John Drake was vicar in 1733, and was succeeded by his son, also called John. The house was probably named after an early member of the family.

Dransfield Close, Road, 10
after the former landowner, William Dransfield, railway contractor, who lived at Ranmoor.

Dunkirk Square, Darnall, was demolished so long ago that few people today know where it was. It was on Main Road, near Britannia Road.

Drill Square, 6
no longer listed; it was first called Queen Anne Street. The name was changed in 1910 and the new name came from the Stalker Drill Works Ltd, which were on the street.

Driver Street, 13
was originally called Railway Street, because of its nearness to the old LNER line at Woodhouse. After Woodhouse became part of Sheffield in 1921 it was renamed to avoid confusion with another Railway Street at Burngreave. I can find no trace of anybody called Driver in the area at the time the street was renamed. It might be a word-association name, railway suggesting engine driver, but that is only a guess.

The Drive, 6
is on the line of the old drive to Wadsley House.

Drummond Crescent, Road, 5
is one of the Southey-Parson Cross streets named after literary figures, but I'm uncertain which. There were three literary Drummonds, Henry (1851-97), theological writer, author of *Ascent of Man*; William Henry (1854-1907), Canadian poet and William (1585-1649), Scottish poet. It could be any one of them.

Drury Lane, 17
possibly from a person called Drury, although the name occurs elsewhere in Yorkshire and is sometimes explained as a corruption of Dowarie Lane, that is. land given as a dowry.

Dryden Avenue, Drive, Road, Way, 5
after John Dryden (1631-1700), English poet and playwright, Poet Laureate from 1670 to 1688.

Duchess Road, 2
after the Duchess of Norfolk.

Dudley Road, 6
not known; name approved, June 1935.

Dugdale Drive, Road, 5
after Sir William Dugdale (1605-1686), antiquary and scholar, who visited Sheffield during a tour of the country to register coats of arms and pedigrees of local gentry. In his record of church monuments called *Monumenta Eboracensia*, he included a list of the stained glass windows in Ecclesfield parish church.

Duke Lane, 1; Duke Street, 2
after the Dukes of Norfolk, land owners and for many years, lords of the manor.

Duke Street, 19
after an old inn, the *Duke William*, which was built in the first few years of the 1800s, and was probably named after William, Duke of Clarence, who later became King William IV.

Duncan Road, 10
I have read suggestions that this road was named after the Rev Norton Fleetwood Duncan, former vicar of Crookes, but it could not have been. The road was approved (for Charles Robinson, solicitor) in 1897 – nineteen years before Mr Duncan became vicar. The only other suggestion I can make is that it had something to do with Duncan Gilmour, who certainly built in the area, but this is only a guess.

Duncombe Street, 6
was built by one of the early freehold land societies and named after Thomas Slingsby Duncombe (1796-1861) radical MP for Hertford, and later for Finsbury, who presented a Chartist petition in 1842. Duncombe visited Sheffield in 1844 to address a meeting and was given a rousing reception by his local supporters.

Dundas Road, 9
is a link with Earl Fitzwilliam, the landowner, or to be more exact, several links. Charlotte, daughter of the third Earl, married Baron Dundas. The fifth Earl also married a Dundas, and Lady Frederica Elizabeth Dundas, who married the seventh Earl, was Lady Mayoress of Sheffield in 1909 when her husband was Lord Mayor. The road was first called Milton Street (the Fitzwilliam family had a seat called Milton Park, near Peterborough, and the Earl's eldest son had the title Viscount Milton). It was changed after

Dykes Hall, Wadsley, was demolished in the 1920s but its name lived on in the names of several streets.

Tinsley came into Sheffield, in 1912.

Dunedin Glen, Grove, 19
after Dunedin, one of the rugby playing centres of New Zealand (see Arms Park Drive). Dunedin is the Gaelic name for Edinburgh.

Dunella Drive, Place, Road, 6
not known; built for the Sutton Trustees as part of Wadsley Hall estate. Names approved, August 1925.

Dun Fields, 3
from an old field name. Dun is the old spelling of Don.

Dunkeld Road, 11
from Dunkeld, a town on the River Tay, Perthshire, where the Dukes of Atholl had one of their seats, Dunkeld House (see Blair Athol Road).

Dunkerley Road, 6
after the Rev Daniel Dunkerley, who was minister at Loxley Chapel from 1802 to 1820, and the Rev David Dunkerley, minister at the same chapel from 1821 to 1825 and again from 1830 to 1833. It was said of Daniel Dunkerley that 'being rather stout, he well became our large pulpit'. Other streets in the area (France Road, Hanson Road, Lee Road and Leaton Close) are named after former ministers at the chapel.

Dunkirk Square, 9
no longer listed; the name probably came from a Darnall field name. Dunkirk was a fairly common field name, one of several foreign names (such as California, Jericho, Klondyke etc.) known as nicknames of remoteness, applied to fields ironically to signify their distance from the farm.

Dunlop Street, 9
was built by the Sheffield, Attercliffe and Carbrook Freehold Land Society (formed 1853) and was first called Dun Street, after the nearby River Don, which was sometimes spelt Dun. To avoid confusion with another Dun Street at Shalesmoor, it was changed in 1872, by simply adding lop to the end of it.

Dunmow Road, 4
seems to have been named after the Essex villages of Little and Great Dunmow. Little Dunmow is famous for the Dunmow Flitch ceremony in which a flitch of bacon is awarded to any married couple who have never quarrelled or wished themselves single again since their wedding day. The rival claims are tried before a jury of six spinsters and six bachelors.

Dunninc Road, 5
after Dunninc, one of the six Saxon lords who held the manor of Ecclesfield at the time of the Norman conquest (Godric was another, hence nearby Godric Road). After the conquest all six lost their influence. Commercial street guides persist in calling this one Dunning Road.

Dun Street, 3
from the nearby River Don, the old spelling of which was Dun.

Durham Lane, Road, 10
Durham Road was first called West Bank Place. It was changed in 1890. There was no special reason for the new name, from the cathedral city of Durham.

Durlstone Close, Crescent, Drive, Grove, 12
not known; names approved 1940.

Durmast Grove, 6
after the Durmast species of oak tree, which has dark, heavy wood and is often used by builders and cabinet makers. It is one of a group of streets which (because they were built near Acorn Hill) were named after some of the 300 different species of oak (see Golden Oak, Holme Oak, Oak Apple Close, Red Oak and Scarlet Oak).

Durvale Court, 17
Dur is one of the ancient spellings of Dore – Dore Vale.

Dutton Road, 6
not known; plans for the road were approved for Mrs Jane Carter of Dykes Hall Road, in 1897.

Dyche Close, Drive, Lane, Place, Road, 8
Dyche Lane, the oldest of the group, is recorded in a document of 1592 as Dikes Lane, and in several later documents as Dyks, Ditch, or Dych Lane. It means there was a ditch nearby.

Dyke Hall Gardens, Place, Road, 6
Dykes Hall was a large old house rebuilt by John Fowler in 1852, owned at various times by William Pashley Milner, solicitor, J.W. Wilson, brewer, and others, and demolished in 1927 for the building of Dykes Hall housing estate.

Dykes Lane, 6
as Dyche, above; from the old word meaning a ditch.

Dyke Vale Avenue, Close, Place, Road, Way, 12
from the valley of the stream known as the Ochre Dyke.

Dykewood Drive, 6
from the nearby Sough Dyke Wood. Sough here is the old word for a bog.

Dyson Place, 11
after Miss Eliza Dyson, who was tenant of the farm at the top of this lane in the 1860s. In the 1865 directory she is listed as having two farms, this one and another at Tinsley.

Eadon Street, 9
no longer listed; named after Robert Thomas Eadon who was a landowner at Attercliffe in the mid-nineteenth century. He was the son of Moses Eadon, of the President Steel Works, served as a town councillor and as a member of Sheffield School Board.

Earldom Close, Drive, Road, Street, 4
were built on Earl Fitzwilliam's land. The earldom was created as an Irish title in July 1716, and as an English title in 1746.

Earl Marshal Close, Drive, Road, View, 4
were built on the Duke of Norfolk's land and named after the ancient office of Earl Marshal, held by the Dukes of Norfolk since 1672. The Earl Marshal is head of the College of Arms, attends the sovereign at the opening and closing of Parliament, and organises state processions and ceremonials, including coronations.

Earl Street, Way, 1
after the earldom of Arundel, a title held by the Dukes of Norfolk since 1660.

Earsham Street, 4
built on the Duke of Norfolk's land and named after an estate in Suffolk also owned by the Duke, Earsham Park, near Bungay.

East Bank Close, Place, Road, View, Way, 2
after the house called East Bank, built in the 1830s by Thomas Turner, later the home of T. Nowil, and later still of Henry Pashley, solicitor. Before East Bank Road was built, the house was described as being on Shrewsbury Bank. East Bank, the house name, is a straightforward descriptive name – the hill to the east of the town centre.

East Cliffe Drive, 2
after the house called East Cliffe, home in the 1850s of Edward Hudson, merchant. The name is a variation on East Bank.

East Coast Road, 9
leads towards what used to be the goods station of the Lancashire, Derbyshire and East Coast Railway, which opened in 1897 and was absorbed by the Great Central Railway in 1907.

Ecclesall Road around 1916. Greystones Cinema, on the left, opened in July 1914.

Eastcroft Close, Drive, Glen, View, Way, 19
from an eighteenth century Mosborough field name. East Croft, to the east of the old Sheffield to Eckington turnpike.

Eastern Avenue, Crescent, Drive, Walk, 2
a variation on the 'east' names, East Bank, East Cliffe, etc. to the east of the city centre.

Eastfield Road, 10
built in the 1890s for Warrington Slater and named from an old Crookes field name, East Field.

East Glade Avenue, Close, Crescent, Place, Road, Square, Way, 12
the glade, or clearing to the east of Birley Moor Road.

Eastgrove Road, 10
followed the 'grove' theme set by Broomgrove, Clarkegrove and Southgrove.

East Parade, 1
on the eastern side of Sheffield Cathedral. The parade was built in 1808 when the old Town Hall at the parish church gates was demolished.

East Road, 2
another variation on the 'east' theme – East Bank, East Cliffe, Eastern etc.

Eastwood Road, 11
was built on land part-owned by Alderman James Neill (see Neill Road), and named after his childhood home, Eastwood House, Rotherham.

East View Terrace, 6
looks eastward.

Eaton Place, 2
after John Eaton, pawnbroker, who represented Park ward on the Town Council from 1873 onwards. He was Lord Mayor in 1900.

Ebenezer Place, Street, 3
from the Ebenezer Chapel, Shalesmoor, which opened in July 1823. During the opening service there was an alarm that the building was falling down and 'the congregation escaped in confusion, breaking 700 panes of glass'.

Eben Street, 9
is a name that was chopped in half. It was originally called Ebenezer Street. To avoid confusion with Ebenezer Street, above, it was changed in 1871 by chopping the last four letters off it.

Ecclesall Road, Ecclesall Road South, 11
from the old words *eccles,* meaning church and *halh,* meaning a hollow, the church in a hollow. Although the present church is not in a hollow, the church it replaced was lower down the hillside and was indeed in a hollow.

Ecclesfield Road, 5
a directional name; the road towards Ecclesfield, which comes from the old words meaning the church in open country.

Eccles Street, 9
was first called Elizabeth Street (after Elizabeth Read of the Read family of Wincobank Hall). It was renamed in 1903, for no particular reason after the town of Eccles in Lancashire

Eckington Road, Way, 19
from the village of Eckington, which is recorded in 1002 as Eccingtune and has been spelt various ways since then – Echinton, Eketon, Eggington, etc. It means the farm belonging to Ecca or Ecci.

Edale Road, 11
from the Derbyshire village of Edale.

Eden Drive, 6
not known.

Edenhall Road, 2
was built on the Duke of Norfolk's land and named after the village of Edenhall, three miles from Penrith, Cumbria. One of the Duke's ancestors, Thomas Howard, of Corby Castle, married Barbara Musgrave, of Edenhall, in 1720.

Edensor Road, 5
from the village of Edensor (pronounced Enza) in Chatsworth Park.

Eden Street, 6
no longer listed; named from a place called Eden in Yorkshire. I don't know which. There are several (see Anlaby).

Edgar Street, 4
not known; built in the 1870s.

Edge Bank, 7
Mary Walton in her *History of the Parish of Sharrow,* says it means the edge of Meadow Bank.

Edgebrook Road, 7
from the stream which runs through Nether Edge, under Abbeydale Road and into the River Sheaf. Once open, and apparently quite a large stream, nowadays it is piped or culverted for much of its length.

Edge Close, Lane, 6
from the geographical feature, Birley Edge.

Edgedale Road, Edgefield Road, Edge Hill Road, Edgemount Road, 7
are all variations on the theme of Brincliffe Edge.

Edgewell Close, Crescent, Drive, Lane, Place, Rise, Way, 6
from the well at Birley Edge. The Edge Well is recorded in a document in 1590.

Edith Walk, 6
from the earlier Edith Street which was fairly obviously named after a lady called Edith but I have not been able to trace her.

Edmund Avenue, Close, Drive, 17
after Edmund West, of Amberden Hall, Essex, who was lord of the manor of Greenhill in the sixteenth century. In 1573 he sold the manor to John Bullocke, of the Inner Temple, London, for £307.

Edmund Road, 2
was built on the Duke of Norfolk's land and named after someone called Edmund in the Duke's family history. There were several Edmunds, but the most likely one is Lord Edmund Talbot, third son of the fourteenth Duke, who unsuccessfully contested Brightside in the elections of 1885 and 1886, and later became MP for South West Sussex.

Edward Road, 9
not known.

Edward Street, 3
was built around 1805, mostly on land belonging to the Church Burgesses. It was obviously named after someone called Edward, but I have not been able to identify him.

Edwin Road, 2
not known; built in the 1890s.

Effingham Lane, Road, Street, 4
from a branch of the Duke of Norfolk's family, the Howards of Effingham. The first Baron Howard of Effingham was a son of Thomas, second Duke of Norfolk. The seventh Baron was created Earl of Effingham in 1731. Effingham is a village near Leatherhead, Surrey.

Egerton Lane, Street, 1
the street was built around 1830 and named after Lord Francis Egerton (1800-1857), Secretary for War. In 1846 he became the Earl of Ellesmere. His sister, Sophia, married the Duke of Norfolk. For some reason, Egerton Street is listed in street directories of the late 1860s and early 1870s as Edgerton Street.

Elcroft Gardens, 19
is an abbreviated form of a Beighton field name recorded in 1796, Elgie Croft.

Eldon Court, Street, 1
after the Earl of Eldon (1751-1838), Lord Chancellor 1801-1806 and again 1807-1827.

Eleanor Street, 9
was approved in 1897 for Frederick Uttley Laycock, solicitor, (see Uttley Street); obviously named after a woman called Eleanor, probably a relative of Mr Laycock's.

Elgin Street, 10
after the Morayshire market town of Elgin; one of a group of streets given Scottish names (see Arran).

Ella Street, 4
after the villages of Kirk Ella and West Ella on the north bank of the Humber. Earl Fitzwilliam's family owned land there.

Ellenborough Road, 6
after Ellenborough House, an old farm nearby, kept in the 1870s by Joseph Ashforth junior. His father had Owling House Farm.

Ellerton Road, 5
after the village of Ellerton on the River Derwent, eleven miles west of Market Weighton. Neighbouring Wheldrake Road was named after another River Derwent village.

Ellesmere Road, Walk, 4
after Lord Francis Egerton, son of the first Duke of Sutherland, who was created Earl of Ellesmere in 1846. Ellesmere is a place in Shropshire. The Earl's link with Sheffield is that his sister Sophia, married the Duke of Norfolk, and Ellesmere Road was built on the Duke of Norfolk's land.

Ellin Street, 1
after the Ellin family who had a cutlery works and a house near The Moor. They started their business in 1784 and operated so successfully that three members of the family held the position of Master Cutler in 1833, 1841, and 1908.

Elliott Road, 6
after Ebenezer Elliott, the corn law rhymer (1781-1849) who lived at Upperthorpe. The road used to be one of a pair along with Montgomery Road, after Sheffield's other famous poet, James Montgomery, but Montgomery Road was renamed Burns Road.

Elliottville Street, 6
uncertain. The street was built about 1870 and may have been named after a field. There was an Elliott Field in the area.

Ellison Street, 3
probably after Joseph Ellison, file and steel manufacturer, whose works were in Wellmeadow Place and who lived in Meadow Street in the early nineteenth century.

Ellis Street, 3
not known.

Elm Crescent, 19
group name – trees. See Ash Street.

Elmfield Avenue, 5
from an old field name.

Elmham Road, 9
was built on the Duke of Norfolk's land and named after six villages south of Bungay, Norfolk, where the Duke had interests – North Elmham, South Elmham St James, South Elmham St Cross, South Elmham St Margaret, South Elmham St Michael, and South Elmham St Peter. It was originally one of a group of streets named after Norfolk villages (see Bannham and Logan).

Elm Lane, 5
the area was known as The Elm in the eighteenth century. There was also an Elm Green and an Elm Farm. Obviously there were elm trees nearby.

Elmore Road, 10
after the eminent Victorian painter Alfred Elmore, who specialised in pictures of romantic historical incidents.

Elm Road, 10
group name – trees (see Chestnut Avenue, 19).

Elmview Road, 9
was originally called Elm View. It was built by the Meadow Hall Freehold Land Society and was intended to be one of three parallel streets named after trees, but the other two – Oak Street and Ash Grove – were never built.

Elmwood Drive, 19
from a nearby house called Elmwood which was built about 1881 for a member of the Wells family of Eckington Hall.

Elstree Drive, Road, 12
probably a link with the builders, Henry Boot and Sons, who won a contract in 1928 to build a garden city at Elstree, mainly for people who worked at the nearby film studios. Boots often named streets after places where they had large contracts elsewhere in the country. Some of their housing developments in the south of England have streets with Sheffield or north Derbyshire names.

Elton Street, 6
no longer listed. First called Ellis Street, it was renamed in 1872 to avoid confusion with another Ellis Street, and although the new name probably came from Charles Isaac Elton, jurist, archaeologist, MP and author, who was prominent at the time of the renaming, the main aim was to choose a name that was similar to the old one.

Elwood Road, 17
I suspect this name comes from a nearby wood called Little Wood. The road could not be called Little Wood Road or it would have been confused with Littlewood Road, 12. It looks as though Elwood (L-wood) was a compromise.

Embankment Road, 10
was near the embankment of the old Pisgah Dam, one of several reservoirs at Crookesmoor which used to supply Sheffield with water.

Emerson Close, Crescent, Drive, 5
after Ralph Waldo Emerson (1803-1882), essayist and poet.

Emily Road, 7
according to Mary Walton, in her *History of the Parish of St Peter, Abbeydale* was built in 1894 and named after a female relative of Joshua Spooner, one-time owner of the Machon Bank estate.

Empire Road, 7
a popular Victorian and Edwardian patriotic street name; most cities have one.

Endcliffe Avenue, Crescent, Edge, 10;
Endcliffe Glen Road,
Endcliffe Rise Road, 11;
Endcliffe Vale Avenue, Road, 11 and 10
Endcliffe is recorded in 1333 as Elcliffe, and in 1577 as Elclyffe. According to the English Place Name Society, it comes from the Old English word *elle*, meaning elder tree – the hill with elder trees.

Endcliffe Grove Avenue, 10
from a house called The Grove. In the

Ellesmere Road, with a crowd of local children outside the Wesleyan Church. The board outside the church is advertising Harvest Festival services.

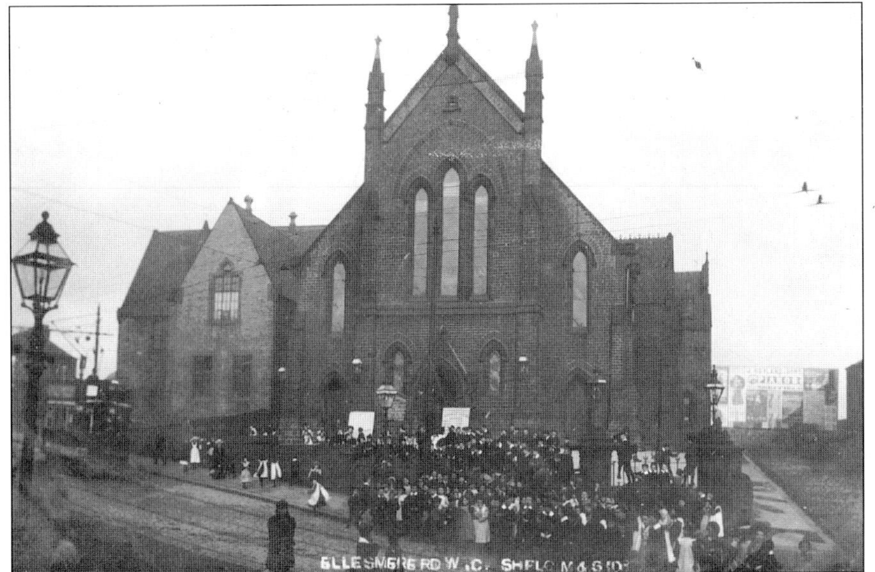

1890s Benjamin Livingstone Marples lived there.

Endcliffe Hall Avenue, 10
from the mansion built in the 1860s on the site of an earlier building by Sir John Brown, businessman, town councillor, alderman, magistrate, twice Mayor, twice Master Cutler. He is said to have spent £150,000 on the hall.

Endcliffe Terrace Road, 11
Endcliffe Terrace was originally the name of one house, home in the 1850s of William Younge.

Endfield Road, 5
from an old field name.

Endowood Road, 7
a name that sometimes crops up as a field name. It means end of the wood, in this case, the adjacent Ecclesall Wood.

Enfield Place, 13
after the Middlesex market town of Enfield.

Ennerdale Avenue, Drive, 19
group name – Lake District locations (see Ambleside).

Epping Gardens, Grove, 19
after Epping Forest, Essex; one of a group of streets named after forests (see Ashdown).

Errington Avenue, Close, Crescent, Road, Way, 2
Errington Road was approved in January 1935 and built on the Duke of Norfolk's land. Other nearby streets approved at the same meeting (Berners, Fellbrigg, Aylward etc) had links with the Duke, but Errington is a mystery unless it comes from the Errington family, who like the Duke, were prominent Roman Catholics.

Erskine Crescent, Road, View, 2
from the fact that a relative of the Duke of Norfolk, Sir Henry Francis Howard, diplomat, married, in 1830, Sevilla, daughter of Lord Erskine.

Eskdale Close, Road, 6
Eskdale Road, built first, was originally called Tuxford Road. It was renamed in 1924 (because there was another Tuxford Road at Attercliffe), after Eskdale in Cumbria.

Esperanto Place, 1
is really the left-over bit of the bottom of Norfolk Street chopped off by Arundel Gate. It was given its own name in honour of the holding of the International Esperanto Congress in Sheffield in 1974.

Essendine Crescent, 8
after the village of Essendine in the old county of Rutland. It was built by Frederick Thomas Walker, constructional builder, who lived at Norton Lees, and was assistant managing director of Ketton Portland Cement Co. He was a former High Sheriff of Rutland, where he owned land. He also built Ketton Avenue, 8.

Essex Road, 2
was built on the Duke of Norfolk's land and named after one of the Duke's ancestors, John Petre, later created Baron Petre of Writtle, who was at various times Sheriff of Essex, MP for Essex and Lord Lieutenant of Essex

Etwall Way, 5
after the village of Etwall, six miles south west of Derby.

Evans Street, 3
probably after James Evans who was a builder and brickmaker living in nearby Monmouth Street in the mid-nineteenth century.

Evelyn Road, 10
built about 1890 by Sheffield Land and Mortgage Corporation Ltd, and probably named after Harry Evelyn Marsh, eldest son of Alderman Harry P. Marsh who was a director of the Corporation.

Everard Avenue, Drive, Glade, 17
not known. The names Everard Avenue and Drive were approved in July 1958.

Everingham Close, Crescent, Road, 5
from the village of Everingham five miles from Market Weighton. Everingham Hall was owned by Lady Herries (see Herries Road) and later by the Duke of Norfolk.

Everton Road, 11
from the village of Everton, Nottinghamshire, three miles south east of Bawtry; one of four streets all named after villages in the Bawtry area, and all ending in 'ton' (along with Newington, Rossington and Wiseton).

Evesham Close, 9
after the Vale of Evesham, famous fruit and vegetable growing area; one of a group of streets named after English vales (see Aylesbury).

Exchange Gateway, 1
from the older name, Exchange Court, the place where horses were changed in the days of coaching inns. There were two coaching inns in the area in the 1790s, the *Mitre*, Fargate and the *Bird in Hand*, Church Lane. Waggons for London, Halifax and Leeds left the *Mitre*, and a Manchester waggon left the *Bird in Hand* every Thursday.

Exchange Street, 2
from Sheffield's first Corn Exchange, built by the twelfth Duke of Norfolk in 1830. The building was demolished to make way for market re-development and a new Corn Exchange was built in Sheaf Street in 1881. This second building was destroyed by fire in 1947.

Exeter Drive, Place, Way, 3
from the older Exeter Street, now no longer listed. Till 1890 Exeter Street was called Egerton Street West. It was renamed after Exeter, the county town of Devon.

Exley Avenue, 6
after Joseph Exley who was a victualler in Langsett Road. Mr Exley was given planning permission to build sixty houses in the avenue in 1909-10. Two years later, permission was granted for more houses, this time to G. Exley.

Eyam Road, 10
from the famous plague village of Eyam, Derbyshire.

Eyncourt Road, 5
not known; name approved February 1920.

Eyre Lane, Street, 1
after Vincent Eyre, Town Trustee 1784-1801, Town Collector 1790-1793, and chief agent in Sheffield for the Duke of Norfolk. As chief agent, Mr Eyre supervised development of the Duke's land between Surrey Street and the River Sheaf.

Fairbank Road, 5
after the Fairbank family of surveyors and mapmakers who, from the 1730s to the 1850s, made meticulous plans of areas in and around Sheffield. Their map books, carefully preserved in the Central Library, are an invaluable reference source.

Fairbarn Close, Drive, Place, Road, Way, 6
from an old farm called Fairbarn which was owned in the eighteenth century by George Bamforth, lord of the manors of Worrall and Wadsley, who lived at High House. When he died in 1730, he left the farm to his widow.

Fairfax Road, 2
after General Fairfax, who was commander of the parliamentary troops in Yorkshire during the English civil war.

Fairleigh, 2
not known; name approved May 1924.

Fairmount Gardens,12
was built in the grounds of a house called Fairmount.

Fairthorn Road, 5
not known; name approved February 1920.

The Fairway, 10
because of its nearness to Hallamshire golf course.

Falconer Lane, 13
the name Falconer is recorded in the area as Fawkeners in a document of 1553, and is thought to come from the family of a man called Robert le Faukener, who lived in the fourteenth century. There was also a Falconer House and a Falconer Wood.

Falkland Road, 11
from the Fifeshire town of Falkland, twenty-one miles from Edinburgh, site of a palace built by James V, which fell into decay in the seventeenth century and was restored by the Marquis of Bute in the 1890s.

Fallon Road, 6
named in 1947 by Wortley Rural District Council after Reuben Fallon and Carry Fallon, who lived on Stannington Road in the 1930s and 1940s.

Falmouth Road, 7
after the Cornish port of Falmouth (see Barmouth).

Falstaff Crescent, Gardens, Road, 5
were named in March 1938 with Launce Road, and both names seem to come from comic characters in Shakespeare's plays, Falstaff from Sir John Falstaff.

Faraday Road, 9
after Michael Faraday (1791-1867) physicist and discoverer of electromagnetic induction which prepared the way for the electric motor and dynamo, the transformer and the telephone.

Faranden Road, 9
was approved (as Farranden Road) in 1893 for the Darnall landowner Col E.W. Stanyforth. Most of the streets on his land were named after members of his family, or places in Yorkshire with which they were connected, but I have not been able to pin down a reason for this one.

Farcroft Grove, 4
from an old field name, Far Croft, mentioned in a document of 1637.

Farfield Road, 3
from an old field name, the meaning of which is obvious. There was also a homestead in the same area called Farfield.

Fargate, 1
until the early eighteenth century Sheffield was only a small group of buildings clustered on the western bank of the River Sheaf, where it joins the Don. Beyond the buildings were fields, orchards, gardens and moorland. At that time, Fargate was out of the centre – the far street – rather than being part of the centre as it is today.

Farish Place, 2
after the Rev Henry Farish, first vicar of St Mary's, Bramall Lane, from 1829 to 1853, and vicar of Ecclesall from 1853 till his death in 1856. Christ Church, Heeley was built as a tribute to him.

Far Lane, 6
a descriptive name; like Far Field, it was a common name signifying that it was some distance from a homestead or settlement.

Farm Bank Road, Farm Road, 2
from The Farm, an ancient building rebuilt in 1824, when it became the Sheffield residence of the Duke of Norfolk. The Duke sold it to the Midland Railway in 1898, and after being British Rail's local headquarters in later years, it was demolished in 1967.

Farm Close, 12
from Charnock Hall Farm.

Farm Crescent, Walk, 19
from Plumbley Hall Farm

Farm Fields Close, 19
was built alongside the play area developed on the fields of Westfield Farm.

Farmstead Close,14
from the nearby Newfield Green Farm.

Farndale Road, 6
was originally called Firbeck Road. It was changed in 1924 to avoid confusion with Firbeck Road, Woodseats. Farndale is a north Yorkshire beauty spot famous for its daffodils.

Farnley Avenue, 6
when it was first built, by Parson Cross Freehold Land Society in 1877, it was called Nelson Road (after Thomas Nelson, mason and builder, who was on the committee of the land society). When the area came into Sheffield, where there was already a Nelson Road, it was renamed, from the Yorkshire village of Farnley.

Farrar Road, 7
after the Rev John Farrar (1802-1884), president of the Wesleyan Methodist Conference in 1854 and (a rare honour), again in 1870. He served in Sheffield for a time and was an acquaintance of John Holland, the Sheffield author.

Far View Road, 5
was built in the 1930s on land formerly belonging to the old Cliffe Farm as part of what was first called the Styring estate. One of the advertised attractions of the estate was that, at 450 feet above sea level, it commanded extensive views over the Ecclesfield area – hence Far View.

Favell Road, 3
was first called Chantrey Road. It was renamed in 1903 after the Rev Henry

Arnold Favell, vicar of St George's Church from 1873 to 1884. His vicarage, built in 1876, stood on this road. He later became vicar of St Mark's and Archdeacon of Sheffield.

Fawcett Street, 3
after the Misses Marianne and Martha Fawcett, who ran a boarding and day academy for young ladies at nearby Bellefield House in the early 1800s.

Fawley Road, 6
no longer listed; named after Thomas Cowley Fawley, of Woodgrove House, Penistone Road, who was given planning permission to build the road, (and Hicks Road) in 1878.

Fearnehough Street, 9
after J. Fearnehough who owned land and property in the street, and in nearby Broad Oaks. He is mentioned in the Town Council minutes in 1890, but I have not been able to find out any more about him.

Fellbrigg Road, 2
is mis-spelt. It ought to be Felbrigg. It was built on the Duke of Norfolk's land and named after the village of Felbrigg, Norfolk.

Fell Place, Road, Street, 9
after the Fell family who were well-known in Sheffield. Mrs Elizabeth Fell, widow of ironmaster John Fell (who built New Hall, Attercliffe) was a local benefactress. She was involved in setting up the Infirmary, gave £1,000 towards its cost – a considerable sum in the 1790s – and the foundation stone was laid in her name. She also helped the Sunday school movement and the charity schools. The three streets were built on the grounds of New Hall.

Fenney Lane, 11
from the old word *fennig,* meaning marshy.

Fentonville Street, 11
the Fenton family had a farm in the area in the early nineteenth century. The farm land was later made into gardens which were known as Fentonville Gardens. The gardens, between Cemetery Road, Washington Road and Sharrow Lane, were built on from the 1870s onwards.

Ferguson Street, 9
not known; built in the 1890s on land owned by the Church Burgesses.

Fern Avenue, 19
there were probably ferns growing on the site.

Ferncroft Avenue, 19
from an old field name, Fern Croft.

Fern Road, 6
was approved in 1867 (with Welbeck Road) for the Welbeck Freehold Land Society. There doesn't seem to have been anyone called Fern connected with the society so this too was probably named from ferns growing on the site.

Ferrars Close, Drive, Road, Way, 9
seems to be a corruption, or mis-spelling of Ferrers, from the village of Higham Ferrers, Northants. The Earls Fitzwillam, lords of the manor of Tinsley, were also lords of the manor of Higham Ferrers in the mid-nineteenth century, and the family held the title Viscount Higham of Higham Ferrers.

Ferriby Road, 6
after the villages of North and South Ferriby on opposite banks of the Humber; one of a group of streets named after villages in the Humberside area (with Hessle and Ganton).

Fersfield Street, 4
from the village of Fersfield, between Diss and Kenninghall, Norfolk. The street was built on the Duke of Norfolk's land. The Duke's ancestors were lords of the manor of Fersfield from the fourteenth century onwards.

Fieldhead Road, 8
from a large house called Field Head, built in the 1780s by John Shore, the banker, and later the home of Alderman Richard Solly. It stood near what is now the Abbeydale Road end of Fieldhead Road and had extensive grounds. It was demolished in the 1870s.

Fieldhouse Way, 4
is an abbreviation of Carr Field House, an old house which stood nearby.

Fielding Road, 6
was built on land owned by the Dixon family of Hillsborough Hall. Florence, daughter of J. Willis Dixon, married, in 1900, Charles William Fielding. Sir Charles, as he later became, was Director General of Food Production in 1918-19, member of several national committees, and a well-known writer on agricultural subjects. He owned 3,000 acres of land in Sussex.

Fife Close, Gardens, Street, Way, 9
Fife Street, built first, was originally called Fowler Street, after John Fowler, a local landowner through whose land it was built. It was renamed in 1903. Fife is a former Scottish county (now an administrative region) between the Firths of Forth and Tay.

Fig Tree Lane, 1
dates back to about 1700 and comes from a house called Figtree Hall which stood nearby. The assumption is that the house had a fig tree in its garden.

Filey Lane, 3 Filey Street, 10
Filey Street was originally called New Porter Street. It was changed in 1890. There was no special reason for the new name which came from the well-known Yorkshire coastal resort.

Finchwell Close, Crescent, Road, 13
Finchwell Road, built first, was originally called Park Lane. It was renamed in 1924 from an old well nearby called the Finch Well. There was also a Finch Well Field.

Findon Crescent, Place, Road, Street, 6
Findon Street came first, built in the 1860s as part of the Dykes Hall estate, and originally called Fowler Street, after John Fowler, owner of the land, who rebuilt, and lived at, Dykes Hall. It duplicated another street name, and it was renamed in 1903, after a village called Findon. There are two, one near Aberdeen (from which the Findon, or Finnon, haddock was named), the other near Worthing in Sussex.

Finlay Street, 3
not known; originally called Arthur Street, it was renamed in 1872.

Firbeck Road, 8
from the village of Firbeck, three miles from Maltby; one of a group of streets with Yorkshire place names.

Fircroft Avenue, Road, 5
from a large house nearby called Fir Croft, which was owned up to 1894 by Stephen Sampson, although it was lived in by Thomas E. Ellison, barrister.

Fir Place, Street, 6
some time during the 1850s, part of

Firth Park Road on an undated picture postcard, but possibly taken in the 1920s.

what is now Walkley became known as Fir View, presumably because there were fir trees somewhere in the area. The two streets, built later, continued the fir theme.

Firshill Avenue, Close, Crescent, Croft, Gardens, Glade, Rise, Road, Walk, Way, 4

from a house called Firshill. When it was advertised to let in 1844, it was described as a mansion with eighteen acres of grassland around it. It was the home of Edward Vickers (1804-1897), of Naylor, Vickers and Co. He lived in it till 1857 when he moved to Tapton Hall, which he re-built.

Firth Park Avenue, Crescent, Road, 5

from the thirty-six acre park given to Sheffield in 1875 by Alderman Mark Firth, industrialist, Mayor (in 1874), Master Cutler (1867-69), and public benefactor. The parkland was originally part of the estate attached to Page Hall.

Fir Vale Place, Road, 5

the name Fir Vale seems to have originated as a house name, which appears in some directories as Firs Vale, presumably because it was in the valley below Firs Hill. The house was the home in the 1880s of Walter Marsh. When it was offered for sale after his death, it had six acres of land and was said 'to contain within itself all the desiderata for a gentleman's residence'

Fir View Gardens, 4

looks across to Fir Vale.

Fisher Lane, 9

after John Fisher, a well-known local farmer who was prominent in the movement which resulted in the building of Darnall Old Wesleyan Chapel in 1822.

Fishponds Road, Fishponds Road West, 13

when the 700-acre Woodthorpe Hall estate was offered for sale in 1844, it was offered 'with its lawns, pleasure grounds, fishpond, rockery, out-offices etc.' The fishpond, reduced in size, was retained as a feature at the corner of Richmond Road and Hastilar Road South when the estate was developed for housing.

Fitzalan Road, 13

Fitzalan is one of the family names of the Duke of Norfolk who was lord of the manor of Handsworth and owned land in the village. Several other streets with names connected with the Duke were given new names in 1923 after Handsworth became part of Sheffield.

Fitzalan Square, 1

as above, from one of the family names of the Duke of Norfolk. Powers to build the square were obtained by the Town

Fitzalan Square in the late 1930s, showing the old stone tram shelter, steps down to the underground Tramways Office, the first C&A building, and on the Haymarket corner, the Fifty Shilling Taylor.

Council in 1869 but the work involved demolishing several properties, including two pubs and a group of houses, and the work was not completed till 1881.

Fitzgerald Road, 10
not known; approved in 1895 for the trustees of John Tasker.

Fitzhubert Road, 2
from Fitzhubert, the first Norman lord of the manor of Eckington in 1086; one of several Manor estate names taken from the old Eckington Court Roll.

Fitzmaurice Road, 9
is a link with the famous Huntsman family who owned land and property in the area. Benjamin Huntsman, of West Retford Hall (1820-1893), who was a descendant of the famous inventor, married Anna Maria Fitzmaurice, daughter of General Fitzmaurice, in 1850.

Fitzroy Road, 2
not known.

Fitzwalter Road, 2
from the sixteenth century marriage between the second Duke of Norfolk's daughter, Elizabeth, and the Earl of Sussex, who was also Baron Fitzwalter.

Fitzwilliam Gate, Street, 1
after the Fitzwilliam family of Wentworth Woodhouse, who owned large areas of land in Sheffield and were lords of the manor of Ecclesall. The seventh Earl Fitzwilliam was Lord Mayor of Sheffield in 1909.

Five Trees Avenue, Close, Drive, 17
from five large chestnut trees which stood on a narrow strip of land between the housing development and Abbeydale Road South. At last count there were only three left.

Flask View, 6
looks towards Damflask Reservoir.

Flat Street, 1
a descriptive name; in the 1797 directory it appears as Flatt Street. Flatt, a word often used in field names, comes from an old Norse word, but it means the same thing.

Flaxby Street, 9
from the village of Flaxby, near Knaresborough.

Fleet Street, 9
not known; possibly from the Lincolnshire hamlet called Fleet. Several of the streets on the New Hall estate were given Lincolnshire names. Elizabeth Fell, née Laughton, who lived at the hall (see Fell Street), came from Lincolnshire.

Fleury Close, Crescent, Place, Rise, Road, 14
after Dr Henry Cornelius Flory, who was descended from the Huguenot family of Fleury. He set up the Myrtle Spring Boarding School in 1837 and ran it until his death in 1863, when he was succeeded by his son. He also owned the toll bar at Myrtle Spring.

Flockton Avenue, Crescent, Drive, Road, 13
from the Flockton coal seam which is found in the area.

Flodden Street, 10
from the Battle of Flodden fought between the English and the Scots in September 1513, won, after fierce fighting, by the English (see Bosworth).

Flora Street, 6
one of three streets built by Joseph Stovin and John Wreaks on the site of the old Infirmary Road barracks, which the two men bought for £2,850 in 1855. All three streets were given girls' names, Florence, Gertrude and Thirza. Thirza was after Mr Stovin's wife and daughter who were both called Thirza. The other two streets were almost certainly named after female relatives of the two men, but I have not been able to identify them. Florence Street was renamed Flora Street in 1872 because there was another Florence Street elsewhere in the town.

Florence Road, 8
uncertain; it appears first in the 1902 directory. It may have something to do with Councillor James Sivil, who built in this area, and whose wife was called Florence.

Folds Crescent, Drive, Lane, 8
from the old Folds Farm, Beauchief. For about fifty years, up to the early twentieth century, George Sampson, agent to E.V.P. Burnell, the owner of Beauchief, was the farmer there.

Foley Street, 4
was built on the Duke of Norfolk's land. In 1849, Lady Mary Charlotte Howard, daughter of the thirteenth Duke of Norfolk, was married to Baron Foley of Kidderminster.

Follett Road, 5
not known; name approved August 1931.

Forbes Road, 6
was first called Storth Road. It was renamed in 1924 after a popular local doctor, Dr Alexander Forbes, who lived at the corner of this road and Langsett Road. Dr Forbes, born in Aberdeen, came to Sheffield in 1890 and worked in Hillsborough for more than fifty years. He was a city councillor, churchwarden at St Bartholomew's, and chairman of the Caledonian Society. He died in 1945.

Ford Road, 11
a link with the Greaves Bagshawe family of Banner Cross Hall, who developed the Banner Cross area (see Blair Athol Road). The Bagshawe family had another home at Ford Hall, Derbyshire, from which this road gets its name.

Foremark Road, 5
after the South Derbyshire village called Foremark; one of a group of streets named after Derbyshire villages.

Forest Edge, 11
from its nearness to Ecclesall Woods.

Forge Lane, 1
from the Vulcan Works of Thomas Ellin and Co, forgers and rollers, which stood between Ellin Street and Forge Lane.

Forncett Street, 4
was built on the Duke of Norfolk's land and named after three villages in Norfolk, Forncett St Mary, Forncett St Peter, and Forncett End. They are about halfway between Norwich and Diss.

Fornham Street, 2
was built on the Duke of Norfolk's land and named after two villages in Suffolk in which the Duke had an interest, Fornham All Saints and Fornham St Martin, about two miles from Bury St Edmunds.

Forres Avenue, Road, 10
from the market town of Forres, twelve miles from Elgin (see Arran Road).

Forster Road, 8
no longer listed; probably named after Joseph Forster, described as a manager, who lived in Oak Street, Heeley, in the 1860s and 1870s at the time road was built.

Fort Hill Road, 9
from the ancient hill fort at Wincobank, a three-acre earthwork fort overlooking the Don Valley which was destroyed during the Roman occupation.

Fossdale Road, 7
from Fossdale, north of Hawes, one of a group of streets named after famous dales.

Fourwells Drive, 12
there were four wells in the vicinity.

Foxdale Avenue, 12
the dale below Fox Wood.

Foxglove Road, 5
group name – flowers (see Acacia).

Foxhall Lane, 10
was originally called Fox Lane, as which it is recorded in a document dated 1442. It was renamed in 1903 after the nearby farm called Fox Hall, which almost certainly took its name from the Fox family who were prominent in Fulwood for many years.

Fox Hill Avenue, Close, Crescent, Drive, Place, Road, Way, 6
from a farm called Fox Hill, which is mentioned in Harrison's survey of 1637 as 'Ffox Hill, a tenement with a dwelling house, stable, barn and other outhouses'. The farm was demolished in the 1930s to make way for housing.

Fox Lane, 12
probably after Thomas Fox, who had a farm on Birley Lane early in the twentieth century.

Fox Lane, 17
usually in researching street names, there are too few clues. In this case there are too many. There was a house on the lane called Fox Hall, and a farm nearby called Fox Farm; over the years, several people called Fox have lived nearby, among them Samuel, farmer in the 1870s, Clement, farmer in the 1890s, Edmund, farmer (at Fox Farm) in the 1920s, and Edmund Fox, joiner and builder in the early 1900s. The lane could have been named after any of them, or even somebody else.

Fox Road, Walk, 6
after B.P. Broomhead Colton-Fox, solicitor (and chairman of Thos. Firth and Sons), who owned most of the property in the road, and in several nearby roads (see Sherde Road and Wales Road). Mr Colton-Fox was killed in 1890 in an accident at Sheffield Victoria Station.

Fox Street, 3
was built on the Duke of Norfolk's land and seems to have been named after the Liberal statesman Charles James Fox (1749-1806). It was built around the time of his death. Among other things, Fox urged full freedom for dissenters and Roman Catholics, a cause which probably endeared him to the Duke, who was a leading Roman Catholic.

Foxwood Avenue, Drive, Grove, Road, 12
from the small wood nearby called Fox Wood. A homestead, a farm and a quarry in the area all had the same name.

Framlingham Place, Road, 2
was built on the Duke of Norfolk's land and named after Framlingham, a market town in east Suffolk. One of the Duke's ancestors, Roger Bigod, third Earl of Norfolk, built a castle at Framlingham which was owned by the family for three centuries.

France Road, 6
after the Rev Thomas France, minister of Loxley Congregational Chapel from 1854 to 1888.

Francis Street, 9
no longer listed; probably after Francis Huntsman, descendant of Benjamin Huntsman. The family owned land at Attercliffe some of which was used for house building in the 1880s and 1890s.

Frank Place, 9
not known.

Fraser Close, Crescent, Drive, Road, Walk, 8
Fraser Road was built first; the original intention was to call it Duffield Road, after James Duffield, of Wilson Cammell's works, Dronfield, for whom it was built. Instead, it was named after a painter called Fraser, but I am not sure which one. There were three, Alexander, John and Robert, all of whom exhibited at the Royal Academy. Mr Duffield collected paintings (see Chatfield, Crosby and Kennedy).

Frederick Road, 7
after Frederick Clarke, for whom houses on the road were built in the 1880s. No address is given for him in the Town Council minutes, but he was probably Frederick Clarke, manager, who is listed in directories of the time as living at Albert Road, Heeley.

Frederick Street, 9
after Frederick Whitby, an official of the Albert Freehold Land Society who built the street in the 1870s. Whitby Road was named after the same man.

Freedom Court, Road, 6
Freedom Road was built by the Freedom Hill Freehold Land Society in the 1860s. One of the aims of the freehold land societies was to give working men the chance to buy houses and with it, as freeholders, the chance to vote. Freedom was much in their minds. One said in its advertising matter 'Qualify yourselves – and proclaim a lasting triumph to the cause of popular and enlightened freedom'.

Freeston Place, 9
not known.

Fretson Road, 2
not known; name approved May 1924.

Friar Close, 6
from the character Friar Tuck; one of a group of Stannington streets named on the Robin Hood theme.

Frickley Road, 11
from the area of Frickley in South Yorkshire.

Frith Close, Road, 12
uncertain; it is first mentioned in the 1921 street directory, although it may have existed before then. The only people of this name I have been able to trace in the area are a Sarah Frith who owned a cottage and several fields not far away, and the Rev W. Frith, who was connected with Gleadless Independent Chapel around the turn of the century.

Fulwood Road, looking towards town, with not a horse or motor car in sight.

Froggatt Lane, 1

probably after James Froggatt, merchant, whose works were in Eyre Street in the early nineteenth century.

Frog Walk, 11

in 1933, when there was a series of readers' letters to the *Sheffield Daily Telegraph* about the origin of this name, one claimed that it came about because a man called Kenyon, who lived nearby, married a French woman. It didn't. Most readers, among them old residents of the area, said there were two walks. The one built first was known as The Old Walk which in local dialect became T'owd Walk, and eventually, Toad Walk, and the later one, named by association, was Frog Walk. It may be much simpler. It may just be that there were frogs around there.

Fulford Close, Place, 9

were built off York Road, and named after a suburb of the city of York. Fulford is south of York, on the road to Selby.

Fulmere Crescent, Road, 5

after William Fulmere, who was vicar of Ecclesfield in the fourteenth century.

Fulmer Road, 11

from the village of Fulmer, near Slough, Buckinghamshire; a link with the Wilson and Harland families (see Denham Road).

Fulney Road, 11

from the village of Fulney, near Spalding, Lincolnshire.

Furnace Lane, Woodhouse Mill, in pre-First World War days. The houses across the bottom of the lane are on Worksop Road, now known as Retford Road.

Fulton Road, 6

was originally called Prospect Road, but there were three Prospect Roads and two were renamed in 1872. The reason for the new name of this one is uncertain. There was a *Fulton Inn* on the street but I have not been able to establish if the street took its new name from the inn (as seems likely) or if the inn was named later from the street. The most famous person called Fulton was the American engineer Robert Fulton, who invented the first practical steamboat, a torpedo boat and a steam frigate.

Fulwood Lane, 11; Fulwood Road, 10

from the area called Fulwood, which is recorded, as Fulwod, in a document of 1332, and is said to come from the old words meaning dirty wood. Part of Fulwood Road was first called Chantrey Road. It changed in 1886.

Furnace Hill, 3

from the steel furnaces built nearby in the 1760s by John Love, who was the first man in Sheffield to make crucible steel (Huntsman's works were outside the town boundary at that time).

Furnace Lane, 13

from an old cast metal furnace set up at Woodhouse Mill in 1755. It operated till the early nineteenth century, and its remains were demolished along with some cottages in 1889.

Furness Close, 6

after Matthew Furness, landlord of the *Robin Hood Inn*, and owner of the land on which the close was built. The Furness family were prominent farmers in the Stannington area.

Furniss Avenue, 17

after Richard Furniss (1791-1857) who was born at Eyam, but moved to Dore as a young man and became something of a celebrity as village schoolmaster, parish clerk, registrar of births and deaths, part-time doctor, surgeon and dentist, legal consultant, surveyor, and poet.

Furnival Gate, Square, Street, 1; Furnival Road, 4

from the de Furnival family (whose name is believed to come from Fourneville, near Honfleur, France), lords of the manor of Sheffield from 1198 to 1383.

Gainsborough Road, 11
when it was made, in 1892, the road was named after the only house on it, Gainsborough House. The man who lived in the house from the 1870s, to the 1890s, was William Henry Pigott, who was an artist, hence the house name. Like the celebrated Thomas Gainsborough, Mr Pigott was a landscape painter.

Gainsford Road, 9
after Alderman Thomas Robert Gainsford (1844-1910), who was born at Darnall Hall, and was on the Town Council (later the City Council) from 1871 till 1907. Known to fellow councillors as 'The member for water', he was the first chairman of the Water Committee, a post he held for 20 years. He was also first chairman of the Derwent Valley Water Board. Outside council, he was a magistrate and chairman of Sheffield Coal Company for many years.

Galley Drive, 19
after William Galley, who was a farmer at west Mosborough in the nineteenth century. For a short time he was also the proprietor of a not very successful pit near Plumbley Lane.

Galsworthy Avenue, Road, 5
after John Galsworthy (1867-1933), novelist, dramatist, essayist, and author of *The Forsyte Saga*.

Gamston Road, 8
from a Nottinghamshire village called Gamston.

Ganton Road, 6
from the village of Ganton, eight miles west of Filey; one of a group of streets named after Yorkshire villages.

Garden Street, 1
from the gardens on the site before Ellins works were built.

Garden Walk, 19
there were gardens on the site.

Garland Close, Croft, Mount, Way, 19
after Thomas Garland, who had a large area of land where these streets were built in the late eighteenth century.

Garland Drive, 6
from a nearby house called Garland Cottage.

Garry Road, 6
was built on land belonging to the Dixon family of Hillsborough Hall and was first called Garth Road. It was changed to Garry Road in 1903. Most of the other streets built on the land were given names associated with the family. When I wrote about the other streets in the *Morning Telegraph* some years ago, a reader at Bridlington, who lived in the Hillsborough area when the Dixon land was developed, wrote to tell me that Garry Road was the last to be named. By then, he said, all the appropriate personal names had been used and Garry Road was named after the family pet. I checked with a surviving member of the family who said he could not confirm this, but it was quite possible.

Garter Street, 4
no longer listed; it was one of three streets built on the Duke of Norfolk's land and given names connected with the College of Arms, Garter Street after the Garter King of Arms (see also Norroy and Windsor). The Dukes of Norfolk, as Earls Marshal, controlled the College of Arms.

Garth Road, 9
not known; it was approved for Col E.W. Stanyforth in 1897 (see Staniforth Road).

Gatefield Road, 7
from the house called Gatefield House, which was built in the 1830s by Samuel Younge, solicitor, and later lived in by T.B. Cockayne, founder of Cockayne's department store. The house, now a social club, took its name from the field on which it was built.

Gatty Road, 5
after Dr Alfred Gatty (1839-1903), who was vicar of Ecclesfield for sixty-three years, edited the 1869 edition of *Hunter's Hallamshire*, and wrote several books of his own, including *Sheffield Past and Present*. His wife, Margaret, was also a writer, and founded and edited a children's magazine, and their daughter, Juliana Horatia Ewing, was a well-known writer of children's stories.

Gaunt Close, Drive, Place, Road, Way, 14
after John Gaunt (1789-1861), of Darnall Hall, one of Sheffield's early benefactors. He paid for the building of St Jude's Church, Moorfields, and left money to the Infirmary, the Public Dispensary (later called the Royal Hospital), schools, charities and religious organisations.

Gayton Road, 4
after the village of Gayton, Norfolk; group name (see Blayton).

Gell Street, 3
from the Gell family, originally of Hopton Hall, near Wirksworth, who became large landowners in the Sheffield area and succeeded to the Broomhall estates through intermarriage with the Jessop family.

George Street, 1
is not shown on the 1771 map of the town, but is mentioned in the 1797 trade directory. It probably refers to King George III, who reigned from 1760 to 1811, but it may have been named after George Woodhead, of Highfield, who owned the land on which it was built from 1787 onwards, and was largely responsible for the street being built. It was originally to have been called Waterhouse Street, from a family called Waterhouse, former owners of the land, part of which was called Waterhouse Croft.

Gerald Street, 9
not known.

Gerard Close, Street, 8
Gerard Street was approved in 1901 for Sheffield Brick Company, and probably named after someone called Gerard, but I cannot identify him. Two other streets planned (but apparently not built) by the company at the same time were to have been called Ellough Street and Rigma Hill.

Gertrude Street, 6
not known; see Flora Street.

Gervase Avenue, Drive, Place, Road, Walk, 8
after the last of the Strelley family to be lord of the manor of Ecclesall, Gervase Strelley, who lived at Beauchief and died in 1609.

Gibbons Drive, Walk, 14
after the wood carver, Grinling Gibbons (1648-1721) whose carving, highly regarded for its beauty and delicacy can be seen in St Paul's Cathedral, Canterbury Cathedral, Windsor Castle, Chatsworth and elsewhere; one of a group of streets named after famous people in the art world (see Constable).

Gibraltar Street, 3
was probably inspired by Britain's successful defence of Gibraltar, acquired in 1711, against attack by the Spanish in 1726. Gibraltar became a Crown colony in 1830.

Gifford Road, 8
after Edric Frederick Gifford, VC, third Baron Gifford, who served with the Ashanti expedition of 1873-74, in the Zulu war of 1879, and later on the staff of Viscount Wolseley; one of a group of streets named after prominent Victorian military men (along with Glover, Staveley and Wolseley).

Gilbert Row, Street, 2
after Gilbert, seventh Earl of Shrewsbury, builder of the Shrewsbury Hospital in Sheffield, and last of his line to be connected with the town. After his death in 1616, his Sheffield properties passed to his daughter, Alethea Talbot, and by her marriage to Thomas Howard, Earl of Arundel and Surrey, the estates passed to the Howard family, Dukes of Norfolk.

Gill Croft, Meadows, 6
from an old Stannington field name recorded as Gilland, in the fourteenth century, Gilleland, and eventually Gyllesfield, in the fifteenth. It was named from someone called Gille, or Gill.

Gilleyfield Avenue, 17
from an old field name. Gilley Meadow, recorded in a document of 1622 and mentioned in the Dore Enclosure awards, is thought to come from a personal name, possibly that of Richard Gilly, who lived in the area in the fourteenth century.

Gillott Road, 6
was built by Parson Cross Freehold Land Society in the 1870s and named after Levi Gillott, of Birley Carr, one of the Society's two trustees.

Gilpin Lane, Street, 6
not known; Gilpin Street was first called George Street. It was changed in 1872.

Girton Road, 9
not known; possibly from the village of Girton, Nottinghamshire.

Gisborne Road, 11
from one of the family names of W.H. Greaves-Bagshawe, former owner of Banner Cross Hall, for whom the road was built (see Blair Athol Road). One of his ancestors, the Rev William Bagshawe, of Ford Hall and Banner Cross, married Anne Foxlowe in 1798. Miss Foxlowe's mother was Dorothy Gisborne, sister of General James Gisborne. The name was kept in the family in later years. Mr Greaves-Bagshawe's grandson was called Gisborne Carver.

The Glade, 10
from its setting amidst trees.

Gladstone Road, 10;
Gladstone Street, 9
after William Ewart Gladstone (1809-1898), English statesman, four times Prime Minister between 1868 and 1894.

Glave Street, 9
after William Glave, painter and paper-hanger, who owned the land on which it was built. There is some doubt about his name which appears in the directories as both Glave and Glaves. The street was built after his death, in the 1870s, by his executors. Samuel Glave, probably one of his relatives, lived in a house nearby and is mentioned in the commissioners' awards for the Attercliffe enclosures in the early nineteenth century.

Gleadless Avenue, Bank, Common, Crescent, Drive, Mount, 12;
Gleadless Court, 2;
Gleadless Road, 2, 14 and 12
from the area called Gleadless. The name appears as Gleydlys in the fifteenth century and is thought to come from the Old English word *glaed*, and to mean the clearing in a glade. The bottom part of Gleadless Road was originally called Sheaf Street.

Glebe Road, 10
was built on what was originally glebe land – land belonging to the church. The church owned quite a lot of land in Crookes. In early days parsons could farm their glebe land or let it, but in later years most glebe land was managed by the Ecclesiastical Commissioners.

Glenalmond Road, 11
from the Glenalmond valley in Perthshire, through which the River Almond flows. The name occurs because of the Murray family's connections with Banner Cross Hall (see Blair Athol Road). The Murray family seat is in Perthshire.

Glencoe Drive, Place, Road, 2
Glencoe Road, built first, was originally part of Stafford Street. It was given a name of its own in 1900, after the village of Glencoe, Natal, which in 1899 was the scene of the first encounter between British and Boer troops at the start of the Boer War.

Glenholme Drive, Place, Road, Way, 13
after a house at Richmond called Glenholme. In the early twentieth century it was the home of A.J. Jackson jr, steel merchant.

Glenmore Croft, 12
from a glen called Glen More in Strathclyde.

Glenorchy Road, 7
from the valley of the River Orchy, Strathclyde.

Glen Road, 7
in the 1860s, there was only one house in the area, Glen Cottage, which took its name from the valley between Brincliffe Edge and Machon Bank.

The Glen, 10
a variation on Endcliffe Glen.

Glentilt Road, 7
from the valley of the River Tilt, north of Blair Castle, Perthshire; a link with the Murray family (see Blair Athol Road).

Glen View, 11
overlooks the Porter Valley.

Glen View Road, 8
overlooks Abbeydale.

Glossop Lane, Road, 10
the building of Glossop Turnpike road was first planned in 1817, and the following year Sheffield Town Trust

Glossop Road was given a temporary triumphal arch for the visit of King Edward VII in 1905.

agreed to pay £200 towards its cost on condition that it entered the town along the route of what is now West Street. It was built as the Town Trust wanted it.

Gloucester Crescent, Street, 10

Gloucester Street was built around the time of the death of William Frederick, Duke of Gloucester, in 1834. After his death the title became extinct, but it was revived in 1928 for Henry, third son of King George V.

Glover Road, 8

after Sir John Hawley Glover RN, who was involved in the 1873-74 Ashanti war; group name (see Gifford).

Glover Road, 17

is mentioned in suburban sections of the Sheffield directories (though not every year) dating back to the 1890s. I have not been able to trace a local person named Glover. It may be from the same man as Glover Road, 8.

Goathland Close, Drive, Place, Road, 13

from the Yorkshire village of Goathland, eight miles from Whitby.

Goddard Hall Road, 5

from the house called Goddard Hall which had twenty-five acres of land around it in the 1840s. For many years it was the home of the Smilter family. In 1891 it was bought for conversion into a children's home. The grounds became part of what is now the Northern General Hospital complex. The Firth Park end of Herries Road used to be called Smilter Lane, after the family who lived at Goddard Hall. S.O. Addy suggested that the name Goddard might be from the old word godardy, meaning a pipe, goit, or canal, after some feature on the building. If so, he said, it would have been named in the same way as Spout House and Launder House (launder being another word for spout).

Godric Road, 5

after Godric, one of the lords of the manor of Ecclesfield before the Norman Conquest. Dunninc was another, hence nearby Dunninc Road.

Golden Oak Dell, 6

one of a group of streets named after varieties of oak trees (see Durmast).

Goodison Crescent, Rise, 6

after Joseph Goodison, farmer and coal owner in the area in the 1840s and 1850s. The two streets were built on what was part of Mr Goodison's nineteen acre farm south of Wood Lane. The land included ten fields and a number of small coal pits.

Goodwin Road, 8

after Charles Goodwin who owned a plot of land at the corner of Chesterfield Road and Thirlwell Road, with two shops and three houses on it. The property was offered for sale in 1873 after his death.

Goore Avenue, Drive, Road, 9

were built on land belonging to the Staniforth family (see Staniforth Road) and named from one of the family ancestors, Elizabeth Goore, who married Thomas Staniforth. Their son Samuel, married Mary Littledale, hence the Littledale estate, of which these three streets are part.

Gordon Avenue, 8

not known; the avenue was first listed in the 1914 directory which makes it somewhat late for it to have been named after General Gordon.

Gordon Road, 11

after General Charles George Gordon (1833-1885) famous for his ten-month defence of Khartoum. The road, one of three named after prominent Victorian military men (along with Stewart and Berresford) was built around the time Gordon was killed.

Gorse Lane, 10

was originally called Back Lane. It was renamed in 1903. There was gorse in the area.

Goulder Place, 9

after the Goulders, Henry, James, Herbert, George and John, who built and owned property in various parts of Attercliffe (and elsewhere) in the nineteenth century. John Goulder still had a joiner's shop and builder's yard on Attercliffe Common in 1905.

Gower Street, 4

from the Leveson-Gower family, Dukes of Sutherland (hence nearby Sutherland Road). The name crops up in Sheffield through a link with the Duke of Norfolk. Henry Charles, the thirteenth Duke of Norfolk married Charlotte Sophia Leveson-Gower, daughter of the first Duke of Sutherland in 1814. Strictly speaking, the name is pronounced 'Looson-Gore', so it ought to be 'Gore' Street.

Grafton Street, 2

like nearby streets, comes from the lineage of the Talbot family who were lords of the manor of Sheffield. Sir Gilbert Talbot, and his descendants, including George Talbot, who became ninth Earl of Shrewsbury, had their family seat at Grafton, Worcestershire.

Graham Knoll, Rise, Road, 10

Graham Road was built first, in the 1860s, as part of the Storth Crescent estate, and named after Sir James Robert George Graham (1792-1861), First lord of the Admiralty, and later Home Secretary under Peel.

Grammar Street, 6

was built on land leased from the governors of the old Sheffield Grammar School, in the 1870s. The grammar school, founded in 1603, was at that time in St George's Square. In 1884 it became part of the Collegiate School, which in turn became part of Wesley College, later renamed King Edward VII School.

Granby Road, 5

was built on land belonging to the Firth family and probably named after the Marquis of Granby who was among the Prince of Wales's party at the official opening of nearby Firth Park in 1875. The Marquis, later Duke of Rutland, was Lord of the Bedchamber to the Prince's father.

Grange Cliffe Close, 11

was built on land that was formerly part of the Abbeydale Grange estate. The Grange was the home of Wilson Mappin, magistrate and director of Sheffield Gas Company. Nearby Hastings Road was known as Grange Road up to 1886.

Grange Crescent, Grange Crescent Road, Grange Road, 11

after the old house called Sharrow Grange which stood on Sharrow Lane. In the 1750s it was a farm owned by Thomas Younge. Later it was the home of Thomas Marrian, brewer. The corporation bought it in 1928 and used it briefly for blind welfare services until new buildings were ready in 1930, when the old house was demolished.

Grange Lane, Grange Mill Lane, 5

from the house called Thundercliffe Grange, built, on the site of an older building, by Thomas Howard, Earl of Effingham, in 1777, and lived in by his family till 1860. In later years it was a home for mentally handicapped children, then it was divided into apartments.

Grange Lane, 13

from the house called Handsworth Grange, sometimes known as Cinder Hill Grange, home for many years of the Stacye family, and later owned by Fisher, Son and Sibray, the seed and nursery firm.

Grange Road, 19

from the house called Beighton Grange, home of the Stone family for thirty years, William Henry Stone, colliery owner, then C.H. Stone, who sold the house in 1898. It had fourteen acres of land.

Grant Road, 6

not known; the road was approved for H.S. Barker in 1898.

Granville Road, Square, Street, 2

from one of the family names of Sophia Leveson-Gower, daughter of George Granville Leveson-Gower, first Duke of Sutherland, who was married in 1814 to Henry Charles, thirteenth Duke of Norfolk. Their son, the fourteenth Duke of Norfolk, was named Henry Granville Fitzalan-Howard.

Granville Road, looking towards City Road, on a less than busy day in the early 1900s.

Grasmere Road, 8

group name; Lake District theme (see Arnside Road).

Grassdale View, 12

overlooks the site of a field called Grassdale, shown on the 1796 Mosborough enclosure map as belonging to Widow Needham.

Grassington Close, Drive, 12

from the North Yorkshire village of Grassington, thirteen miles from Skipton.

Grassmoor Close, 12

from an old field name, Grass Moor.

Grassthorpe Road, 12

was originally called Thorpe Road. It was changed in 1924, and Grassthorpe, the name of a Nottinghamshire village, was simply an adaptation of the old name.

Gray Street, 3

after Joshua Gray who was a well-known scissor manufacturer in Sheffield in the 1830s. The street was built alongside his house.

Gray Street, 19

after John Gray who owned land on Mosborough Green, including part of Church field, at the time of the land enclosures.

Greasbrough Road, 9

was originally called Wentworth Road, after the stately home of Earl Fitzwilliam on whose land it was built. It was renamed in 1912, after another part of the Earl's estate, Greasbrough, near Rotherham.

Greaves Close, Lane, 6

Greaves is an old Stannington family name. There have been farmers called Greaves in and around the village for more than 300 years. Harrison's survey of 1637 mentions Robert, Edward senior, Edward junior, George, Richard and Elizabeth Greaves, all of whom held land in the area.

Greaves Road, 5

from Greaves Farm on Yew Lane. As with Greaves Close and Lane, above, the name has been common in the area. The 1856 directory lists three farmers called Greaves around Ecclesfield, John, Samuel and William.

Greaves Street, 6
after a former landowner. It was built in the early 1850s on land belonging to John Greaves.

Greenfield Close, Drive, Road, 8
from an old field name. It appears in an 1870 advertisement offering for sale a house, stables, cowhouse, outbuildings, orchard and a four-acre croft called The Green Field, having a frontage to the Sheffield and Chesterfield turnpike road.

Greengate Close, Lane, Road, 13
from an old field name – Greengate Close, The late Ernest Atkin, in his *Historical Notes and Memories of Woodhouse*, said there was a gate, painted green, at the top of Greengate Lane to prevent cattle straying.

Greenhill Avenue, Parkway, Road, Greenhill Main Road, 8
Greenhill, recorded in the twelfth century as *Greenhilheg*, and later as *Grenhill*, *Grenylle* and *Grennell* is a straightforward descriptive name.

Greenhouse Lane, 10
no longer listed; it was named after the nearby Green House Farm, so named because it was near to a piece of common land called Andrew Green.

Greenhow Street, 6
Greenhow is said to mean green hillside, but the meaning was either an accident or a coincidence in this case. The street was originally called Green Street. It was renamed in 1872 to avoid confusion with another street of the same name.

Greenland Close, Court, Drive, Road, View, Walk, Way, 9
Greenland Road, built first, was sometimes called the Greenland Engine Road (after a nearby engine which took water from a coalpit), and sometimes the Greenland Arm Road (from the old Greenland arm of the canal, which was filled in many years ago). The name came originally from two fields at Attercliffe called Far Green Land and Near Green Land.

Green Lane, 3
is mentioned in Harrison's survey of 1637. It comes from the old area of common land called West Bar Green.

Green Oak Avenue, Crescent, Drive, Grove, Road, View, 17
after the *Green Oak Inn* which was built about 1820 on the then new turnpike road from Sheffield to Baslow. It was offered for sale, with two closes of land and a blacksmith's shop adjoining, in the *Sheffield Independent* of 1st December 1821, when it was described as newly-built. There was also a toll bar nearby called the Green Oak bar.

Greenock Street, 6
was originally called Green Street. It was renamed in 1903 and the new name was an effort to keep as near as possible to the old one. Greenock is a Scottish port on the Firth of Clyde.

Greenside Mount, 12
not known.

The Green, 9
from the old area of common land, Darnall Green, which was enclosed in 1811 at the same time as Attercliffe Common and Oakes Green.

The Green, 17
one of a group of definitives, along with The Grove, The Crescent, The Quadrant.

The Greenway, 8
refers to the area of grassland which was retained as a feature when the street was built.

Greenwood Avenue, Close, Crescent, Drive, Road, Way, 9
comes from the family line of the Staniforth family, owners of the land (see Staniforth Road). Samuel Staniforth married Mary Littledale (which is why the development was called the Littledale estate). Their daughter, Sarah, married Frederick Greenwood, of Keighley.

Greenwood Lane, 13
Greenwood is an old family name in Woodhouse. John Greenwood is mentioned in accounts of 1743 for supplying stone for highways, and there were Greenwoods in the village from then up to modern times, notably as builders. One of them, William Greenwood, who was also a member of Handsworth Parish Burial Board, lived in a house at the corner of this lane in the mid-1800s.

Greenwood Place, 9
no longer listed; G.R. Vine says in his *History of Attercliffe* that it was named after Sharp Greenwood, manufacturing chemist at the nearby Attercliffe Chemical Works. Mr Greenwood died in 1876 when his gig collided with a dray at Meadowhead.

Gregg House, Crescent, Road, 5
from Gregg, sometimes Greg, house, a farmhouse built about 1680, formerly owned by the Parkyn family. The name is thought to be a contraction of the personal name Gregory.

Gregory Road, 8
was built in the early 1870s by Heeley Central Freehold Land Society and named after John Gregory, builder and contractor, of Mount Pleasant Road, Highfield. Mr Gregory and his son, John Gregory junior, property broker in London Road, were involved with the land society.

Gresham Road, 6
was originally called Wilson Road. It was renamed in 1886 to avoid confusion with another Wilson Road. There was no strong local reason for the new name, which presumably came from the village of Gresham, Norfolk.

Gresley Road, Walk, 8
after William Gresley, abbot of Beauchief Abbey in the fifteenth century.

Greystock Street, 4
from an old title formerly held by the Duke of Norfolk's family, the barony of Greystock. When Edward, the ninth Duke, died in 1777 without leaving any children, the Dukedom was passed on, but several baronies, including that of Greystock, went into abeyance.

Greystones Avenue, Close, Court, Crescent, Drive, Rise, Road, 11
the name Greystones may simply have been a descriptive name for some local feature, but according to some sources, grey stones were commonly used in Saxon England to mark boundary lines.

Greystones Grange Crescent, Road, 11
were built in the grounds of a house called The Grange, home of A.J. Arnold up to 1922 after which it seems to have been let to boarders.

Greystones Road, on a picture postcard posted in June 1919.

Greystones Hall Road, 11

after the house called Greystones Hall which was built by Samuel Greaves in the early nineteenth century on the site of an earlier house which once belonged to a member of the Bright family. Later, Alderman Michael Hunter lived at the hall, and in the 1920s and 1930s it was used by the builders W. Malthouse Ltd, as an estate office when they were building the Greystones Hall estate. It was demolished for the building of flats.

Grimesthorpe Road, 4

from the area called Grimesthorpe which was recorded in 1297 as *Grimestorp*, later as *Grymysthorp*, and *Grimstrop*. It is said to mean Grim's outlying farmstead from the old Norse personal name *Grimr*.

Grimsell Close, Crescent, Drive, Way, 6

according to S.O. Addy, the local historian, grimsell means black. He says the old Dutch word, *grimsel*, meant soot. The Grimsell streets at Foxhill got their names from an old field called The Grimsells, presumably so named because the soil was dark coloured.

Grinders Hill, 1

named after one of the city's best-known occupations. Grinding went on in the area.

Grinders Walk, 6

as above. Wadsley, like Sheffield, had a flourishing cutlery trade. At one time there were more than one hundred cutlers' shops in the area. Many of them took their knives for sharpening down to the Loxley valley where there were twenty-one water mills between Low Bradfield and Malin Bridge. The walk went down to the grinders' wheels.

Grindlow Close, Drive, 14

group name – Peak District theme; after the place called Grindlow, near Great Hucklow.

Grizedale Avenue, Close, 19

group name – forest theme; after the Grizedale Forest, Cumbria.

Grosvenor Square, 2

uncertain; it was built in 1885 for trustees of the Cecil estate, and may simply have been a copy of the well-known London square's name.

Grouse Croft, Street, 6

Grouse Street, built first, was originally called Bank Street. It was changed in 1872 to avoid confusion with Bank Street in the town centre. The new name is a complete mystery.

Grove Avenue, 6

from the house nearby called Wadsley Grove, home at various times of John F. Machen, steel manufacturer, Rev John Livesey, vicar of St Philip's Church, George Longden, the builder, Councillor Mrs A.E. Longden, Sheffield's first woman Lord Mayor, and Aaron Patnick. When it was offered for sale in 1888, the house had three acres of land.

Grove Avenue, 17

from the road it was built off, The Grove.

Grove Road, 7

from the house called Mill Grove at Millhouses, once the home of J.B. Mitchell-Withers, architect and surveyor. In the 1860s it had three acres of land.

Grove Road, 17

was once the access to a house called Totley Grove, which was built in the late seventeenth century and was enlarged and altered several times. When the nearby Midland Railway line was built the road no longer led to the house but it retained its old name.

Grove Square, 6

was built in an area formerly known as Wood Grove. There was also a house nearby called Grove Lodge, home in the 1850s of William Hobson (hence nearby Hobson Avenue).

Grove Street, 3

no longer listed; named after an old house at Pitsmoor called Grove House. In the early nineteenth century it was the home of Joseph Haywood, solicitor, who had chambers in Paradise Square. A nearby road was named after him.

The Grove, 6; The Grove, 17

definitives which avoid the need to think up a name.

Grove Walk, 17

was built off Grove Road.

Guernsey Road, 2

group name – Channel Islands theme (see Alderney Road).

Guest Road, 11

not known. Plans were approved in 1898, and the road, like many in the area, was built for Mrs Harland and Mrs Thompson, of the Wilson family. Most of the roads on their land were named after members of the family or other places in the country where they owned land or had interests, but I have not been able to track down anybody called Guest in the family history.

Guildford Avenue, Close, Drive, Rise, View, Walk, Way, 2

after Guildford, Surrey, probably because of the Duke of Norfolk's extensive interests in Surrey.

Gun Lane, 3

was first called Nursery Lane, from the old nursery land nearby. It was renamed in the 1860s from the public house it ran alongside, the *Great Gun*, which started as a beerhouse run by Waltham Cowham in 1848.

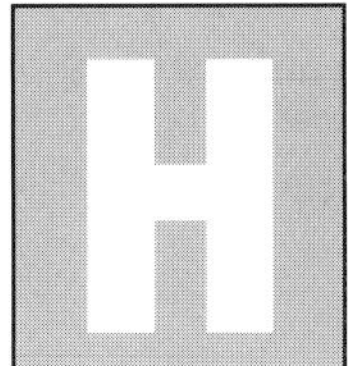

Hackthorne Road, 8
after the Lincolnshire village of Hackthorne; group name (see Aisthorpe Road).

Haddon Street, 3
was originally called Burton Street, from the same source as Burton Road. It was renamed in 1886. The new name was from the Derbyshire stately home, Haddon Hall. Like other streets nearby, it has a link with the Dukes of Rutland. Haddon Hall was one of the family seats, and the family also held the title Baron Manners of Haddon.

Haden Street, 6
after William Haden, owner of the land through which the street was built in the early 1870s. Mr Haden was a grocer in Meadow Street, and miller at the Old Park Mills, Neepsend Lane.

Hadfield Street, 6
after George Hadfield (1787-1879) radical MP for Sheffield from 1852 to 1874, who helped to form the Anti-Corn Law League.

Haggard Road, 6
after Sir Henry Rider Haggard (1856-1925), author of *King Solomon's Mines, She, Allan Quartermain*, and other popular adventure novels. Nearby Rider Road is also named after him.

Hagg Hill, 6
Harrison's survey of 1637 mentions 'a common called The Hagg'. S.O. Addy, in his *Sheffield Glossary*, says Hagg comes from the Old Icelandic word *hagi*, meaning pasturage.

Hagg Lane, 10
from the area nearby called Bell Hagg.

Hague Lane, 2
no longer listed; named after William Hague, mason, beerhouse owner, shopkeeper and property owner, who died in 1894. He owned the *Oxford Hotel*, four shops and fourteen cottages in the area.

Haigh Moor Close, Road, 13
from the Haigh Moor coal seam which is found in the area.

Hail Mary Drive, 13
from the nearby Hail Mary Hill and Hail Mary Wood, which are included in a list of the 1839 tithe awards. The name probably originates from the fact that the land was owned by the church.

Halcyon Close, 12
not known; halcyon is another name for the kingfisher. It also means calm, peaceful, or happy, from the expression halcyon days, a period of calm and tranquility during which, it was believed, kingfishers did their breeding. Presumably the intention was to convey the impression that Halcyon Close was a quiet, peaceful spot.

Hale Street, 8
after George C. Hale, secretary of Sheffield Brick Company Ltd, who built the street (see Aizlewood Road).

Halesworth Road, 13
was first called Arundel Road, after the stately home of the Duke of Norfolk, lord of the manor of Handsworth. It was renamed in 1929, after Handsworth had become part of Sheffield, to avoid confusion with Arundel Street in the city centre. The new name came from the town of Halesworth in east Suffolk, nine miles from Beccles.

Halfway Drive, Gardens, 19
from the place called Halfway which took its name from an inn called the Halfway House, recorded in the eighteenth century. Most of the places called Halfway in England (and there are seven, plus one called Halfway House and two others called Halfway Houses) got their names in the same way, from inns that were half way between villages or towns and were usually old coaching stops.

Halifax Road, 6
a directional name; it was part of the old Sheffield to Halifax turnpike road which was set up by an Act of Parliament in 1777.

Hallamgate Road, 10
from the house called Hallam Gate which stood on the site of what is now a university hall of residence. In the mid-nineteenth century it was the home of the Spooner family, from whom nearby Spooner Road took its name.

Hallam Grange Close, Crescent, Croft, Rise, Road, 10
were built on land that was formerly part of Hallam Grange Farm. In the 1880s the fifty-seven acre farm was owned by Samuel Parker and farmed on a yearly tenancy by John Wragg.

Hallam Lane, 1
probably after Samuel Hallam, pen and pocket knife manufacturer, whose workshop was nearby in the 1840s.

Hallamshire Close, Drive, Road, 10
were built on what used to be Hallam Fields. T. Walter Hall, the local historian, showed the fields on a map he prepared for a paper called *The Aula in Hallam*, in which he set out to show that the old lost village of Hallam was nearby.

Hallcar Street, 4
from the old Hall Carr Wood. By the end of the eighteenth century much of the wood had gone but a house called Hall Carr House stood in Carlisle Street for many years.

Hallgate Road, 10
not known; name approved in 1927. Possibly a reference to nearby Tapton Hall.

Halliwell Close, Crescent, 5
after James B. Halliwell who had Lapwater Farm at Birley Carr in the early 1900s. Most of the farmland was built on.

Hallowmoor Road, 6
not known; built in the late 1920s. Hallowmoor sometimes appears in old documents as Allamoor.

Hall Park Head, Hill, Mount, 6
Harrison's 1637 survey mentions a seventy four-acre area of Stannington called Haw Park. Joseph Hunter, the historian, referred to it as Haugh Park. S.O. Addy, the later historian, said haw meant hall and that the hall in question was probably a building shown on a 1747 Fairbank map as 'The Mannor House'. Addy believed that the hall of Waltheof, lord of Hallamshire, was in the area.

Hall Road, 9 and 13
the section in Sheffield 13 was originally called Bernard Road, after Bernard Edward, twelfth Duke of Norfolk. It was renamed (to avoid confusion with Bernard Road in the city centre) in 1925, and the new name was from Handsworth Hall, built by the sixth Earl of Shrewsbury. His son Gilbert, seventh Earl, was born there. The other section of Hall Road was built in the

Handsworth Hill was never an official street name, it was a name widely used by residents of Darnall and Handsworth when they were referring to two bits of road. One, shown here, was really a section of Main Road, from Darnall up to the railway bridge. The other, beyond the railway bridge and near the Triangle Estate, was part of Handsworth Road.

1930s and there was talk of joining the two bits, which were separated by a field. The join never happened, and now the two pieces of road are separated by the Parkway.

Hallyburton Close, Drive, Road, 2

were built on the Duke of Norfolk's land and named from the fact that one of the Duke's relatives, R. Mowbray Howard, married, in 1912, Audrey Cecilia Campbell, daughter of Charles Hallyburton Campbell, nephew of the first Baron Campbell.

Halsall Avenue, Drive, Road, 9

were built on land belonging to the Staniforth family and named from the family lineage. Margery Halsall married Charles Goore, and their daughter, Elizabeth, married Thomas Staniforth (see Staniforth Road).

Halsteads, 13

not known.

Halton Court, 12

after the village of East Halton, Humberside; one of a group of streets given Humberside place names (with Barlby and Winterton).

Hamilton Road, 5

was built for Mark Firth around the time of the opening of Firth Park by the Prince of Wales in 1875. It was named after the Marquis of Hamilton, MP for County Donegal, who was Lord of the Bedchamber to the Prince from 1866 to 1885 and came with him on his visit to Sheffield.

Hammerton Close, Road, 6

after Joseph Hammerton who was a farmer in the area in the 1860s and 1870s.

Hammond Street, 3

after Thomas Hammond who was a property owner in the area. The 1841 directory describes him as a 'gentleman' and lists him as having two homes, one in Hammond Street, the other in Hammond Place.

Hampton Road, 5

after Thomas Hampton, steel manufacturer and merchant, who lived at Home Cottage, Crabtree, in the nineteenth century. He was linked with several companies, notably the Phoenix Bessemer Steel Co Ltd, Rotherham, of which he was managing director. He was also a trustee of the Ark Permanent Mutual Benefit Building Society.

Handley Street, 3

from an eighteenth century farmer called Handley. The 1830 Sheffield Local Register says of him 'Handley of Oldcarr, who took in a great many cows; hither the lasses came in great numbers every night to milk them'

Hands Road, 10

was first called Hands Lane. It changed in 1909. It was named after Thomas Hand, silversmith, who lived and worked at Commonside in the nineteenth century. It probably started out as Hand's Lane.

Handsworth Avenue, Crescent, Road, 9 and 13

from the area called Handsworth, spelt Handesuuord in Domesday Book, and after that, Handelesworth, Handisworth, Hannesworth, etc. It is said to mean the enclosure belonging to a person called Hand, possibly a shortened form of the name Handwulf. Up to 1924 Handsworth Road was called Main Road.

Handsworth Grange Close, Crescent, Drive, Road, Way, 13

from the house, Handsworth Grange, sometimes called Cinder Hill Grange, which stood near the corner of Grange Lane and Beaver Hill Road. It was the home of the Stacye family for many years, and was later owned by Fisher, Son and Sibray Ltd, who had extensive nurseries in the area. It was demolished in the 1960s.

Hangingwater Close, Road, 11

from a field called Hangingwater Field, probably because it sloped steeply towards the River Porter (see Hanmoor).

Hangram Lane, 11

S.O. Addy, the local historian said this name came from the Anglo Saxon word *Hangra* (plural *hangran*) meaning a meadow or plot of grass, usually by the side of a road. The village of Angram in the West Riding is said to get its name from the same source.

Hanmoor Road, 6

an area of common land called Han More is referred to in a document of 1465. It is also mentioned, as Hanmore, in Harrison's survey of 1637. It appears in another old document as Hangmoore, which suggests that it may come from the old word *hangende*, meaning hanging or steep. There were also three fields at Stannington called Han Moore Close.

Hannah Road, 13

one of a group of streets named after members of the Watson family – George Watson Builders Ltd. The family owned the land on which the streets were built and the family firm built them.

Hanover Court, Square, Street, Way, 3
after the royal house of Hanover. Hanover Street was built in the 1780s, during the reign of King George III, Britain's third ruler in the Hanover line which ended with the death of Queen Victoria in 1901.

Hanson Road, 6
after the Rev John Hanson, minister of Loxley Chapel from 1833 to 1851; one of a group of streets named after former ministers of the chapel.

Harbord Road, 8
after the Harbord family, Cecil R. Harbord and Gordon Harbord, who were estate agents, insurance brokers and coal merchants at Woodseats in the early 1900s. They owned land nearby and Cecil Harbord lived at the corner of Abbey Lane and Harbord Road.

Harborough Avenue, Close, Drive, Rise, Road, Way, 2
one of several Manor estate street names taken from the early history of the manor of Eckington. The 1649 list of Eckington field names included one called Harborough Frith, sometimes spelt Harbour Frith.

Harbury Street, 13
was originally called Hope Street. It was changed in 1924 and the new name, a random choice, came from the village of Harbury in Warwickshire.

Harcourt Crescent, Road, 10;
after Sir William George Granville Venables Vernon Harcourt (1827-1904), grandson of a former Archbishop of York, one-time leader of the Liberal Party, who was Home Secretary at the time Harcourt Road was built in the 1880s.

Hardcastle Drive, Gardens, Road, 13
after Hannah Hardcastle who ran a dame school at Woodhouse in the early 1800s, one of three small schools in the village at that time. There have been Hardcastles at Woodhouse for more than 200 years, many of them stonemasons or builders, and there are still some there today.

Hardwick Crescent, 11
after the stately home of Hardwick Hall, Derbyshire; one of three streets built for J.Y. Cowlishaw in 1897, all named after stately homes (along with Osberton and Sandbeck).

Hardy Place, 6
was built around 1870 and first called Hardy Street, possibly after William Hardy, joiner, builder and contractor in the late nineteenth century, first in Corporation Street, later in Spring Street.

Harefield Road, 11
from the parish of Harefield, Middlesex. The road was built on land owned by the Wilson family. Louisa Ellen Wilson married the Rev Albert Augustus Harland, one-time curate of Ecclesall, who was vicar of Harefield for fifty years. Several other streets on Wilson land at Sharrow Vale, Psalter Lane and Hunters Bar were named after places near Harefield (Denham, Pinner and Fulmer).

Harewood Road, 6
from Harewood, near Leeds, where the Earl of Harewood has his family seat.

Harewood Way, 11
as above; one of a group of streets named after stately homes.

Harland Road, 11
after the Rev Albert Augustus Harland (see Harefield Road, above). He and his wife had seventeen children, one of whom, Albert Harland, was MP for Ecclesall. The Rev Harland died in 1921.

Harleston Street, 4
was built on the Duke of Norfolk's land and named after the small market town of Harleston, near Bungay, Norfolk, where the Duke was lord of the manor.

Harley Road, 11
was built on land belonging to Earl Fitzwilliam and named after the hamlet of Harley near the Earl's family seat at Wentworth.

Harmer Lane, 1
goes back to the early nineteenth century and possibly earlier. In one document there is a reference to a piece of land called Harmer's Open. The name almost certainly comes from a former landowner or tenant but I don't know which. A firm called Harmer and Co is listed at Wicker Foundry in 1814-15.

Harney Close, 9
after George Julian Harney (1817-1897), Chartist leader, who spent several years in Sheffield in the early 1840s. He was a friend and confederate of Samuel Holberry, the local Chartist leader.

Harold Street, 6
was built on land owned by the Burgoyne family around 1875 and named after somebody called Harold but I don't know who. There does not seem to have been a Harold in the Burgoyne family tree.

Harrison Lane, 10
after the Harrison family who lived at Bole Hill Farm for some years. The first of them, Ralph Harrison, came to Sheffield from Cheshire in the 1820s and settled here.

Harrison Road, 6
after Miss Eliza Harrison, the well-known benefactress, of Weston Hall, the house which later became Weston Park Museum. As well as owning land and property at Weston Park, Miss Harrison owned a ten-acre farm at Malin Bridge. After her death in 1873 the Malin Bridge land was sold as building land.

Harris Road, 6
not known; built in the 1890s.

Harrogate Road, 9
no longer listed; was built on land owned by the Staniforth family and named after the Yorkshire town of Harrogate (see Staniforth Road).

Harrowden Court, Road, 9
from a title held by ancestors of Earl Fitzwilliam, former lord of the manor of Tinsley. The Watson Wentworth family held the title Baron Harrowden from 1734 to 1782.

Harrow Street, 11
was first called Andrew Lane. It was renamed (because there was another Andrew Lane in The Wicker) in 1886, after the Harrow district of Middlesex.

Harry Firth Close, 9
after Councillor Harry Firth who represented Attercliffe on the City Council and served as a South Yorkshire county councillor. He died in 1979.

Hartford Close, Road, 8
not known; names approved October 1937. There are several places in Britain called Hartford.

Harthill Road, 13
a link with the Parker family of Woodthorpe. Hugh Parker, born 1808, married Sarah Alderson, daughter of the Rector of Harthill, where the couple were married.

Hartington Avenue, Road, 7
was built as part of the Oakdale estate in 1875 and named after the Marquis of Hartington who was elected leader of the Liberals in the House of Commons that year. He became Duke of Devonshire in 1891.

Hartopp Avenue, Close, Drive, Road, 2
were built on the Duke of Norfolk's land and named after Sir J.W. Cradock Hartopp, who married one of the Duke's relatives, Charlotte Frances Howard (see also Cradock Road).

Hartshead, 1
Mary Walton, in her *Street Names of Central Sheffield*, says 'Almost certainly the Hart's Head was the sign of an inn or shop – the hart's head is the crest of several local families. The inn may have been the predecessor of the *Dove and Rainbow* . . .'

Harvest Lane, 3
is mentioned in Harrison's survey of 1637 as Harvis Lane, so it could come from a person called Harvey or Harvie. It is more likely to have come from the fact that the lane led towards the town mill, in the Mill Sands area, where corn was ground for several hundred years.

Harvey Clough Road, 8
from the name of an old field, Harvey Clough, which was part of Cow Mouth Farm, Norton Lees. Harvey was possibly the name of a former owner or tenant. Clough usually indicates a small, narrow glen or ravine.

Harwell Road, 8
was built on the Cecil estate in 1906 at the same time as Gamston Road, and both were named after places in Nottinghamshire. Harwell is a hamlet near Everton.

Harwich Road, 2
after the seaport of Harwich, Essex, sixteen miles east of Colchester; one of a group of streets named after places in Essex (along with Dovercourt, Stock and Warley). The Duke of Norfolk, on whose land they were built, was lord of the manor of Dovercourt.

Harwood Close, Street, 2
after Mrs Elizabeth Harwood, who owned land in the Highfield area in the nineteenth century. Described in directories as a 'gentlewoman' she lived at Sharrow Lodge in the 1840s.

Harwood Drive, Gardens, 19
after Mrs Elizabeth Harwood, above. As well as owning land in the Highfield area, she owned land at Mosborough, including the 116-acre Plumley Hall estate.

Haslam Crescent, 8
after Christopher Haslam, a Dronfield chaplain, who was appointed by the canons of Beauchief Abbey in 1490 to teach singing and grammar to 'boys or novices'. He was paid twenty-six shillings and eightpence per annum, with food and a room in the abbey provided.

Haslehurst Road, 2
after Charles Haslehurst, partner in the Norfolk Brewery, Broad Street, up to his death in 1851, and a well-known resident of the Park district.

Hastilar Close, Road, 2
the position of hastilar is mentioned in the old Eckington Court Roll, from which many Manor estate streets names were taken. A hastilar or hastler, was a messenger or letter carrier in medieval England, usually taking orders from a court to outlying areas.

Hastings Mount, Road, 7
Hastings Road, built first, was originally called Grange Road, after the thirteen-acre Abbeydale Grange estate nearby. The name was changed in 1886 to avoid confusion with similar names elsewhere, and the new name was from the Sussex coastal town. Hastings Mount was called Copse Avenue up to 1934.

Hatfield House Court, Croft, Lane, 5
from the farm sometimes called Renathorpe Hall, sometimes Hatfield Farm, and later, Hatfield House. Nicholas Hatfield, who died in 1558, left it to his son, Alexander, and he left it to his son, Ralph, after which it passed out of the Hatfield family. In later years it was the home of William Hunter, ancestor of Joseph Hunter, the Sheffield historian.

Hatherley Road, 9
after William Page Wood (1801-1881), lawyer, judge, and Lord Chancellor from 1868 to 1872, who was created Baron Hatherley of Hatherley, Gloucestershire; one of a group of streets named after famous legal men.

Hathersage Road, 17
a directional name; the road leads to Hathersage.

Hatton Road, 6
not known.

Haugh Lane, 11
was built on Earl Fitzwilliam's land and named after the villages of Upper and Nether Haugh, near the Earl's family seat at Wentworth.

Haughton Road, 8
not known; built (with Helmton Road) between 1905 and 1907.

Havelock Street, 10
was built in the 1850s and named after Sir Henry Havelock, English soldier, who commanded a division in the Persian war of 1856 and a year later, during the Indian Mutiny, fought at Lucknow. He died in 1857, around the time this street was being built.

Havercroft Road, 8
from the coal mining area of Havercroft, three miles from Royston; one of a group of streets given Yorkshire place names.

Hawke Street, 9
after Peter Benjamin Hawke, who owned the land through which the street was built in 1868. He is not listed in directories of the time as living in Sheffield and I know nothing more about him.

Hawkshead Road, 4
after the village of Hawkshead, near Ambleside, Cumbria; one of a group of streets named after places in the Lake District.

Hawksley Avenue, Road, 6
after George Hawksley, prominent resident of Owlerton, and owner of more than forty acres of land in the area. Mr Hawksley, who died in 1873, lived at Eagle House, Bradfield Road. These two streets were built on his land.

Haymarket in the early 1900s, with the Royal Hotel where Castle Market stands today, and the long-demolished Norfolk Market Hall, right.

Hawksworth Road, 6
after Charles Wardlow Hawksworth, estate agent and property developer, who built houses in the street and lived in one of them.

Hawley Street, 1
after the Hawley family who owned land and buildings in the area of Campo Lane and Hawley Croft in the eighteenth century. Joseph Hawley of this family was a Town Trustee from 1713 till his death in 1724, and was Town Collector for three years. His son, William, was a candidate for the Town Trust in later years but failed to be elected.

Hawthorn Avenue, 19
there were hawthorn bushes in the area.

Hawthorne Street, 6
built in the early 1860s by Rivelin View Freehold Land Society and apparently named from bushes on or near the site. The final E is missing in some early documents.

Hawthorn Road, 6; Hawthorn Terrace, 10
from hawthorn bushes in the area.

Haxby Place, Street, 13
Haxby Street was first called High Street. It was changed in 1924 after Normanton Springs became of Sheffield, where there was already a High Street. The new name came from the north Yorkshire village of Haxby.

Haybrook Court, 17
from the nearby stream, the Old Hay Brook, recorded in the eighteenth century and said to come from the ancient words *ald haeg*, meaning old fence, or enclosure.

Hayes Court, Drive, 19
after John Ibbotson Hayes, who was master at Mosborough village school in the 1820s and 1830s. He was also registrar of births and deaths for the village, and actuary of Eckington Savings Bank.

Hayfield Crescent, Drive, Place, 12
after the Derbyshire village of Hayfield, between Chapel-en-le-Frith and Glossop; one of a group of streets with Derbyshire names. The old song *Come Lasses and Lads* was written about Hayfield Fair.

Hayland Street, 9
was first called Hawley Street; it was renamed in 1903. The new name seems to have been a random choice.

Haymarket, 1
formerly called Bull Stake; according to Mary Walton in her *Street Names of Central Sheffield*, the new name was adopted about 1830, 'when the then Duke of Norfolk made one of the family's several unsuccessful attempts to establish a hay and corn market in the town'.

Haywood Road, 3
no longer listed; named after Joseph Haywood, solicitor, with chambers in Paradise Square in the early nineteenth century, who lived nearby, at Grove House, Pitsmoor.

Hazelbadge Crescent, 12
from a house called Hazelbadge Hall, Bradwell Dale; one of many Frecheville streets given Derbyshire names.

Hazelhurst Lane, 8
from the nearby Hazelhurst Farm, recorded in 1404 as Haselhurste. It means hazel copse, or wood.

Hazelbarrow Close, Crescent, Drive, Grove, Road, 8
from the de Haselbarrow family who lived at Norton in the thirteenth century. According to S.O. Addy, the local historian, they took their name from the estate on which they lived, Haselbarrow, meaning hazel grove, or wood.

Headford Street, 3
uncertain; it is mentioned in the 1825 directory and may have something to do with an old crossing of the nearby River Porter.

Headland Drive, Road, 10
from an old Crookes field name, or to be more precise, four old field names. The four fields, three owned by the Spooner family at the time of the enclosures, one by John Parker, were known as Rough Head Lands.

Heathcote Street, 4
probably after George Heathcote, who was the blacksmith at Crabtree in the 1870s.

Heather Lea, Avenue, Place, 17
from an old field name. When the site was offered for sale as building land in July 1910, it was described as four closes of freehold land known as Heather Lea', containing a total of eleven acres fronting Causeway Head Road.

Heather Road, 5
group name – flowers theme (see Acacia).

Heathfield Road, 12
possibly from a local field name, although I have not found any reference to a field of this name in the area.

Heath Road, 6
probably after Henry Heath who was a joiner and builder at Wadsley in the late nineteenth century.

Heath Street, 9
no longer listed; was originally called Edith Street. It was renamed in 1886 because it duplicated Edith Street, 6. The new name, a random choice, seems to have come from the village of Heath, Derbyshire.

Heavygate Avenue, Road, 10
from the *Olde Heavy Gate Inn*, one of Sheffield's oldest inns, built in 1696. In 1896, to mark the inn's 200th anniversary, a sheep was roasted in the yard and everyone who came by was given a sandwich and a drink.

Heeley Bank Road, 2
from the hillside known as Heeley Bank. A nineteenth century farm nearby was called Heeley Bank Farm. The name Heeley, mentioned in documents of the fourteenth century as Heghlegh, is said to mean high meadow, or field.

Heeley Green, 2
was first called Heeley Green Road, a name given to it in 1805 by the Enclosure Commissioners because it was built through the green, hitherto an area of common land covering the area between the modern Gleadless Road and Myrtle Road, stretching as far as Penns Road.

Helmsley Avenue, 19
from the village of Helmsley, North Yorkshire, twelve miles from Thirsk; one of a group of streets given Yorkshire place names.

Helmton Drive, Road, 8
not known; built (with Haughton Road) 1905-1907.

Helen Road, 9
no longer listed; was built in 1868 for the Second Attercliffe and Darnall Freehold Land Society and was first called Ellen Road – possibly from Mrs Ellen Potter, midwife, who lived in Howden Road, was involved with the society and owned several houses on the road.

Helston Rise, 7
uncertain; probably from the Cornish town of Helston, famous for its furry dance and birthplace of Bob Fitzsimmons, the last British World Heavyweight Boxing Champion.

Hemper Grove, Lane, 8
Hemper Lane is part of the old turnpike road between Greenhill and Bradway. It is mentioned as Hemp Lane in Holmesfield Court Rolls of 1674, but it has also been known at various times as Hempyard or Hempard Lane, and it is thought that hemp was grown in the area.

Hemsworth Road, 8
from the area called Hemsworth, the spelling of which has changed over the years – Hemenlisworth, Himisworth (in 1300), Himsworth (in 1560), etc. Dialect experts say it means the enclosure belonging to Hemele, the same origin as Hemsworth, near Wakefield.

Hendon Street, 9
was originally called Henry Street, after one of the Dukes of Norfolk, who were lords of the manor of Handsworth. It was changed in 1923, after Handsworth became part of Sheffield (where there was another Henry Street). The new name, from the district of Hendon, north London, was an effort to keep it similar to the old name.

Henley Avenue, 8
after the south Oxfordshire town famous for its annual regatta.

Henry Lane, 10
no longer listed; named after Henry Watson, son of John Watson, who farmed Broomhall Park in the early nineteenth century, then leased the land for building (see Bangor Street).

Henry Street, 3
was built in the 1840s and named after someone called Henry but I don't know who.

Heppenstall Lane, 9
after a man called Price Heppenstall who owned land and property in the lane in the late eighteenth century. There were other Heppenstalls in the area later who may have been his descendants.

Herbert Road, 7
was built in 1867 by the Montgomery

Hemsworth Road was still very much out in the country when this photograph of its corner with Ashbury Road was taken.

Freehold Land Society and named after someone called Herbert but I don't know who.

Herdings Court, Road, View, 12
from the old farmstead called The Herdings. On a stone above the door is the date 1675 but parts of the building are believed to be older. When Gleadless Valley housing estate was built, The Herdings was converted for community use.

Hereford Street, 1
was laid out and named (with Cumberland Street) by the Enclosure Commissioners in 1788. It was probably named after Viscount Hereford.

Hereward Road, 5
one of a small group of streets named from the legend of Hereward the Wake, subject of a novel by Charles Kingsley. (See Bourne and Crowland Roads).

Hereward's Road, 8
is mentioned in the 1815 Enclosure Act but is probably much older. One theory is that it was part of an ancient route from Ashover through Chesterfield to Sheffield. There are references in old documents to Hereward's Street and Hereward's Road at various places along the way but the precise route is not known.

Heron Mount, 2
group name on the theme of birds. (See Curlew Ridge.)

Herries Avenue, Drive, Place, 5; Herries Road, 5 and 6; Herries Road South, 6
from the Duke of Norfolk's family history. One of the Duke's ancestors, the Hon. Angela Mary Charlotte Fitzalan-Howard, married Lord Herries in 1875. Henry, fifteenth Duke of Norfolk, married Gwendolen, Baroness Herries, in 1904. As Duchess of Norfolk, she officially opened Herries Road in 1925.

Herschell Road, 7
after Sir John Herschell (1792-1871) the famous astronomer. Both Herschell and the Rev John Farrar (after whom nearby Farrar Road was named) were acquaintances of the Sheffield author John Holland.

Hesley Road, Terrace, 5
the area known as Hesley, from which these streets get their names, is recorded as Hesteley in the fourteenth century, and later as Hesseley. It means the forest clearing used for horses.

Hessey Street, 13
was first called Spring Street. It was renamed in 1924. The original intention was to call it Seamer Street (from the place called Seamer, near Scarborough) but it eventually became Hessey Street, after John Hessey, local grocer and well-known character in Parkwood Springs, which he represented on the old Handsworth Urban Council. He was also prominent in the local Wesleyan Chapel.

Hessle Road, 6
after the town of Hessle, near Hull. Nearby Ferriby Road is named after a pair of villages near Hull, North Ferriby and South Ferriby.

Hibberd Place, Road, 6
not known; Hibberd Road appeared for the first time in the 1925 street directory and was named after the earlier Hibberd Lane which had been shown in the directories since 1913 but existed before that date. The only person called Hibberd I have been able to trace in the area was a cutler called Samuel Hibberd in the 1870s, but he lived some distance from the lane.

Hickmott Road, 11
after Harry Herbert Hickmott (1858-1900) who was joint owner of the land on which this and four other streets were built in the late 1890s. Mr Hickmott was born at Rotherham, educated at Sheffield and Wolverhampton, and was a solicitor. He was Town Clerk of Rotherham from 1888 till his death (see Neill Road).

Hicks Lane, Street, 3
after Thomas Hicks, joiner and builder, who lived in Woodside Lane in the 1860s. In 1864 Mr Hicks advertised some of the houses he had built in Hicks Street – 'newly painted and papered' – at rents varying from 2s 6d (12½p) to 4s (20p) per week.

Hides Street, 9
after Henry Timm Hides, pawnbroker, jeweller, silversmith and outfitter, who had shops in The Moor, Pond Street, and New Meadow Street, and owned property at Carbrook.

Higgitt Road, 9
probably after William Higgitt, who lived nearby in the 1870s and may have owned property in the area.

Highcliffe Court, Drive, Place, Road, 11
refer to the nearby Greystones Cliffe.

High Court, 1
just what it is, a court off High Street.

Highfield Lane, 13
from an old field name. Several fields in the area are shown on Greenwood's 1771 map as High Fields.

Highfield Place, 2
from an old house called Highfield. It was demolished in the 1870s.

Highfield Rise, 6
from an old Stannington field name, High Field, mentioned in Harrison's survey of 1637. High Field was a very common English field name.

Highgate, 9
simply means high road, or high street, indicating a road, or cattle way of some importance. There are at least twelve Highgates or High Gate Lanes in Yorkshire.

Highgreave, High Greave Avenue, 5
from an old field name. When it was offered for sale in 1870, it was described as 'a croft called High Greave consisting of three acres, one rood, eighteen perches' at that time rented to Henry Hobson.

High Hazels Close, Mead, 9
from the nearby High Hazels Park, which in turn took its name from the private house (later a museum, later still a golf clubhouse) which in the mid-nineteenth century was the home of William Jeffcock, first Mayor of Sheffield. But the name is older than the house. A homestead called High Hazels, and a field called High Hazels Close are referred to in a survey of 1802. The name refers to the trees at the top of the hill.

High House Road, Terrace, 6
from the house called High House which was owned by the Bamforth family, lords of the manor of Owlerton, the last of whom, George Bamforth, died childless in 1739, when the lordship

passed, through his sister, to the Burton family. The house later became a brewery.

High Lane, 12
indicates, as with High Street, or High Road, a thoroughfare of some importance in the locality.

High Matlock Avenue, Road, 6
from the area called Little Matlock, because of its alleged scenic similarity to the Derbyshire town. This was mainly due to a Unitarian minister, the Rev Thomas Halliday, who married well, then paid for the land to be laid out in terraces etc. According to one of his critics, this involved him 'wasting his substance paying men 14s (70p) a week for lying on their bellies to plant privet on ledges'.

Highnam Crescent Road, 10
a mystery. The name was approved (along with Moor Oaks Road, Marlborough Road and Elmore Road) in 1878. In the first reference to it in the Town Council minutes, it is spelt 'Highman' Crescent Road.

High Storrs Close, Crescent, Drive, Rise, Road, 11
S.O. Addy, the local historian, said High Storrs came from the old Icelandic word *storr*, meaning coarse, grass which cattle would not eat – an area of coarse grass on a hill.

High Street, 1, 17, 19
the name High Street for the main street of any locality evolved from the Roman practice of building roads on proper foundations, and so making them higher than the surrounding land. Longer Roman roads, previously sunken tracks worn away by use, thus became 'high' ways and main streets in populated areas became 'high' streets. High Street in the centre of Sheffield has been the subject of argument among local historians for the last two centuries. On his 1736 map of the town Ralph Gosling, a respected surveyor of the time, showed it as 'Prior Gate', not High Street. R.E. Leader, the local historian said it had always been High Street and that Gosling's name for it was 'an unaccountable freak' (although he conceded, somewhat unwillingly, that it was referred to as 'High Street or Prior Gate' in a property transfer deed dated 1748). Leader said the name Prior Row was used to refer to the whole of the north side of High Street from Market Place to the church gates, but that the name Prior Gate was born on Gosling's map.

Another local historian, T. Walter Hall, was less adamant. He found it difficult to believe that a man of Gosling's standing could have made such a mistake and thought it had been called Prior Gate at some time.

Five other High Streets, at Attercliffe, Grimesthorpe, Normanton Springs, Park and Walkley, were renamed to avoid confusion with High Street, 1 (see Attercliffe Road, Bard Street, Haxby Street, Highton Street, Upwell Street).

High Street Lane, 2
originally ran off High Street, Park, which was renamed Bard Street in 1872.

Highton Street, 6
was originally called High Street. To avoid confusion with other High Streets, it was renamed in 1872. The new name was concocted to keep it as near as possible to the old one.

High Trees, 17
from the oak, beech and sycamore trees which were preserved at the entrance to the street when it was built.

High Wray Close, 11
from a house called High Wray on Millhouses Lane. In the 1920s it was the home of William Bayldon Barber, stock and share broker. The house, probably named after the village of High Wray, near Lake Windermere, had a daffodil wood which was opened to the public occasionally to raise money for charities.

Hill Close, 6
from the nearby hill.

Hillcote Close, Drive, 10
not known.

Hillfoot Road, 3; Hillfoot Road, 17
both are near the bottom of hills.

Hillsborough Place, Road, 6
from the area called Hillsborough, which was originally known as just The Hills. It appears in various documents as Hylls (in 1538), The Hilles (1567), and Hills (1654). The 'borough' seems to have been added as an afterthought in the late eighteenth or early nineteenth century. According to some accounts, the name Hillsborough was first applied to Hillsborough Hall as a tribute to Lord Downshire, of Downshire, County Down, who had held the title Earl of Hillsborough, and was Secretary of State for the Colonies in the late eighteenth century.

Hillside, 19; Hillside Avenue, 5; Hillside Crescent, 19
straightforward descriptive names for streets on the sides or top of hills.

Hill Street, 2
was there in the early nineteenth century before the area was extensively built up. In the absence of anybody called Hill in the locality around that time, it can only refer to the incline – hardly much of a hill – from Moorfoot to Highfield.

Hill Turrets Close, 11
from the house called Hill Turrets at the corner of Ecclesall Road South and Bents Road. Early this century it was the home of George Clark, magistrate and councillor for Nether Hallam ward for three years.

Hinchcliffe Walk, 3
after William Hinchcliffe who had a beerhouse in St Stephen's Road (at the side of the walk) from the 1860s to the 1890s.

Hinde House Crescent, Croft, Lane, 4
from the old farm known as Hinde House. In 1900 the farmer was George Henry Helliwell, and in the 1920s it was Jabez Cowley.

Hinde Street, Hindewood Close, 4
as Hinde House Crescent, above.

Hirst Common Lane, 6
from the old word hyrst, meaning a wood – the common near a wood. Two areas nearby are known as Upper Hirst and Lower Hirst. Nearby Midhurst Road was originally called Hirst, or Hurst, Road.

Hoban Street, 9
no longer listed; named after the man for whom it was built in 1899, J. Hoban, about whom I know nothing.

Hobart Street, 11
was built on land owned by George Wostenholm and possibly named – like his home, Kenwood – from a place in New York State, USA, the town of Hobart.

Hobson Avenue, Place, 6
after William Hobson who lived at a house called Grove Lodge, Hillfoot, in the 1850s. The area around the house was known as Wood Grove.

Hodgson Street, 3
after George Hodgson, steel maker and roller, whose Vulcan Works were off what was then called South Street and is now called The Moor. A lane near the works was called Hodgson's Court. By 1833 it had become Hodgson Street.

Holbeck Street, 9
from the suburb of Leeds called Holbeck; one of a group of Attercliffe streets (with Baildon and Manningham) given Yorkshire names.

Holberry Close, Gardens, 10
originally called Havelock Square; renamed in 1982 after the Chartist leader Samuel Holberry who died after being imprisoned for planning an uprising of working people in Sheffield in the 1840s.

Holbrook Avenue, Green, Rise, 19; Holbrook Drive, Road, 13
from the area called Holbrook, at Mosborough, which appears as Holbroke in a document of 1489, and as How Brook in the seventeenth century. It comes from the old words *hol broc*, meaning the brook in the hollow, in this case the Short Brook which runs into the River Rother.

Holdings Road, 2
was approved for the Duke of Norfolk in 1895. The reason for the name is not clear unless it refers to the Duke's holdings of land in the Sheffield area.

Holdsworth Street, 8
after Albert Holdsworth, of Claremont Place, who was a shareholder in the Sheffield Brick Co Ltd, builders of the street.

Holgate Avenue, Close, Crescent, Drive, Road, 5
after Robert Holgate (1481-1555), Archbishop of York from 1545 to 1554.

Holkham Rise, 11
from Holkham Hall, family seat of the Earl of Leicester; group name – stately homes (see Alton).

Holland Place, Road, 2
after John Holland, author, journalist, editor of the *Sheffield Iris*, and later of the *Sheffield Mercury*, friend and biographer of James Montgomery.

Holland Street, 1
after Alwin Hibberd Holland, who was a grocer and flour dealer in West Street in the 1840s and 1850s and owned property in the area.

Hollindale Drive, 12; Hollinhouse Lane, 6; Hollins Close, Court, Drive, 6; Hollinsend Avenue, Place, Road, 12; Hollins Lane, 6
all come from *hollin*, the old word meaning holly, which used to be extensively grown as a winter fodder, particularly for sheep. It was grown in the area of all these streets.

Hollis Croft, 1
after Thomas Hollis, son of a Rotherham blacksmith of the same name, who did well in business and became one of Sheffield's earliest benefactors, setting up almshouses, a school and a charity, all of which, like this street, bore his name.

Hollis Croft, 13
not known.

Hollis Terrace, 6
no longer listed; after William Hollis, joiner and builder, who lived in Spring Vale Road in the 1870s and 80s and built houses in the area.

Hollow Lane, 19
from a local geographical feature called The Hollow – a dip in the ground.

Hollybank Avenue, Close, Crescent, Drive, Road, Way, Holly Gardens,12
as Hollinsend, from the holly grown locally for winter feed.

Holly Lane, Street, 1
the lane is mentioned in the Burgery records of 1609 as 'Blynde Lane or Hollin Lane'. Hollin is the old form of holly, so presumably at one time there was some in the area.

Hollythorpe Crescent, Rise, Road, 8
is a mixture of the names of two old houses, The Hollies and Thorpe House. Up to the 1930s they were the only two houses in the area.

Holman Street, 9
no longer listed; after Nicholas Robert Holman, tillage merchant and corn factor in Newhall Road in the 1870s, when he developed this street. He lived at Bank House, Attercliffe, at the time, and later moved to Ashgate Road.

Holme Close, Lane, 6
Holme Lane is mentioned in Harrison's survey of 1637. There was a Holme Field nearby. Holme is a common element in English place names. It usually means water meadow. As the lane runs near the River Loxley, it seems a logical explanation in this case.

Holmhirst Close, Drive, Road, Way, 8
from the old Holmhirst Farm which stood roughly where Holmhirst Way is today. Holmhirst Road led to it. The name certainly goes back to the early 1700s and probably earlier. Holmhirst Land Co Ltd offered the land for building purposes in 1880 at prices 'from two shillings per yard upwards'.

Holme Oak Way, 6
after a variety of oak trees. Group name (see Durmast).

Holmshaw Drive, Grove, 6
after Robert Holmshaw, scissor grinder, founder (and for many years president and treasurer) of the Scissor Grinders' Union, and one of the pioneer members of Sheffield Trades Council. He died in 1891 at the age of 73.

Holtwood Road, 4
after the house called Holtwood, built and lived in for many years by Samuel Smith, miller. Two months after his death in January 1903 the house was offered for sale with three acres of land. The road was built about 1907.

Holy Green, 1
after Thomas Holy, who lived in a house on South Street (now The Moor) towards the end of the eighteenth century. He was a well-known resident and one of the town's earliest followers of John Wesley. When Wesley came to Sheffield in 1786 he called on Mr Holy whose house continued to be known as Holy Green House long after his death.

Holyoake Avenue, 13
was built on farmland owned by Brightside and Carbrook Co-operative Society and named after a keen sup-

porter of co-operation, George Jacob Holyoake (1817-1906), English social reformer, author, and Chartist. He wrote *A History of Co-operation*.

Holywell Road, 4 and 9
was built (with Southwell Road) for Henry Unwin's trustees in the 1890s. Both roads appear to have been named in an attempt to continue the 'well' theme already established by Upwell Street and Birdwell Road. When it was first built, Holywell Road was only a short road off Upwell Street.

Homestead Close, Road, 5
before the site was developed, there was a homestead there.

Honeysuckle Road, 5
group name – flowers (see Acacia).

Hoober Avenue, 11
was built on Earl Fitzwilliam's land and named after the area of Hoober near the Earl's seat at Wentworth.

Hoole Lane, Road, 10
after Charles Hoole, well-known grocer and tea dealer, who lived at Hallam Gate for many years up to his death in 1876.

Hoole Street, 6
was built by Whitehouse Lane Freehold Land Society and named after Francis Hoole, solicitor, town trustee, town councillor for thirteen years, and Mayor in 1853. He lived at The White House.

Hooley Road, 13
after William John Hooley (1817-1886) clothier, well-known resident of Woodhouse, lay preacher for more than fifty years, member of Handsworth local board and overseer of the poor. He was involved in the Stand Greave Freehold Society which built this and other roads.

Hooton Street, 4
was built on Earl Fitzwilliam's land and named after the South Yorkshire village of Hooton Roberts, where the Earl owned land and was lord of the manor.

Hopedale Road, 12
from Hopedale, the old name for the Hope Valley. Many Frecheville streets were given Derbyshire names, mainly because the builder Charles Boot, lived in Derbyshire, at Thornbridge Hall.

Hopefield Avenue, 12
possibly from a local field name. In another example of the name, elsewhere in Yorkshire, Hope Field is said to come from the old word hop, meaning a side-valley.

Hope Street , 3
not known.

Hopwood Lane, 6
from an old field name, Hopwood Tofts, mentioned in Harrison's survey of 1637 as nine acres of arable land held by Rowland Revell of Steele Farm. The land is still known as Hopwood Tofts.

Horam Road, 6
was built in the nineteenth century for Philip Ashberry who lived at nearby Wellfield House. Horam was a family name. His brother, and co-principal in the family firm, was Bernard Horam Ashberry.

Horndean Road, 5
one of a pair of roads (Idsworth the other) named after places in Hampshire. Horndean is a town five miles from Havant.

Horner Road, 7
after Henry Horner who was secretary of the Mount Pleasant Land Society formed in the late 1860s to develop the area around the house known as Mount Pleasant at Highfield. Mr Horner, a millwright, lived in Sharrow Lane.

Horninglow Close, Mount, Road, 5
from the Derbyshire village of Horninglow; one of a group of streets named after places in South Derbyshire.

Horsewood Road, 13
not known.

Houndkirk Road, 11
from the nearby Houndkirk Moor. According to S.O. Addy, Houndkirk (sometimes spelt Ankirk, or Hankirk) came from the Anglo Saxon word *ent*, meaning a giant. Giants, he said, were thought to live on rocks and mountains.

Hounsfield Lane, Road, 3
after George Hounsfield, partner in Sheffield Coal Company, director of the Midland Railway, chairman of Sheffield and Rotherham Bank, and of Sheffield Water Company, treasurer of Sheffield Gas Company, magistrate and Church Burgess, who on his death in 1870, left £20,000 to be given out in pensions to the poor, known as the Hounsfield Charity.

Houstead Road, 9
from the nearby Bowden Houstead wood (see Bowden Wood Avenue).

Howard Lane, Street, 1
from Howard, the family name of the Dukes of Norfolk, for many years lords of the manor of Sheffield and substantial landowners.

Howard Road, 6
before the road was built, there was a house called Howard House in nearby Steel Bank, and an area called Howard Hill, but which came first, the hill or the house, and where the name originated, I do not know.

Howden Road, 9
the Howdens were an old Attercliffe family who owned property in the area from the time of William Howden (1663-1721) and Thomas Howden (1782-1837). The property later passed by marriage to the Fowler family.

Hoyland Road, 3
one of three roads built by the Hillfoot Freehold Land Society in the 1870s; probably named after John Hoyland, who was a blacksmith in Harvest Lane at the time.

Hoyle Street, 3
after John Hoyle, who lived at Upperthorpe from the 1820s to the 1840s. In later years he had a house in Meadow Street. Early directories describe him only as a 'gentleman'. He probably owned land in the area.

Hucklow Drive, Road, 5
after the village of Great Hucklow, six miles from Bakewell; one of a group of streets named after Derbyshire villages.

Hudson Road, 13
not known.

Humble Road, 3
no longer listed; it was built in the 1880s for Bernard Wake, the well-known solicitor, and named after his wife who, before their marriage, was Miss Jane Humble, daughter of the steward to Sir George Sitwell.

Humphrey Road, 8
probably after John Humphrey who

The old toll bar after which Hunters Bar was named.

owned Greenoak Cottage, Greenhill in the early 1900s. The cottage had an acre of land, gardens and a paddock.

Hunsley Street, 4

was built in the 1860s by Sheffield and Grimesthorpe Freehold Land Society and named after the secretary of the society, John Hunsley, of the *Queen's Head Inn*, Castle Street, where the society's meetings were held. He was also a director of the Seventh Borough Building Society.

Hunstone Avenue, 8

after Ernest Hunstone, who was a farmer at Little Norton around the turn of the century.

Hunter Hill Road, 11; Hunter House Road, 11

after John Hunter, whose farm Hunter House, was built some time in the 1600s, and gave its name to Hunter Hill, a strip of woodland called Hunter Plantation, and Hunter's Bar. His descendants lived at the farm for about 200 years.

Hunter Road, 6

not known – built around 1880.

Hunters Gardens, 6

not known.

Hunters Lane, 13

was originally called Back Lane. Its new name came from Joseph Hunter, who owned the land through which it passed. He also owned a nearby quarry. Another man called Hunter, George Cavill Hunter, butcher, owned the farm and five cottages at the Richmond Road end of the lane. The two were probably related.

Huntingdon Crescent, 11

built in the mid-1930s and probably named from a nearby house called Huntingdon House.

Huntingtower Road, 11

from the Murray family's links with Banner Cross Hall in the eighteenth and nineteenth centuries. Huntingtower is a Perthshire village not far from the Murray family seat. Its name was also used as the title of a novel by John Buchan.

Huntley Grove, Road, 11

ought really to be Huntly; they were built on land that was formerly part of W.H. Greaves-Bagshawe's Banner Cross estate. It was said of him that no commoner had a more illustrious pedigree. His family lines were linked to King Edward I and to a large number of peers, including the Earls of Huntly.

Huntsman Road, 9

was built on the Duke of Norfolk's land in 1911. The Watch Committee first agreed it should be called Wilney Road, after the village of Wilney Green, four miles west of Diss, Norfolk. A fortnight later they changed their minds and decided to name it after Benjamin Huntsman, pioneer of crucible steel-making.

Hurl Drive, Hurlfield Avenue, Court, Drive, Road, View, 12

from an old field name. Hurle Field is shown on a 1771 map. S O Addy said in his *Sheffield Glossary* that hurling a field meant to harrow it after its second ploughing. Hurlfield Road was originally called Hagg Lane. It was renamed in 1928.

Hurlingham Close, 11

from the London district of Hurlingham. The Hurlingham Club is the home of polo. The close was named at the same time as Ranelagh Drive and Sunningdale Mount, all three from places with sporting links. Planning permission was granted for all three in 1939 but building was delayed by the Second World War.

Hursley Close, Drive, 19

from Hursley Forsest, Hampshire; one of a group of streets named after forests (see Bramshill).

Hutchinson Lane, Road, 7

after George Hutchinson, of Blackburn, who owned the land on which they were built. He sold a small piece of his land to the Corporation in 1902 for the widening of Abbeydale Road.

Hutcliffe Drive, Hutcliffe Wood Road, 8

from the nearby Hutcliffe Wood, which is recorded in 1603 as Hudclyff Wood and is thought to come from the ancient name *Huda* – Huda's Cliff. Locals sometimes used to refer to it as 'Uttley' Wood. Hutcliffe Wood Road was originally just an off-shoot of Abbey Lane. It was not extended through the wood and down to Archer Lane until the mid-1930s.

Hutton Croft, 12

was built on the site of what used to be Hutton's Yard, ten stone terraced cottages which were owned in the mid-nineteenth century by Mary Hutton, widow of Ezra Hutton, sicklesmith, who originally came from Ridgeway.

Hyacinth Close, Road, 5

group name – flowers (see Acacia).

Hyde Road, 8

no longer listed; when first built (by Heeley Central Freehold Land Society in 1870) it was called Wilson Road, after an official of the society. It was renamed in 1886 after Hyde, the market town in Cheshire.

Hyde Park Terrace, Walk, 2

the name Hyde Park is a comparatively modern one. A clue to its origin may lie in an entry in the Sheffield Local Register for the 27th March 1826 which says that a cricket ground was opened at 'Hyde (High) Park', which seems to suggest that Hyde was a nineteenth century corruption of High – the high part of the Park district.

Ibbotson Road, 6
was built by Lower Walkley Freehold Land Society in 1875 and named after one of the instigators and officials of the society, Benjamin Ibbotson, who lived in Providence Road, Walkley.

Idsworth Road, 5
one of two streets (Horndean is the other) named after places in Hampshire. Idsworth Park is near the village of Horndean.

Ilkley Road, 5
after the Yorkshire town once well-known for its mineral springs, and even better known for the nearby moor upon which it is dangerous to go courting hatless.

Industry Road, 9
was built in 1863 by Attercliffe and Darnall Freehold Land Society as a scheme for seventy houses on a nine-acre site. When they didn't name their streets after their own officials the land societies often opted for worthy, idealistic names like Freedom, Providence and Industry.

Industry Street, 6
was named in the same way as Industry Road, 9, above, but in this case the street was built by the Whitehouse Lane Freehold Land Society in the 1870s.

Infield Lane, 9
from an old field name. It was a fairly common name usually meaning the near, or inner, field.

Infirmary Road, 6
after the General Infirmary (later the Royal Infirmary) built on Upperthorpe Meadows, and opened in October 1797. The hospital owned more than thirty acres of surrounding land, and when this road was built in the 1830s, part of it passed through Infirmary-owned land.

Ingelow Avenue, 5
after Jean Ingelow (1820-1897), English poet and novelist; one of a group of streets named after well-known literary figures.

Ingfield Avenue, 9
from an old field name. Ing comes from an old word meaning meadow or pasture.

The Royal Infirmary, opened – as the General Infirmary – in October 1797, is no longer a hospital. Much of it has gone. But the road named after it remains.

Inglewood Court, Avenue, 19
after the Inglewood Forest, Cumbria; one of a group of streets named after forests (see Bramshill).

Ingram Court, Road, 2
not known; built on the Duke of Norfolk's land, it first appeared in the 1907 street directory.

Inkersall Drive, 19
after an eighteenth-century landowner, Elizabeth Inkersall, who was allocated lands in the 1795 enclosures.

It isn't hard to see why the lane on which these cottages stand at Whiteley Woods came to be known as Ivy Cottage Lane. There is more ivy to be seen than cottage.

Inman Road, 9
no longer listed; named after Nathan Inman, partner in Inman and Hayhurst, lead and glass merchants, Exchange Street. Both partners speculated in housing.

Ironside Close, Place, Road, Walk, 14
after Alderman Isaac Ironside (1808-1870) radical and social reformer, member of the town council and controversial director of the Sheffield New Gas Company in the 1850s (as which he was portrayed in the *Stirrings in Sheffield on Saturday Night*).

Irving Street, 9
not known; the street was approved in 1897 for the Darnall landowner, Col E.W. Stanyforth (see Staniforth Road). Most of the streets built on his land were named after members of his family or places in Yorkshire with which they were connected, but I have not been able to find any appropriate place or person called Irving in the family history.

Islay Street, 10
after the Hebrides island of Islay; one of a group of streets given Scottish names.

Ivanhoe Road, 6
was first called Ivy Road. It was changed in 1906 to avoid confusion with similar sounding names. There was no special reason for the new name (of a popular novel by Sir Walter Scott) except that it retained the first two letters of the old one.

Ivy Cottage Lane, 11
from a nearby cottage. There were several Ivy Cottages in Sheffield but this was probably the best-known, being near to the popular beauty spot, Forge Dam.

Ivy Grove, 10; Ivy Lane, 19; Ivy Park Court, Road, 10;
ivy creeps into English place, street, house and farm names rather a lot. Presumably there was (and may still be) some in the area of all these streets.

Ivy Hall Road, 5
from the house called Ivy Hall. In the 1890s it was the home of Dennis Davy, agent of the Roundwood Colliery Co Ltd.

Jacobs Close, Drive, 5
is the revival of an old street name. There used to be a lane called Jacobs Lane nearby. The reason for Jacobs Lane is not known but it was probably from a person called Jacob.

Jamaica Street, 4
was built on the Duke of Norfolk's land and named from the Duke's family history. Thomas Howard, ninth Baron Effingham (1747-1791) was Governor of Jamaica from 1789 till his death.

James Andrew Close, Crescent, Croft, 8
after James Smith Andrew, farmer, who lived at Greenhill Hall in the early 1900s. He was a member of Norton Rural Council, Norton Parish Council, and Norton Association for the Prosecution of Felons. He also represented Norton-cum-Beauchief on Ecclesall Guardians.

James Street, 9
uncertain; it was built in the 1870s and from then till about 1900 it appeared in directories as St James Street. From 1902 it appeared as James Street.

Janson Street, 9
was first called Lamb Pool Lane (from a nearby pool), then it became Johnson, or Johnson's Lane (after Henry Johnson, owner of Prospect House, nearby). It was changed again in 1872 to avoid confusion with another Johnson Lane, off Nursery Street. The new name was simply a slight adaptation of the old name.

Jardine Close, Street, 9
after Robert Jardine, farmer at nearby Poplar Farm, Newman Road, in the 1890s. Before moving to Wincobank, he farmed at Longley. He died around 1904.

Jarrow Road, 11
was first called Plantation Road. It was changed in 1886 because there was another road with a similar name. There was no special reason for the new name, from the town of Jarrow in County Durham.

Jasmine Avenue, 19
group name – flowers (see Aster).

Jaunty Avenue, Close, Crescent, Drive, Lane, Mount, Place, Road, View, Way, 12
after Jonathan Rhodes, nineteenth century land and colliery owner, of Charnock Hall, who was something of a character and was widely known locally as Jonty, or Johnty. His small colliery stood on what was described in an advertisement of 1893 as 'Johnty Lane', a name that was later corrupted to Jaunty Lane. Jonty is still used occasionally in the Sheffield area as a nickname for boys called Jonathan. Ten streets carry the name Jaunty. Since they were built, Corporation policy has changed and now, no more than three or four streets in a group are given the same name.

Jedburgh Drive, Street, 9
Jedburgh Street was originally called Johnson Street, after a former landowner, John Johnson. It was renamed in 1903 after the Scottish border town of Jedburgh. Jedburgh Drive was originally Milton Street.

Jeffcock Road, 9
after Sheffield's first Mayor, William Jeffcock, coal owner, who was a member of the Town Council from 1843 to 1853. He built and lived in the nearby house called High Hazels.

Jeffery Green, 10
not known.

Jeffrey Street, 2
not known; built in the 1890s.

Jenkin Avenue, Close, Drive, Road, 9
from Jenkin, or Ginkin, Lane, which is mentioned in Harrison's survey of 1637. The origin is uncertain. It may come from the surname of someone who lived in the area. There was also a Jinkin Hill at Ranmoor, and another at Holmesfield, and a Jinkin Wood at Rotherham. S.O. Addy says in his *Sheffield Glossary* that it is unlikely that all these names derived from the surname Jenkin, or Jinkin, because the name is not common in the Sheffield area. He suggested that it might come from Jenkin being the pet form of John, and Jinkin Hill might be the hill down which the fire wheel was rolled on St John's Eve.

Jenkinson Street, 6
no longer listed; named after Arthur

Jenkinson, bricklayer and builder, who built some of the houses in the street in the 1870s and lived in one of them.

Jepson Road, 5

was built about 1870 by Wincobank Freehold Land Society and named after a man who was connected with the Society, Jepson Milner, tool manufacturer. There were already several Milner Roads in the area, hence the use of his first name.

Jericho Street, 3

after an old area of Sheffield called Jericho, a remnant of what J.D. Leader called 'a curious fancy for importing inappropriate Biblical names from the Old Testament' Another area of the old town was known as Egypt.

Jermyn Avenue, Close, Crescent, Drive, Square, Way, 12

from an old field name. Jermyn Meadow is on a list of fields in the Eckington area made in 1796. Frecheville used to be part of the manor of Eckington.

Jersey Road, 2

after the largest of the Channel Islands; group name (see Alderney).

Jessamine Road, 5

group name – flowers (see Acacia).

Jessel Street, 9

after Sir George Jessel (1824-1883) who was Solicitor General and Master of the Rolls; one of a group of streets named after famous legal men (see Brett).

Jessop Street, 11

a name given by the Enclosure Commissioners in 1788; it comes from the Jessop family of Broom Hall, and in particular, Bethia Jessop (1704-1781) one of the freeholders who petitioned Parliament for enclosure in 1779. She died before the commissioners completed their report.

Jew Lane, 1

one theory is that it was the part of town where Jews lived, but there is no evidence to support this. In old directories the name appears as Jehu Lane, and there are several theories for this name. One is that the Earl of Shrewsbury's coachman used to shout 'Jehu' to his horses as he drove down the lane. This seems somewhat far-fetched. Jehu is, however, the name applied to coach drivers, specially reckless ones, and there was a coach driver called Thomas Evenhand living in the lane in the 1820s. The likeliest explanation seems to be that it came from a person's name. Early directories list a man called Jehu Ibbotson living in the area, so it may have been him.

Jobson Place, Road, 3

after Henry Jobson, merchant and landowner in the Infirmary Road area in the early nineteenth century, He was involved in an exchange of land with the General Infirmary in 1814.

John Calvert Road, 13

was originally called Calvert Road. It was renamed in 1924 after Woodhouse became part of Sheffield where there was already a Calvert Road. The original intention was to call it Colwyn Road, but this was not approved by the City Council and it was named instead John Calvert Road, after John Calvert, widely admired Congregational minister of Zion Chapel, Attercliffe, for nearly forty years. He would not use the title 'Reverend' and twice tried to retire, but his congregation would not let him. He finally retired in 1895, and went to live at Southport where he died in 1922 at the age of 96.

Johnson Lane, Street, 3

after a person called Johnson but I don't know who. Johnson Street is listed in the 1825 directory and there were several people called Johnson living in the area at that time.

John Street, 2

uncertain; it appears first as a short street off Bramall Lane in the 1849 directory and may have been named after John Sheldon, local landowner (see Sheldon Lane).

John Ward Street, 13

was first called Ward Street. It was changed in 1924 after Woodhouse area came into Sheffield (where there was already a Ward Street). When the change came before the City Council for approval one member asked who was John Ward and nobody seemed sure except that he was a former resident of Woodhouse. The likely answer is John Ward, stonemason (and probably builder as well) who lived in Woodhouse in the mid-1800s.

Joiner Street, 3

after Samuel Redfearn who lived in a cottage called Nursery House near what is now Nursery Street in the 1820s. He was a joiner and carpenter. By the 1840s, he was described as joiner and builder. Joiner Lane was built alongside his house. His son, Samuel jr, was also a joiner and builder, first in Harvest Lane, later in Andrew Street.

Jordanthorpe Parkway, 8

from the area called Jordanthorpe which appears – as Jurdanthorpe – in a deed dated 1543. Thorpe usually means outlying farm, or hamlet. Jordan, or Jurdan, is thought to come from a person's name.

Joshua Road, 7

after Joshua Spooner who was an extensive landowner in Sheffield, with estates at Crookes and Tapton, as well as Machon Bank (see also Spooner Road, 10).

Jowitt Road, 11

after George Jowitt who lived in Brincliffe Edge Road for many years up to his death in 1955. He was the founder of George Jowitt and Sons, grinding wheel makers. In 1951 his firm gave £30,000 to pay for the Broomcroft old people's home. He was also a pioneer cyclist in Sheffield.

Jubilee Road, 9

plans for the road were approved in May 1897 and it was named to mark the Diamond Jubilee of Queen Victoria's reign which was widely celebrated the following month.

Julian Road, Way, 9

after Canon John Julian, former Wesleyan minister, who became the first vicar of Wincobank (from 1875-1905). He devoted his life to the study of hymns and their history, collected more than 6,000 volumes of hymns from all over the world, composed some himself, and wrote the monumental *Dictionary of Hymnology* which was published in 1892.

Jumble Road, 11

according to S.O. Addy, the local historian, Jumble Hole was the name given

Kenwood Park Road, part of George Wostenholm's US-style layout.

to any rough, bushy, uncultivated hollow. At the time he was compiling his *Sheffield Glossary* in the 1880s, he said Jumble Road was a dyke several yards deep, covered with bushes and briars – a typical jumble hole. Jumble Hole Lane, Thorpe Hesley, got its name in the same way.

Junction Road, 11

may be from the fact that it joins Psalter Lane and Ecclesall Road, or from the junction of several roads at Hunters Bar.

Junction Road, 13

from the Woodhouse junction of the old Manchester, Sheffield and Lincolnshire Railway which was opened to passengers in 1849. The village's first railway station was Woodhouse Junction. It closed to passengers in 1875 and was replaced by the present station.

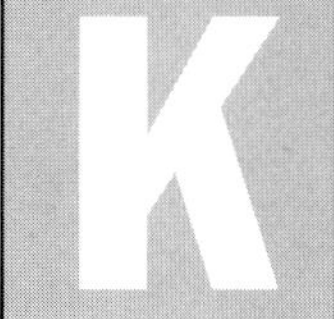

Kaye Place, 10

formerly Kaye's Place, after David Kaye, joiner and builder, who built houses in the area and lived in this street in the 1870s.

Kearsley Road, 2

probably comes (like Ward Place and Asline Road) from the Ward family who lived at nearby Mount Pleasant in the first half of the nineteenth century. One of the girls in the family married John Kearsley of Manchester. The couple had two daughters described by Thomas Asline Ward in his diaries as 'very agreeable women'.

Keats Road, 6

after John Keats (1795-1821) poet, whose first volume of poems was published in 1817, only four years before his death. Some of his best remembered works are the odes *To a Nightingale*, and *To Autumn*, and the ballad, *La Belle Dame Sans Merci*. One of a group of streets named after literary figures.

Keeton's Hill, 2

probably after an early resident of the area, William Keeton, who is listed in the 1820s directories as a 'gentleman' which suggests that he was reasonably well heeled.

Kelvin Place, Walk, 6

from the public house, the *Kelvin Grove*, built in the 1840s and kept for some years by George Frederick Bywater, who was also a fireworks manufacturer and 'Pyrotechnic artist'. When it opened it was not just a public house. It had a range of gymnastic apparatus (swings, ropes, climbing horse, leaping board, etc) for the use of visitors, and a band played one night a week. The admission charge was fourpence, 'threepence of which will be allowed in refreshment'. There was probably a Scotsman behind it. Kelvin Grove is a district of Glasgow named from the River Kelvin.

Kenbourne Grove, Road, 7

from a nearby house called Kenbourne which was probably named as a variation on the theme of Kenwood. The 'Ken' theme was followed in the names of several other nearby houses – Kenbrook, and Kenhurst, for example. Kenbourne Road was originally called Buckley Road. It was changed in 1889.

Kendal Place, Road, 6

from the town of Kendal, Cumbria.

Kenilworth Place, 11
one of two small streets (Marmion Road the other) built around 1905 and named after works by Sir Walter Scott, the novelist. His novel called *Kenilworth* was published in 1821.

Kennedy Road, 8
after the Victorian painter William Denholm Kennedy (1813-1865) who exhibited at the Royal Academy almost every year from 1833 till his death. The road was built for James Duffield of Wilson Cammells Works, Dronfield. Mr Duffield was a collector of paintings.

Kenninghall Close, Drive, Mount, Place, Road, 2
were built on the Duke of Norfolk's land and named from the village of Kenninghall, Norfolk, where one of the Duke's ancestors built a palace set in a 700-acre park in the sixteenth century. The palace fell into disrepair and was pulled down in 1650.

Kent Road, 8
was built through a field called Kent Storth Meadow. At the time of Harrison's survey in 1637 there was a wood in the area called Kent Storth Wood and the field was probably named from the wood.

Kenwell Drive, 17
was built to plans approved in 1937. The name seems to have been some kind of variation on the name of the builder, O. Edwin Hanwell, of Twentywell Lane.

Kenwood Avenue, Bank, Road, 7; Kenwood Park Road, 7
on his many visits to the United States George Wostenholm, the cutler, particularly admired the village of Kenwood, near Oneida Lake, New York State. He was impressed by its layout and its avenues of trees. When he built a new house for himself at Sharrow he called it Kenwood, and when he developed the 150 acres he owned around the house – from Moorfoot to Nether Edge – he set out to emulate the American layout. The estate was known as Kenwood Park. There were twenty-six acres of pleasure grounds around the house designed by Robert Marnock, the celebrated landscape gardener.

Kenyon Alley, 3; Kenyon Street, 1
from the firm of John Kenyon, later Joseph and John Kenyon, merchants, filesmiths and sawmakers, whose works were nearby in the eighteenth and nineteenth centuries.

Keppel Place, Road, 5
after Viscount Keppel who was a friend of Thomas Wentworth, first Marquis of Rockingham. When Keppel was acquitted at a court martial in 1778 the Marquis, by way of celebration, started to build a monument at Scholes (where there is another Keppel Road). When the Marquis died in 1782 the monument, a 115-foot high column known as Keppel's Column, was completed by his nephew and heir, Earl Fitzwilliam.

Kerwin Close, Drive, Road, 17
from the surnames of the owners of the land on which they were built, Mr Kershaw and Mr Winstone. The first three letters of both men's names were joined to make Kerwin.

Kestrel Green, 2
group name – birds (See Curlew Ridge).

Keswick Close, 6
uncertain; probably from a place called Keswick but there are several, the best known of which is in Cumbria. There are two others in Norfolk, and an East Keswick, near Wetherby.

Kettlebridge Road, 9
according to G.R. Vine, in his *Story of Old Attercliffe*, there was a blacksmith called John Kettle whose workshop was nearby and who repaired tools for men building the Manchester, Sheffield and Lincolnshire Railway line. Mr Vine had the story third-hand and it lacks verification.

Ketton Avenue, 8
from Frederick Thomas Walker, constructional builder, who built some early prefabricated houses in the area in the 1930s. Mr Walker was assistant managing director of Ketton Portland Cement Co, and a former High Sheriff of Rutland, where he owned land (see also Essendine Crescent).

Kew Crescent, 12
not known; presumably from the area of Kew, London, site of the famous gardens.

Keyworth Place, 13
Keyworth is one of the old family names in the village of Woodhouse. The history of the village is littered with Keyworths. Lionel Keyworth was a tanner there in 1680, John and Thomas Keyworth, also tanners, were there in 1730 and the name continued in the village till modern times.

Keyworth Road, 6
probably after Charles Keyworth who was proprietor of the New Patent Plastic Brick Company, Wadsley Bridge, in the 1890s.

Khartoum Road, 11
from the capital city of the Sudan which stands at the confluence of the Blue Nile and the White Nile. The city was destroyed by the Arabs in 1885 (when General Gordon was killed), then retaken by the British, under General Kitchener, in 1898, around the time this road was built for Mrs Thompson and Mrs Harland (both members of the Wilson family).

Kildale Gardens, 19
from the North Yorkshire village of Kildale, five miles from Stokesley; one of a group of streets given Yorkshire names.

Kilner Way, 6
from the kilns that were on the site before it was developed for housing. It was the site of a brickworks operated by the Sheffield Brick Co Ltd, Halifax Road.

Kilton Hill, Place, 3
from the earlier Kilton Street (no longer listed) which was built on the Duke of Norfolk's land and named after the village of Kilton, near Worksop, which was once part of the Duke's Worksop estate.

Kilvington Avenue, Crescent, Road, 13
a link with the Parker family of Woodthorpe. Henry Yarborough Parker, born 1814, married Maria Margaret Kilvington in 1842.

Kimberley Street, 9

not known; plans were approved in 1881 for the Goulder brothers who built extensively at Attercliffe. It may have come from the Nottinghamshire village of Kimberley, the Norfolk village of Kimberley, the South African diamond mining city, or the Earl of Kimberley who was Secretary for the Colonies when the street was built.

King Ecgbert Road, 17

after King Ecgbert, King of Wessex from the year 802, who conquered Mercia and other parts of England, and when the Northumbrians surrendered to him at Dore in 827 became the first king to be recognised by the whole country. The Saxon Chronical describes how he led an army to Dore but the Northumbrians, not prepared for a fight, submitted to him. He died in 839.

Kingfield Road, 11

according to Mary Walton in her *History of the Parish of Sharrow*, the road was built in 1850 through a field belonging to Henry King.

King James Street, 6

was built (like nearby Grammar Street) in the 1870s on land leased from the governors of the old Sheffield Grammar School. It was named from the fact that King James granted a charter incorporating the governors of the school in 1604.

Kingslake Street, 9

uncertain; it was built for William Glave and the intention may have been to name it Kinglake, after Alexander William Kinglake, author of an eight-volume history of the Crimean War. Another of Mr Glave's streets had a Crimean connection – Alma Street, from the Battle of Alma.

Kingsley Park Avenue, Grove, 7

uncertain; the name of the avenue was approved in January 1936 and may come from the district of Northampton called Kingsley Park because of Earl Fitzwilliam's Northampton interests.

Kingston Street, 4

from Kingston, the capital of Jamaica. Like nearby Jamaica Street, it was built on the Duke of Norfolk's land. One of the Duke's ancestors, Thomas Howard, ninth Baron Effingham, was governor of Jamaica in the late nineteenth century.

King Street, 3

was first called Pudding Lane. According to some sources it was renamed for the Coronation of King George III, but it was in the list of street names as 'Pudding Lane, or King Street' in 1732, six years before George III was born. It is more likely that it was renamed for the accession of King George II in 1727.

Kingswood Avenue, Close, Croft, Grove, 19

from King's Wood, an area between Wentworth and Elsecar; four of a group of streets given Yorkshire place names.

Kinharvie Road, 5

from a place called Kinharvie in Dumfries and Galloway, on a Scottish estate once owned by Lord Herries. When the last Lord Herries died without heir in 1908 the English title became extinct, but the Scottish barony passed to his first daughter who was Duchess of Norfolk. The Scottish estate, including Kinharvie, then passed into the ownership of the Duke of Norfolk.

Kinnaird Avenue, Place, Road, 5

not known; the name of Kinnaird Road was approved in August 1931. There are three places called Kinnaird in Scotland, a Kinnaird Mansion and a Kinnaird Castle.

Kipling Road, 6

after Rudyard Kipling (1865-1936) the famous author (of *The Jungle Book*, *Puck of Pook's Hill*, *Barrack Room Ballads*, etc) one of a pair, with Rudyard Road.

Kirby Close, 9

from the now-demolished Kirby Road which was built for the Staniforth family and named after the village of Kirby Overblow, south of Harrogate, where the family also owned land (see Staniforth Road).

Kirkbridge Road, 9

from the stream called the Kirk Bridge Dike, sometimes called Darnall Brook, about two miles long, rising near the old Corker Bottom coal pit and joining the Don near Bold Street. It was once an open stream but as Attercliffe was built up it was culverted.

Kirkby Avenue, Drive, Road, View, Way, 12

Kirkby is an old Gleadless name. There was a Kirkby Farm for many years, recorded in 1649 as Kirkeby Farm and thought to have been named after Henry Kirkeby who lived in the area in 1570.

Kirkdale Crescent, Drive, 13

not known; the name was approved in March 1936. An area of Liverpool is called Kirkdale.

Kirkstall Road, 11

from the Kirkstall area of Leeds which is well-known for its Cistercian abbey founded in the twelfth century, and for an obelisk marking the fact that it is equi-distant from London and Edinburgh – 200 miles from both capitals.

Kirkstone Road, 6

from the area and pass called Kirkstone between Windermere and Patterdale in the Lake District.

Kirk Street, 4

was originally called Conway Street. It was renamed in 1872 and the new name is a mystery. The only person called Kirk living in the area at the time was George Kirk, butter dealer in nearby Gower Street, but I have not been able to link him with Kirk Street in any way.

Kirton Road, 4

from a village called Kirton. There are three villages with this name, one in Lincolnshire, one in Nottinghamshire and one in Suffolk. It was probably the Suffolk Kirton because the street was built on the Duke of Norfolk's land, one of a group of streets named after places ending 'ton' (see Blayton).

Kitchen Street, 8

no longer listed; it was originally called Kitchin Street and was named after a group of shareholders in the Sheffield Brick Co Ltd, who developed this street and others nearby. There were ten people called Kitchin holding shares in the company, two of whom, Ashworth Kitchin and Clifford Kitchin were barristers. I can't explain why the spelling changed.

Knab Close, Croft, Rise, Road, 7

from an old farm which is referred to in the Ecclesall Enclosures of 1788 as Prior Nab Farm and was later known as Nab,

or Knab Farm. *Nab* is an old word meaning the top of a hill. Nab Lane and Nab House, Gleadless, come from the same word.

Knaresborough Road, 7
was built as part of the Oakdale Estate at Millhouses and presumably named after the Yorkshire town of Knaresborough.

Knowle Close, 6;
Knowle Croft, Lane, II;
Knowle Road, 5;
Knowle Top, 19
all come from the old word *cnoll*, meaning a mound, or small hill.

Knutton Crescent, Rise, Road, 5
after the Rev Immanuel Knutton who was vicar of Ecclesfield in the seventeenth century. He died in 1655 and was buried at Ecclesfield.

Kyle Close, Crescent, 5
not known; there is a River Kyle in North Yorkshire which flows into the River Ouse, and there are several places called Kyle in Scotland. But these two streets were named in May 1937 along with other streets named after literary figures. If it belonged with others this too should have a literary theme but I have not been able to find an author or poet called Kyle.

Ladies Spring Drive, Grove, 17
from the nearby Ladies Spring Wood, shown as Lady Spring on a 1760 map. Names like this are usually an abbreviation of Our Lady and indicate Church ownership. In this case the name is probably a link with Beauchief Abbey which owned much of the land round about.

Ladybank Road, 19
from the nearby Ladybank Wood which is recorded in 1773. The explanation is probably the same as Ladies Spring above.

Ladysmith Avenue, 7
from the town in Natal, South Africa, which was under siege for four months during the Boer War. Its relief caused rejoicing throughout England, and a good many streets were named after it. The town itself was named after the wife of Sir Henry Smith, one-time Governor of the Cape.

Laird Avenue, Drive, Road, 6
Laird Road was originally called Crabtree Lane. It was renamed in April 1903 to avoid confusion with the Crabtree area near Firvale. Reason for the new name is not known.

Laverack Street, Handsworth, was built on land that was formerly part of the nurseries of John and Thomas Laverack.

Lambcroft Lane, 13
from an old field name. When it was offered for sale in 1883, Lamb Croft was said to be three roods seventeen perches in size. Another field nearby was called Calf Croft.

Lamb Drive, Road, 5
there are two possibilities. Some streets in the area were named after famous literary figures and others after local farmers. This could be either Charles Lamb (1775-1834), the English essayist; or Arthur Lamb, who farmed on Penistone Road up to the turn of the century. My money is on Charles.

Lambert Street, 3
was built across a field called Lambert Croft, which was named after its owner, Matthew Lambert, linen draper and merchant in Market Place, Town Trustee and Church Burgess, who inherited the land from his brother and built a furnace on the croft in 1764.

Lamb Hill Close, 13
from an old field name recorded as Lam Hill in 1565. It is a common English field name and means just what it says – the hill where lambs grazed.

Lancaster Street, 3
from a link with the Duke of Rutland. The seventh Duke was Chancellor of the Duchy of Lancaster.

Lancing Road, 2
was built on the Duke of Norfolk's land and named after the place called Lancing, near Worthing, Sussex. The Duke had interests in the Lancing area.

Landseer Close, Drive, Place, Walk, 14
after Sir Edward Henry Landseer (1802-1873) the English artist who became very popular as an animal painter with pictures like *Monarch of the Glen*. He also designed the famous lions in Trafalgar Square, London. Group name (see Constable).

Langdale Road, 8
after Langdale Tarn and Langdale Pikes, Cumbria; group name – Lake District theme (see Arnside).

Langdon Street, 11
not known; built about 1870. There are several places in the country called Langdon.

Langley Street, 9
probably after Alderman Batty Langley, timber merchant, magistrate, Mayor in 1892, and later Liberal MP for Attercliffe. He lived at Langhill, Manchester Road.

Langsett Avenue, Close, Crescent, Grove, Rise, Road, Walk, 6
from the area called Langsett, recorded as Langseside in the thirteenth century and said to mean the long hillside – presumably the steep slope on the north side of the Little Don Valley.

Lansdowne Road, 11
was made in 1858 and probably named after a leading politician of the day, the third Marquis of Lansdowne, who was Chancellor of the Exchequer in 1806-07 and held office in successive governments. He died in 1863.

Larch Hill, 9
group name – trees (see Alder Lane).

Lark Street, 6
one of a pair (brace?) of streets named after birds (along with Thrush Street).

Latham Square, 11
after Thomas Latham who lived at Hill Top, Bents Green, and owned land on which the first houses in this street were built in the 1890s.

Lathkill Close, Road, 13
from the well-known Derbyshire dale and river, said by Izaak Walton's fishing chum, Charles Cotton, to be the purest stream he had ever seen with the best trout in England.

Lauder Street, 4
not known; approved, with Wade Street, for the Church Burgesses in 1908.

Laughton Road, 9
seems to be named after a place called Laughton, but I don't know which. It was built with Bubwith Road (named after a Humberside village) and Walling Road (named after the Walling Fen area of Humberside), but I can't find a place called Laughton on Humberside.

Launce Road, 5
possibly after Launce, the servant to Proteus in Shakespeare's *The Two Gentleman of Verona* (see Falstaff).

Laverack Close, Street, 13
were built on land that used to be part of the nurseries of John and Thomas Laverack, market gardeners. A blacksmith's shop and a large oak tree were removed for the building of Laverack Street. The story is that John Laverack had no children but the Duke of Norfolk, lord of the manor, told him that his name would be perpetuated in the street name.

Laverdene Avenue, Close, Drive, Road, Way, 17
an adaptation of the name of the builder (in the 1930s) James Laver, of Abbeydale Park Rise.

Laverock Way, 5
uncertain; the name was approved, with others on the Stubbin estate, in February 1920. Laverock is the old word for lark. There is a Laverock Hall near Keighley.

The Lawns, 11
was built on what used to be part of the Banner Cross estate. An old map of the estate shows an area of flat land described as 'The Lawns' where this street now stands.

Lawrence Street, 9
not known.

Lawson Street, 10
was built on church land and named after the Lawson family, Marmaduke and Andrew, of Boroughbridge, who owned the advowson of Sheffield parish church from the 1820s to the 1870s.

Laxey Road, 6
from the town and holiday resort of Laxey on the Isle of Man; one of a group of streets given names of places in the Isle of Man.

Leadbeater Drive, Road, 12
uncertain; the names, approved in January 1957, may come from Thomas Leadbeater, builder at Woodseats, who did some work in the area.

Leader Road, 6
was built in the 1860s as part of the Dykes Hall estate. All three members of the Leader family of Sheffield, Robert, and his sons, John Daniel and Robert Eadon, were members of the committee which developed the 192-plot estate and this road was named after them.

Leadmill Road, 1 and 2; Leadmill Street, 1
from an old leadmill set up in the 1750s, first run by five partners, later taken over by John Barker and Thomas Rawson (the brewer), and closed about 1870. The building was demolished in 1907.

Leake Road, 6
was originally called Palmer Road. It was changed in 1924 to avoid confusion with Palmer Road, Darnall. The new name was from the village of Leake, near Thirsk, north Yorkshire. I'm told locals used to refer jokingly to this road as 'Onion Street'.

Leamington Street, 10
from the town of Leamington. It was built (with Warwick Street) in the late 1890s for Mr S.S. Bower, and both streets were given Warwickshire names.

The Lea, 19
refers to a nearby area of open ground.

Leaton Close, 6
after the Rev F.T. Leaton, minister of Loxley Chapel from 1914 to 1919; one of several streets named after former ministers at the chapel.

There's something of a contrast on this old photograph of Leopold Street – Broomhead's Dining Rooms on the left hand side looking towards the Town Hall and the Grand Hotel on the right.

Leavy Greave, Leavy Greave Road, 3
come from the Middle English words meaning a leafy copse. The name is mentioned in sixteenth-century documents.

Leawood Place, 6
from a farm called Leawood, overlooking Matlock, Derbyshire; one of a small group of streets given names from Matlock area.

Ledstone Road, 8
I suspect this ought to be Ledston, from the village of that name north of Castleford. Other streets nearby have Yorkshire place names (although there is a village called Ledstone in Devon).

Lee Croft, 1
from an old field named after its tenant, probably 'Widdowe Lee', listed in Harrison's 1637 survey as paying £5 rent for a tenement and croft.

Leedham Close, Road, 5
from a pair of houses nearby, built in the 1890s and called Leedham Villas.

Leeds Road, 9
was first called Lord Street. It was renamed in 1886, after the city of Leeds.

Lee Moor Lane, 6
from an area known as Lee Moor, lee meaning a forest clearing.

Lee Road, 6
after the Rev John Lee, minister at Loxley chapel from 1889 to 1913; one of several streets named after former ministers at the chapel.

Lees Hall Avenue, Place, Road; Lees Nook, The Lees, 8
Lees Hall, once the home of the Parker family, later owned by other families, was a large house standing where Newfield School was later built. Its two-feet thick walls were oak panelled and the staircase was so substantial that it is said someone once rode a shire horse upstairs for a wager. Lees in this case comes from Norton Lees.

Leicester Walk, 3
not known; the name occured first with Leicester Street (no longer listed) which was built for the Church Burgesses in the 1830s.

Leigh Street, 9
not known; probably after a place called Leigh, but there are several, the best known of them is the one twelve miles from Manchester.

Leighton Drive, Place, Road, 14
after Frederick (later Lord) Leighton (1830-1896), the English artist who was president of the Royal Acadamy in 1878, was knighted the same year and became a Baron in 1896; one of a group of streets named after artists (see Constable).

Lemont Road, 17
from a house called Lemont at Green Oak. In 1916, just before the road was built, it was the home of Frank H. Roberts, engineer.

Lennox Road, 6
after Lennox Burton Dixon, one time president of the Silversmiths' Association, and a member of the Dixon family of Hillsborough Hall and the firm of James W. Dixon, Cornish Place; one of a group of streets named after members of the Dixon family who owned the land on which they were built.

Lenton Street, 2
was first called Malthouse Lane. It was renamed in 1886, after the Lenton district of Nottingham.

Leonard Close, 2
after Leonard, son of Lord Dacre, lord of the manor of Eckington from 1540 till his death in 1563. Leonard succeeded his father as lord of the manor and as Lord Dacre, then lost all his titles when he joined the Northern Rebellion and took part in the attempt to free Mary, Queen of Scots, in the 1570s.

Leopold Street, 1
was one of several street improvements approved by the Town Council in 1873. Its completion in 1879, coincided with the visit of Prince Leopold, Queen Victoria's youngest son, for the official

opening of Firth College, and it was named after him. Prince Leopold, who held the title Duke of Albany, died in 1884 at the age of 31.

Leppings Lane, 6
leppings is the old name for stepping stones across a stream or river. They were also called leppen stones, or hippen stones. Last century the leppings across the river at Hillsborough were a well-known feature of the area.

Lescar Lane, 11
there was a Lescar grinding wheel at Sharrow Vale as early as the sixteenth century. This street and a local public house took their names from it.

Leslie Road, 6
after Lt-Col John H. Leslie, Royal Artillery, military historian and ordnance expert. After 20 years in the army, 15 of them in India, he came to Sheffield, took charge of the ordnance department at Vickers Ltd, where he later became a director, and lived for about four years at Dykes Hall. While in Sheffield, he was District Commissioner of Boy Scouts, Deputy Leiutenant of the West Riding, and Alexandra Rose Day organiser.

Leverton Drive, Gardens, 11
from Leverton Street (no longer listed) which was first called Garden Street, because it was built across garden land. It was renamed in 1872 to avoid confusion with Garden Street in the town centre. The new name was from the villages of North and South Leverton, near Retford.

Leveson Street, 4
was built on the Duke of Norfolk's land and named from the fact that the 13th Duke married, in 1814, Lady Charlotte Sophia Leveson-Gower, daughter of the Duke of Sutherland.

Lewis Road, 13
was approved in August 1932 and almost certainly named after someone called Lewis but I don't know who.

Leyburn Road, 8
was called Stanhope Road when it was built in the 1890s. It was renamed in 1924 and its new name was from the village of Leyburn, Wensleydale.

Leyfield Road, 17
from the name of several old fields which are listed in the Dore and Totley Enclosure Act of 1809 – Great Ley Field, Near Ley Field, Round Ley Field and Little Ley Field. Ley in place names usually indicates an area that has been cleared of trees.

The old leppings, or stepping stones, from which Leppings Lane was named.

Liberty Close, Drive, Hill, Place, Road, 6
is another of the idealistic names favoured by freehold land societies (Freedom, Industry, Providence, etc). The society that bought land hereabouts in 1857 named it Liberty Hill and called itself the Liberty Hill Benefit Building Society.

Lichford Road, 2
was built on the Duke of Norfolk's land and named from the marriage of his ancestor Bernard, son of Henry Frederick, Earl of Arundel, to Catherine, widow of Sir Richard Lichford, of Dorking, Surrey, in 1672.

Lifford Street, 9
was built on Earl Fitzwilliam's land and named from the fact that William Fitzwilliam, first Baron Fitzwilliam, held the Irish title Baron Fitzwilliam of Lifford, County Donegal.

Lightwood Lane, 8
from the area called Lightwood, spelt *Lyghtwoode* in the sixteenth century. S.O. Addy, the local historian, said it probably came from the Anglo Saxon word *lyt*, meaning small, that is a small wood.

Lilac Road, 5
group name – flowers (see Acacia).

Lilac Road, 19
group name – flowers (see Aster).

Limb Lane, 17
there is reference to an area nearby as Lymme in a fourteenth century document. Language experts say it comes from the old word *lemo* meaning elm. There is also a Limb Brook.

Limbrick Close, Road, 6
from the Limbrick grinding wheels (spelt Limerick in some early documents) which were working in the late 1700s, were later converted to a wire mill, mainly producing crinoline wire, and were rebuilt as grinding wheels in the 1870s.

Lime Street, 6
one of a trio along with Ash Street and Wood Street.

Lime Street, 19
group name – trees (see Chestnut).

Limpsfield Road, 9
was built on land owned by Mrs Alice Barry, daughter of a Sheffield merchant, Henry Greaves Walker. Mrs Barry gave a nearby recreation ground to the city. She lived near Limpsfield, Surrey.

Linaker Road, 6
not known; built in the 1890s.

Linburn Road, 8
was originally called Linacre Road, after the Linacre family of R. and J. Linacre, scythe, sickle and reaping hook manufacturers, of Cobnar Works and Cobnar House. The name was changed in 1903, and the new name was concocted to keep it similar to the old one.

Lincoln Street, 9
was first called Thomas Street but there were several Thomas Streets and this one was renamed in 1886, after the city of Lincoln.

Linden Avenue, 8
linden, meaning lime tree – lime tree avenue.

Lindley Road, 5
not known; built in the early 1900s and first shown in the 1905 directory.

Lindsay Avenue, Close, Crescent, Drive, Road, 5
after Sir David Linday (1490-1555) Scottish poet and satirest. His poems have been described as forthright attacks on 'unthrift, sloth, falsehood, poverty and strife'. One of a group of streets named after literary figures.

Lingfoot Avenue, Close, Crescent, Drive, Place, Walk, 8
from an old field name. Lingfoot Field is recorded in the tithe awards of 1845 but the name is probably much older than that. Ling usually meant land where heather grew.

The Link, 10
a link between Forres Avenue and Forres Road.

Linley Lane, 12 and 13
from an old farm nearby called Linley Farm. The name appears as Lyndeley in a document of 1330 and language experts say it means lime tree wood or clearing.

Linscott Road, 8
the other roads with which it was built (Chatfield, Crosby, Kennedy, Fraser) were all named after artists. The man for whom they were built, James Duffield, was an art collector. But I have not been able to find an artist called Linscott. There was, however, a Belgian artist called Linschoten, and it is just about possible that Linscott may be an attempt to anglicise his name.

Lismore Road, 8
was originally called Livingstone Road, after Dr David Livingstone, the missionary and traveller (the parallel road being Stanley Road, after Sir Henry Morton Stanley, the explorer, whose name is often linked with his). But there was another Livingstone Road, so this one was renamed in 1903. Lismore was a random choice. There is an island called Lismore in Argyllshire and a town called Lismore in County Waterford.

Lister Avenue, Close, Crescent, Drive, Place, Way, 12
name approved 1951; possibly from the firm of G.R. Lister and Son, asphalters and road makers, of Young Street Works. The firm certainly made some of the roads in Gleadless area.

Lister Lane, 3
probably after John Lister who was a joiner and builder in nearby Allen Street at the time the lane was built in the early 1870s.

Lister Road, 6
was built in 1875 by Lower Walkley Freehold Land Society and named after the secretary of the society, Henry Pickering Lister, accountant, estate and financial agent, rent and debt collector, who lived at Upperthorpe and had offices in Figtree Lane.

Lister Street, 9
after Stephen Lister who lived in nearby Station Road, Darnall, in the late 1800s. In the 1883 directory he is listed as a butter and egg dealer at Norfolk Market Hall, but in later directories he is also described as a market gardener at Darnall.

Little Common Lane, 11
from an old area of common land referred to as 'the Lyttle Comen' in a document of 1587. It was within the triangle now formed by this lane, Ecclesall Road South and Abbey Lane. The lane was originally called Common Lane but in 1903 it was renamed to avoid confusion with another Common Lane.

Littledale Road, 9
was built on land belonging to the Staniforth family and named after someone in the family pedigree, Mary Littledale, who married Samuel Staniforth, son of Thomas (see Staniforth Road).

Little John Copse, 6
after Little John, one of Robin Hood's merry men; one of a group of streets named from links with the legendary Sherwood outlaw because of his supposed connections with the Loxley area.

Little Lane, 4; Little Lane 12
exactly what they are, little lanes.

Little London Place, Road, 8
uncertain; but the name Little London occurs as a location or field name in five other parts of south west Yorkshire and in most cases is thought to be a corruption of the Old Norse word *lundr*, meaning a grove, or small wood. There was a field called Little London Holme at Ecclesall, and a Little London Wheel near Bell Hagg.

Little Matlock Gardens, Way, 6
from the area known as Little Matlock (see High Matlock).

Little Norton Avenue, Drive, Lane, Way, 8
Little Norton was once a small hamlet quite separate from the village of Norton. In later years it was submerged under new building. In a will dated 1535 it is mentioned as Lytyll Norton, and in a document dated 1384, as Parva Norton.

Littlewood Drive, Lane, Road, 12
the lane, which appeared first, leads to a small area of woodland – a little wood.

Liverpool Place, Street, 9
a link with Earl Fitzwilliam. William Charles, Viscount Milton, son of the fifth Earl, was married at St George's, Hanover Square. London, in 1833, to Lady Selina Jenkinson, daughter of the Earl of Liverpool.

Livesey Street, 6
was originally called Cemetery Road because it was near a cemetery. It was renamed in 1872 after the Rev John Livesey who was vicar of St Philip's Church for thirty-nine years up to his death in August 1870.

Livingstone Road, 9
not known; it was built in the 1880s, and may have been a belated tribute to David Livingstone, the explorer, who died in 1873.

Lloyd Street, 4
not known; approved in 1898 for 'J.B. Firth and others'.

Loakfield Drive, 5
from an old field name. Lokefield, or Lookefield, believed to be a corruption of Le Oak Field, is mentioned in documents of the sixteenth century.

Lock Lane, 9
from the nearby lock on the Sheffield and South Yorkshire Canal known as Jordan Lock.

Lock Street, 6
not known; originally called New Queen Street, it was renamed in 1872.

Lodge Lane, 6 and 10
from the old Rivelin hunting lodge (see Lodge Moor Road).

Lodge Moor Road, 10
the moor above Rivelin Lodge, a hunting lodge built for the Earl of Shrewsbury in the early 1600s, and mentioned in Harrison's survey of 1637.

Lofthouse Road, 6
was approved in 1898 for H.S. Barker. Since nearby streets were given Yorkshire names, this one is probably from the village of Lofthouse near Wakefield.

Logan Road, 9
was originally called Shelfanger Road, from the village of Shelfanger, near Diss, Norfolk. It was renamed in 1909 after John William Logan, railway contractor, who lived at High Hazels while his firm was building additional lines between Darnall and Woodhouse for the Great Central Railway in the 1870s. He seems to have done a bit of farming on the side. His stock, including three horses, four beasts, farming implements, and eighteen tons of straw, was offered for sale in 1876. By the 1890s, Mr Logan was MP for Leicestershire.

Lomas Close, Lea, 6
after the Lomas family who have been prominent in the Stannington area for many years.

London Road, 2
a directional name; it has been the route to London since stage coach days. It was a rough journey for coaches. They crossed Little Sheffield Moor, forded the River Porter, went up a lane to Highfield, branched off to Heeley and Newfield Green at the start of a three, or four-day trip.

Longacre Close, Way, 19
from an old field name.

Longford Close, Crescent, Drive, Road, Spinney, 17
after Nigel de Longford, lord of the manor of Totley (and Dore) at the time of King Henry III. He succeeded to the lordship by marrying an heiress.

Long Henry Street, 2
no longer listed; originally it was called Henry Street (after an ancestor of the Duke of Norfolk) but there was another Henry Street so this one was changed by putting Long in front of it. Although the street has gone the name is preserved in one of the rows at Park Hill Flats.

Long Lane, 6 (Loxley); Long Lane, 6 (Stannington); Long Lane, 10
are all simple descriptive names. Lanes with this name are often straight, which makes them seem longer. Their straightness and their names were usually due to the enclosure commissioners who were fond of laying out straight roads as convenient boundaries between allotments of land, and just as fond of calling them 'Long Lane' (see Long Line).

Longley Close, Crescent, Drive, Lane, 5
from the area known as Longley which is mentioned (as Longlegh) in a document dated 1384. It means long clearing, or field.

Longley Hall Grove, Rise, Road, Way, 5
from the house, Longley Hall, built in the early eighteenth century and bought about 1907 by Sheffield Board of Guardians. When the Guardians were abolished in 1930 the hall passed into Corporation ownership, and the fifty acres of land attached to it were used mostly for housing.

Long Line, 11
was first called Long Lane, but there were so many Long Lanes that some had to be renamed. This one was built during the Dore enclosures of the early nineteenth century (see Long Lane).

Longstone Crescent, 12
from the villages of Great and Little Longstone, Derbyshire, on the edge of the Thornbridge Hall estate owned by Charles Boot at the time his firm built this street (and many others) at Frecheville.

Long Walk, 10
descriptive name; the walk used to be longer than it is now. In the 1880s it stretched from Crookes (the road) to Clough Head and the first part of it was along what is now Stannington View Road.

Lonsdale Road, 6
after Kirkby Lonsdale, Cumbria; one of a small group of streets with Lake District names (with Bowness and Kirkstone).

Loosemore Drive, 12
after Sgt Arnold Loosemore, of Sheffield, who won the Victoria Cross for bravery in 1917. Single-handed and armed with a machine gun, he wiped out a German position and rescued a wounded comrade. On another occasion he won the Distinguished Conduct Medal. Sgt Loosemore died, aged twenty-seven, in 1924.

Lopham Street, 3
was built on the Duke of Norfolk's land and named after the Norfolk villages of North and South Lopham, near Diss.

Lord Street, 2
no longer listed; built on the Duke of Norfolk's land and named after him as lord of the manor.

Lound Road, 9
uncertain; it was built in 1935, and the name may be from a personal name (although I haven't found anybody of this name in the area), or from the old word *lundr*, meaning wood. There was plenty of woodland nearby.

Louth Road, 11
from the Lincolnshire market town of Louth. It was built on land that once belonged to the Younge family. It passed to the Otter family through the marriage of Elizabeth Younge to Francis Otter, of Ranby Hall, Wragby, Lincs. After his death, in July 1875, the estate was inherited by his son, Francis Robert Otter, also of Ranby Hall. It was during his ownership that the land was developed for housing, and several of

the streets that were built were given Lincolnshire names.

Love Lane, Street, 3
probably from one of Sheffield's early steel makers, John Love, who started a works in the West Bar area in 1760 and was in business there till 1801.

Lovell Street, 4
was built on the Duke of Norfolk's land and named after someone in his ancestry. John, the seventh Earl of Arundel, was married in 1428 to Maud, daughter of Robert Lovell.

Lovetot Street, 9
after the Lovetot family who were lords of the manor of Sheffield from 1100 to 1180. The family name came from Louvetot, a small village near Rouen, France.

Lowburn Road, 13
not known; approved February 1934.

Lowedges Crescent, Drive, Place, Road, 8
from an old field name. A twenty-eight acre farm in the area which was run by John Smith in the 1840s had three fields called Bate Low Edge, Lower Bate Low Edge, and Moor Low Edge. The farm itself was called Lowedges Farm. The word low was commonly used in north Derbyshire to mean hill – the fields on the edge of the hill.

Lowfield Avenue, 12
from an old field name.

Lowhouse Road, 5
from an old farm at Shiregreen which was called Low House Farm. In the 1890s Thomas Kirton and William Mott, farmers and dairymen, were listed as living there.

Low Matlock Lane, 6
from the area known as Little Matlock (see High Matlock).

Low Road, 6
descriptive name; the road below Stannington Road.

Lowther Road, 6
not known; built around 1900.

Loxley New Road, Loxley Road, 6
from the area called Loxley which is recorded as Lockeslay or Lokkeslay, in the fourteenth century. It is believed to come from the old English personal name *Locc* and to mean the forest glade belonging to Locc. Loxley New Road was an unimaginative bit of naming for a road that was new in 1899.

Loxley View Road, 10
looks across towards Loxley, or did when it was first built.

Lucas Street, 4
was built in the 1860s for Earl Fitzwilliam and probably named after Thomas Lucas, who was a builder and joiner in nearby Fawcett Street around that time.

Luke Lane, 6
not known; according to the Rev H. Kirk-Smith in his *History of Wadsley*, it was formerly called Pig Street, because of the number of people who kept pigs in the area. The new name may have come from a personal name but in some parts of Yorkshire to luke means to pull up weeds from a field of corn, from an old Icelandic word, *lok*, meaning weed.

Lumley Street, 4 and 9
was built on the Duke of Norfolk's land and named after one of his ancestors, John Lumley (1533-1609) who became Baron Lumley in 1547. He was a friend of the Earl of Arundel and married Jane Fitzalan, the earl's eldest daughter. After his death the title Baron Lumley became extinct.

Luna Croft, 12
not known; possibly from a field name.

Lundwood Close, Drive, Grove, 19
from the area called Lundwood, Barnsley; many of the new streets at Mosborough have been given Yorkshire names.

Lupton Crescent, Drive, Road, Walk, 8
from the Lupton family who lived at Greenhill Hall. John Lupton, a successful farmer, moved into the hall at the beginning of the nineteenth century and he and his family lived there for about thirty years.

Luton Street, 9
was originally called Brook Street. It was renamed in 1886 after the Bedfordshire town of Luton.

Lydgate Hall Crescent, 10
from the house built in the early nineteenth century, once the home of Horatio Bright, later of Daniel Doncaster. The surrounding land was developed in the 1930s, by which time the hall was in use as a boarding house.

Lydgate Lane, 10
a lidgate, or litgate, was a barrier, sometimes a swing-gate, across a road, or a latched gate across a path, designed to allow people through but prevent cattle straying. There was a field called Litgate Field at Crookes. The word, which is not exclusive to this area, is often pronounced lidyet, or lijjit.

Lyminster Road, 6
was built on the Duke of Norfolk's land and named after the Sussex village of Lyminster, near the Duke's estate at Arundel.

Lyndhurst Close, Road, 11
after Lord Lyndhurst, prominent politician around the time the road was built in 1878. He was at various times Attorney General, Lord Chancellor, and Chief Baron of the Exchequer.

Lynmouth Road, 7
after the coastal resort of Lynmouth, Devon – see Barmouth.

Lynn Place, 9
probably from King's Lynn, Norfolk. The Dukes of Norfolk owned land in the King's Lynn area and the seventh Duke was High Steward of Lynn.

Lynton Road, 11
from the Devon coastal resort of Lynton, 14 miles from Barnstaple.

Lyons Close, Road, Street, 4
were built on the Duke of Norfolk's land and named from the marriage of Henry, Earl of Arundel to the youngest daughter of Baron Lyons in 1839. The couple met in Greece. Henry had been sent there to avoid him marrying a Miss Pitt. Disraeli is said to have quipped that the Earl had escaped the Pitt only to fall into the Lyons' mouth.

Lytton Avenue, Crescent, Drive, Road, 5
after Edward George Earle Bulwer-Lytton, later Lord Lytton (1803-1873) the English novelist and playwright; one of a group of streets named after literary figures.

Machon Bank, Nether Edge, was named after a well-known local family.

Machon Bank, Machon Bank Road, 7
from the Machon family, who were landowners in the area for nearly 200 years.

Mackenzie Crescent, 10
not known.

Mackenzie Street, 11
after the Rev Alexander Mackenzie, vicar of St Paul's Church, Sheffield, from 1778 to 1816. He was a very popular man in the town, and at six-feet-four-inches one of the tallest. He lived near this street.

Madehurst Gardens, Rise, Road, View, 2
were built on the Duke of Norfolk's land and named after the village of Madehurst, near the Duke's stately home at Arundel, Sussex.

Magpie Grove, 2
group name – birds (see Curlew Ridge).

Maidstone Road, 6
was originally called Mount Pleasant Road. It was renamed in 1924 to avoid confusion with Mount Pleasant, Sharrow. The new name was from Maidstone, the county town of Kent.

Main Avenue, 17
was built, about 1912, through a field called Main Furlong and took its name from the field.

Main Road, 9
up to the 1870s was part of the Sheffield to Worksop turnpike road, the main road through Darnall. It lost its status, but kept its name, when Staniforth Road was built.

Main Road, Main Street, 12
one was the main road through Ridgeway, the other, originally called Smithy Road (from the old blacksmith's shop), was the main street of Hackenthorpe.

Majuba Street, 6
from the military action at Majuba Hill, Natal, in 1881. A small British force which captured the 7,000ft hill was attacked and defeated early next morning by the Boers. The name comes from the Zulu word meaning hill of doves.

Makin Place, Road, 9
no longer listed; named after William Makin and his sons, steel converters and rollers, who set up their factory nearby about 1820.

Malinda Street, 3
almost certainly after a woman called Malinda, but I don't know who she was. It is listed in the 1838 directory but not in the 1825 directory.

Malin Road, 6
from the area called Malin Bridge, which took its name from a person, probably Malin Stacie who held land in the area in the seventeenth century.

Maltby Street, 9
was originally called Clay Lane. There was another Clay Lane so this was renamed, in 1886, after the village of Maltby, near Rotherham.

Malting Lane, 4
malting is another word for malt house, a place where malt is prepared and stored. Since this lane was very close to both the railway and canal warehouses, the likelihood is that one of the warehouses was a malt house.

Manchester Road, photographed around 1908.

Malton Street, 4
was built on Earl Fitzwilliam's land and named after one of his ancestors who was created Baron Malton in 1728. He later became Thomas, first Marquis of Rockingham. The Fitzwilliams had strong links with the Yorkshire market town of Malton. They owned land there and the sixth Earl was MP for Malton from 1837 to 1841 and again from 1846 to 1847.

Maltravers Close, Crescent, Place, Road, Terrace, Way, 2; Maltravers Street, 4
were built on the Duke of Norfolk's land and took their name from a title held by the Duke, Baron Maltravers.

Malvern Road, 9
not known; it was first shown as a small road off Industry Road in the 1907 directory, and with two houses on it in the 1908 directory; presumably from the Worcestershire beauty spot.

Manchester Road, 6 and 10
directional name; it was part of the old Sheffield to Manchester turnpike road built under an Act of Parliament of 1818 and opened in 1821. Before that the main route to Manchester was through Ringinglow.

Mandeville Street, 9
Vine says it was originally called Meadow Street (from a field name) and that it was renamed in the 1870s. The name Mandeville is a mystery. There was a fourteenth century writer called Sir John Mandeville and there are several place names with Mandeville in them, none of which satisfactorily explains a street name in Darnall.

Manners Street, 3
like surroundings streets, is a link with the Duke of Rutland whose family name is Manners.

Manor Laith Road, 2
from an old farm called Manor Laith Farm which stood on White's Lane. Laith is an old word meaning barn.

Manor Lane, Way, 2
from the old Manor Lodge, built in the early 1500s by George, fourth Earl of Shrewsbury, to provide himself with a new house that was a bit more comfortable than Sheffield Castle. The lodge was part-demolished in 1700s, suffered from vandalism, and became a ruin.

Manor Oaks Close, Place, Road, 2
from a house called Manor Oaks which was the home of William Bradley up to the 1870s. The house was almost certainly named from the fact that Manor Park was originally famous for its oak trees, described glowingly by John Evelyn in his book *Sylva, or Discourse on Forest Trees*, published in 1679.

Manor Park Avenue, Close, Court, Crescent, Drive, Place, Rise, Road, Way, 2
from the old Manor Park Farm, nearby. The farm took its name from the 100-acre park, with its beautiful trees and hundreds of deer, which once surrounded Manor Lodge. It remained parkland until the seventeenth century when many of the trees were felled and it was converted to farmland.

Manor View, 19
not known.

Mansel Avenue, Court, Crescent, Road, 5
after the Rev Edward Mansel, vicar of Ecclesfield from 1693 till his death in 1704. He built a vicarage, since rebuilt, and left sixteen acres of land to his successors on condition that a sermon was preached, or the catechism expounded, every Sunday afternoon from Easter to Michaelmas.

Mansfield Drive, Road, 12
Mansfield Road was part of the old Sheffield to Mansfield turnpike, more often called the Gander Lane turnpike, set up by Act of Parliament in 1779.

Manton Street, 2
was built in the 1840s on the Duke of Norfolk's land and named after Manton, near Worksop, once part of the Duke's extensive estate at Worksop. He owned a large plantation there.

Manvers Road, 6
from Earl Manvers (nearby Thoresby Road is named after the Manvers family seat at Thoresby, near Mansfield). The Nottinghamshire theme was continued in the names of the houses built on the two streets – Sherwood Villas, Welbeck Villas, Ollerton Villas, Gateford Villas, Rufford Villas, etc.

Manvers Road, 19
after Earl Manvers, of the Pierrepont family, who were lords of the manor at Beighton for more than 200 years.

Maplebeck Drive, Road, 9
from the village of Maplebeck, seven miles north west of Newark, Notts.

Maple Croft Crescent, Road, 9;
from an old field name, Maple Croft, recorded in 1630.

Maple Grove, 9
group name – trees (see Alder Lane).

Mappin Street, 1
was first called Charlotte Street, after Princess Charlotte, only child of King

George IV, and wife of King Leopold I of the Belgians. It was renamed in 1922 after Sir Frederick Thorpe Mappin (1821-1910) cutlery manufacturer, town councillor, Town Trustee, Master Cutler (in 1855), Mayor (1877), Freeman (1900), benefactor (Mappin Art Gallery etc.) and moving force behind the foundation of Sheffield University. The university's Mappin Hall is on the street.

Marcham Drive, 19
after Henry de Marcham, a Beighton man who was an English bowman at the Battle of Crecy in 1346. His name is recorded in a Muster Roll made sixteen months after the battle.

March Street, 9
was originally called Brook Street. It was renamed in 1886 after the Cambridgeshire market town of March.

Marchwood Avenue, Drive, Road, 6
three of six streets named after neighbouring villages near Southampton, three after the village of Marchwood, the other three after the village of Ashurst.

Marcus Drive, 3
was built on the Duke of Norfolk's land and named Marcus Smith, who worked for the Duke from 1820 till his death in 1871, latterly as his Sheffield agent.

Marden Road, 7
after the house alongside which it was built in 1905, Marden House, on Sandford Grove Road.

Margaret Street, 1
was built on the Duke of Norfolk's land and named after one of the Duke's ancestors, Lady Margaret Mowbray, daughter of Sir Thomas Mowbray, first Duke of Norfolk in the Mowbray line, and wife of Sir Robert Howard. By their marriage, much of the Mowbray wealth passed to the Howard family.

Margate Drive, Street, 4
Margate Street, built first, was originally called Sharpe Street (after Thomas Sharpe, of Mulberry Street, committee member of Sheffield and Grimesthorpe Freehold Land Society, who built it in the 1870s). It was renamed in 1886 after the Kent resort of Margate.

Margerison Street, 8
was built by Sheffield Brick Company in 1881 and probably named after someone in the building business called Margerison. The trouble is there were several of them. The one involved here was probably either Alfred Margerison, slater and slate merchant, one of a number of Margerisons in the slate business, who also built houses, some of them in the Abbeydale Road area; or Tom Margerison, builder and contractor, listed at Saxon Road in the 1905 directory.

Margetson Crescent, Drive, Road, 5
after James Margetson, Archbishop of Dublin, and then Armagh, in the seventeenth century. He was taken to Ireland as Chaplain by Lord Wentworth, Lord President of the North.

Marion Road, 6
not known; built in the 1890s.

Market Place, 1
probably the least used street name in Sheffield. It is where the market used to be held. The old market cross stood near the top of Angel Street, but by the late eighteenth century, as the town grew, the market was moved to a less busy site. The original charter for the town's markets dates back to 1296.

Market Square, Street, 13
from the butter and egg market held near the village cross at Woodhouse. According to Le Tall, it stopped about 1748.

Markets Road, 9
from the Parkway Wholesale Markets which opened in November 1961 to replace the old Castlefolds wholesale market in the city centre.

Markham Terrace, 8
not known; built about 1890.

Mark Lane, 10
from the Anglo-Saxon word *mearc*, meaning a boundary mark. The boundary between Hallam and Ecclesall was nearby.

Marlborough Road, 10
after John Spencer-Churchill, seventh Duke of Marlborough, who was Lord Lieutenant of Ireland at the time the road was built in the 1870s. The name Marlborough was often used for houses and streets simply because it had a classy aura.

Marlcliffe Road, 6
was originally called Marlborough Road but it duplicated Marlborough Road, 10, and was renamed in 1906. The new

The caption on this postcard says 'Market Place & Angel Street'. Market Place is one of the city's least used street names.

name was contrived to stay as near as possible to the old one.

Marmion Road, 11
one of two streets built around 1905 (the other Huntingtower Road), and both named after works by Sir Walter Scott. *Marmion* was a narrative poem by Scott published in 1808.

Marples Close, Drive, 8
from the earlier Marples Street, no longer listed; the street was named after John Marples, of Wadsley Grove, who was a prominent shareholder in the firm that built the street in the 1880s, Sheffield Brick Co. Ltd (see Aizlewood).

Marriott Lane, Road, 7
Marriott Road, built first, was originally called Wood View Terrace. It was renamed Marriott Lane in 1910, and later became Marriott Road. The name was taken from the wood it viewed, Marriott Wood, thought to have been named after a local person.

Marr Terrace, 10
was originally called Market Place. It was renamed after the village of Marr, near Doncaster, to keep it similar to the old name.

Marsden Lane, 3
was originally called Masdin Lane, after Joshua Masdin, pen, pocket and table knife manufacturer at Brocco Street in the 1840s. It was listed in the directories as Masdin Lane for more than twenty years but some time in the 1870s it became Marsden Lane.

Marshall Road, 8
after William Marshall who had about fifty acres of land in the Woodseats area at the time of the enclosures.

Marsh Close, 19
from the area nearby known as Eckington Marsh.

Marsh House Road, 11
from the old farm sometimes called Marsh Farm, sometimes Marsh House. In the early 1900s Benjamin Roberts was farmer there.

Marsh Lane, 10
after Harry Parker Marsh, for whom it was approved in 1907. Mr Marsh, of Marsh Brothers and Co, Pond Steel Works, was a magistrate, Town Council member, Lord Mayor in 1907, Church Burgress, and secretary of Sheffield Chamber of Commerce.

Marstone Crescent, 17
was built (with Stonecroft Road) in 1934 by Charles Lindley Marcroft, builder, who lived nearby. Marstone and Stonecroft seem to be concoctions of the name Marcroft and the word stone.

Marston Road, 10
from the battle of Marston Moor where Royalist forces were beaten by Cromwell's Parliamentarians in 1644; one of a group of four streets named after British battles (see Bosworth Road).

Martin Crescent, 5
from a field called Martin Pickle (Pickle from the old word *pightel*, meaning enclosure) which was recorded in 1758.

Martin Lane, Street, 6
no longer listed; Martin Street was first called King Street. It was built on land owned by the Addey family. Ownership passed to the Martin family when Miss Addey married Edward Martin, well-known Sheffield surgeon. To avoid confusion with King Street in the town centre, it was renamed, after the Martin family, in 1872.

Mary Street, 1
was built on the Duke of Norfolk's land and named after someone in the Duke's family, probably Mary Charlotte, born 1822, daughter of the thirteenth Duke, and sister of the fourteenth.

Masefield Road, 13
after John Masefield (1878-1967), Poet Laureate. It was called Masefield Avenue when it was approved in February, 1934. In September 1934 it was renamed Masefield Road.

Mason Crescent, 13
after the builders J.C. Mason Ltd, who were involved in house building in the area in the 1930s. Between 1935 and 1938 they built more than 100 houses and shops around Hastilar Road South.

Mason Lathe Road, 5
after the Mason Lathe Farm (lathe meaning barn), which stood nearby. When the farm was offered for sale in 1876 it had twenty-five acres of land including fields called Mason Field, Upper Mason Field, Lower Mason Field and Far Mason Field, all, like the farm itself, thought to have been named after a former owner.

Massey Road, 13
after Thomas Massey, cobbler in Woodhouse in the early 1800s and something of a character. Known as The Woodhouse Rhymer, he was challenged by the local doctor to write a poem about him. Having seen the doctor on his ass, he wrote a poem that started

It happened on a certain day,
I met two asses by the way,
the one like monk, with gorged hide,
upon his brother was forced to ride.

By all accounts the doctor was not amused.

Masters Crescent, Road, 5
after Edgar Lee Masters (1868-1950) American poet, winner of the Mark Twain Medal in 1921; one of a group of streets named after literary figures.

Mather Avenue, Crescent, Drive, Road, Walk, 9
was built on land belonging to the Staniforth family (see Staniforth Road). One of the Staniforth ancestors, Richard Goore (after whom Goore Road was named) married Alice Mather.

Matilda Lane, Street, Way, 1
some accounts say the name comes from Maude de Lovetot, who married Gerard de Furnival about 1198, but the lady was better known as Maud, not Matilda. Matilda Street, which was built first, was on the Duke of Norfolk's land and it was originally called Duke Street – after the Duke himself. It was renamed in 1871. My first feeling was that it was renamed after the Duke's sister, Lady Adeliza Matilda (1829-1904) who married Lord John Manners MP in 1855. I still favour this explanation but some people are convinced that the name came from the *Matilda Tavern* which was built on the street in the 1840s. The tavern is said to have been named after Queen Matilda, wife of William the Conqueror.

Matlock Road, 6
was originally called Wharncliffe Road. It was renamed in 1886 after the Derbyshire town of Matlock.

Matthews Lane, 8
after Matthew Bolton who lived in a cottage at the Backmoor end of the lane in the 1800s. In some early references it appears as Matthew's Lane.

Matthew Street, 3
after James Matthews, penknife manufacturer, who is listed in the 1825 directory at 27 Shalesmoor. Matthew Street was built alongside his house soon after this date.

Maugerhay, 8
there are several theories for this name, recorded as Mackehay in 1573, Makerhay in 1588, and Maggerhay in 1593, but language experts believe it comes from an ancient personal name and means Malger's, or Mauger's enclosure.

Mauncer Crescent, Drive, Lane, 13
from an old Woodhouse field name which appears on a map of 1776 as Monser. In a document of 1684 it is also spelt Mornsall. Fields with names that include morn, or morning, were often eastward-facing.

Maun Way, 5
from the River Maun, Nottinghamshire, which flows through Mansfield and Ollerton; one of a small group of streets named after rivers.

Mawfa Avenue, Crescent, Drive, Lane, Road, Walk, 14
from an old lane in the area called Mawfa, or Morfa, Lane. Addy suggested that it came from the Middle English word *morfen* (meaning moor-fen), and a similar old Welsh word meaning marsh. At the time he was writing in the 1880s, he said the land around the lane was indeed wet and swampy.

Maxey Place, 8
was built by Heeley Central Land Society and named after William Maxey, of Thirlwell Mount. In directories of the 1850s and 1860s, Maxey is described as 'clerk and farmer'. He may also have been involved in the land society.

Maxfield Avenue, 10
after Joshua Maxfield, of J. and J. Maxfield, piercers and stampers, who was an overseer and town councillor for Nether Hallam. He lived for some years at a house called Holly Bank, at the corner of Crookesmoor Road and Northumberland Road, where this street was later built. He died in 1900.

Maxwell Street, Way, 4
were built on the Duke of Norfolk's land and named from the fact that one of the Duke's ancestors, Philip John Canning Howard, married Alice Clare Maxwell, niece of Lord Herries in 1875. There was another, later, link between the two families. The fifteenth Duke's wife, who was Baroness Herries in her own right, was also a Maxwell. Maxwell Way was originally called Writtle Street (from another of the Duke's relatives, Baron Petre of Writtle, Essex). It was renamed at the request of residents.

Mayfield Road, 10
from the nearby Mayfield Valley. Language experts say the name might come from a person called May, from the old word mea, meaning pasture, from the old word maege, meaning maiden, or, most likely of all, from the Maythorn, or hawthorn.

May Road, 6
after Princess May of Teck who was to have married the eldest son of King Edward VII, Albert Victor, Duke of Clarence and Avondale (after whom nearby Clarence and Avondale Roads were named). But the Duke died in 1892 at the age of twenty-eight before the wedding could take place. Money collected by Sheffield ladies for a wedding present was spent instead on a wreath.

May Tree Close, Croft, Lane, 19
May trees are common hawthorn trees also called hedgethorns, whitethorns, or quickthorns. Presumably there were some in the area of these streets.

Meadow Bank Avenue, 7; Road, 11
from an old field name. The avenue was built through Mow Meadow Bank, a field shown on eighteenth century maps.

Meadow Crescent, 19; Meadowcroft Gardens, Glade, Rise, 19
from old field names.

Meadow Gate Lane, 19
was originally called Meadow Gate, meaning the road leading to the meadow. Two nearby fields were called Upper and Nether Meadow Gate Close.

Meadow Grove, Meadow Grove Road, 17
from two fields which stretched down the hill from Totley Hall Lane, one called the Meadow, the other called Far Meadow.

Meadow Hall Road, 9
from an old farm called Meadow Hall, sometimes Mead Hall, built in the seventeenth century. John Marshall was farmer there in 1900.

Meadowhead, Meadowhead Avenue, Close, Drive, 8
Meadowhead, mentioned in Norton parish registers as early as 1699, means the top of the meadow.

Meadow Street, 3
from the old Upperthorpe meadows which covered quite a large area up to the 1790s. The founders of the General (later Royal) Infirmary bought about thirty acres of the meadows in 1792 on which they built their hospital. Land left over was leased out for building.

Meadow Terrace, 11
from an old field name.

Meadow View Road, 8
a variation on Meadowhead.

The Meads, 8; Meadway Drive, The Meadway, 17
were all built on or near former meadow land. Mead is another word for meadow.

Medlock Close, Crescent, Croft, Drive, Road, Way, 13
Medlock Road, the first to carry the name, was originally called Clough Road. But when the Handsworth area came into Sheffield, where there was another Clough Road, it was renamed (in 1924) after the Medlock area of greater Manchester.

Meersbrook Road in Edwardian times.

Meersbrook Avenue, Road, 8
from the stream, the Meers Brook, the name of which means a dividing line or boundary (as in mere stones, or boundary stones). For many years the stream was the boundary between Yorkshire and Derbyshire.

Meersbrook Park Road, 8
from the nearby public park, formerly part of the estate of Meersbrook House, acquired by the Corporation in 1886, made into a park, with additions in 1928 and 1946.

Meetinghouse Lane, 1
from the Quaker meeting house built nearby in 1709, rebuilt in 1739, badly damaged in the 1940 blitz, completely rebuilt on Hartshead in the 1960s and later rebuilt again.

Meetinghouse Lane, 13
from the Quaker meeting house built at Woodhouse about 1660, and rebuilt in 1885.

Melbourne Avenue, 10
after William Lamb, second Viscount Melbourne (1779-1848) Irish Secretary from 1827 to 1828, Home Secretary 1830-35, and Prime Minster 1835-41.

Melbourn Road, 10
appeared in the directories for thirty years as Melbourne Road (which means it was probably named after Viscount Melbourne, above). Some time between 1902 and 1905 it lost its last letter.

Melfort Glen, 10
from Loch Melfort, on the east coast of Strathclyde; one of several streets given Scottish names.

Mellington Close, 8
uncertain; it was named in 1939, possibly after the village of Mellington in the Montgomery district of Powys.

Melrose Road, 3
uncertain; Melrose is a small town on the River Tweed. It does have a remote link with Sheffield. Waltheof, grandson of Waltheof the Saxon lord of Hallamshire, was Abbot of Melrose.

Melton Grove, 19
from the village of High Melton, near Doncaster; one of a group of streets named after places in South Yorkshire.

Melville Road, 9
uncertain; possibly from Melville Castle, former seat of Viscount Melville, on the bank of the River Esk, Midlothian (See Campbell Road).

Mercia Drive, 17
from the Anglo-Saxon kingdom of Mercia (see King Ecgbert Road).

Meredith Road, 6
not known; it appeared first in the 1901 directory.

Merlin Way, 5
was approved in February 1920 along with Ribble, Maun and Calder Ways, and since the other three are all named after rivers, the assumption must be this was too. The only one I can find is a stream called Merlin's Brook, near Haverfordwest. It seems very small though, compared with the others.

Merton Lane, Rise, Road, 9
Merton Lane, built first, was originally called Malthouse Lane, from the malthouse of George Ellis, farmer and maltster at Wincobank in the mid-1800s. It was renamed in 1903, after the Merton district of London.

Methley Close, 12
after John and Ellen Methley who were teachers at Gleadless Endowed School in the 1870s.

Meynell Crescent, Road, 5
after Alice Meynell (1850-1922) English poet, remembered for *The Rhythm of Life*, *The Colour of Life*, and an anthology called *The Flower of the Mind*; one of a group of streets named after literary figures.

Mickley Lane,
from the area called Mickley which is referred to as Mickelee in a thirteenth century document. It means a great clearing.

Middlecliffe Close, Court, Rise, 19
from an old field name. Middle Cliffe Field is mentioned in the Beighton enclosure awards.

Middlefield Close, Croft, 17
from an old field name. Middle Field, one acre, three roods, eighteen perches, was owned in the mid-1800s by John Shearwood and rented by George Thorpe.

Middle Hay Close, Place, Rise, View, 14
from an old Gleadless field name, Middle Hayfield. Two other fields nearby were called Roe Hay and Bottom Hay.

Middleton Street, 9
no longer listed; named after John Middleton, local landowner in the 1860s. He is mentioned in the Town Council minutes and in nineteenth century property advertisements but I know nothing about him. In the late 1920s, some of the property on the street was sold by trustees of the late Charles Middleton, builder and property repairer, who may have been a descendant.

Mickley, the area after which Mickley Lane was named, is recorded in a thirteenth century document.

Middlewood Road, 6

from the name of an old wood. A charter written in 1350 refers to land lying between 'Medel Wodde and the park of Waddesley'.

Midfield Road, 10

the abbreviation of an old field name, Middle Field.

Midhill Road, 2

from the old house called Midhill, because of its situation. In the 1850s and 1860s it was the home of William Renton.

Midhurst Road, 6

was originally called Hurst Road. It was renamed in 1924 and the new name was an attempt to keep some similarity to the old one. Midhurst is a place in Sussex.

Midland Road, 8

from the old Midland Railway which owned extensive land and property at Heeley, most of which was auctioned in 1890.

Midland Street, 1

from the Midland Railway. The company was given planning permission in August 1900 to build fifty-five houses in Clough Road, Shoreham Street, Margaret Street and a new street. This was the new street.

Milburn Court, Grove, 19

from the Milburn Forest, Cumbria; one of a group of streets named after British forests (see Bramshill).

Milden Road, 6

was originally called Miller Road, after George Miller, railway contractor, who helped to build the Manchester, Sheffield and Lincolnshire Railway line. He bought Wadsley House estate in 1851 and lived there till his death in 1884. The name was changed in 1924 and the new name, chosen for its nearness to the old name, came from the village of Milden in Suffolk.

Miles Close, Road, 5

were built on the Duke of Norfolk's land and named after someone called Miles in the Duke's family. He had several relatives of this name, including the eighth Baron Beaumont and the tenth Baron Beaumont. It was probably one of them. The present Duke is also called Miles, but he says the streets were not named after him.

Milford Street, 9

was originally called Fitzwilliam Street, after Earl Fitzwilliam. There was another Fitzwilliam Street so this one was renamed in 1886, apparently after the Welsh seaport of Milford.

Milldale Road, 17

was built near the site of an eighteenth century lead mill which later became a cutler's wheel and later still, a rolling mill. It closed in 1886.

Miller Croft, 13

from the fact that there used to be a windmill nearby. It stood on what was then called Stubbin Lane and is now Stradbroke Road. It was built about 1800 but by the 1860s it had fallen into disrepair.

Miller Road, 7

was built by Sheffield Brick Company. At first I thought perhaps the name was an oblique reference to the other business in which the chairman of the Brick Company, Councillor John Aizlewood, was involved – as head of the Crown Corn Mills. It may have been. But there was a John Miller, plumber and painter in the Abbeydale Road area at the time the road was built and if he was involved in the work, it might have been named after him.

Middlewood Road in the 1930s, with Holme Lane on the right, and a proper, old fashioned ironmonger on the left.

Millhouses Lane, 7 and 11
was a narrow, unnamed track till 1779 when it was set out under the Ecclesall Enclosure Act as a road to be called Millhouses Lane. The name came from the area called Millhouses, which means the houses near the mill. Bits of the old mill can still be seen in Millhouses Park. The old mill pond was filled in when the park was made.

Mill Lane, 3
is near the site of the old town corn mill.

Mill Lane, 17
as Milldale, above.

Millmount Road, 8
was originally called Milner Road after the Milner family who lived at nearby Meersbrook House until the late nineteenth century. To avoid confusion with Milner Road, Attercliffe (named after a member of the same family) it was renamed in 1903 and the new name was chosen for its similar sound to the old one.

Millsands, 3
is where the old town corn mill used to be. There was a mill on the site for more than 800 years. The last one was demolished in the late 1930s.

Millthorpe Road, 5
from the place called Millthorpe, near Holmesfield; one of a group of streets with Derbyshire place names.

Millwood View, 6
the original recommendation was to call it Mill View, because it looked out over several old mill sites in the Loxley Valley. When it reached the council sub committee the name was changed to Mill Wood View, presumably because it also overlooked several wooded areas.

Milner Road, 9
no longer listed; it was named after Gamalial Milner (1747-1825) who was a large landowner in Attercliffe township in the early 1800s and was one of the Twelve Capital Burgesses.

Milnrow Crescent, Drive, Road, View, 5
possibly after the nineteenth-century vicar of Milnrow (a district of Greater Manchester, two miles east of Rochdale), the Rev M.R. Baines, who collaborated with the Rev Alfred Gatty over details of the Scott monument in Ecclesfield church when Gatty was preparing a new edition of *Hunter's Hallamshire*.

Milton Lane, 3; Milton Street, 1 and 3
from the title Viscount Milton held by the Fitzwilliam family, who were lords of the manor of Ecclesall. The title was usually held by the Earl's eldest son.

Milton Road, 7
not known; the road was built in the 1880s for Miss Newbould, daughter of John Newbould, mortgagee of Thomas Steade, the builder. It was one of several roads built for her after Steade went bankrupt.

Minna Road, 3
was built on the Duke of Norfolk's land and named after one of his ancestors, Augusta Mary Minna Catherine, youngest daughter of Baron Lyons of Christchurch, who married the Earl of Arundel in 1839. The Earl later became Duke of Norfolk, and she became Duchess.

Minto Road, 6
was originally called Milner Road after William Pashley Milner, solicitor, who lived at Dykes Hall. It was renamed in 1903, apparently after Gilbert John Murray-Kynynmound-Elliott, fourth Earl of Minto, distinguished soldier, Governor General of Canada, and later Viceroy of India, who died in 1914.

Mitchell Road, 8
not known; built in the late 1870s as part of the Holmhirst estate.

Mitchell Street, 3
after Samuel Mitchell (1773-1828), merchant, Town Trustee and landowner, who lived at Western Bank, and was one of the original promoters of the Sheffield Savings Bank.

Moffatt Road, 2
not known; the name was approved in September 1937. I have checked with a member of the family of the firm which built it and he did not know the origin of the name. There is a place called Moffatt in Scotland.

Molineaux Close, Road, 5
not known; name approved in August 1931.

Molloy Place, Street, 8
after Patrick 'Paddy' Molloy, builder, carter and demolition contractor, who had premises in Hollis Croft and Broad Lane, and built houses at Heeley, Brightside and elsewhere. He and his brother John took over the carting business of their father, James Molloy, after his death. They did the preparatory excavations for the building of the Town Hall. Patrick, who died in 1919, lived for a time in one of his own houses, 17 Molloy Street.

Mona Avenue, Road, 10
uncertain; built about 1884. The name may have something to do with the Mona Loan and Investment Co, the principals of which, William Clague and Christopher Henry Stembridge, both lived nearby. In any event, the name probably came originally from a woman called Mona but I have no idea who she was.

Monckton Road, 5
was originally called Milner Road, but there were four Milner Roads in Sheffield and three, including this one, were renamed in 1903. There were sixty-two roads renamed at the time and some of the new names were arbitrary to say the least. I can't think of a reason for this one unless it was a tribute to Sir John Braddick Monckton, Town Clerk of London from 1873 till his death in 1902 (shortly before the renaming).

Moncrieffe Road, 7
was originally called New Machon Bank Road. It was renamed as being too cumbersome in 1890. The first idea was to call it Bakewell Road, but this was changed to Moncreiffe, from the middle name of Miss Annie Moncreiffe Rundle, who lived at Kenwood for twenty years up to her death in 1922. She was the sister-in-law of George Wostenholm, cutler, the man who developed much of Sharrow and Nether Edge.

Monmouth Street, 3
possibly after the Duke of Monmouth. He led a revolt against James II (whose Catholicism had aroused considerable fear in England) and after his defeat and capture, was executed at Tower Hill in 1685.

Mons Street, 9
was originally called Blucher Street, after Marshal von Blucher, Prussian military commander and ally of Britain at the Battle of Waterloo. In 1919, by which time German names had become

wildly unpopular in Britain, it was renamed after the Belgian town of Mons, where a major battle in August 1914 resulted in heavy British losses.

Montagu Road, 6
no longer listed; named after Montagu George Burgoyne, who owned the land on which it was built. The Burgoyne family were lords of the manor of Owlerton from the late eighteenth century onwards

Montague Street, 11
no longer listed; named after Samuel Montague. Apart from the fact that he applied to the Town Council for permission to build in the area in 1874, I know nothing about him.

Montenay Crescent, Road, 5
from an old field name, Mountenay Croft, recorded in 1698. The field probably got its name from the Mounteney *(sic)* family who were large and influential landowners in Ecclesfield area from the thirteenth to the sixteenth centuries. Thomas, fifth Lord Furnival, lord of Hallamshire, married a member of the family, Joan de Mounteney, in the fourteenth century.

Montfort Drive, 3
from the earlier Montfort Street, no longer listed, which was built on the Duke of Norfolk's land and named from a title now extinct. Margaret, daughter of the second Lord Furnival, lord of the manor of Sheffield, married the third Baron Montfort in the fourteenth century.

Montgomery Avenue, Drive, Road, 7
after James Montgomery (1771-1854), journalist, poet, and hymn writer. He was a friend of George Wostenholm, the cutler who built Kenwood and developed the land around it, including Montgomery Road. Before Kenwood was built the two men were close neighbours at The Mount, Broomhill.

Montgomery Terrace Road, 6
was built in 1852 on land owned by the Infirmary and named after James Montgomery (above) who was a supporter of the Infirmary from its early days and was chairman of its weekly board for twenty-five years. To mark his long connection with the hospital he planted an oak tree in the grounds in 1851.

Montrose Road, 7
a name linked with the Murray family, Dukes of Atholl (see Blair Athol Road). One of the Duke's ancestors married Lady Agnes, daughter of the Earl of Montrose.

Moonshine Lane, 5
from the area called Moonshine which is shown on Greenwood's 1817 map of Yorkshire and is mentioned in the 1849 tithe awards. The origin of the name is a mystery. Although it is more likely to refer to some geographical feature, it is not entirely impossible that it had something to do with illegal liquor. In this sense the word is usually thought to be modern American but it was in use in England in the 1700s and is known to have been used in reference to illicit gin in north Yorkshire in the 1790s.

Montgomery Road, Sheffield, in the early 1930s. The tramway route along the road, from City to Nether Edge, was closed and converted to buses in 1934.

Moorbank Close, Drive, Road, 10
Moorbank Road, built first, was originally called Moorbrook Road. It was renamed in 1924. Moorbank refers to the hillside below Lodge Moor.

Moor Crescent, 19
from Mosborough Moor.

Moorcroft Avenue, Close, Drive, Road, 10
from Lodge Moor.

Moor End Road, 10
from the house called Moor End (at the end of Crookes Moor). From 1863 till 1885 it was the home of Alderman Robert Leader (1809-1885), editor and proprietor of the *Sheffield and Rotherham Independent*. From 1885 to 1899 it was the home of his son, John Daniel Leader (1835-1899), author, historian and journalist. Both men were Town Trustees and magistrates.

Moore Street, 3
appears on the 1832 map and in most early directories as Moor Street, which suggests that it was named after the Little Sheffield Moor. By the 1850s some directories still called it Moor Street and some said Moore Street, but by the 1870s they all called it Moore Street.

The Moor as it was in the 1930s, with St Paul's Church just visible in the distance, the not-long-opened British Home Stores on the right, and trams running down the centre of the road. At that time, The Moor was still a relatively new name for the road.

Moorfields, 3
an abbreviation of Shalesmoor Fields.

Moorgate Avenue, 10
from Moorgate House, Crookesmoor Road. In the 1860s, it was the home of John Wilson Hawksworth JP, of Wilson Hawksworth, Ellison and Co, steelmakers, of Carlisle Works, Carlisle Street East.

Moorland Place, 6
from the area known as Hanmoor.

Moorland View, 10
descriptive; looks towards moorland.

Mooroaks Road 10
from the house called Moor Oaks (another reference to Crookes Moor). In the early 1800s it had more than six acres of land around it. Till his death in 1862 it was the home of George Ronksley. Later, Charles Marsden, paper manufacturer, lived there.

Moorside Close, 19
was built at the side of Mosborough Moor.

Moorsyde Avenue, Crescent, 10
seem to have been named from their nearness to the Bole Hills, which, while they are not strictly moors, are distinctly moorish.

The Moor, 1
was originally called South Street, because it was the main route south out of town. It did not become The Moor until February 1922 (a change imposed because the old name clashed with another South Street in the Park area). The new name came from the fact that in early days the road crossed an open area called Little Sheffield Moor.

Moorthorpe Gardens, Green, Way, 19
from the area of Moorthorpe, near South Elmsall; one of a group of Mosborough streets given Yorkshire names.

Moor Valley, 19
the valley between Birley Moor and Mosborough Moor.

Moor View Drive, Road, 8;
Moor View Terrace, 11
all have views of the Derbyshire moors.

Moorwood Lane, 6
from a wood called Moor Wood, referred to in a document of 1366 as Morwood, and in the 1379 poll tax return as Morewood.

Mordaunt Road, 2
after a lady of doubtful reputation. The road was built on the Duke of Norfolk's land. Henry, seventh Duke of Norfolk, married, in 1677, Lady Mary Mordaunt, daughter and heiress of Henry Mordaunt, Earl of Peterborough. They were later separated and the Duke divorced her in 1700 by Act of Parliament because of her misconduct.

Morgan Avenue, Close, Road, 5
after Lady Morgan (1783-1859) Irish novelist and wife of Sir Charles Morgan, physician. She made her name with her third novel, *The Wild Irish Girl*. One of a group of streets named after literary figures.

Morland Close, Drive, Place, Road, 14
after George Morland (1763-1804) British painter. He painted mostly country subjects, gipsies and farm interiors. In later years he drank excessively and he died in poverty. One of a group of streets named after artists.

Morley Road, 6
was first called Cross Lane. It was

renamed in 1887 after Albert, Earl of Morley, Liberal peer and Under Secretary of State for War from 1880 to 1885. He visited Sheffield and toured Cammell's steelworks.

Morpeth Gardens, Street, 3
from the earlier Morpeth Street, which was named after George William Frederick Howard, Lord Morpeth (1802-1864) MP for the West Riding from 1832 to 1841 and from 1846 to 1848. He attracted 8,000 people to one of his meetings in Sheffield. Lord Morpeth, related to the Duke of Norfolk, became seventh Earl of Carlisle in 1848.

Morrall Road, 5
not known; built in the late 1960s.

Mortimer Street, 1
was built on the Duke of Norfolk's land and named from the fact that one of the Duke's ancestors, Richard, fourth Earl of Arundel, married Phillipa Mortimer, daughter of Edmund, Earl of March, in 1390. Richard was attainted, and executed in 1397.

Mortlake Road, 5
was originally called Melbourne Road, after the place in Derbyshire called Melbourne. It was renamed in 1903 (to avoid confusion with Melbourn Road, 10) after the area of Mortlake, near Richmond, Surrey.

Morton Street, 3
no longer listed; named from Joseph Morton and Son, merchants, stove grate and fender manufacturers, of Bellefield Works, at the corner of Bellefield Street and Fawcett Street. The factory was built about 1853 and was sold by Mortons in 1869.

Mosborough Hall Drive, 19
from the house called Mosborough Hall, built in the fifteenth century, home of the Burton family in the seventeenth century, Joseph Stone, merchant, in the eighteenth century (when it was modernised), the Staniforth family, and in the nineteenth century, of Charles Rotherham, who was born in the village in poor circumstances, and became a wealthy businessman. The house was converted into a hotel in the 1970s.

Mosborough Moor, 19
from the moorland through which the road was built.

Mosborough Parkway, 19
from the area called Mosborough, recorded as Moresborough in the eleventh century and later as Mouresborough, and believed to mean a fortified place on the moor.

Mosborough Road, 13
from the family history of the Parker family of Woodthorpe. John Parker, born 1664, married Mary Staniforth of Mosborough.

Moseley Lane, 1
no longer listed; named after the *Moseley's Arms* public house. In the 1840s, Thomas Moseley ran a public house called the *Old London Apprentice* at 81 West Bar. About 1848 he moved a few doors along to what appears to have been a new house which he named after himself, the *Moseley's Arms*. Some time in the 1850s Levi Ibbotson took it over but kept the old name which is still in use today.

Moses Street, 9
no longer listed; named after Moses Ellis, who owned the land through which the street was built in the late 1860s.

Mossdale Avenue, Moss View, Moss Way, 19; Moss Grove, 12
from the stream, the Moss Brook, which runs through Mosborough.

Moss Road, 17
no longer listed; named from the old bridle road across Totley Moss, moss in this sense meaning flat, marshy ground.

Motehall Drive, Place, Road, Way, 2
like many Manor estate names this one is linked with the history of Eckington Manor. A list of Eckington field names made in 1649 includes a field called the Mote (or Moote) Hall Yard. A mote hall was a place where meetings took place.

Mountain Street, 9
from an old Attercliffe field name. When the field was offered for sale in 1864 it was advertised as Mountainy Field. At that time it produced a tithe rent of fourteen shillings a year.

Mountford Croft, 17
after George Mountford, who made scythes, hay and straw knives, etc, at Totley Forge in the 1850s. He was also tenant of more than thirty acres of land.

Mount Pleasant Road, 7
no longer listed; from the house called Mount Pleasant which was built in 1777 for Francis Hurt Sitwell, who used it as a second residence (his first being at Renishaw). It later became a pauper lunatic asylum, a girls' school, then Government offices. It is now a community centre. Mount Pleasant was a very common English place or house name. Several other areas in and around Sheffield had the same name.

Mount Road, 3
from the hilly terrain at Parkwood Springs.

Mount Street, 11
from the area known as The Mount at Highfield.

Mount View Avenue, Gardens, Road, 8
were built by the Mount View Benefit Building Society in the 1850s. The society and the streets were named from the fact that the site looked across to The Mount at Highfield, and to the house called Mount Pleasant.

Mowbray Street, 3
was built on the Duke of Norfolk's land and named from the fact that one of his ancestors, Sir Robert Howard, married Lady Margaret Mowbray in the fifteenth century.

A.J. Mundella (1825-1897), Liberal MP for Brightside.

Mulberry Street, 1
owes its name to King James I who had the notion, in about 1607, that silkworms should be bred in England. County lieutenants were asked to help, books and instructions on breeding were sent out, and mulberry trees were planted to provide food for the silkworms. The back of High Street used to be gardens so mulberry trees may have been planted there.

Mulehouse Road, 10
is near the route of the old Racker Way, the bridle path from Sheffield to Stannington, along which mules used to carry goods. The assumption is that somewhere nearby there was a mule house, where they were fed and watered.

Mundella Place, 8
after Anthony John Mundella (1825-1897) who was MP for Sheffield from 1868 to 1885, and MP for Brightside from 1885 to 1897. He served as president of the Board of Trade and was a member of the Cabinet. His keenest interests were the poor law, industrial affairs and education.

Murdock Road, 5
not known; name approved March 1938.

Murrayfield Drive, 19
from the famous Scottish Rugby Union ground; one of a group of streets with rugby connections (see Arms Park Drive).

Murray Road, 11
from the Murray family's links with Banner Cross Hall. Lord John Murray, army general and son of the Duke of Atholl, married a grand-daughter of John Bright, owner of the hall. Their daughter married General William Foxlowe, who later assumed his wife's family name, Murray. He had the hall rebuilt, but died before it was finished (see Blair Athol Road).

Musgrave Crescent, Drive, Place, Road, 5
comes from the Duke of Norfolk's ancestry; Thomas Howard, of Corby Castle, married Barbara Musgrave, sister of Sir Christopher Musgrave, in 1720.

Mushroom Lane, 3 and 10
the name came from an old rule in some parts of England which allowed a settler to acquire rights to a piece of land if he built a cottage on it overnight and had smoke coming from the chimney next morning. A cottage built in this way was referred to as Mushroom Hall, on account of its overnight growth. According to a Sheffield Almanack published in the 1850s, the Mushroom Hall near this lane was built by a man called Ben Pinder on the night of 10 April 1789.

Muskoka Avenue, Drive, 11
have names which came originally from the name of a Chippawa Indian chief, Nesqua Ukee, which means 'not easily turned back in battle'. The chief gave his name to the Muskoka district of Ontario, Canada, which is now a well-known tourist area. Two of the men involved in developing the two Sheffield streets, brothers Albert George, and Alfred Christopher Burnett, visited Canada, were impressed by the Muskoka district, and used the name for the new streets when they returned to Sheffield.

Myers Grove Lane, Myers Lane, 6
Harrison's survey of 1637 mentions 'an intacke called Myers (wood and some arable) lying betweene Loxley water and Stannington Wood'. Myers means wet or marshy ground.

Mylnhurst Road, 11
from a house called Mylnhurst, built in the 1870s by Major William Greaves Blake JP, of Stephenson Blake and Co, typefounders of Upper Allen Street. It was later the home of the Walsh family, and in 1933 was converted into a school.

Mylor Road, 11
was built on Greaves-Bagshawe land and seems to have been named from *mylor*, the old Celtic word meaning prince, referring to the family's Scottish ancestry.

Myrtle Road, 2; Myrtle Springs, 12
from the white flowered shrub called the myrtle. Apparently there were some in the area.

Myton Road, 9
was built on land owned by the Staniforth family (see Staniforth Road) and named after the village of Myton-on-Swale, North Yorkshire.

Nairn Street, 10
from the Scottish town of Nairn, on the Moray Firth; one of a group of streets with Scottish names (see Arran Road). Nairn Street was originally part of Bute Street. It was given its own name in 1909.

Napier Street, 11
after Sir Charles Napier (1786-1860), British admiral. The street was built at about the time he died.

Narrow Walk, 10
descriptive name. It is shown on the 1850 Ordnance Survey when the area around it was still fields.

Naseby Street, 9
was originally called School Lane because of the school nearby. It was renamed in 1886, along with two other School Lanes, and the new name was from the village of Naseby in Northamptonshire.

Nathan Close, Drive, Grove, 19
after a nineteenth century resident of Mosborough, Nathan Staton, sicklesmith, who ground his sickles at the Carlton Wheel.

Navan Road, 2
like many Manor estate names, comes from the early history of Eckington. The lord of the manor of Eckington from 1721 to 1733 was James D'Arcy, Baron D'Arcy of Navan, Ireland.

Needham Way, 7
after George William Needham, farmer, who had Carter Knowle Farm around the beginning of the twentieth century.

Neepsend Lane, 3
there is some doubt about the origin of the name Neepsend. It is referred to in a document of 1297 as Nipisend, and is later recorded as Nepeshende. The likeliest explanation seems to be that it means the end of the hill from the old English word *Hnipa*, meaning steep hill.

Neill Road, 11
after James Neill, City Council member from 1901 to 1904, head of James Neill and Co, Composite Steel Works, and Master Cutler in 1923. Mr Neill was co-owner (along with H.H. Hickmott)

of the land on which the road was built in 1899.

Nelson Road, 6
after Admiral Lord Nelson, one of a pair with Wellington Road, named after another British military hero.

Nesfield Way, 5
from the village of Nesfield, near Ilkley.

Nether Edge Road, 7
Nether Edge, meaning lower edge or escarpment, was the name of a farm in the eighteenth century. Two other farms in the area, shown on the 1795 Fairbank map, were called Upper Edge and Edge End. The other two names went out of use but Nether Edge lived on as the name of a district.

Netherfield Road, 10
from an old field name, meaning lower, or bottom field.

Nethergate, 6
gate in this sense means road, the lower, or bottom road, which is what it is.

Nethergreen Road, 11
Nethergreen is referred to in a document of 1771 and again by the enclosure commissioners in 1791. It means the lower green – lower in relation to other greens at Fulwood.

Nether Shire Lane, 5
from the area called Nether Shiregreen, another way of saying lower Shiregreen. It used to be a separate little community in the Southey manor of Ecclesfield township.

Netherthorpe Place, Road, Street, Walk, 3
thorpe meaning a hamlet or settlement, and nether meaning lower, indicating that it was below another hamlet or settlement. In this case the one higher up was called Upperthorpe.

Nettleham Road, 8
from the village of Nettleham, near Lincoln, which is where the Bishops of Lincoln lived for many years. One of a group of streets given Lincolnshire names (see Aisthorpe Road).

Neville Close, Drive, 3
probably from the de Neville family who were lords of the manor of Sheffield for a short time in the fourteenth century.

Newark Street, 9
from the Nottinghamshire market town of Newark.

Newbould Crescent, 19
from an old field name. Newbould Field, recorded in a Mosborough survey of 1798, was probably named after a former owner or tenant. There are several people called Newbould mentioned in the same survey.

Newbould Lane, 10
after William Newbould who owned land in the area. Both The Mount and Wesley College (later King Edward VII School) were built on his land.

Newburn Drive, Road, 9
from an old house, Newburn House, home in the 1890s of Samuel Pope, who is described in directories as a manager.

Newbury Road, 10
from Newbury, near Reading, scene of two Civil War battles, in 1643 and 1644; one of a group of streets named after British battlefields (see Bosworth Road).

Newcastle Street, 1
after Thomas Pelham, Duke of Newcastle, Prime Minister from 1754 to 1756 and again from 1757 to 1762.

New Cross Drive, Walk, Way, 13
from an old field name. A survey of Handsworth and Woodhouse made in 1802 mentions two fields called Lower New Cross and Upper New Cross.

Newent Lane, 10
was originally called New Lane (as which it appears in Harrison's survey in 1637). It was changed to avoid confusion with another New Lane elsewhere and Newent, a market town in Gloucestershire, was simply an adaptation of the old name.

Newfield Crescent, Croft, Lane, 17
from an old field name. The field, which fronted Newfield Lane, was part of Upper Causeway Head Farm. When the farm was offered for sale in 1897, it included 'three closes of land called The New Field' measuring just over twelve acres.

Newfield Farm Close, 14
from the nearby farm which was owned by the Alderson family up to the 1870s, and at that time had more than fifty acres of land.

Newfield Green Road, 2
from the area of land called Newfield Green. It is many years since the field was new. There is a reference dated April 1566 to a court held at Sheffield at which 'Edward Tallilour surrendered a messuage called Newfeld Greene, lying in Heyley to the use of John Calton'.

Newhall Road, 9
from the building called New Hall which was built by John Fell in the 1720s. Said to be a fine, brick mansion, 130 feet long, it was surrounded by meadows and gardens and had a lawn sloping down to the River Don. It changed hands several times and was

Newlyn Road in the early twentieth century, with Derbyshire Lane cemetery visible on the horizon.

pulled down in the 1870s. Newhall Council Schools were built near the site of the hall.

Newington Road, 11
from the village of Newington, near Bawtry (see Everton Road).

Newlands Drive, Grove, Road, 12
from a field name which is mentioned in a survey made in 1798. Newlands, a common English field name, usually indicated an area cleared and converted to pasturage.

Newlyn Place, Road, 8
from the Cornish holiday resort of Newlyn, near Penzance. One story is that it was much favoured by the man who developed the two roads but I don't know if this is true.

Newman Close, Court, Drive, Road, 9
from a family name of the Bardwell family. When Frederick Bardwell paid for the building of St Thomas's church, vicarage and schools at Wincobank in the 1870s, he dedicated the church to his parents, Thomas Newman Bardwell and Martha Bardwell, and to his brother, Thomas Newman Bardwell junior.

Newmarch Street, 9
was built on land owned by Earl Fitzwilliam and named from a title held by the Fitzwilliam ancestors, Baron of Newmarch and Oversley (hence nearby Oversley Street).

Newsham Road, 8
was originally called Fisher Road. It was renamed in 1917 after John George Newsham, of Carrfield Avenue, Meersbrook, who was a member of the old Norton parish council and later, from 1909 to 1922, Conservative member of Sheffield City Council for Heeley ward.

Newstead Avenue, Close, Drive, Grove, Rise, Road, Way, 12
Newstead is a common English name for villages, hamlets, farms, or even individual houses. It means simply new place. The most famous Newstead is the Nottinghamshire village near which stands Newstead Abbey, home of the Byron family.

New Street, 1
a name that quickly becomes out of date, although most towns and cities have one. Gosling's map of 1736 shows only Figtree Lane, but New Street is shown on the Fairbank map of 1777.

New Street, 19
as above, a name that is only accurate for a limited time.

New Street Lane, 2
was named from a nearby street, once called New Street, but renamed Stepney Street in 1886. Although the reason for it had gone, the lane kept its old name.

Newton Lane, 1
after a local property owner in the middle of the nineteenth century, Jonathan Newton.

Niagara Road, 6
from a piece of wild exaggeration. The road, a nearby works, and Sheffield Police sports ground all took their names from a weir across the River Don known locally as the Niagara Falls. It is quite a large weir but it is a long way short of Niagara Falls.

Nicholson Place, Road, 8
after Benjamin Nicholson, of Shoreham Street Works, who died in 1888. He owned land and houses in Nicholson Road, Nicholson Place, and elsewhere in the city, much of it built as an investment. He lived at Nelson Villa, Whirlowdale Road.

Nichols Road, 6
Nichols was a common name in the Stannington-Rivelin area throughout the nineteenth century. The 1865 directory lists Elias Nichols, spring knife manufacturer; John Hives Nichols, farmer and tax collector; John Ward Nichols, farmer and pocket knife maker;

Framed by trees, Newman Road, Wincobank, as it was in 1954. Its name came from the Bardwell family.

Thomas Nichols, blacksmith; and William Nichols, farmer. Likeliest candidate for the origin of the street name is Edward Nichols who was a farmer at Rivelin.

Nidd Road, 9
from the River Nidd which flows from Great Whernside past Pateley Bridge and joins the Ouse north of York. The road was built on Staniforth family land (see Staniforth Road).

Nightingale Street, 9
was built by the Albert Freehold Land Society, and in the absence of anybody called Nightingale connected with the society, the assumption must be that it was given the name Nightingale because it was built near Florence Street. If so, it was a curious thing to do because Florence Street was not named after Florence Nightingale but after the Italian city of Florence. The whole thing became even more complicated in 1906 when Florence Street was renamed Vine Street.

Nile Street, 10
from the Battle of the Nile, 1798, in which British ships commanded by Admiral Nelson attacked and defeated a force of French ships to prevent them supporting Napoleon in Egypt. Out of seventeen French ships, thirteen were sunk. A row of houses near this street was called Nelson Place.

Nodder Road, 13
after the Nodder family who owned land at Woodthorpe. John Nodder (1680-1732) lead merchant, of Woodhouse, also owned lead mines at Hucklow and Eyam, served on the Town Trust and the Church Burgesses. His son, John (1715-1772) was an attorney and Town Trustee.

Noehill Place, Road, 2
from the name of an old cottage at Mosborough called Noehill House; another of the Manor estate names taken from the ancient history of Eckington manor.

Nook End, Nook Lane, 6
from a house called The Nook. It had about two acres of land with it and was the home of George Greaves up to his death around 1901. Nook usually means a corner, or hollow, but according to Addy, in the Sheffield area it meant a cutting on a moor made for cultivation or the building of a house.

The Nook, 10
from an old farmstead nearby called Barber Nook, nook having the same meaning as in Nook End, above. In the 1856 directory, Samuel Gillatt, farmer and cattle dealer, is listed at Barber Nook.

Norborough Road, 9
was built on Earl Fitzwilliam's land and named from a family title. From 1746, the third Earl was allowed to use the title Earl Fitzwilliam of Norborough in the county of Northamptonshire.

Norfolk Lane, 1; Norfolk Road, 2; Row, Street, 1
from the Dukes of Norfolk, lords of the manor and leading landowners in Sheffield from the seventeenth century to modern times. In terms of street names, the extent of the Norfolk land ownership, and of the Norfolk influence, can be gauged by the fact that so many of the streets explained in this book are named after individual Dukes, their wives, or other close relatives, their ancestors, homes, titles, estates elsewhere in the country, and in one case, after a school one of the Dukes attended.

Henry, 15th Duke of Norfolk, first Lord Mayor of Sheffield (in 1897), and the city's first Freeman. During the time he was Duke, from 1860 to 1917, much of his Sheffield land was developed for housing and nearly all the streets built for him were given names associated with the Dukedom.

Norfolk Park Avenue, Drive, Road, 2
from the park owned by the Duke of Norfolk, private for many years, although public access was allowed. The Duke presented the fifty-one acre park to the city in 1909. Norfolk Park Avenue was first called Norfolk Avenue. It was renamed in 1930.

Norgreave Way, 19
from an old field name. It was recorded in the seventeenth century as Norgreaves, and it means the northerly grove or copse.

Normancroft Close, Crescent, Drive, Way, 2
in 1982, when parts of the Manor estate were modernised, the City Council held a competition for new street names. The winning entry (from the council's own housing officials) suggested naming groups of streets after ancient tribes – Celts, Romans, Saxons, etc. These four were named after the Normans.

Normandale Avenue, Road, 6
from an old field name which is shown on a map made in 1760. S.O. Addy in *The Hall of Waltheof*, suggests that it means the dale of the northmen, or Norwegians, indicating the site of a Scandinavian settlement.

Norman Street, 9
not known; the first reference I have found to it is in the Town Council minutes for 1866 when building plans submitted by Earl Fitzwilliam were approved.

Normanton Gardens, 4
from the older Normanton Street, no longer listed, which was built on Earl Fitzwilliam's land and named after the town of Normanton, three miles from Wakefield, which was part of the Badsworth estate inherited by one of the Earl's ancestors, the second Marquis of Rockingham.

Normanton Grove, Hill; Normanton Spring Court, Road, 13
from the area called Normanton Spring. There are several places in Yorkshire and Derbyshire called Normanton and language experts say the name means the settlement of the northmen, or Norwegians, indicating an ancient Scandinavian settlement. The name sometimes appears in old documents as Northmanton.

Norris Road, 6
not known. It was built around 1900.

Norroy Street, 4
was built on the Duke of Norfolk's land and named from the title of one of the officers of the College of Arms, the Norroy King of Arms. At the time the street was built the Duke was head of the College of Arms and his nephew was Norroy King of Arms.

North Church Street, 1
was originally called North Street, which was simply a directional name. It was changed in 1872 to avoid confusion with another North Street. The word church was added because it was the direct route to the parish church from West Bar.

Northcote Avenue, Road, 2
after Sir Stafford Henry Northcote (1818-1887), English politician, successively Secretary for India, Chancellor of the Exchequer, Leader of the House of Commons and Foreign Secretary. In 1885, he became Earl of Iddesleigh. The road was built around the time of his death in January 1887.

Northern Avenue, 2
runs north-south through the Arbourthorne estate.

Northfield Avenue, Road, 10
from an old field name. Harrison's survey of 1637 mentions North Field as being held, together with a tenement and other land, by John Spooner. Northfield Road was originally called Dark Lane. It was renamed in 1893.

North Hill Road, 5
descriptive name.

Northlands Road, 5
from an old field name recorded in a document of 1451 as Notland.

North Quadrant, 5
a quadrant is a quarter of a circle, which is what this is. There are two streets called quadrants at Firth Park, this and nearby West Quadrant.

North Street, 6
a directional name.

Northumberland Road, 10
after Hugh Percy, Duke of Northumberland, MP for Buckingham, Launceston and then Northumberland, Viceroy of Ireland in 1829-30 and Chancellor of Cambridge University. The road, first called Northumberland Street, and much shorter than it is now, was built around the time of the Duke's death in 1847.

Norton Avenue, Lane, 8
from the village of Norton, which means north enclosure or farmstead. It is a common name among English villages. Harold Armitage, in his book *Chantreyland,* said he had counted seventy-six places called Norton and there were probably more.

Norton Church Road, 8
from the church of St James the Great which dates from the twelfth century and contains memorials to members of the Blythe family, two of whom became Bishops, and to Sir Francis Chantrey, the famous sculptor, all of whom were natives of Norton.

Norton Green Close, 8
refers not to the village green as might be expected, but to a bowling green which has been traced back to 1681. The house built adjacent to the green was called Norton Green and was the home of James Addy, father of Sidney Oldall Addy, and later of Sir Nathaniel Creswick.

Norton Hammer Lane, 8
the Hammer part of the name comes from the Old English word *hamm,* meaning land or enclosure beside a river, in this case the River Sheaf.

Norton Lees Close, Crescent, Lane, Road, Square, 8
lees means a clearing, pasture, or meadow. The name Norton Lees goes back to at least the fourteenth century.

Norton Park Avenue, Crescent, Drive, Road, View, 8
from Norton Park, the 150 acres of land that surrounded Norton Hall and was owned by the lord of the manor in former times. Most of the land was bought in 1925 by Councillor (later Alderman) J.G. Graves, the Sheffield benefactor. When he gave the land to the city part of it became Graves Park.

Norwich Row, 2
from the earlier Norwich Street, no longer listed, which was built on the Duke of Norfolk's land and named from the Duke's family connections with the city of Norwich. From 1672 till 1777 the Dukes of Norfolk also held the title Earl of Norwich. They had a palace in the town until 1711, and the fifteenth Duke built the Cathedral church of St John, Norwich.

Norwood Avenue, Close, Drive, Road, 5
Norwood means north wood, which is how it sometimes appears in old documents. The name of the Norwood area of London came about in the same way.

Norwood Grange Drive, 5
from the house called Norwood Grange.

Nottingham Cliff, Street, 3
from the Duke of Norfolk's family history. Charles, second Baron Howard of Effingham, and grandson of the first Duke of Norfolk, was also created Earl of Nottingham in 1597. The title became extinct in 1681.

Nowill Court, Place, 8
probably after Thomas Nowill, Britannia metal spoon manufacturer at Club Gardens, who I suspect was involved with one of the local freehold land societies.

Nunnery Drive, Terrace, 2
from the Nunnery Colliery which used to be nearby. The Nunnery Colliery Co Ltd, owned a number of pits, including one at Handsworth. The company is said to have taken its name from the ancient Benedictine nunnery at Wallingwells, near Woodsetts, which owned land at Handsworth.

Nursery Lane, Street, 3
when Sheffield was little more than a large village, the lord of the manor's nursery gardens were in this area.

Nuttall Place, 2
after Alderman William Nuttall, of Norfolk Road, who came to Sheffield as a young man, set up a flourishing grocery business, and became an overseer, JP and Town Council member. He was an alderman from 1890 till his death in 1912.

Oak Apple Close, 6

one of a group of Stannington streets which – because they were built near Acorn Hill – were given names connected with the oak tree (see Durmast).

Oakbank Court, 17

from the much older name Akley Bank, which is nearby. Akley means oak field.

Oakbrook Court, View, 10; Road, 11

from the stream, the Oak Brook, which runs into the River Porter. When Mark Firth built a house in the area in the 1860s he named it Oakbrook because the stream ran through its grounds. The Prince and Princess of Wales stayed with him at Oakbrook in 1875 when they visited Sheffield for the opening of Firth Park.

Oakdale Road, 7

stands in an area once well-known for its oak trees. One, a landmark for many years, known as the Montgomery Oak (because of a legendary connection with James Montgomery, the poet and journalist) stood at the junction of Oakdale Road and Oak Hill Road. It was cut down in March 1922 because it was becoming dangerous.

Oakes Green, 9

from an old area of open land known as Oakes Green, eight to ten acres in size, and probably named after the Oakes family who were well-known locally. Matthew Oakes, tailor, born about 1625, had five sons, all apprenticed to the cutlery trade, and their decendants were still living in Attercliffe up to the mid nineteenth century.

Oakes Park View, 14

from the area of land called Oakes Park, surrounding the house called the Oakes, home from the late seventeenth century of the Bagshawe family. The house was named from oak trees in the area.

Oakes Street, 9

not known.

Oakham Drive, 3

was built off Rutland Road and named after Oakham, the old county town of Rutland.

Oak Hill Road, 7

see Oakdale Road, above.

Oakholme Road, 10

from the house at Broomhill called Oakholme. In the 1850s it was the home of Thomas Wilson, merchant and manufacturer, of the well-known Sycamore Street firm John Wilson and Son. Most of the land surrounding the house was acquired by Sheffield University.

Oakland Road, 6

one of several streets built by Hillsborough Freehold Land Society and named (with Beechwood Road) on the trees theme. Hawksley Road, named after G.W. Hawksley (see Cannock Street), became part of Oakland Road in 1903.

Oakley Road, 13

was built on the Duke of Norfolk's land and named after the Norfolk village of Oakley, near Diss.

Oak Park, Place, 10; Oak Road, 12

presumably from oak trees in the area.

Oak Road, 19

group name – trees (see Chestnut).

Oaks Fold; Oaks Fold Avenue, Road; Oaks Lane, 5

from the name of an old Shiregreen farm known at various times as Woolley Grange, The Oaks and Oaks Fold, mentioned in a document of 1582.

Oak Street, 8

there was a belt of oak trees nearby. In the 1850s the street was known as Great Oak Street.

Oak Street, 19

group name – trees (see Ash Street).

Oakwood Avenue, 5

from an old Ecclesfield field name.

Oakworth Close, Drive, Grove, View, 19

from the Yorkshire village of Oakworth, near Keighley.

Oborne Street, 3

no longer listed; after Walter Oborne, merchant, who owned land and property in the area. He was chairman of the Don Navigation Co, and agent for Mrs Fell of New Hall.

Occupation Lane, 12

an 'occupation' lane, or road, meant that it was not a turnpike, or a parish road, but was privately owned by the people who had built it for themselves and their tenants. Here, it became a specific name.

Ochre Dyke Close, Lane, 19

from the stream called the Ochre Dyke, which runs from Birley Moor through Beighton to the Rother. It was named from its colour, supposedly caused by deposits of iron oxide in the water.

Odom Court, 2

after Canon William Odom, vicar of St Simon's, Eyre Street, 1879-88, but best remembered as vicar of Heeley from 1888 till his retirement in 1916. He wrote several books about Sheffield including *Hallamshire Worthies,* and *Historic Personages in Sheffield.* His grave is only yards away from this street, in Heeley parish churchyard.

Ogden Place, 8

was built as part of the Douglas Haig Memorial Homes which were opened by Princess Mary in 1929, and named after the Ogden Trust which gave £3,600 towards the cost of the buildings.

Oldale Close, Court, Grove, 13

after a peculiar Woodhouse character, Godfrey Oldale, who died about 1864, the last of an old local family. His wife whitewashed their house once a week, and when she did the ceilings he held the tub on top of his head. She also whitewashed certain parts of the house once a day, coal-tarred her bonnet, black-leaded her husband's shoes daily, and scrubbed him with a brush weekly. When they moved house the whitewash on the walls of their old house was an inch and a half thick.

Old Ecclesall Road, 11

exactly what it is, the old bit of road that was the original route of Ecclesall Road before Moorfoot was redeveloped.

Oldfield Avenue, Close, Grove, Road, Terrace, 6
from a field name. Old Field was recorded in 1423. By the sixteenth century it seems to have had an alternative name, Odamfield.

Old Fulwood Road, 10
the original route of Fulwood Road before it was straightened.

Old Hall Road, 9
was built through the grounds of Attercliffe Hall, a building which dated back to the seventeenth century. It was pulled down in 1868, but part of it, the servants' quarters, survived till the 1930s, then that too was demolished.

Old Hay Gardens, Lane, 17
Old Hay Lane was recorded in 1770 as Ouday Lane which, according to language experts, comes from the ancient words *ald haeg*, meaning old fence or enclosure. The name was also used as a field name and as the name of a stream, the Old Hay Brook.

Old Lane, 19
straightforward descriptive name.

Old Park Avenue, Road, 8
from the Old Park Wood which took its name from the old Beauchief Park, the 200-300 acres of land that surrounded Beauchief Abbey.

Old Retford Road, 13
used to be part of the main road from Sheffield to Worksop and Retford. At first it was called Worksop Road. In February 1924 it was renamed Retford Road (because there was another Worksop Road at Attercliffe), and when a new, wider stretch of road was built, the old section, no longer part of the main road, became Old Retford Road.

Old Street, 2
straightforward descriptive name.

Oldwell Close, 17
from a well which stood in Totley Hall Lane. The stonework of the well was preserved and incorporated as a feature in the wall at the entrance to the close.

Olive Crescent, 12
not known; built in the 1960s.

Olive Grove Road, 2
from a house nearby called Olive Grove, built in 1837.

Olive Road, 19
from the name of the builder's wife.

Oliver Road, 7
not known; approved, December 1934.

Olivers Drive, Mount, 9
were built on land belonging to the Oliver brothers, of the eighty-seven acre High Hazels Farm. They built Olivers Mount in 1933. One of the brothers, Herbert Oliver, was a city councillor.

Olive Terrace, 6
from an old mill nearby called Olive Mill, part of which used to be a paper mill. In 1794 Widow Goodison, Matthew Ibberson, and John Hibbard were partners in the mill. Later it was run by Joshua Woodward. A house nearby was called Olive House. The chances are that the name came from a lady, possibly Widow Goodison.

Olivet Road, 8
was originally called Olivant Road (after a person called Olivant. There was a George Olivant living at Woodseats in the 1890s. It may have been him). It was renamed, for no obvious reason, in the 1890s. An olivet is an oval-shaped imitation pearl. Its choice as a Sheffield street name seems to have been nothing more than an effort to stay as near as possible to the old name.

Omdurman Street, 9
no longer listed; named from the town of Omdurman, Egypt, where, on the second of September 1898, General Kitchener, commanding an Anglo-Egyptian force, defeated the Dervishes, avenging the death of General Gordon and restoring British influence in the area. The street was built soon afterwards.

Onchan Road, 6
from the village of Onchan, near Douglas, Isle of Man; one of a small group of streets named after places in the Isle of Man (with Colby and Laxey).

Onslow Road, 11
not known; plans were approved in 1893 for G.T.W. Newsholme, the well-known chemist.

Orange Street, 1
from the Royal house of Orange which took its name from a town in Holland. Prince William of Orange became King William III of Britain, ruling as joint sovereign with his wife Mary, daughter of King James II.

Orchard Close, Crescent, 5; Orchard Lane, 19
were built on or near orchards.

Orchard Lane, Place, Street, 1
according to old maps the area between Fargate, Church Lane (now Street), and Balm Green, used to be Brelsforth Orchards, or it may have been Brelsworth's, or even Brinsworth's. Nobody is sure of the spelling. Anyway, it was an orchard.

Orchard Road, 6
was built through Orchard Field, one of twenty-one acres of fields owned in the early nineteenth century by Jonathan Haigh, who lived at nearby Walkley Hall at the time.

Ordnance Place, 9
from the nearby Royal Ordnance Factory.

Orgreave Lane, Place, Rise, Road, Way, 13
from the area called Orgreave which was mentioned in Domesday Book as Nortgrave, meaning the pit from which ore was dug.

Oriel Mount, Road, 10
not known; Oriel Road, built first, was approved in 1899 for H.I. Dixon of Stumperlowe Hall and the famous silver firm. There was a house nearby called Oriel House, but I have not been able to sort out if the street was named after the house or vice versa.

Ormond Close, Drive, Road, Way, 8
after John Ormond, sometimes called Urmon, who, by his marriage to Joan Chaworth, became lord of the manor of Norton in the early sixteenth century. The couple had three daughters and through them the lordship passed to the Denhams and the Babingtons.

Orpen Drive, Way, 14
after Sir William Orpen (1878-1931) Dublin-born artist best known as a portrait painter. During the First World War he was an official war artist and many of his war pictures were presented to the nation. One of a group of streets named after artists.

Orphanage Road, 3
from the National Union of Teachers girls' orphanage which was opened at Barnsley Road, Firshill, by Lady Mappin in September 1887. When the Firshill lease ran out the orphanage moved to Page Hall in 1895.

Osberton Place, 11
was approved in 1893 (with Sandbeck Place) for J.Y. Cowlishaw, and named after Osberton Hall, two miles from Worksop, Notts, seat of the Foljambe family.

Osborne Close, Road, 11
after Thomas Osborne, file manufacturer, who bought three fields in the area in the 1830s and built a house which he called Osborne Cottage. The road was made soon after.

Osgathorpe Crescent, Drive, Road, 4
from the area called Osgathorpe, near Firvale, one of the berewicks of the manor of Hallam in Domesday Book. It means the farm belonging to Osga, or Osgar.

Osmaston Road, 8
was originally called Osborne Road after Thomas and George Henry Osborne, file manufacturers and general merchants at Woodseats in the nineteenth century. It was renamed in 1903 after a place called Osmaston in Derbyshire. There are two places with this name, one near Derby, the other near Ashbourne.

Osprey Gardens, 2
group name – birds (see Curlew Ridge).

Oswestry Road, 5
built for the Duke of Norfolk. One of the Duke's ancestors, Thomas, fourteenth Earl of Arundel, was given the title Baron Oswestry.

Otley Walk, 6
from the earlier Otley Street (no longer listed). Otley Street was originally called Cliffe Street. It was changed in 1886 because it was a duplicate name. The new name came from the Yorkshire town of Otley.

Otter Street, 9
not known. Vine says in one of his books that there were otters in the river at Attercliffe in times past. The street was near the River Don originally, but the river was diverted at this point.

Ouseburn Croft, Road, Street, 9
were built on land belonging to the Staniforth family (see Staniforth Road). Ouseburn Street, built first, was originally called Hammerton Street, after the village of Kirk Hammerton on the River Nidd. It was renamed in 1926 after the villages of Great and Little Ouseburn, near York.

Ouse Road, 9
was built on Staniforth land (see Staniforth Road) and named after the River Ouse, formed by the joining of the Ure and the Swale at Boroughbridge. The name Ouse comes from the old Celtic word Usso, meaning water.

Outram Road, 2
after Henry Outram, file manufacturer, of Canal Works, who lived at Beech House, Birkendale. He was Liberal town councillor for Park ward from 1884 till 1890. He died in 1894.

The Oval, 5
retains the name of a feature which stood in the grounds of Brush House, the building which later became Firth Park Grammar School. John Booth, who lived at the house, planted an oval avenue of trees with a path between them. The street of today is the exact shape and size of the oval of trees. The grounds of the house were built on in the 1920s.

Overcroft Rise, 17
from an old Totley field name. Four neighbouring fields were called Barn Croft, Little Croft, Anthony Croft and Over Croft.

Overdale Gardens, Rise, 17
from an old house nearby called Overdale. Up to his death in 1909 it was the home of William Richards, well-known pawnbroker.

Overend Close, Drive, Road, Way, 14
after Mrs Maria Overend who gave more than £15,000 to the Infirmary, £20,000 to the Church Burgesses, and paid for the rebuilding of Tinsley Church. Her husband, William Overend QC, was chairman of the Trade Outrages Commission in 1867.

Oversley Street, 9
was built on Earl Fitzwilliam's land and named from a title held by two of the Earl's ancestors, Thomas Wentworth and William Wentworth. In the seventeenth century both men held the title Baron of Newmarch and Oversley. The title later became extinct.

Overton Road, 6
was originally called Wharncliffe View Road. It was changed in 1906 and the new name was from a village called Overton. There are ten villages called Overton but the inspiration in this case was probably Overton near York.

Owen Close, Place, Walk, 6
after Wilfred Owen (1893-1918) a poet whose work emerged from the First World War when he was a patient in a war hospital with Siegfried Sassoon. One of a group of streets named after literary figures.

Owler Lane, 4
was built in the late nineteenth century and took the name of a much older lane which had been known for many years as The Owlers. Owler is an old name for alder, the tree.

Owlerton Green, 6
from the area of common land called Owlerton Green, shown on old maps within the triangle now formed by Penistone Road, Bradfield Road, and this street.

Owlet Lane, 4
an owlet is a young owl but what its relevance to this lane is I don't know.

Owlings Place, Road, 6
from an old farm in the area called Owling House. In the 1870s the farmer there was Joseph Ashforth. His son, also Joseph, had another farm called Ellenborough House (hence Ellenborough Road).

Owlthorpe Greenway, Lane, Rise, 19
from a small hamlet called Owlthorpe, near Mosborough Moor.

Ox Close Avenue, 17
from a Bradway field name which was in use in the sixteenth century and possibly earlier. There was also an Oxclose Farm.

Oxford Street, 6
was built in the 1840s on land belonging to George Addey, one of a group of streets the names of which seem to have been copied from famous London street names. As well as Oxford Street, there were Bond Street (now gone) and Burlington Street.

Oxspring Bank, 5
after Joseph Edward Oxspring who was the farmer at nearby Wardsend House Farm. Mr Oxspring, who died in 1930, was one of the best known farmers in the city, co-founder, and first secretary, of the Sheffield branch of the NFU.

Oxted Road, 9
was built on land owned by Mrs Alice Barry, daughter of Henry Greaves Walker, a well-known merchant in Sheffield for fifty years. Mrs Barry lived at Oxted, Surrey. She gave some of her land nearby to Sheffield Corporation in May 1898 for use as a recreation ground.

Paddock Crescent, 2
from an old farm nearby called Paddock, or Paddocks Farm. The land around it was built on in the 1930s.

Padley Way, 5
after the places called Nether Padley and Upper Padley, near Hathersage; one of a group of streets given Derbyshire place names.

Page Hall Road, 4
when Thomas Broadbent, merchant and banker, wanted to build a house in 1773 he chose a site called Page Field and called the house he built Page Hall. The house had several owners before it was bought by Mark Firth in 1874. He gave part of the land around it to make Firth Park.

Paget Street, 9
nothing known.

Pagoda Street, 9
from the Pagoda Works of Joseph Whitehead and Co, umbrella rib manufacturers. Pagoda was their trademark. The works were originally in Washford Road. In 1892 the firm moved to the Newhall Road area and named their new factory Pagoda Works. The short street leading to the works took the same name. The firm went into liquidation in 1901 and the premises were sold.

Palgrave Crescent, 5
after Francis Turner Palgrave (1824-1897) poet and critic, Professor of Poetry at Oxford University but best remembered as the editor of *Golden Treasury of English Songs and Lyrics*, first published in 1861.

Palmer Road, 9
not known; approved (with Calvert and Clipstone Roads) for the Greenland Freehold Land Society in 1869. Probably named after someone connected with the society.

Palmerston Road, 10
after Henry John Temple, third Viscount Palmerston (1784-1865), statesman. After being Foreign Secretary and Home Secretary he was Prime Minister from 1855 to 1857 and again from 1859 till his death. He visited Sheffield in 1862.

Palmer Street, 9
after Sir Roundell Palmer (1812-1895), later Lord Selborne, who was Lord Chancellor of England 1872-1874 and 1880-1885, and had three Attercliffe streets named after him, this one, nearby Roundel Street (wrongly spelt) and Selborne Street (see Brett).

Palm Lane, Street, 6
not known; Palm Street is not listed in the 1856 directory but it appears in the 1859 directory.

Paper Mill Road, 5
from the Hallamshire Paper Mills, Ecclesfield, which were set up in 1858 and carried on business till 1907 when they closed. The buildings had previously been used as a cotton mill.

The Parade, 12
parade, meaning a walkway.

Paradise Lane, Square, Street, 1
some time in the 1730s Joseph Broadbent, member of a Sheffield Quaker family and successful businessman, built a row of five houses on Hick Style Field and for reasons known only to him called them Paradise Row. The lane, square and street, built much later, took their names from the houses.

Park Avenue, 10
from nearby Endcliffe Park.

Park Crescent, Lane, 10
from the old Broomhall Park, the land surrounding Broom Hall. In the 1830s the nearest houses to the hall were those on Park Lane, set in open countryside.

Parkers Lane, Road, 10
after William Parker, 'gentleman', who lived at Nelson Place, Glossop Road, in the 1840s and owned three and a half acres of freehold pasture land around Parkers Road. The land was offered for sale in 1845 as 'a most inviting situation for a country residence.'

Parkers Lane, 17
there have been several well-known people called Parker living at Dore, including two vicars, but this lane seems to have been named after Elisha Parker, farmer and post office keeper in the village from the 1860s to the 1890s.

Parkfield Place, 2
was built in 1905 on the site of Park

Field House which had stood since the 1790s. The house took its name from Far Park Field, so named because it was near the southern boundary of the old Sheffield Park.

Park Grange Close, Croft, Drive, Mount, Road, View, 2
from the house called Park Grange, home for many years of the Roberts family, notably Samuel Roberts, partner in a silver-plating firm, pamphleteer, writer, and anti-slave trade campaigner, who moved to the house after his marriage in 1794 and lived there till his death in 1848.

Parkhead Court, Crescent, Road, 11
from the old manorial park held by Sir Robert de Ecclesall in the fourteenth century. The park was extensive and included Ecclesall Woods. Its south western boundary, and highest point, was Park Head.

Park House Lane, 9
from the house called Park House (presumably from Tinsley Park), home in the 1870s of William Brookes, of William Brookes and Son, edge tool manufacturers, Howard Works, Lovetot Road.

Parkin Street, 6
probably after John Parkin, of the firm Blake and Parkin, file, saw, machine knife, railway spring and steel manufacturers, of Meadow Works, Meadow Street. Mr Parkin lived in a villa (and owned property) at Upperthorpe in the 1850s.

Park Road, 6
from nearby Deer Park.

Parkside Lane, 6
from the area known as Parkside, Stannington.

Parkside Road, 6
is alongside Hillsborough Park.

Park Spring Close, Drive, Grove, Place, Way, 2
from the house called Park Spring at East Bank, home in the 1860s of Francis Colley, leather and gutta-percha dealer, and later of Thomas Cole, co-founder of the Cole Brothers store.

Park Square, 2
like Park Hill and the Park district, the name comes from the old Sheffield Park which, in the Middle Ages, covered nearly 2,500 acres, was eight miles in circumference and stretched from the town centre out to Handsworth and Gleadless. It contained hundreds of large oak trees and about 1,200 deer roamed in it.

Parkstone Delph, 12
not known; delph usually indicates a quarry.

Park View Avenue, 19
from a house called Park View, on nearby Rotherham Road. In the 1960s it was the home of J.D. Drabble.

Park View Court, 8
from its nearness to Graves Park.

Residents of Parkside Road had a lot to put up with until the 1950s when Sheffield Wednesday played at home, not least a long line of parked trams waiting to take fans home.

Park View Road, 6
overlooks Hillsborough Park.

Park View Terrace, 9
looks towards Tinsley Park.

Parkway Avenue, Close, Drive, 9
from the Park district (see Park Square).

Parkwood Road, 3; Parkwood Road North, 5
from the wood called Old Park Wood, hardly anything of which remains. While acting as agent for the Duke of Norfolk, Joseph Banks, attorney and Town Trustee, who lived at Shirecliffe Hall, cut a carriageway between Old Park Wood and Cook Wood to make it easier to get his carriage to Sheffield.

Parsley Hay Close, Drive, Road, 13
from the Derbyshire hamlet of Parsley Hay, once a station on the Cromford and High Peak Railway.

Parsonage Close, 19
from the old Mosborough parsonage on nearby South Street.

Parsonage Crescent, Street, 6
were built by Walkley Parsonage Freehold Land Society, so named because the site was near the vicarage in Walkley Road. The man behind the society, accountant Walter Sissons, also lived in Walkley Road. The vicar at the time, the Rev Thomas Smith (vicar from 1869 to 1901) was a character. He once read his own obituary notice in a local newspaper, congratulated the editor on what it said, then next day preached a sermon from the text: 'Can these dry bones live?'

Parson Cross Road, 6
Parson's Crosse Lane is mentioned in Harrison's survey of 1637, but the origin of the name is a mystery.

Partridge View, 2
group name – birds (see Curlew Ridge).

Passhouses Road, 4
after a small group of cottages known as Pass Houses, from their owner, William Pass, colliery owner, who lived at the house called Pitsmoor Abbey (see Abbeyfield).

Paternoster Row, 1
a mystery; it may be a copy of Paternoster Row, London, (the street

where rosaries were made). There is no evidence that rosaries were ever made in the area of the Sheffield street.

Patmore Road, 5
after Coventry Kearsey Deighton Patmore (1823-1896), English poet and critic who was librarian at the British Museum from 1847 to 1868. Originally Patmore Street, it was changed to Patmore Road in 1926.

Paulet Road, 2
no longer listed; it was named after Sir Amyas Paulet (sometimes spelt Amias Poulet), harsh, intolerant puritan, who was appointed Keeper of Mary Queen of Scots during her imprisonment in England and kept the post till her death. He had previously been English Ambassador to France.

Pawson Place, 7
after Henry Pawson, co-founder (with Joseph Brailsford) of the once-famous Pawson and Brailsford business and trustee of the Mount Pleasant Land Society which built this street and others nearby.

Paxton Court, 12
was built by a solar heating co-operative and named after Sir Joseph Paxton (see below), pioneer of the use of solar energy.

Paxton Lane, 10
from Sir Joseph Paxton's links with the nearby Botanical Gardens. For many years it was believed that Paxton, designer of the Crystal Palace, had designed the glass pavilions in the gardens. In fact they were designed by B.B. Taylor in the Paxton style and Sir Joseph was chairman of the committee which judged the submitted designs.

Payler Close, 2
after Nathaniel Payler who was lord of the manor of Eckington from 1738 to 1749; one of many Manor Estate streets named from the ancient history of Eckington.

Paythorne Avenue, 8
no longer listed; it was named after the village of Paythorne, Ribblesdale, and became part of Warminster Road in 1935.

Peakdale Crescent, 12
from the hamlet of Peak Dale, near Buxton; one of a group of streets given Derbyshire names.

Pearce Road, Walk, 9
not known; Pearce Road appears in early directories as Pearse Road. It was built in the 1890s.

Pearson Place, 8
after the Rev Henry Pearson, vicar of Norton from 1812 to 1844 and his son, the Rev Henry Hollingworth Pearson who succeeded his father and was vicar from 1844 to 1888.

Pear Street, 11
one of two streets built off Ecclesall Road in the nineteenth century, both named after fruit. The other, Plum Street, was renamed Plumpton Street in 1872.

Pear Tree Road, 5
from an old field name; Peare Tree Field, described as eleven acres of pasture, is included in Harrison's survey of 1637 among lands held by Richard Burrowes, gentleman, of Shirtcliffe Hall Farm.

Pedley Avenue, Close, Drive, Grove, 19
after John Pedley, who was one of the trustees of the turnpike road at Mosborough in the late eighteenth century.

Peel Street, Terrace, 10
after Sir Robert Peel (1788-1850), Lancashire-born statesman, who, as Home Secretary, set up the police force and was later Prime Minister three times, in 1834, 1839 and 1841.

Pelham Street, 9
possibly a link (like other Attercliffe street names) with the Howards of Effingham, one of whom, Francis Howard, married Philadelphia Pelham in 1673. She was the daughter of Sir Thomas Pelham of Laughton, Sussex.

Pembrey Court, 19
from the Pembrey Forest, Dyfed; one of a group of streets named after British forests (see Ashdown Gardens).

Pembroke Street, 11
not known; the earliest lease I have come across on the street is 1848.

Pendeen Road, 11
from the Cornish village of Pendeen.

Penistone Road, 6
a directional name, the road to Penistone. The name Penistone means the town on the pen, or hill. At 700 ft above sea level it is said to be the highest market town in England.

Penley Street, 11
not known; it was built in the 1880s. There is a village called Penley in Clwyd, three miles east of Overton. It may be from that.

Penns Road, 2
not known; built about 1870.

Penny Lane, 17
the word penny occurs quite often in English place and field names – Penny Hill, Penny Croft, Penny Piece etc. It usually indicates that in ancient times the land referred to produced a rent of one penny.

Penrhyn Road, 11
from a house called Penrhyn Villa which was built on Psalter Lane in the early 1870s. It was the home of Joseph Waterhouse Goodwin, accountant and estate agent, who had offices in Church Street. Penryhn is a slate quarrying district of Clwyd. There is also a village called Penrhyn in Anglesey.

Penrith Close, Crescent, Road, 5
from a title held by a branch of the Duke of Norfolk's family. Sir Esme William Howard, son of Henry Howard of Greystoke, Cumberland, was created Baron Howard of Penrith in 1930.

Penrose Place, 13
was named in 1922 at the same committee meeting as nearby Corwen Place. Corwen comes from the Welsh village of that name and it seems likely that Penrose is an Anglicised version of another Welsh place name, Penrhos. There are four places in Wales with this name.

Penthorpe Close, 12
after Thomas Penthorpe (1806-1849), Sheffield Chartist and associate of Samuel Holberry, who died in poverty in the workhouse.

Pentland Gardens, 19
from the Pentland Hills in Scotland; one of a group of streets named after British hills (see Blackdown Avenue).

Penton Street, 1
nothing known.

Percy Street, 3
from the Duke of Rutland's family history. One of the Duke's ancestors, Mary, daughter of Viscount Canterbury, married Hugh Percy, Bishop of Carlisle, in the early nineteenth century.

Perigree Road, 8
from the old wood called Perigree Wood, the name of which comes from an old family called Perigoe who lived nearby. A Fairbank map of 1778 shows land held by Edward Perigoe.

Periwood Lane, 8
an abbreviation of Perigree Wood, above.

Perkyn Road, Terrace, 5
probably after John Perkyn who lived at Ecclesfield in the sixteenth century. His name appears in a list of Ecclesfield feoffees of 1534.

Peterborough Close, Drive, Road, 10
from Peterborough Cathedral; one of a group of streets named after churches (along with Rochester, St Albans, Westminster, Winchester and Worcester).

Petre Drive, Street, 4
were built on the Duke of Norfolk's land and named after a relative of his, Lord Petre, who was a trustee of the Duke's estate. The Petre family and the Duke's family, both strongly Roman Catholic, were linked by marriage in the eighteenth century.

Petworth Drive, 11
from Petworth House, the Sussex stately home, formerly owned by Lord Leconfield. He gave it to the National Trust in 1947. One of a group of streets named after stately houses.

Peveril Road, 11
built in the 1890s. Peveril is the name of a well-known castle at Castleton, and of the principal character in Scott's novel, *Peveril of the Peak*. The street name is possibly something to do with the Bagshawe family of Banner Cross Hall, who had close links with the Peak District.

Pexton Road, 4
one of a group of six roads the names of which seem to have been chosen primarily because they all end in the letters 'ton' (see Blayton).

Pinstone Street as it looked around 1913.

Phillimore Road, 9
was built in 1898 for Frederick Uttley Laycock, who owned property in the area. Mr Laycock was a solicitor and named the road after a famous legal family – Joseph Phillimore, advocate, Professor of Civil Law, and MP, and his sons, Sir Robert Joseph Phillimore, judge and expert on ecclesiastical law, and John George Phillimore, jurist and MP.

Phillips Road, 6
after Miss Fanny Payne Phillips and Miss Mary Payne Phillips, who, together with Mrs Henrietta Harrison, of Boroughbridge, gave seventy-five acres of Loxley Common to Sheffield Corporation in 1912. They were relatives of Dr Henry Payne who lived at Loxley House for many years up to his death in 1895.

Phoenix Road, 12
from an old public house nearby called the *Phoenix*.

Pickering Road, 3
was originally called Prospect Road. It was renamed in 1872 after Joseph Pickering, polishing paste manufacturer, who served on the Town Council from 1871 to 1873 and was connected with the Parkwood Springs Land Society which built this road and others nearby.

Pickering Street, 9
was originally called Pickering Road. It was named after Charles Pickering who kept a beerhouse in Clifton Street, Carbrook, in the 1870s and built houses, some in Pickering Street and some in Clifton Street.

Pickmere Road, 10
not known; it was approved for trustees of the late John Tasker in 1895. Pickmere is the name of a village in Cheshire, and Pick Mere is a lake near the village.

Pilgrim Street, 3
was built in the 1890s on the Duke of Norfolk's land and possibly named from the fact that the Duke made a pilgrimage to the Holy Land in April 1890.

Pinfold Lane, 3; Pinfold Street, 1
a pinfold, from the old word *pindan*, to shut in, was a cattlepen. In Sheffield, a man called the pinder, elected by the Court Leet, had the task of rounding up stray cattle and putting them in the pinfold till the owners turned up and paid a small fee for their release. The remains of the old pound at the end of Pinfold Lane were not removed till the late 1930s.

Pingle Avenue, Road, 7
from an old field name. A pingle was a small field, from the Middle English word *pingel*. Up to the early 1900s there was also a Pingle Head Farm in Millhouses Lane.

Pinner Road, 11

from the place called Pinner in Middlesex. The road was built for the Wilson family, one of whom, Louisa Ellen Wilson, married the Rev Albert Augustus Harland. Mr Harland was curate of Ecclesall for a time. He later served fifty years as vicar of Harefield, Middlesex, hence the appearance of several Middlesex names among streets built for the family in this area.

Pinstone Street, 1

started as Pincher Croft Lane (from a field name), then became Pinson Street, and at some time changed to Pinstone Street. Nobody knows quite why.

Piper Close, Crescent, Road, 5

from a seventeenth century house nearby called Piper House. S.O. Addy said the name probably came from one of the paid pipers who were employed to call out the hours of the night, rather than from a local surname.

Pipworth Road, 2

no longer listed; like many Manor Estate names it was borrowed from the history of Eckington, where there was (and still is) a Pipworth Lane and a field called Pipworth Tongue Head.

Pisgah House Road, 10

from a house called Pisgah House at Crookesmoor, once the home of John Jobson Smith JP, stove grate manufacturer. In the nineteenth century part of Crookesmoor was known as Mount Pisgah, possibly because it overlooked Sheffield. Mount Pisgah, east of Jordan, was the site from which Moses looked over the promised land.

Pitchford Lane, 10

from Pitchford's Farm, the only building shown in the area on a Fairbank map made in 1791. It was farmed in the late eighteenth century by John Pitchford, and later by his grandchildren. The lane led to the farm.

Pit Lane, 12

there were several pits in the Intake area in the nineteenth century and this lane led to one of them, Woodthorpe Colliery.

Pitsmoor Road, 3

from the area called Pitsmoor which is recorded in early documents as Orepitts, and means the place where ore was dug.

Pitt Close, Lane, 1

after William Pitt (1759-1806), MP for Appleby 1781, Chancellor of the Exchequer 1782, Prime Minister from 1783 to 1801 and again from 1804 till his death.

Plantation Road, 8

was built through a plantation called Lady's Spring Wood, owned in the early nineteenth century by Sheffield Church Burgesses.

Plantin Rise, The Plantin, 19

from an area of land nearby known as The Plantin. According to the *English Dialect Dictionary*, in Yorkshire and Derbyshire, the word plantin meant a plantation or coppice.

Platt Street, 3

not known. Originally called Summer Street; renamed, 1872.

Platts Drive, 19

after William Platts who was elected chairman of Beighton parish council at its first meeting on 4 December 1894.

Pleasant Close, Road, 12

were built in the 1930s. The name seems to have been an effort to give them an attractive sounding name.

Plover Court, 2

group name – birds (see Curlew Ridge).

Plowright Close, Drive, Mount, Way, 14

not known; names approved August 1959.

Plumbley Hall Road; Plumbley Lane; Plumbley Wood Lane, 19

early documents refer to the area as Plumleg but by the fourteenth century it had become Plumley. It means plum tree clearing. Plumley Lane is recorded in 1794. Plumbley Hall Road is from Plumbley Hall Farm. In the 1840s, when Joseph Drabble was farmer there it had 116 acres.

Plum Lane, 3

was originally called Pear Street, as which, it was unofficially closed in 1855. A local timber merchant who owned land on both sides of the street closed it at each end. Local newspapers reported that he had 'stolen' the street. Sheffield Highway Board called on him to explain his action and reopen the street. He did. He said he thought he owned it. The name was changed in

Pitsmoor Road, on the right, and the old Pitsmoor Toll Bar at the junction with Burngreave Road. The postcard was issued in the early 1900s, but I suspect it is a copy of a much earlier photograph because the toll bar gates are still in position.

1872 because there was another Pear Street, and for the new name one fruit was substituted for another.

Plumpers Road, 9
from the old *Plumpers Inn*, later rebuilt and called the *Plumpers Hotel*. Plumpers were people who, acting as a group, cast all their votes in an election for one candidate. In 1807 the voters of Tinsley were plumpers. They cast all their votes for Lord Milton, son of Earl Fitzwilliam, which is how the inn and the road, both built on Fitzwilliam land, got their names.

Plumpton Street, 11
no longer listed. It was originally called Plum Street. It changed to Plumpton in 1872 to avoid confusion with another street. Plumpton means plum orchard.

Plum Street, 3
from Plum Lane, above.

Plymouth Road, 7
one of a group of streets the names of which seem to have been chosen because they were all places ending with 'mouth' (see Barmouth).

Polka Court, 3
from the earlier Polka Street, no longer listed, the origin of which is not known.

Pollard Avenue, Crescent, Road, 5
after a former tenant of the land, John Pollard, cowkeeper, who also had a farmhouse nearby, owned by William Vickers.

Pomona Street, 11
from the *Pomona Inn* which was once the centre of a pleasure ground known as the Pomona Gardens. An 1852 advertisement described them as 'the largest public gardens in Sheffield' with 'a splendid collection of evergreen and flowering shrubs, musical meetings every Monday, Wednesday and Friday nights, tea and dinner parties, and a choice stock of wines, spirits and bitter beer'. The gardens, and the inn, took their name from Pomona, Italian goddess of fruit and gardens.

Pond Close, Road, 6
from an old farm nearby, Pond Farm, on the opposite side of Stannington Road.

Pond Hill, Street, 1
there were several ponds and water wheels in the area from the sixteenth century to the nineteenth. On the 1771 Fairbank map of Sheffield one of the ponds is called Mill Dam and another Forge Dam.

Poole Place, Road, 9
throughout the 1880s the directories call it Pool Road and it seems to have taken its name from Pool House, which was the home of Isaac Heward, pruning shear manufacturer. Even after the road was shown as Poole Road, the house was still shown in later directories as Pool House. My guess is that there was a pool somewhere near.

Pool Square, 1
from Barkers Pool.

Poplar Avenue, 19
group name – trees (see Chestnut Avenue).

Popple Street, 4
after Abraham Popple, builder and contractor in the late nineteenth century. He lived in Janson Street and built houses and shops in Page Hall Road, Owler Lane and Popple Street.

Porter Brook View, 11
overlooks the River Porter. S.O. Addy said the river name came from the old Icelandic word *parta*, or *partera*, meaning to part or divide. Another theory is that it came from a local surname.

Porter Lane, 1; Porter Terrace, 11
from the River Porter, above. Porter Lane is recorded in the 1600s.

Portland Lane, 1
after William Henry Cavendish Bentinck, Duke of Portland, Prime Minister 1783, Home Secretary 1794 to 1801, and Prime Minister again from 1807 to 1809.

Portland Road, 19
not known.

Portland Street, Walk, 6
seems to have no local significance. Portland was an up-market name in Victorian times, for streets, houses, and pubs, partly through Portland Place, London, which was built in the 1770s, but mostly through association with the Duke of Portland.

Portobello, Portobello Lane, Street, 1
from Porto Bello, a village in the Caribbean named by Columbus in 1502. It means beautiful harbour. Porto Bello was the scene of a famous British naval action. Sir Francis Drake was buried at sea off Porto Bello Bay.

Portsea Road, 6
was built by a freehold land society and originally called Providence Road, a name much favoured by land societies for its implications of prudence and foresight. It was changed in 1903 to avoid confusion with Providence Road, Walkley (also built by a land society)

The Pomona Hotel, Ecclesall Road, before it was rebuilt. It was named, like Pomona Street, after the Italian goddess of fruit and gardens.

and the new name was from the place called Portsea, near Portsmouth.

Powell Street, 3
after the man who built the first few houses in the street, James Powell, builder and bricklayer, who had premises in nearby Mitchell Street. He must have been pleased with the houses. He moved into one of them himself. By the 1870s Mr Powell owned property all over the area. It was offered for sale in 1883 after his death.

Powley Road, 6
not known; name approved 1938.

Poynton Wood Crescent, Glade, 17
from the nearby Poynton Wood, thought to have been named after a person, possibly John Poynton who lived in the area in the sixteenth century.

Prescott Road, 6
was originally called Townhead Road. It was renamed in February 1922. The new name may have been an arbitrary choice after a place called Prescott (there are three), or it may have been a belated tribute to R.M. Prescott, Town Clerk of Sheffield from 1907 to 1913.

Preston Street, 8
after George Henry Preston, joiner and builder, of Langdon Street, who built thirty-seven houses in Preston Street and Chippinghouse Road in the 1880s.

Prestwich Street, 9
was originally called Princess Street, probably for the same reason as Princess Street, Attercliffe. Because it duplicated the Attercliffe name it was renamed in 1903 from the place called Prestwich, Lancashire, a random choice.

Priestley Street, 2
after Harvey Priestley, landlord of the *Truro Tavern* in the nineteenth century. He owned a nearby field called Priestley's Field on which the local football team played its matches.

Primrose Avenue, 5
group name – flowers (see Acacia).

Primrose Crescent, 19
group name – flowers (see Aster).

Primrose Hill, 6
was built in the 1890s for M.G. Burgoyne, well-known local landowner. Presumably there were primroses in the area at one time.

Primrose View, 8
from Primrose Meadows, once an open rural area around the River Sheaf. Parts of the meadows were tipped and built on. Heeley Baths, neighbouring houses and factories were all built on what used to be the meadows.

Traffic congestion at the top of Prince of Wales Road, on the left, has not changed a great deal since the 1950s, though the trams have rather altered.

Prince of Wales Road, 2 and 9
was built with the help of a £60,000 Government grant for unemployment relief, named – with his permission – after the Prince of Wales (later Duke of Windsor) and officially opened by Sir Henry Maybury, Director General of Roads, in October 1921. The Darnall end of the road was originally called Owlergreave Road, from a field name, Owler Greave, meaning alder field.

Princess Court, 2
was built off Prince of Wales Road and named by association, after the Princess of Wales.

Princess Street, 4
was built on the Duke of Norfolk's land and named after one of his ancestors, Princess Anne, fifth daughter of King Edward IV, who married Thomas, third Duke of Norfolk at the end of the fifteenth century. She died in 1511, leaving no children, and the Duke married as his second wife Elizabeth Stafford, daughter of the Duke of Buckingham.

Priory Avenue, Place, Road, Terrace, 7
from a farm called Priory Farm, probably owned at one time by the Priors of Worksop. The farm stood till about 1860, but its fields, called Priory Fields, remained till some years later.

Proctor Place, 6
probably after Edward Proctor, mason, builder and contractor in Hillsborough area in the 1870s. He lived at Burrowlee.

Prospect Court, Drive, Place, Road, 17; Prospect Road, 2
were all built on sites which commanded good views. Because of Sheffield's hills a good many building sites had commanding views so Prospect was a popular nineteenth century street name. In addition to these, there were Prospect Roads at Parkwood Springs (later renamed Pickering Road), Walkley (later renamed Fulton Road), and Crookesmoor (later renamed Redcar Road). Prospect Road, 17, was first called Bradway Bank. It was renamed in 1937.

Providence Road, 6
providence, like industry and freedom, was one of the idealistic names often used by freehold land societies when

Psalter Lane, when the roadside trees were much smaller and there were fewer vehicles on the road.

they built their houses and streets. This particular road was built by the Rivelin View Freehold Land Society in the 1860s.

Psalter Court, Lane, 11

like Saltergate, Chesterfield, it was the route by which salt came into town. S.O. Addy said that the initial letter P was a vulgar affectation added later and had no significance. Stories of monks walking along the road singing hymns were romantic nonsense, he said.

Purbeck Court, Grove, Road, 19

from the Purbeck Hills, Dorset; one of a group of streets named after hills (see Blackdown).

Pye Bank Close, Drive, Road, 3

Harrison's survey of 1637 mentions 'a meadow called Pigh Hill' in this area. Pigh is the old Middle English word meaning a small enclosure or croft. By the time of Gosling's map in 1736, Pigh Hill had become Pye Bank.

The Quadrant, 17

from its shape, although strictly speaking a quadrant is a quarter of a circle, and this isn't.

Quail Rise, 2

group name – birds (see Curlew Ridge).

Quarry Hill, 19; Quarry Lane, 11; Quarry Road, 13; Quarry Road, 17; Quarry Vale Grove, Road, 12

were all built near old quarries.

Queen Mary Close, Crescent, Road 2

after Mary Queen of Scots who was imprisoned in Sheffield from 1570 to 1584. Nearly one-third of her life was spent under guard in Sheffield. She was executed at Fotheringay Castle, Northamptonshire, at the age of forty-three.

Queen's Road, 2; Queen's Road, 19; Queen's Row, 3; Queen Street 1; Queen Street, 19

one of the commonest of all English street names. Most of them were in honour of Queen Victoria who reigned from 1837 to 1901 and who probably had more stations, parks, hotels, public houses, halls, towns, cities, waterfalls, medals, embankments – and streets – named after her than any other person in British history. Queen Street, 1, is an exception. It is listed in the 1797 directory so it was obviously named after an

These old properties at Pyebank were demolished for redevelopment in 1906. They had been marked with white crosses when this picture was taken.

earlier queen, probably Queen Charlotte, wife of King George III.

Queen Victoria Road, 17
no doubt about this one. After Queen Victoria, as mentioned above. It was originally called Victoria Road. Renamed in 1935.

Quiet Lane, 10
was originally called Carr Lane, like nearby Carr Bridge, from the old word meaning marshy land. But there were at least five other Carr Lanes, and this was one of several to be renamed.

Local historian T. Walter Hall regretted the new name. It was doomed to be a misnomer, he said. He suggested it should be called Jowett Hill, which would preserve an ancient Hallamshire place name, but his idea was not accepted and it became Quiet Lane, a descriptive but not particularly significant name.

The new section of Retford Road, between Handsworth and Woodhouse Mill, soon after it opened in the 1920s. The old route went – and still goes – off to the right. There are fewer trees and more buildings in the area today. Retford Road was originally called Worksop Road.

R

Raby Street, 9
was built on Earl Fitzwilliam's land and named from a title held by the Earl's ancestors, Baron Raby. Raby is a place in Durham.

Racker Way, 6
from an ancient pack horse track called the Racker Way which went through this area. It was mentioned in a thirteenth century deed and its name came from the Old English word *hraca*, meaning a narrow hill path.

Radford Street, 3
was built across land owned by the Church Burgesses and named after the Rev Thomas Radford who was minister at St Paul's Church from 1775 to 1788 and the first minister of St James's Church from 1788 till his death in 1816. He was also chairman of the Infirmary Board from 1810 to 1815.

Radnor Close, 19
from the Radnor Forest in Wales; one of a group of streets named after British forests (see Ashdown).

Raeburn Close, Place, Road, Way, 14
after Sir Henry Raeburn (1756-1823) Scottish portrait painter. He taught himself to paint and married Countess Leslie after painting a portrait of her. He was a member of the Royal Academy and was knighted in 1822. One of a group of streets named after artists (see Constable).

Rails Road, 6
from an old field name. Rails Field is shown in a Fairbank map made in the 1770s.

Railway Street, 3
no longer listed; it was off Rock Street, Pitsmoor. It was named from its nearness to the Sheffield-Woodhead-Manchester railway line.

Rainbow Avenue, Close, Crescent, Drive, Grove, Place, Road, Walk, Way, 12
from the Rainbow Forge which was built on the Shire Brook near Hackenthorpe by George Sheppard about 1800. It was one of several waterwheels on the stream, mostly making scythes and sickles.

Raisen Hall Place, Road, 5
from a seventeenth century house called Raisen Hall which took its name from Thomas Raysin, son of John Raysin. In old documents it appears as Raysin, Rayson, and Reason Hall. In later years the Denton family lived at the hall for six generations.

Raleigh Road, 2
presumably after Sir Walter Raleigh, the Elizabethan explorer.

Ralston Close, Croft, Grove, Place, 19
from a Yorkshire village called Ralston.

Rampton Road, 7
from the place called Rampton, Nottinghamshire. It was built in 1886 as part of the South View Gardens estate. Several streets in the area were named after places in East Nottinghamshire, Gamston and Leverton among them.

Ramsey Road, 10
not known; built 1901.

Ranby Road, 11
from Ranby Hall, Wragby, Lincolnshire. It was built on land that first belonged to the Younge family. Elizabeth Younge married Francis Otter, of Ranby Hall, Wragby, and by the time this road was built the land had been inherited by their son Francis Robert Otter, also of Ranby Hall.

Randall Place, Street, 2
from the Randall Steam Joinery Works and Moulding Mills founded in the

1860s by John Thomas Johnson, who came to Sheffield in 1864 and died in 1911 at the age of eighty-five. Why he chose the name Randall for his works is not known but the name obviously had some significance for him because he also named his house, at Machon Bank, Randall House.

Ranelagh Drive, 11
from the place called Ranelagh, London, famous as a polo centre, and the home of the Ranelagh Club.

Rangeley Road, 6
not known; built in the 1890s.

Range Road, 4
from the rifle range in the old quarry in Wincobank Lane which was used by the Howard Rifle Club in the early 1900s.

Ranmoor Chase, Court, Crescent, Road; Ranmoor Park Road, 10
from the area called Ranmoor, in ancient times, Ran Moor, listed in Harrison's survey of 1637 as twenty-five acres in size. Some old documents call it Rand Moor. It is believed to come from the old word *rand*, meaning edge, or border – the moor on the border.

Ranmoor Cliffe Road, 10
in old place names a cliff was not necessarily steep or rocky. Any old hillside would do. In this case one side of the Porter Brook valley became known as Ranmoor Cliffe and the other side as High Cliffe.

Ranskill Court, 9
from the earlier Ranskill Road, no longer listed, which was originally called Woodside Road and was renamed in 1912 after Ranskill, two miles from Blyth, Nottinghamshire.

Raseby Avenue, Close, Place, 19
from a man called Raseby, a local landowner, whose name appears on an eighteenth century property roll.

Ratcliffe Road, 11
was built across a narrow strip of land owned at the time of the Ecclesall Enclosure Act by a man called Isaac Ratcliffe.

Ravencarr Place, Road, 2
from Raven Carr, an eighteenth century field name in Eckington, one of many Manor Estate streets named from the ancient history of Eckington area

Ravenfield Close, 19
from the village of Ravenfield, near Rotherham; one of a group of streets given South Yorkshire names.

Raven Road, 7
was originally called Speeton Road, from the village of Speeton between Bridlington and Filey. It was renamed in 1905. I do not know the reason for the new name.

Ravenscroft Avenue, Close, Court, Crescent, Drive, Oval, Place, Road, Way, 13
from the house called Ravenscroft at Richmond, which first appears in the directories of 1914-15 as the home of Leonard Jackson, steel manager. The house, in Smelter Wood Road, later became a home for the elderly.

Ravensworth Road, 9
a link with the Bright family who owned the Carbrook estate in the seventeenth century. Sir John Bright's third wife (of four) was Frances Liddell, of Ravensworth Castle, Durham. His daughter by an earlier marriage, Catherine, also married one of the Ravensworth Liddells.

The Ravine, 5
descriptive name, from a nearby geographical feature.

Rawson Spring Avenue, Road, Way, 6
from Rawson Spring Wood, which was named after its one-time owners, the Rawson family, who were prominent in Sheffield affairs for about 500 years. A spring wood consisted of young trees. The name occured frequently in and around Sheffield.

Rawson Street, 6
from the same family mentioned above. Mary, John, William and George Rawson crop up frequently in Harrison's survey of 1637 as landowners and in a variety of other activities. John Rawson was Master Cutler in 1625 and the family played a leading part in town life.

Raynald Road, 2
not known; name approved May 1924.

Rectory Terrace, 9
no longer listed; it was off Upwell Street. Brightside vicarage was on the terrace until a new vicarage was built in Beacon Road.

Redbrook Croft, Grove, 19
from the place called Redbrook in Yorkshire.

Redcar Road, 10
was originally called Prospect Road. It was changed in 1886 because there was another Prospect Road, and the new name came from Redcar, the Yorkshire market town eight miles from Middlesbrough.

Redfern Avenue, Court, Drive, Grove, 19
after Samuel Redfern who was the saddler in Mosborough village (see also Saddler).

Red Hill, 1
is recorded in Harrison's survey of 1637 as a meadow called Red Hill, just over two acres in size, held at the time by John Trippett. The name is thought to come from the colour of the soil.

Redland Lane, 7; Red Lane, 10
as with Red Hill, the names are believed to come from the colour of the soil.

Redmires Road, 10
follows part of the ancient road known as Long Causeway. The name Redmires, which is mentioned in Harrison's survey of 1637, refers to the local soil – red and boggy. Soldiers who trained at Redmires camp in the First World War knew it well.

Red Oak Lane, 6
from a variety of oak tree. One of several streets named after oak trees because they were built on Acorn Hill.

Redthorn Road, 13
from the red flowered variety of hawthorn bushes that used to be common near the site.

Reed Street, 3
no longer listed; it was off Broomhall Street and named after Lancelot Reed, born Northumberland, who came to Sheffield and established a timber busi-

ness, L.G. Reed and Co, first in Ecclesall Road, later on Broomhall Street. He also operated as a builder.

Regent Street, 1; Regent Terrace, 3
like the street of the same name in London, were named after King George IV who, before he became king in 1820, was Prince Regent for nine years.

Remington Avenue, Drive, Road, 5
after Thomas and Richard Remington who were among forty-one Yorkshire gentry who signed a petition to the king in 1640 complaining about the compulsory billeting on local people of 'unruly soldiers . . . to whose violences and insolences we are so daily subject'. Details of the petition are given in Eastwood's *History of Ecclesfield*.

Renathorpe Road, 5
from Renathorpe Hall, later known as Hadfield Farm, then Hatfield House, which is mentioned in Harrison's survey of 1637. The name is a corruption of Reynaldthorpe, a village which stood in the thirteenth century on high ground between the present locations of Sheffield Lane Top and Shiregreen Lane.

Reneville Close, Crescent, Drive, 5
after Jordan de Reneville, son of Adam de Reneville, who was lord of the manor of Cowley in the Twelfth century. The manor later passed to the Mountenay family, and was later sold to the Earl of Shrewsbury.

Reney Avenue, Crescent, Drive, Road, Walk, 8
after John Reney, village blacksmith at Greenhill in the middle of the eighteenth century. The 1856 directory lists two possible descendants of his, Thomas Reaney, blacksmith at Greenhill, and William Reaney, blacksmith at Bradway.

Renshaw Road, 11
after Miss Mary C.M. Renshaw, who owned land at Ecclesall. She sold some of it to Sheffield Corporation for the widening of Ringinglow Road.

Renton Street, 11
originally called Mill Lane; it was renamed in 1872 after Robert Renton, anvil, vice, and tool manufacturer, of Askam Brothers and Renton (later known as Renton's), Napier Street.

Reservoir Road, 10
there were several reservoirs at Crookesmoor – Old Great Dam, Ralph Dam, Misfortune Dam, Godfrey Dam, New Dam – and in the late eighteeth and early nineteenth centuries Sheffield's water supply came either from them or from the White House dams at Hillsborough. As new and larger reservoirs were built those at Crookesmoor were closed one by one.

Retford Road, 13
was originally called Worksop Road. It was part of the old Sheffield to Worksop turnpike road. The name was changed in 1924 because there was another Worksop Road at Attercliffe.

Revill Lane, 13
Revill was an old family name in the village of Woodhouse. John Revill was a freeholder in the village in 1657 and is thought to be the man from whom this lane was named.

Rex Avenue, 7
not known; was built (with Dewar Drive and Stowe Avenue) for H. Andrews.

Reynard Lane, 6
is a corruption of an old field name, Reynold Close.

Rhodes Street, 2
after Joseph Rhodes who had property in the area in the mid-nineteenth century. The street name was from a group of houses he owned called Rhodes Row.

Ribblesdale Drive, 12
one of a small group of streets named after dales.

Ribble Way, 5
from the River Ribble which flows seventy-five miles from Whernside, Yorkshire, through Lancashire to the Irish Sea; one of a small group of streets named after British rivers.

Riber Close, 6
from Riber Castle, near Matlock; one of several streets given names of places near Matlock because they were built in the area of Sheffield called Little Matlock.

Ribston Court, Road, 9
were built on land owned by the Staniforth family (see Staniforth Road) and like many streets built on the family's land were named after a place in Yorkshire. Ribston is a small village on the bank of the River Nidd, south of Knaresborough. It also gave its name to an apple, the Ribston Pippin, said to have been grown from a seed brought to this country from Normandy.

Richards Court, Road, 2
after Benjamin Richards, a clothier in the Market Place in the nineteenth century, who lived at Sale Hill and was co-founder of Sheffield and District Property Co Ltd, the firm which built Richards Road.

Richmond Avenue, Grove, Place, Road; Richmond Hill Road, 13
from the area called Richmond, once a rural little hamlet, and spelt Rychemond in the fourteenth century. It comes from the old French words meaning strong hill, the same origin as the town of Richmond in north Yorkshire. According to Canon Ferraby in his *Groundwork of the History of Handsworth*, the name came originally from a place called Richemont in France.

Richmond Hall Avenue, Crescent, Drive, Road, Way, 13
there seems never to have been a Richmond Hall. The house referred to was probably Richmond House, a house and farm with sixty-five acres of land occupied up to 1874 by William Stacey. When it was offered to let that year it was said to be 'a very desirable residence for a retiring tradesman who may have a taste for amateur farming'.

Richmond Park Avenue, Close, Crescent, Croft, Drive, Grove, Rise, Road, 13
from the estate called Richmond Park, consisting of a house called Richmond and extensive grounds, owned for many years by the Young family, latterly Bernard Joseph Young JP, who died in 1910, and then his son, Smelter Joseph Young. The house was demolished about 1950 and the site taken over by the Corporation.

Richmond Street, 3
was built on the Duke of Norfolk's land and named from the fact that Mary, daughter of Thomas, the third Duke, was married in the 1530s to Henry Fitzroy, Duke of Richmond and illegitimate son of King Henry VIII.

Richworth Road, 13
seems to be concocted from the names of Richmond and Handsworth.

Riddings Close, 2
from an old Mosborough field name. Riddings field was awarded to Joseph Naylor in the 1795 Mosborough enclosures. One of many Manor Estate streets named from the ancient history of Eckington manor.

Rider Road, 6
one of a quartet of literary roads. This and Haggard Road were named after Sir Henry Rider Haggard (1856-1925) author of *She*, *King Solomon's Mines* etc. The other two were named after Rudyard Kipling.

Ridgehill Avenue, Grove, 12
a variation on nearby Ridgeway Road.

The Ridge, 10
was built on the site of a house called The Ridge, once the home of Sir Ashley Ward, Master Cutler in 1939, and later of Sir Gerard Young, Master Cutler in 1961, and Lord Lieutenant of South Yorkshire.

Ridge View Close, Drive, 9
overlooks the old Roman Ridge on Wincobank Hill.

Ridgeway Crescent, Drive, Road, 12
a directional name. It goes towards the village of Ridgeway which was mentioned in a document of 1201 as Regeway, and gets its name from the road which runs along a ridge. Part of Ridgeway Road was originally called Gladstone Road (after the statesman).

Riggs High Road, Riggs Low Road, 6
from two fields called the Riggs which were part of the nearby Griffs Farm. Riggs in this context means ridges.

Ringinglow Road, 11
Hunter's Hallamshire says several ancient documents refer to 'a great heap of stones called Ringin Lowe', suggesting that it was the site of an ancient barrow, as at Arbour Low, Derbyshire. The name was originally spelt Ringinglowe Road but the City Council decided to drop the last letter in 1915. (They took the last letter off Stumperlowe at the same time and then put it back on again in 1922).

The caption on this photograph describes Rivelin Valley Road as 'The New Road', which dates it roughly. The road opened in 1907.

Ringstead Avenue, Crescent, 10
according to the builder's grandson, the name was suggested because the crescent formed a ring with other roads in the area.

Ringwood Crescent, Drive, Grove, Road, 19
from the Ringwood Forest, north of Bournemouth; group name – forests (see Ashdown).

Ripley Street, 6
after Harry Ripley, builder, contractor, brick manufacturer, and land owner. He lived at Wadsley House in 1900 and a company called Hillsborough Estates Ltd was formed to buy and develop his land.

Ripon Street, 9
like surrounding streets, was named after a prominent nineteenth century lawyer, Fredrick John Robinson, first Earl of Ripon (1782-1859), MP for Ripon, who was at various times Chancellor of the Exchequer, Secretary for War, Leader of the House of Lords and briefly (as Viscount Goderich), Prime Minister in 1827 (see Brett).

Rippon Crescent, Road, 6
were built by a freehold land society and named after someone linked with the society, possibly James Rippon, grocer in Infirmary Road, who represented Nether Hallam ward on the Town Council from 1867 to 1873.

Rising Street, 3
was built on the Duke of Norfolk's land and named after Castle Rising, a village four miles from King's Lynn, Norfolk. The old castle from which the village was named was given to the third Duke of Norfolk by King Henry VIII as a reward for his services. It was sold by the seventh Duke to pay debts.

Rivelin Bank, 6
the hill by the Rivelin.

Rivelin Park Court, Crescent, Drive, Road, 6
from the area of public open space nearby acquired by the Corporation in 1934 for use as parkland. A children's paddling stream and playground were added in 1951 as part of the Festival of Britain celebrations.

Rivelin Road, Street, Terrace, 6
from the well-known river called the Rivelin which is recorded as Riveling in a document dated 1310. Dialect experts say it means rivulet, or small river.

Rivelin Valley Road, 6
from the valley through which the river passes. The road was opened in 1907.

Riverdale Avenue, Road, 10
from the house called Riverdale, home of Charles Henry Firth, of the famous Sheffield family. In the town directories of 1876 and 1879 the house appears as 'Riversdale', but from 1881 onwards it appears as Riverdale.

River Lane, 1
from the River Sheaf (see Sheaf Street).

Riverside Close; River Terrace, 6
from the River Loxley.

Roach Road, 11
was approved in 1903 for Mrs Harland and Mrs Thompson, of the Wilson family, owners of the land. Most of the streets built for these two ladies were named after members of their family, or places with which they were associated, but Roach is a mystery.

Robert Road, 8
probably after Robert Jones, builder, of Greenfield Road, who built many houses in this area in the 1930s.

Robertshaw Street, 3
no longer listed; it ran from St Phillips Road to Brightmore Street. It was originally called Robert Street, after Robert Mitchell, merchant, and a member of the family who owned land in this area. To avoid confusion with Robert Street, Shalesmoor, it was renamed in 1872 and the new name was concocted to keep it similar to the old one.

Robertson Drive, Road, 6
after John T. Robertson, joiner and builder in the late 1800s who built and owned property in the Walkley Area.

Robey Street, 4
not known; first appeared in the 1902 directory.

Robinbrook Lane, 12
from the stream, the Robin Brook, which was mentioned in a document of 1570 as Robbyn Brooke. It flows into the Moss Brook.

Robin Hood Chase, 6
one of a small group of streets named after the legendary Sherwood outlaws, because of Robin Hood's supposed links with Loxley. Harrison's survey of 1637 mentions a croft 'wherein is ye foundation of an house or cottage where Robin Hood was born'.

Robin Hood Road, 9
was originally called School Street. It was renamed to avoid confusion with another street of the same name. The new name seems to have been purely fanciful, with no particular relevance to Wincobank.

Robin Lane, 19
dates back to the eighteenth century and is thought to have come from a person's name, but whose name is not known.

Robinson Road, 2
from the brickyard of James Robinson and Son at the end of Blagdon Street. Robinsons were brick manufacturers in the Park district for more than 100 years.

Rochester Close, Drive, Road, 10
from Rochester Cathedral; one of a group of streets named after churches (see Peterborough).

Rockingham Close, Gate, Way, 1
after the Marquis of Rockingham who was lord of the manor of Ecclesall in the days when Ecclesall manor stretched right down to Sheffield Moor.

Rockingham Lane, Street, 1
although the explanation may be the same as the streets above, it seems more likely (since the two are surrounded by other streets named after prime ministers), that they were named after Charles Watson-Wentworth, Marquis of Rockingham (1730-1782), who was Prime Minister from 1765 to 1766, and again in 1782. He died after three months of his second term of office.

Rockley Road, 6
probably from the area known as Rockley at Worsbrough which has historical connections with Hillsborough.

Rockmount Road, 9; Rock Street, 3
from the rocky nature of the ground nearby.

Rodger Road, 13
after a member of the Watson Family who owned the land on which the streets were built (see David Close).

Rodley Lane, 2
after John Rodley who lived in this lane in the early nineteenth century. In the 1841 directory he is described as a 'letter carrier and manufacturer of galvanic machines and insulated wire for galvanic uses'.

Rodman Drive, Street, 13
Rodman Street was originally called George Street (after George Travis who owned most of the houses in the street). It was renamed in 1924, when Woodhouse came into Sheffield, where there was another George Street. The new name was after Willie Rodman, well-known member of the old Handsworth Urban District Council and of the Handsworth and Woodhouse school and burial boards.

Rodney Hill, 6
from the *Admiral Rodney* public house which was named after George Brydges Rodney, great English seaman (1719-1792). There was also a Rodney Club in Sheffield, named after him. He visited the town in 1790 and presented his portrait to the club.

Roebuck Road, 6
was built in the 1850s and named after John Arthur Roebuck (1801-1879) radical MP for Sheffield from 1849 to 1868 and supporter of the freehold reform movement which flourished in the Walkley area. At about the time the road was built his Sheffield constituents gave him 1,100 guineas and presented him with his portrait to mark his work for the town.

Roe Lane, 3
from the nearby Roe Wood. It was first called Roe Wood Lane. One theory is that roe refers to deer, but the stronger theory is that it comes from the old word *wro*, or *wroo*, meaning a nook of land, because of the 200ft. diameter earthwork in the wood, thought to have been the homestead of an ancient Celtic family.

Rokeby Drive, Road, 5
from the Rokeby family who lived at nearby Thundercliffe Grange in the fifteenth and sixteenth centuries.

Roland Row, 2
not known.

Rolleston Road, 5
from the south Derbyshire village of Rolleston; one of a group of streets named after places in south Derbyshire.

Rollet Close, 2
after Peter Rollet who was confidential secretary to Mary Queen of Scots when she was imprisoned in Sheffield. Rollet suffered from consumption, died in 1574 and was buried in Sheffield.

Rollin Drive, 6
there have been Rollins living in the Owlerton-Hillsborough area from the

early nineteenth century to modern times, most of them connected with the Slack steelworks. At the time this avenue was named (in 1937) there were five people called Rollin living in the area and it was probably named after one, or all, of them.

Romandale Garden, 2
one of the new Manor Estate names agreed by the City Council in 1982, all taken from ancient tribes – Celts, Saxons, Normans, and in this case, the Romans.

Roman Ridge Road, 9
from the ancient earthwork rampart and ditch from Sheffield to Mexborough across Wincobank Hill, traces of which can still be seen. It is known as the Roman Ridge, or Roman Rig, but it may well have been pre-Roman, possibly built by the ancient Britons and adapted by the Romans.

Romney Garden, Road, 2
the road is no longer listed; it was probably named after George Romney (1734-1802), the English historical and portrait painter considered among late Victorian artists to be next in importance to Reynolds and Gainsborough.

Romsdal Road, 10
was named – somewhat surprisingly – from the Romsdal Valley in Norway. It was one of three Norwegian names approved for streets at Crookes by the Watch Commitee in 1909. The other two were Bergen Road (after the seaport and second city of Norway) and Hardanger Road (after Norway's largest fiord). The other two were either not built, or if they were, did not last long. They were shown on at least one street map at the time but they were not included in any of the directories. Why Norwegian names were chosen I have no idea.

Ronald Road, 9
was built on land owned by the Staniforth family and named after Ronald Thomas Stanyforth, an officer in the 17th Lancers, who was Comptroller to the Duke of Gloucester in the 1930s. He was the son of Lt-Col Edwin Wilfrid Stanyforth, of Kirk Hammerton Hall, York. who inherited the family's Sheffield land (see Staniforth Road).

Ronksley Crescent, Road, 5
after James Ronksley, member of a well-known Stannington and Rivelin family, who owned a farm at Stannington and land at Shiregreen.

Ropery Row, 2
from the name of a much older small street off South Street, which was named from the fact that there was a rope manufacturer on it. In the 1850s there were two rope makers on South Street, Thomas Bagshaw at number five, and Samuel Sayles at number thirty-seven.

Rosamond Avenue, Close, Court, Drive, Glade, Place, 17
probably after Rosamond Hawksworth, who married Cyril Arthington, of Hazelbarrow, in the sixteenth century. Rosamond was a Roman Catholic and she was named by the Earl of Shrewsbury in a list of 'Popish Fugitives' he compiled for Derbyshire. She was one of several Norton people named.

Rosa Road, 10
was built in 1901 for John Middleton. My guess is that it was named after one of his female relatives, possibly his wife.

Roscoe Bank, Court, Drive, Mount, 6
from a field name which probably originated from a person's name. It is shown on the 1851 map.

Roscoe Road, 3
from a field name, Roscoe Fields, where open-air meetings were held in the early nineteenth century. The origin of the name is uncertain. It could be from a personal name.

Rose Avenue, 19
group name – flowers (see Aster).

Rosedale Garden, Road, 11
were built on Wilson family land and named after the Rosedale Valley and Abbey on the North Yorkshire Moors.

Rose Hill, 5
no longer listed; it was named after a Brightside land-owner, Benjamin Rose who died about 1852. He owned the *White Swan* public house near Brightside railway station and had sixteen acres of land adjoining what was then Jenkin Lane and is now Jenkin Road.

Roselle Street, 6
was originally called Rose Street, after a man called Rose. When the area came into Sheffield, where there was another Rose Street, it had to be changed (in 1903). The new name was an attempt to stay as near as possible to the old one.

Rosemary Road, 19
one of a group of streets named after trees. The Rosemary is a hardy evergreen, more of a shrub than a tree.

Roslin Road, 10
from the Midlothian village of Roslin, one of a group of streets named after places in Scotland (see Arran).

Rosser Avenue, 12
not known.

Rossington Road, 11
from the place called Rossington between Doncaster and Bawtry; one of a group of streets the names of which all end in 'ton' (see Everton).

Ross Street, 9
was originally called Russell Street, after Earl John Russell, the Victorian statesman. It was renamed in 1903, probably after Edward Ross, secretary of the Manchester, Sheffield and Lincolnshire Railway for forty-two years. The street led to the MS & L's Darnall goods yard.

Rothay Road, 4
after the river that rises near Grasmere, Cumbria; one of a group of streets with Lake District names.

Rothbury Close, Court, 19
from the Rothbury Forest, Northumberland; one of a group of streets named after British forests.

Rotherham Road, 13; Rotherham Road, 19 (Beighton); Rotherham Road, 19, (Halfway)
are all directional names. They lead towards Rotherham.

Rotherham Street, 9
from the town of Rotherham.

Rothervale Close, 19
the valley of the River Rother (see below).

Rother Valley Way, 19
one of the north-south grid roads at Mosborough, both named after river

valleys. Rother, recorded as Roder in 1164, means chief river, or full river.

Rotherwood Avenue, 13
Rotherwood is mentioned in *Hunter's South Yorkshire*, published in 1828 and simply means the wood by the river Rother. A nearby house was also called Rotherwood. It was the home of Richard Sorby, a coal owner, in the 1850s.

Rough Bank, 2
no longer listed; it means what it says, a hillside of rough ground.

Roundel Street, 9
is wrongly spelt and has been ever since it was built. It ought to be Roundell. It was named, like nearby Palmer Street, and Selborne Street, after Sir Roundell Palmer, first Earl of Selborne (1812-1895), former Lord Chancellor of England (see Brett).

Rowan Tree Dell, 17
from rowan trees in the area. The tree is common around Sheffield. It is sometimes referred to as the mountain ash. In some parts of the country it is known as quickbeam, or 'fowler's service tree', because bird snarers used to bait their traps with its berries.

Rowdale Close, 12
from the place called Rowdale in Derbyshire.

Rowell Lane, 6
not known; Rowell and Rowell Cliffes are referred to in a document of 1824.

Rowland Road, 2
after Rowland Hodgson (1772-1837) who lived in Highfield Terrace in the early nineteenth century. He was a well-known churchman (his father, the Rev Rowland Hodgson, was vicar of Rawmarsh), a Town Trustee and friend of James Montgomery.

Rowland Street, 3
not known; built about 1870.

Rowsley Street, 2
one of a pair with Cromford Street; both named after Derbyshire villages. Rowsley, between Bakewell and Matlock, is well-known for its seventeenth century inn, the *Peacock*.

Roxton Avenue, Road, 8
from the house called Roxton House on Abbey Lane. The man who lived in the house in the 1920s, Job Grant, inspector for the Blackburn Philanthropic Assurance Co Ltd, owned eight acres of land nearby including the land on which Roxton Road was built. There is a village called Roxton near Bedford.

Roydfield Close, Drive, Grove, 19
from an old field name, Roide Field, recorded in 1608. By the time of a survey made in 1798 it had become The Royd, or Royd Field. It is thought to have come from the Old English word *rodu*, meaning a clearing.

Royds Lane, 4
from an area referred to as The Rodes in a fourteenth century document and as the Royds in the seventeenth century. It means a clearing, as Roydfield, above.

Royston Avenue, Close, Croft, 19
from the area of Royston, near Barnsley; one of a group of streets given South Yorkshire names.

Rubens Row, 2
from the earlier Rubens Street (no longer listed) which was built on the Duke of Norfolk's land and named after the artist Peter Paul Rubens (1577-1640). Rubens painted several of the Duke's ancestors, including the magnificent portrait of Aletheia Talbot, heiress of Sheffield, Countess of Arundel, which now hangs in the Alte Pinakothek in Munich.

Rudyard Road, 6
after the author Rudyard Kipling (see Kipling Road).

Rufford Court, Rise, 19
from Rufford Park, Nottinghamshire. Rufford Abbey, set in the park, was the home of Lord Savile for many years.

Rugby Street, 3
from the Warwickshire town of Rugby.

Rundle Drive, Road, 7
from the maiden name of Mrs Eliza Maria Wostenholm, third wife of George Wostenholm, the cutler, who developed much of Sharrow and Nether Edge. When Mrs Wostenholm died she left the family home at Kenwood to her sister, Miss Annie M. Rundle, well-known local benefactress, who lived at Kenwood till her death in 1922.

Rupert Road, 7
not known; the road was built in 1862 for the Montgomery Freehold Land Society, and obviously named after someone called Rupert but I don't know who he was.

Rural Lane, 6
was originally called Fox Lane. It was changed in 1903 and given a fairly meaningless new name which was presumably intended to be descriptive.

Rushby Street, 4
after David Rushby who was a builder and joiner. He built houses in Baretta and Rushby Streets in the 1880s.

Rushdale Avenue, Mount, Road, Terrace, 8
Rushdale was the name of a little valley through which the Meers Brook ran. According to J.H. Stainton in *The Making of Sheffield*, it was a delightful spot with many oak trees on either side of the stream.

Rushleigh Court, Rushley Avenue, Close, Drive, Road, 17
from an old field name. When the field was offered for sale in 1878 it was described as 'a close of land called The Rushley situated in the township of Dore and containing one acre, one rood and eight perches or thereabouts'.

Ruskin Square, 8
after John Ruskin (1819-1900) art critic and author, who visited Sheffield in the 1870s and set up his educational museum in the town, first at Walkley, then, from 1890, at Meersbrook Park, where it remained till 1953.

Russell Court, 11
not known; all the other courts on the development are named after stately homes.

Russell Street, 3
after the statesman, Earl Russell (1792-1878) who was involved in the 1832 Reform Bill and the repeal of the Corn Laws, and served at various times as Home Secretary, Foreign Secretary, and Prime Minister.

Rustlings Court, 10; Rustlings Road, View, 11
Rustlings Road was built first, in the 1880s, and named from the farm whose land it passed through, Rustlings Farm. There is a record of Russling Park in

Rustlings Road in the 1950s.

the area on a Fairbank map of 1755. One theory is that it means rush-lands.

Ruthin Street, 4
not known; Ruthin is a Welsh market town on the River Clwyd, site of a thirteenth century castle.

Ruth Square, 10
was built in 1906-7 and almost certainly named after a lady called Ruth but I don't know who she was.

Rutland Park, 10
was originally called Belvoir Crescent, after Belvoir Castle, seven miles from Grantham. Perhaps someone thought that Sheffielders might have difficulty with the pronunciation of Belvoir. Whatever the reason, it was quickly renamed Rutland Park, Belvoir Castle being the family seat of the Dukes of Rutland.

Rutland Road, Way, 3
Rutland Road, built first (in the 1860s) was named from the fact that George, sixth Earl of Shrewsbury, lord of Hallamshire, married Gertrude, daughter of Thomas Manners, Earl of Rutland. They had four sons. After Gertrude died, in 1566, the Earl ('in an evil hour,' he said later) married Bess of Hardwick.

Rydalhurst Avenue, 6
from the house called Rydal Hurst House which was built in the eighteenth century and was first called Fox Lane House. It was bought by John Ridal in the 1850s and after his death, was rebuilt, enlarged and renamed by his son, also called John, in 1876.

Rydal Road, 8
group name – places and features in the Lake District. Rydal is the name of a Lake District village, lake and waterfall.

Ryecroft Glen Road; Ryecroft View, 17
A Rye Croft House is mentioned in the 1822 Enclosure Act, but the name almost certainly came from an old field name.

Ryefield Gardens, 11
from an old field name.

Ryegate Crescent, Road, 10
from the house called Ryegate, built about 1897, home of Alderman Arthur Neal, solicitor, MP for Hillsborough from 1918 to 1922, president of the Chamber of Commerce and director of Sheffield United FC. He died in 1933 and four years later the house became an annexe to the Children's Hospital.

Ryhill Drive, 19
from the place called Ryhill, near Royston; one of a group of streets given Yorkshire place names.

Ryle Road, 7
after the Rt Rev John Charles Ryle, first Bishop of Liverpool, who had links with the Wostenholm family of Kenwood Park, Sheffield. Some years after the death of George Wostenholm, his widow was married again, to Mr T.E. Beaumont. The ceremony was performed by Bishop Ryle. When Mrs Beaumont died in 1887, she left the Bishop a legacy in her will.

Rylstone Court, Grove, 12
from the village of Rylstone, five miles north of Skipton; one of a group of streets given Yorkshire place names.

Sackville Road, 10
not known; it was built (with Fitzgerald and Pickmere Roads) in 1896 for the trustees of John Tasker.

Saddler Avenue, Close, Green, Grove, 19
were named, like the nearby Redfern streets, after Samuel Redfern who was the saddler in Mosborough village.

St Aidan's Avenue, Close, Drive, Mount, Place, Road, Way, 2
from nearby St Aidan's Church which was built for £1,000 and opened in November 1912, first as a chapel of ease to St John's. It later became the centre of a new parish.

St Albans Close, Drive, Road, 10
from St Albans Cathedral; one of a group of streets named after British churches. St Alban was a young Roman soldier who gave sanctuary to a priest, was converted to Christianity, and was executed for his beliefs.

St Andrew's Close, Road, 11
from St Andrew's Church which was built on a site given by Sir John Brown, the industrialist, and consecrated by Archbishop Thomson in August 1869.

St Anthony Road, 10
from an old well at Crookes called St Anthony's Well. St Anthony is the patron saint of hogs and swineherds.

St Barnabas Lane, Road, 2
from the church of St Barnabas, Highfield, the foundation stone of which was laid on 11 June 1874, St Barnabas Day. It was consecrated by the Archbishop of York on 16 October 1876 and later became the first church in Sheffield to be lit by electricity.

St Charles Street, 9
from the Roman Catholic church of St Charles which was built in 1868 at a cost of £4,500 on a site given by William Wake.

St Elizabeth Close, 2
from the St Elizabeth home of the Little Sisters of the Poor which opened in 1908 and was closed, because of the high cost of necessary renovation, in 1980. The former old people's home and day centre was then demolished.

The Peace Gardens now occupy the site of St Paul's Church. The church was closed in 1937 and demolished, and the original gardens opened two years later. The church's name lives on in St Paul's Parade.

St George's Close, Court, Terrace, 3

from St George's Church which was named partly as a display of loyalty. The first stone was laid on 19 July 1821, the day of King George IV's coronation. For the first and only time, the town guns fired a royal salute to mark the occasion.

St James Row, Street, 1

from St James' Church, Townhead Street, which was built in 1879 and badly damaged in the 1940 blitz. The ruins were cleared in 1950. It was dedicated to St James as a compliment to the Rev James Wilkinson, former vicar of Sheffield. St James Row has had two other names. It was originally called Virgin's Walk. Then it became West Parade (opposite East Parade), and lastly it became St James Row.

St James Walk, 13

from the nearby Woodhouse Mill Church, opened in October 1892 as a mission church to St James', Woodhouse. It never had a dedication of its own and was known as St James' Mission Church.

St John's Close, Gardens, Road, 2

from the church of St John the Evangelist, Park, built on a site given by Henry Charles, Duke of Norfolk, and consecrated by Archbishop Vernon Harcourt in July 1838.

St Joseph's Road, 13

from St Joseph's Roman Catholic Church which was consecrated in 1881. St Joseph's School, attached to the church, opened in 1901.

St Lawrence Road, 9

from St Lawrence's Church, Tinsley, which was built on the site of a Norman building. It was rebuilt in 1878 by Mrs Maria Overend in memory of her first husband, George Hounsfield, businessman, magistrate and Church Burgess.

St Mark's Crescent, 10

from St Mark's Church, Broomhill, which was consecrated in May 1871. The church was destroyed by fire bombs in the 1940 blitz and a new church incorporating the spire of the old one was consecrated in 1963.

St Mary's Gate, Road, 2

from St Mary's Church, Bramall Lane, which was built between 1826 and 1830 and consecrated on 21 July 1830. In 1839, during the Chartist agitation, an unsuccessful attempt was made to fire the church.

St Paul's Parade, 1

from St Paul's Church which stood on the site of the Peace Gardens (previously called St Paul's Gardens). The church was built in 1720, after which there was no service in it for twenty years because of a dispute over the patronage. It was consecrated in 1740, closed in 1937 and demolished. The gardens opened in 1939 and were rebuilt in the late 1990s.

St Joseph's Road, Handsworth, in the 1920s; St Mary's Church in the distance, St Joseph's church school on the left, and the boundary wall of Handsworth council school on the right.

St Peter's Close, 1
from Sheffield Cathedral which is dedicated to St Peter and St Paul.

St Philip's Lane, Road, 3
from St Philip's Church which was named in honour of Philip Gell, of Hopton, Derbyshire, who gave the land for the church in the 1820s and laid the first stone. The church was demolished in 1952 after being closed for several years.

St Quentin Close, Drive, Mount, Rise, View, 17
from an old well nearby called Quintinewelle in old documents, possibly named by the Beauchief Abbey monks after St Quentin. But it might also have been because it was the fifth well (quin meaning five) or because it was near a quintain, or tilting post.

St Ronan's Road, 7
was built by Thomas Steade and named in 1881. The reason for the name is uncertain. There were several saints called Ronan, one a seventh-century Scottish hermit, another a Scottish bishop. The name was popularised in Sir Walter Scott's novel called *St Ronan's Well*. There was a well near the site of the road but I do not know if it had a name.

St Stephen's Road, 3
no longer listed; it was named from St Stephen's Church, Fawcett Street, which opened on 13 December 1857 and was consecrated in 1858 by Archbishop Musgrave. The entire cost of the church was met by Henry Wilson of Westbrook.

St Thomas Road, 10
from the church of St Thomas, Crookes, which was built by subscription in 1839, and enlarged in 1857 and 1889.

St Thomas Street, 1
not known.

St Wilfrid's Road, 2
from St Wilfrid's Roman Catholic Church, the site for which (at the corner of Shoreham Street and Queens Road) was given by the Duke of Norfolk. The church opened in October 1879. It was badly damaged in the 1940 blitz.

Sale Hill, 10
S.O. Addy thought the name was ancient and came from the Old Norse word *sel*, meaning a shed on a mountain pasture. The street was built on church land and it seems more likely that it was named after Canon Thomas Sale, vicar of Sheffield from 1851 to 1873.

Sales Street, 3
no longer listed; it was named after J.H. Sales, property owner in Sales Street, Fowler Street and Pye Bank.

Salisbury Road, 10
was built in the 1870s by Crookes View Land Society and named after James Edward Salisbury, stay busk manufacturer, who lived at Holywell House and was involved in several local land societies.

Salmon Street, 11
possibly from the town called Salmon in New York State, USA. It was built on George Wostenholm's land and several names used in the area (including Mr Wostenholm's home, Kenwood, and Washington Road) were given American names.

Sambourne Square, 3
no longer listed; it was named after Thomas Sambourne, Sheffield's first speculative builder. An attorney, with an office in Paradise Square, he leased land from large estate owners in the 1790s and built small houses for sale. He later emigrated to America.

Samson Street, 2
not known.

Samuel Close, Drive, Place, Road, 2
after Samuel Roberts, merchant, writer, pamphleteer, anti-slave trade campaigner, and campaigner against the use

St Philip's Church, on the triangle of land between the junction of Penistone Road and Infirmary Road, was demolished in 1952, but the road named after it is still there.

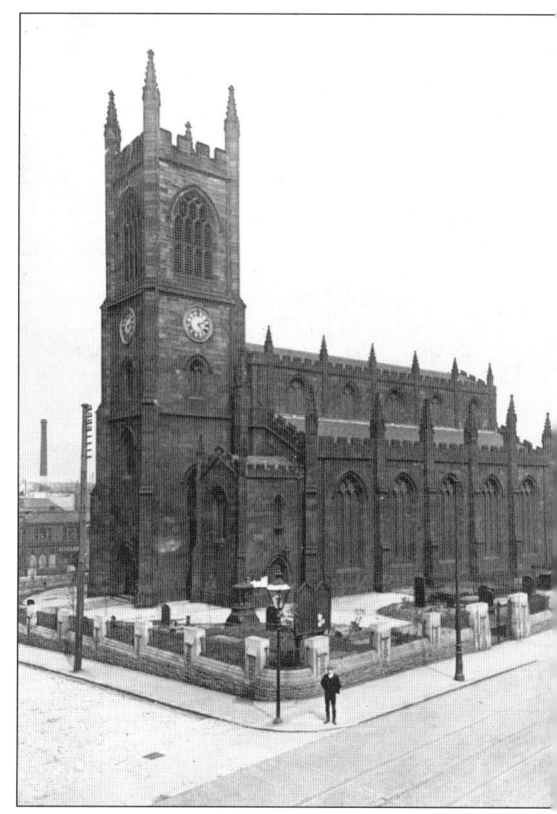

of boys as chimney sweeps. He lived nearby at a house called Park Grange from 1794 till his death in 1848.

Sandbeck Place, 11
was built (with Osberton Place) for J.Y. Cowlishaw in the 1890s and named after Sandbeck, near Maltby, for many years the seat of the Earls of Scarbrough.

Sandby Court, Croft, Drive, 14
after Paul Sandby (1725-1809), painter. He was born at Nottingham, was an original member of the Royal Acadamy and is sometimes referred to as the father of the watercolour school. One of a group of streets named after artists.

Sanderson Road, 9
from Sanderson Brothers and Co. Ltd, who owned a large area of land around this road, on part of which their factory stood. About 1880, the firm moved to Newhall and sold the Attercliffe land.

Sanderson Street, 9
after John Sanderson, partner in Sanderson Brothers and Co. Ltd, who moved house from Darnall to New Hall in 1840 and lived at the hall till his death in 1852. The firm's new works were built on land that was formerly part of the New Hall estate.

Sandford Grove Road, 7
after Henry Barlow Sandford who was solicitor to the Sheldon family estate for whom the road was built. He was also a town councillor.

Sandhurst Place, 10
apparently from the Berkshire village of Sandhurst where the Royal Military College was built in 1812.

Sandringham Road, 9
from the place called Sandringham in Norfolk.

Sands Close, 14
from two old fields called Sands Closes, one about one-and-a-half acres, the other two-and-a-quarter acres, mentioned in a survey made in 1802. They were owned at that time by John Nodder.

Sandstone Avenue, Close, Drive, Road, 9
from the old sandstone quarries on Wincobank Hill. In the 1850s James Wilkinson was the quarry owner.

Sandy Acres Close, Drive, 19
there was a sandpit nearby, alongside what used to be Eckington Road and is now Eckington Way.

Sandygate Grove, Lane, Road, 10
Sand Gate is mentioned in a document of 1771. It means a sandy road or cattle way.

Sandygate Park; Sandygate Park Crescent, Road, 10
the area became known as Sandygate Park because when plans were prepared in 1913 the idea was to lay out the development as a park, with carriage drive, grass margins, trees, a central reservation, croquet lawn, tennis courts, and houses, each in at least half-an-acre, spaced in echelons so that every one had an open view.

Sarah Street, 3
no longer listed; named after a member of the Mitchell family who owned the land. I don't know which. There were five women called Sarah in different generations of the family.

Sark Road, 2
group name – Channel Islands (see Alderney).

Saunders Place, Road, 2
after Alderman George Lemon Saunders who was a member of Sheffield Town Council from 1851 to 1854 and again from 1858 till his death in 1870. From 1859 onwards he was an alderman.

Savage Lane, 17
from a Dore field name, Savage Acres, occupied in 1820 by Thomas Savage, after whom the field was probably named.

Savile Street, Savile Street East, 4
were built on the Duke of Norfolk's land and named from the fact that the Duke's ancestor, Thomas, son of the sixth Duke, married Mary Elizabeth Savile, daughter and heiress of Sir John Savile, of Copley, Yorkshire, in the seventeenth century.

Sawdon Road, 11
was built on land owned by the Wilson family and named after the village of Sawdon, inland from Scarborough, on the edge of the North York Moors.

Saxonlea Avenue, Court, Crescent, Drive, 2
one of the ancient tribal names introduced on the Manor estate in 1982, in this case the Saxons.

Saxon Road, 8
not known; the road was built in 1878 on land formerly owned by the Midland Railway.

Scarborough Road, 9
from the Yorkshire coastal resort.

Scargill Croft, 1
from a field owned in the seventeenth century by Thomas Scargill, or Scargell, who was a collector of rents for the Burgesses. The name was a common one in Sheffield. R.E. Leader wrote: 'from 1560 to 1689 Scargills and Shemelds pervaded the affairs of the town'. Sheffield parish registers contain fifty-eight baptisms under the name of Scargill between 1560 and 1619, fourteen Scargill marriages between 1562 and 1599 and nineteen Scargill burials from 1562 to 1605.

Scarlet Oak Meadow, 6
from a variety of oak tree; one of several streets named after oak trees because they were built on or near Acorn Hill (see Durmast).

Scarsdale Road, 8
was originally called Green Lane. It was renamed in 1903 after a house at the top of the lane called Scarsdale House, sometimes called Scarsdale Villa. It was the home in the 1890s of Edward Lister, butcher and farmer. Scarsdale was the name of an ancient wapentake of Derbyshire.

Scholey Street, 3
was originally called School Lane, from a house in Andrew Street which was used in the early nineteenth century as a cottage school. The name was changed in 1872 because there were several School Lanes, and the new name was chosen for its similar sound.

School Avenue, Close, 19
were built near what was then called Eckington Grammar School and later became part of Westfield Comprehensive School.

School Green Lane, 10
from an old farm called School Green Farm which had a school attached to it. When the property was offered for sale in 1835 it consisted of farm, stables, ten closes of land, a cottage, schoolroom, and gardens. The farm was occupied by Joseph Bennett at that time and the schoolroom was used by the churchwardens and overseers of Upper Hallam township.

School Lane, Street, 2
from the old St John's National Schools in Duke Street.

School Lane, 6
from the nearby school opened in 1911, later known as Stannington Infants.

School Lane, 8
from Greenhill School.

School Lane, School Lane Close, 8
from Norton School.

School Road, 19
from Beighton School which opened in 1880 as a board school, later became a council school, then a secondary modern, and later still became Brookhouse junior mixed.

School Road, 10
was originally called School Lane; it was named from Crookes Endowed School which was set up with money bequeathed by William Roncksley in 1723.

School Street, 19
from the old Mosborough village school founded about 1680 by Joseph Stones, who left a house and land for the purpose of educating fifteen poor children of Mosborough free of charge. The school was enlarged in the 1870s.

Scofton Place, 9
from the Nottinghamshire village of Scofton between Worksop and Retford.

Scotia Close, Drive, 2
is a link with the imprisonment of Mary Queen of Scots in nearby Manor Castle. Until the eleventh century Scotland was known as Caledonia. Then part of it became Scotia, from the tribe that lived there, the Scots. The name Scotland was not established till the twelfth century.

Scotland Street, 3
on the 1771 Fairbank map of Sheffield and in the 1774 trade directory, it appears simply as 'Scotland'. One theory is that it was the area of the town where immigrants settled, although most of them seem to have been Irish rather than Scots. This may have been a fine distinction in eighteenth-century Sheffield.

Scott Road, Street, 4
Scott Road was built first, in 1880, on the Duke of Norfolk's land, as a small *cul de sac* off Barnsley Road. It was named from the Duke's family history. The fourteenth Duke's eldest daughter, Lady Victoria Alexandrina, married James Robert Hope-Scott, of Abbotsford, in 1861. She was his second wife. His first was the granddaughter of Sir Walter Scott, the novelist.

Scowerdons Close, Drive, 12
from the old farm called Scowerdons Farm which seems to be a corruption of several field names. When the farm was offered for sale in 1848 it had forty-one acres of land including four fields called the Long Scourdine, the Nether Scourdine, the Great Scourdine and the Under Scourdine, collectively known as the Scourdines.

Scraith Wood Drive, 5
from a nearby wood. In the early nineteenth century when it was called Scraith Spring Wood it covered six acres and was owned by Miss Hannah Rawson who also owned a seven-acre field nearby called Scraith Field. The word scraith, mentioned as screth in a document of 1557, and as scrath in Harrison's survey of 1637, means a landslide, or scree.

Seabreeze Terrace, 13
the legend is that the man who built it had a good win on a horse called Sea Breeze. The horse, referred to in record books as Seabreeze, all one word, won The Oaks and the St Leger in 1888 but it is unlikely that anybody won a large amount of money on it in either of these races. It started at 7-4 in The Oaks and 5-2 in the Leger.

Seabrook Road, 2
was built on the Duke of Norfolk's land and was originally called Segrave Road, from one of the Duke's ancestors, Margaret, daughter of Thomas of Brotherton, Earl of Norfolk, who married John, fourth Lord Segrave, in 1338. It was renamed in 1921 to avoid confusion with Seagrave Road, 12, and the new name was concocted to keep it similar to the old one.

Seagrave Avenue, Crescent, Drive, Road, 12
after S.W. Seagrave, well-known nurseryman and horticulturist, who lived at a house called Ashbrook on Seagrave Road and had a nursery and a plot of land on the opposite side of the road.

Seaton Close, Crescent, Place, Way, 2
after Mary Seaton, attendant to Mary Queen of Scots throughout her imprisonment in Sheffield. She was said to be the finest dresser of a woman's hair in the country and the only one of the Queen's six waiting women of any reputation.

Sedan Street, 4
was built in the 1870s and named from the Battle of Sedan, a town in the Ardennes area of France, which took place in 1870. It was the decisive battle in the Franco-Prussian war and after it Napoleon III surrendered to the Germans.

Sedgley Road, 6
probably from the place called Sedgley, near Dudley in the West Midlands.

Sefton Court, Road, 10
probably from Sefton Park (see Belsize Road).

Selborne Road, 10; Selborne Street, 9
were both built for lawyers and both named after Sir Roundell Palmer, later Earl of Selborne (1812-1895) who was Solicitor General, Attorney General, and Lord Chancellor twice, 1872-74 and 1880-85 (see Brett).

Selby Road, 4
from the Yorkshire town of Selby, fourteen miles from York.

Photographs like this, of Shalesmoor in the 1950s, will perplex future collectors of unmarked postcards, for virtually nothing recognisable remains of the buildings.

Sellers Street, 8
was built by Sheffield Brick Company Ltd and named after Alfred Sellers, of Victoria Villas, Shirebrook Road, who was a director of the company.

Selly Oak Grove, Road, 8
from the nearby Selly Oak Wood, named from the Selioke family (spelt various ways) who lived in the Norton area in the fourteenth and fifteenth centuries, owned land and manufactured iron.

Senior Road, 9
after Alderman George Senior, magistrate and chairman of George Senior and Son Ltd, who was chairman of the Parks Committee when nearby High Hazels Park was opened in 1895, and as Lord Mayor officially opened High Hazels Museum in December 1901.

Serpentine Walk, 8
from a stretch of water called the Serpentine which was filled in when Norton Park Avenue was built.

Sevenfields Court, Lane, 6
not known.

Severn Road, 10
was originally called Salisbury Road. It was renamed in 1886 because there was another Salisbury Road. The new name was a random choice, from the River Severn which flows into the Bristol Channel.

Severnside Drive, Gardens, Place, Walk, 13
is a revival of an old name. In his *Historical Notes on Woodhouse*, Ernest Atkin mentions a document of 1791 which referred to an encroachment in 'Sevenside Lane'. This, said Councillor Atkin, was one of the old names for what is now Station Road. In the modern street names Sevenside (which probably came originally from an old field name) has become Severnside.

Sewell Road, 19
after William Sewell, a miner well-known in Mosborough and Eckington. He was chairman of the Miners' Association, a local magistrate, and councillor.

Shalesmoor, 3
Mary Walton says in her *Street Names of Central Sheffield* that the old name was Sherramoor, meaning a boundary, from the Old English word *Scearu*, meaning cut, or divided.

Sharpe Avenue, 8
despite its spelling, I think this street was named after Tom Sharp who was a farmer at Greenhill in the early 1900s. In 1929-30 the Corporation bought land from Mr Sharp's trustees for the building of Greenhill Avenue.

Sharrard Close, Drive, Grove, Road, 12
after Albert Sharrard who lived at Jessamine Villa, Hollinsend, in the early 1900s. He was a partner in the firm of Sharrard and Hydes, spoon and fork manufacturers, of Trafalgar Street.

Sharrow Lane, Mount, Street, 11; Sharrow View 7
from an area called Sharrow which comes from the old word *sherra*, meaning land shared between a number of people.

Sharrow Vale Road, 11
the valley below Sharrow (see above).

Shaw Street, 9
after George Shaw who farmed at Brightside in the 1870s. His farm, a homestead and six fields totalling thirty-six acres, was offered for sale as building land in 1876.

Sheaf Bank, 2; Sheaf Square, Street, 1
from the River Sheaf, spelt Sceth in the thirteenth century and later, Sheath. It is thought to come from the old word meaning a divider, or boundary line.

Sheaf Gardens Terrace, 2
from the pleasure grounds known as the Sheaf Gardens. R.E. Leader, in his *Reminiscences of Old Sheffield*, said the

gardens, which stretched from Clough Lane to the River Sheaf, were 'considered second to none in the neighbourhood'.

Shearwood Road, 10
was approved in 1869 for Miss Elizabeth and Miss Ellen Shearwood, daughters of John Shearwood, well-known Sheffield solicitor, land and property owner, in the early nineteenth century. He lived at Sharrow Mount, owned land at Dore and property in the town centre. His estate was the subject of protracted legal disputes after his death.

Sheephill Road, 11
straightforward; the hill where sheep grazed.

Sheffield Parkway, 2 and 9
from the fact that its junction at the city end is at the bottom of the Park district.

Sheffield Road, 9; Sheffield Road, 12; Sheffield Road, 13
are all directional names – the roads all go towards Sheffield.

Sheldon Lane, 6; Sheldon Road, 7; Sheldon Street, 2
although they are in different parts of the city they were all named after the same man, John Sheldon, who owned a large amount of land and property in the town centre, at Little Sheffield, Worrall, Loxley, Walkley, Fulwood, Dronfield and Stannington. He was alotted land at Little Sheffield (near Moorfoot) in the enclosure awards of 1788, and had sixteen acres of land at Stannington. After his death, the auction of his estate in May 1850 took two days.

Sheldon Row, 3
from the earlier Sheldon's Yard which was probably named after Joseph Sheldon, bricklayer and builder in The Wicker in the 1820s.

Shelf Street, 2
was originally called Sheaf Street. It was renamed in 1872 by simply changing one letter to keep it as near to the old name as possible. Shelf is the name of a village near Bradford.

Shenstone Road, 6
probably from the place called Shenstone, near Lichfield, Staffordshire. Several nearby streets have Staffordshire names.

Shepcote Lane, Way, 9
from the Old English words meaning the place where sheep were kept.

Shepherd Street, 3
uncertain; the first leases in the street date back to the early 1800s when there were several people of this name living in the town. But there is mention of a seven-acre field in the area, called Sheppard Field, in Harrison's Survey of 1637 and it may come from that.

Shepperson Road, 6
was built on land owned by the Dixon family of Hillsborough Hall and named after James Willis Dixon's wife who was Miss Anne Shepperson before they married.

Sherde Road, 6
was built on land owned by B.P Broomhead Colton-Fox, well-known nineteenth century Sheffield solicitor, whose first wife was the daughter of Capt Staveley Sherde, of Sherde Manor, Wales, near Sheffield.

Sherwood Glen, 7
not known; the street was approved in October 1937. There was a house called Sherwood somewhere in the area which might account for the street name. On the other hand it could have been suggested by the fact that the area was surrounded by trees.

Shipman Court, 19
after Joseph Shipman, village schoolmaster at Mosborough in the 1860s.

Shipton Street, 6
was originally called Chapel Street from a nearby chapel in Addy Street. It was renamed in 1872 from the place called Shipton, north of York.

Shirebrook Road, 8
was originally called Victoria Road, after Queen Victoria. It was renamed in 1887 from the nearby Meers Brook which was for many years the boundary between Yorkshire and Derbyshire.

Shirecliffe Close, Lane, 3; Shirecliffe Road, 5
from the area called Shirecliffe, recorded as Shyrclyf in 1366 and Sherclyffe in the sixteenth and seventeenth centuries. Language experts say it comes from the Old English word *scir*, meaning bright or gleaming – bright hillside.

Nowadays, Sharrow Lane is busier than it was when this photo was taken in the early 1900s. It has changed beyond recognition, but the name is the same.

Shiregreen Lane, Terrace, 5
from the area called Shiregreen, thought to mean the place, or green, on the shire boundary, perhaps the northern boundary of Hallamshire.

Shirehall Crescent, Road, 5
from an old house called Shire Hall, sometimes called Shire House.

Shirland Lane, 9
was originally called Back Lane. It was renamed from a house called Shirland House, sometimes called Shirland Cottage, built in the 1820s and for more than forty years home of the Deakins, a well-known Attercliffe family. At various times later it was also known as Beardshaw House and Baltic House, because Vickers George Beardshaw of Baltic Steelworks lived in it.

Shirley Road, 3
was originally called Back Lane. It was renamed in 1899 from an old field name, Shire Ley, meaning open pasture.

It was a fairly common field name. There was a field called Shire Ley at Sharrow which became Shirle, as in Shirle Hill.

Shore Court, Lane, 10
after the Shore family, bankers, businessmen, and extensive landowners in Sheffield. William Shore lived at a house called Tapton Hill, near Shore Lane. The house was later rebuilt and renamed Tapton Hall.

Shoreham Street, 2 and 1
was built on the Duke of Norfolk's land and named after the Sussex town of Shoreham. In ancient times the Dukes of Norfolk were lords of the manor of both New and Old Shoreham.

Shortbrook Bank, Close, Croft, Drive, Road, Walk, Way, 19
from the stream called the Short Brook which rises above Moss Way and joins the Rother near Station Road.

Shortridge Street, 9
after John Shortridge who owned land and property in this street and in Chippingham Street and Place (see Chippinghouse Road).

Shorts Lane, 17
uncertain; several fields at Dore were called Short Lands. It may have something to do with them.

Short Street, 9
descriptive name; for many years there were only two buildings on the street, both shops.

Shrewsbury Road, 2
from the seven Earls of Shrewsbury who were lords of the manor of Sheffield from the fourteenth to the seventeenth century.

Shubert Close, 13
a document of 1764 refers to a stream called 'Shoulder Broad Brook, sometimes called Shoe-Broad Dyke'. By the 1880s it had become Shubbard Dyke, later corrupted to Shubert. In old field and place names, Shoe-broad (and shoulder-broad and shovel-broad) indicate narrowness.

Shude Hill, Lane, 1
comes (like nearby Bakers Hill) from its nearness to the old town bakehouse. S.O. Addy, the local historian, said shudes, or shoods, were the husks of oats. Shude Lane was first called Forge Lane.

Sicey Avenue, Lane, 5
Brian Woodriff, in his book *Forkmaking and Farming at Shiregreen* says this name came from an ancestor of his, a man called Sicey Ellis, and that it was originally Sicey's Lane.

Siddall Street, 1
probably after Samuel Siddall, described as 'gardener, goldsmith and tailors' shearmaker', who lived on Broad Lane at the end of the eighteenth century.

Sidney Street, 1
was built on the Duke of Norfolk's land and named from his family history. The second Duke's grandson, Thomas Radcliffe, who became Earl of Sussex in the sixteenth century, married Frances Sidney, daughter of Sir William Sidney.

Siemens Close, 9
after Sir William Siemens (1823-1883), the German scientist and inventor, who settled in England in 1844, took British nationality in 1859, and was knighted in 1883. The furnace he invented revolutionised steel production.

Silkstone Close, Crescent, Drive, Place, Road, 12
from the Silkstone coal seam which is beneath the site.

Silver Birch Avenue, 10
from silver birch trees in the area.

Silverdale Close, Court, Crescent, Croft, Gardens, Glade, Road, 11
the dale below Silver Hill.

Silver Hill Road, 11
there is a story that a hoard of silver was found in the area in the early 1800s but there is no evidence to support this. S.O. Addy thought the name was just another way of saying that it was a sunny hill position. There are five other Silver Hills in Yorkshire, and two other Silverdales, and in most cases the name is thought to be a description of the local soil – silver or rich coloured.

Silver Mill Road, 2
was originally called Folly Road. It was renamed after a nearby silver mill in 1909. (S.O. Addy says in his glossary that Granville Street, running from South Street to Dyers Hill, was formerly called The Folly, 'from a foolish attempt by one whose name is forgotten to work a mine there').

Silver Street, 1
from the number of silver workers who had workshops in the street. Some of them were still there in the late 1700s and early 1800s; Jonathan Watkinson (1776), William Patten (1780), Hannah Watkinson (1792), John Ashforth, Joseph Cutts and Thomas Anderton (1825). Before they moved to Cornish Place, James Dixon and Son, one of the best known of all the silver firms, had premises in Silver Street.

Sims Street, 1
not known.

Singleton Crescent, Grove, Road, 6
not known; approved in 1898 for the trustees of M.G. Burgoyne.

Sitwell Place, Road, 7
after Francis Hurt (1728-1793), who changed his name to Sitwell when he succeeded his uncle to the Sitwell estate at Renishaw. Francis Hurt Sitwell, as he became, built the house called Mount Pleasant at Highfield in 1777 and used it as his second residence for some years. His son, Sitwell Sitwell, sold the house in 1794.

Skelton Close, Drive, Grove, Lane, Walk, Way, 13
after an old local landowner, Nancy Skelton, who had several houses and a yard on Skelton Lane.

Skelton Lane, 19
probably after Nicholas Skelton who lived in the Beighton area in the seventeenth century.

Skelton Road, 8
was originally called Alpine Road, because of its steepness. But there was another Alpine Road and this one was renamed in 1903. The new name was from the nearby works of C.T. Skelton and Co, manufacturers of spades, shovels and tools. The head of the firm, Sir Charles Thomas Skelton (1833-1913), Mayor of Sheffield in 1894, knighted after Queen Victoria's visit to open the Town Hall in 1897, owned land in the Heeley area.

Skelwith Close, Drive, Road, 4
from Skelwith Bridge and Skelwith Force waterfall, near Ambleside; one of a group of streets given Lake District names.

Skinnerthorpe Road, 4
from a farmstead, or perhaps a hamlet, which is referred to in a document of 1558 as Skynnerthorpe. It is thought to come from a personal name – Skynner's farmstead.

Skipton Road, 4
from the place called Skipton in north Yorkshire; one of a group of streets all of which have names ending 'ton'.

Skye Edge Avenue, Road, 2
Skye Edge is a descriptive name for the high ridge overlooking the city centre. It seems to have been an early nineteenth-century concoction. There is no mention of it in early reference books, but the 1853 Ordnance Survey shows an area called Sky Edge and a small wood called Sky Edge Plantation. The letter 'e' on the end of Sky, added later, serves no purpose.

Slate Street, 2
uncertain; it was built (with Delf Street) on the Duke of Norfolk's land to plans approved in 1897. Delf, or delph, usually means a quarry. There was a quarry nearby but it was a stone quarry, not a slate quarry. It may have produced roofing stones.

Slayleigh Avenue, Drive, Lane, 10
from an old field name recorded in the seventeenth century as Slalee and later as Slay Lee. It is thought to mean the field or clearing where sloes were grown.

Sleaford Street, 9
was originally called Victoria Street. It was renamed in 1886 after the Lincolnshire market town of Sleaford, an arbitrary choice.

Slinn Street, 10
from Slinn's Farm which was nearby. Its owners, Charles and George Slinn, sold the land for building in the 1870s.

Slitting Mill Lane, 9
there was a bar and slitting mill in the area run by John T. Young and Co. It is shown on a 1766 Fairbank map. There was also a Slitting Mill Farm.

Smithywood Crescent, Woodseats, was originally called White House Crescent, from this house, though it looks as if the paint was peeling when it was photographed in the 1860s.

Smallage Lane, 13
not known.

Smalldale Road, 12
from Smalldale, near Bradwell; one of many Frecheville streets given Derbyshire names.

Smeaton Street, 11
uncertain; probably from the north Yorkshire villages of Great and Little Smeaton.

Smelter Wood Avenue, Court, Crescent, Drive, Lane, Place, Rise, Road, Way, 13
from the nearby wood, the name of which comes from a local family. The Smelter family lived at Richmond from the middle of the seventeenth century and owned land and property in the area for 250 years.

Smithfield, 3
S.O. Addy said he thought it could mean the field belonging to the blacksmith, and it could. But it could just as easily be named after somebody called Smith because there have been plenty of them in the locality. The likeliest is George Smith, Master Cutler in 1749, whose ten children and twelve apprentices all lived in a large house in its own grounds in Peacroft (now part of Solly Street). He died in 1776. Some of the leases in Smithfield date from the early 1770s. One of Mr Smith's sons, the Rev John Smith, was head of Sheffield Free Grammar School and another, the Rev George Smith, was curate of Ecclesall.

Smithfield Road, 13
from an old farm called Smithfield House. The 1862 directory lists the farmer as William Smith, which probably explains the farm's name.

Smith Street, 9
after the man for whom it was approved in 1898, T. Smith, builder in the Darnall area.

Smithywood Crescent, Road, 8
up to the middle of the nineteenth century Smithy Wood stretched almost from Little London area up to Meersbrook Park. Now only a few scattered trees remain. There was a smithy in the area. Smithywood Crescent was originally called Whitehouse Crescent (from a house nearby called the White House). It was renamed in 1926.

Snaithing Lane, 10
snaithing used to be a common field name in and around Sheffield, thought to come from the Anglo Saxon word meaning a small piece. S.O. Addy said when the name was applied to a road or track it signified a zig-zag path up a hillside.

Snaithing Park Close, Road, 10
from Snaithing Park, the seventeen acres of land around the house which was built and lived in for some years by Alderman William W Harrison, electro

plate manufacturer and magistrate. The land was offered for sale for building purposes in the late 1880s.

Snig Hill, 3
several explanations have been offered but the most likely is that the name comes from the old practice of snigging a load up a hill – bringing it up a bit at a time, or giving it some kind of additional help, with a pole under the rear wheels, or with a secondary horse which was known as a snig horse.

Arnold Muir Wilson, city councillor and solictor, told the story of coming out of a hearing in a Lancashire town and seeing a man with an outfit on which it said 'Scissor Grinder – Sheffield'.

Determined to check the man's credentials, Councillor Wilson asked: 'Are you from Sheffield?'

'Oh, yes,' said the man.

'Do you know Snig Hill?'

'No,' said the man. 'But I know his brother, Charley.'

Snow Hill Row, 2
from an earlier name, Snow Hill, which has gone out of use. Snow Hill is mentioned in the 1797 directory and is probably much older than that. Several cities have a Snow Hill, including London and Birmingham. Fairfield says the one at London was originally Snore Hill, from an old word meaning twist, that is, a twisting lane. There is nothing to show that the Sheffield name comes from the same source and it seems to mean, as with other hills or fields of the same name, the hill where the snow lay thickest and longest.

Snow Lane, 3
not known; it was built on land belonging to the Church Burgesses in the 1760s.

Soap House Lane, 13
from the Victoria Soap Works, Woodhouse Junction, which were the works of Hibbard, Richardson and Co, soap, grease and oil manufacturers in the 1880s. The Hibbard in the firm's title was John Hibbard, of Lamb Hill, Richmond.

Solferino Street, 11
from the village of Solferino, Lombardy, northern Italy, where, in June 1859, a combined force of French and Piedmontese defeated the Austrians and freed Lombardy from Austrian domination.

Solly Street, 1
after Isaac Solly, born 1724, member of a well-known Sheffield family who ran the firm of Solly Brothers, iron masters, and were linked by marriage with the Hollis family, founders of the Hollis Hospital. His grandson was Alderman Richard Solly. Peacroft (from an old field name) became part of Solly Street in 1898.

Somercotes Road, 12
from the place called Somercotes, near Alfreton, Derbyshire.

Somerset Road, Street, 3
were built on the Duke of Norfolk's land and named from the marriage of the sixth Duke about 1652 to Lady Anne Somerset, eldest duaghter of the Marquis of Worcester. She died in 1662.

Somerville Terrace, 6
was originally a row of houses rather than a street. It was named after Mary Somerville (1780-1872), eminent scientific writer after whom Somerville College, Oxford, was named. Sir Francis Chantrey did a bust of her for the Royal Society.

Sorby Street, 4
from the firm of John Sorby and Sons, edge tool, joiners' tool, sheep shear, file, saw, spade and shovel manufacturers on Spital Hill in the early nineteenth century.

Sothall Close, Court, Green, 19
Sothall is recorded in 1356 as Swothalge, later as Swootall, Swothall and by the sixteenth century, Sothall. It is thought to come from the personal name Swota – Swota's nook of land.

Southall Street, 8
not known; the name was approved (with Arthington Street and Whiting Street) in December 1908, so it was probably something to do with the Arthington Trust (see Arthington Street).

Southbourne Road, 10
was originally called Westbourne Road East (a cumbersome and slightly contradictory name at best). It was changed in 1886 and its new name (giving it yet another compass point) was from a house called Southbourne, once the home of Robert James Tennant, of the brewing family, and later of Alderman Joseph Gamble.

Southcroft Gardens, Walk, 7
Southcroft Gardens was previously called Arthur Street. It was changed in the early 1980s. The new name was in fact an old one. South Croft was the name of a field in the Abbeydale Road area. In the late 1700s it was part of land belonging to the homestead called Broadfield.

Southend Place, Road, 2
were among the last batch of streets named on the Wybourn estate in April 1933 by which time, it seems, ideas for street names were hard to find. Southend Road was at the south end of the estate.

Southern Street, 9
was built in 1890 for Samuel Grey Richardson, magistrate and former Master cutler. It was named after Francis Southern, his business partner in the firm of Southern and Richardson, Don Cutlery Works, Doncaster Street.

Southey Avenue, Close, Crescent, Drive, Hill, Place, Rise, Walk, 5
from the area called Southey, recorded as Southalgh in the thirteenth century, later as Suthagh, Southawe, and Southall. It means south enclosure.

Southey Green Close, Road, 5
from the old area of common land called Southey Green, one of several commons totalling 749 acres in the Ecclesfield parish when Harrison's survey was made in 1637.

Southey Hall Drive, Road, 5
from the house called Southey Hall, home in 1641 of George Carr, later of the Haywood family. It was demolished in 1937.

Southgrove Road, 10
continued the 'grove' theme already established in other street names nearby – Broomgrove, Clarkegrove, etc.

The caption on this picture postcard describes it as a view of 'South Street, Sheffield', which is what it was called up to February 1922. Since then it has been better known as The Moor.

South Lane, 1
from the old name of what is now called The Moor. Up to 1922 The Moor was called South Street (because it was the main route south). This lane was originally off South Street.

South Parade, 3
made more sense when it was one of a pair with North Parade (off Russell Street), but with North Parade gone, it means very little.

South Road, 6
directional name.

Southsea Road, 13
from the Hampshire coastal resort near Plymouth.

South Street, 2; South Street, 19
directional names.

**South View, 19;
South View Close, Rise, 6**
descriptive names. Streets built on south-facing slopes often advertise the fact. Those built on north-facing slopes rarely do.

South View Crescent, Road, 7
were built on garden land known as South View Gardens.

Southway, 19
directional name.

Southwell Road, 4
was built (with Holywell Road) for trustees of the late Henry Unwin in 1895 and seems to have been named after the place called Southwell in Nottinghamshire, possibly to retain the 'well' theme since both roads were built near Upwell Street.

Spa Brook Close, Drive, 12
the nearby stream is actually called the Shire Brook, but this name could not be used because it would have been confused with Shirebrook Road 8. Spa Brook was as near as possible to it.

Spa Lane, Spa Lane Croft, 13
from a modest little spa at Woodhouse, an enclosed spring which stood at the top of Spa Lane, with a room in which to undress and iron rings in the wall for visitors to grip as they bathed.

Spa View Avenue, Drive, Place, Road, Terrace, Way, 12
looks towards Birley Spa where a bath house was built in the early 1840s and the grounds around it laid out and planted. The water was reputed to have medicinal properties for many years before the bath was built. In later years the grounds became derelict and were acquired by Sheffield Corporation as an amenity area.

Speeton Road, 6
from the north Yorkshire village of Speeton, four miles from Filey.

Spencer Road, 2
was built by Sheffield and District Property Co Ltd, in 1872 and named after a founder-member of the company, Joseph Spencer, of Westbourne Road, clerk to Sheffield Board of Guardians for forty-three years. He died in 1899.

Spinkhill Avenue, Drive, Road, 13
from the village of Spinkhill, Derbyshire

Spitalfields, 3
from an old field name, meaning hospital fields, as in Spital Hill.

**Spital Hill, 4;
Spital Lane, Street, 3, and 4**
from the hospital founded in the area in the twelfth century by William de

Lovetot, lord of the manor, and dedicated to St Leonard. Spital is an abbreviation of hospital.

Spofforth Road, 9
from the village of Spofforth, Yorkshire, standing on the River Crimple. The Percy family had a fortified manor house there the ruins of which can still be seen (see Staniforth Road).

Spooner Road, 10
from the Spooner family, Joshua Spooner and his sons, William and Peter, who lived at Tapton House and owned land in the area. When Joshua died he left five-sixths of his money to William and one-sixth to Peter, who was lame 'and would not need so much'. William died in 1874 and the money passed to Peter, but he died two years later.

Spoon Glade, Way, Spoonhill Road, Spoon Lane, 6
after a former resident of Stannington, although which one is not certain. There were several people called Spoon in the area. Harrison's survey of 1637 recorded two, John Spoune, or Spoone, and Richard Spoone.

Spotswood Close, Drive, Mount, Place, Road, 14
after James Spotswood who was one of the trustees of Gleadless Independent Chapel which was built in the 1820s. Mr Spotswood was appointed a trustee in 1887.

Spout Copse, Lane, Spinney, 6
from an old house called Spout House, recorded as Spowt House in a document of 1547. According to some accounts there were three houses around Stannington with this name. One suggestion is that the name comes from an architectural feature of the house, perhaps a rain pipe.

Spring Close Dell, Mount, View, 14
from an old field name, Spring Close.

Springfield Avenue, Close, Glen, Road, 7
from an old Millhouses field name. Spring Field, which seems to have been quite large, is shown on a Fairbank map made in 1757. At that time it was one of the fields on George Hatfield's farm.

Spring Hill, Spring Hill Road, 10
from a stream, the exact course of which is uncertain because it was obscured by buildings many years ago.

Spring House Road, 10
from the house called Spring House, owned for many years by George Eadon, auctioneer and sharebroker, who owned other land and property in the area (including another house called Spring View, below). It had twenty-six acres of land attached. After Mr Eadon's death in 1871 it was offered for sale as building land.

Spring Lane, 2
there was a spring nearby.

Spring Street, 3
from the stream called Bower Spring.

Springvale Road, Walk, 6 and 10
the spring from which they were named flowed from Steel Bank down the valley to the Don. It was used to supply water to the Infirmary from a reservoir at the bottom of Upperthorpe Road till 1861 when the Infirmary went over to the town supply.

Spring View Road, 10
after a house called Spring View; like Spring House (see above) it was owned by George Eadon, auctioneer and sharebroker.

Spring Water Avenue, Close. Drive 12
there was a spring near the site.

Springwood Road, 8
from a nearby wood.

Spurr Street, 2
after Peter Spurr who lived at Heeley Bank in the early nineteenth century. The 1835 directory describes him as 'gentleman'. Heeley Bank was at some time a farm.

Stacye Avenue, Rise, 13
from the Stacye family of Ballifield Hall and Cinder Hill, a Quaker family well-known in Handsworth area for hundreds of years. One of them, Mahlon Stacye, emigrated to America in 1666 and founded the settlement of Trenton (see Trenton Close).

Stafford Lane, Road, Street, 2
were built on the Duke of Norfolk's land and named from one of the Duke's ancestors. William, son of the Earl of Arundel, married Mary, sister of the fifth Baron Stafford and was himself created Viscount Stafford in 1640.

Stainmore Avenue, 19
from the Stainmore Forest, Cumbria, one of a group of streets named after British forests (see Ashdown Gardens).

Stainton Road, 11,
probably (in view of the other Lincolnshire names round about) from the village of Stainton le Vale, near Market Rasen.

Stair Road, 4
not known; built in the 1890s. There are two villages called Stair, one in the Lake District, the other in Scotland, but there is no obvious connection with either of them. In field names stair usually means steep.

Stalker Lees Road, Stalker Walk, 11
from an old field name. As well as the field, Nether Stalker Lees, there was also a wood called Great Stalker Wood.

Stamford Street, 9
not known.

Stanage Rise, 12
from the area called Stanage, Derbyshire, one of a group of streets given Derbyshire names.

Stancer Street, 3
no longer listed, named after Joseph Stancer who was a grocer in Harvest Lane in the 1860s and 1870s and also had premises in Portland Street.

Standish Avenue, Close, Drive, Road, 5
were built on the Duke of Norfolk's land and named from the marriage of one of the Duke's ancestors, Elizabeth Howard, daughter of Sir Francis Howard, of Corby Castle, Cumberland, to Edward Standish in the seventeenth century.

Standon Crescent, Drive, Road, 9
Standon Road was originally called Station Road, from the nearby Meadowhall and Wincobank railway station. It was renamed in 1903 and the new name was chosen to keep it similar to the old one.

Staneford Court, 19
after William Staneford who is listed as one of the freeholders of Beighton in 1633. He was granted land as a reward for his military service.

Stanground Road, 2
not known, name approved May 1924.

Stanhope Road, 12
after the Rt Hon Edward Stanhope MP (1840-1893) who was Colonial Secretary in 1886-87, and Secretary for War from 1887 to 1892 when this road was built. He is remembered for his reform of army administration and for establishing the Army Service Corps.

Staniforth Road, 9
the Attercliffe end of the road was originally called Pinfold Lane. The name Staniforth was from a family who owned land in the area for hundreds of years. Thomas Staniforth was mentioned in the Capitation Tax lists of 1379. By the time Staniforth Road was built in 1870, the land was owned by the Rev Thomas Staniforth. He owned a large amount of land in Sheffield and elsewhere. His Sheffield land stretched from the railway bridge at the bottom of Staniforth Road up to what is now Prince of Wales Road.

Although he owned Darnall Hall, and a house in the Lake District, he lived at Kirk Hammerton Hall, near York, and owned a large area of land there too. In his younger days he was an athlete and rowed stroke for Oxford in the first University boat race. In fact, he was involved in getting the race started. After his death in 1887, his estate passed to his great nephew, Edwin Wilfrid Greenwood, of Swarcliffe Hall, Yorkshire, who then assumed by Royal Licence the name and coat of arms of Stanyforth (reverting to the older spelling of the name).

Lt-Col Stanyforth, as he later became, owned most of the Sheffield estate when it was developed for housing purposes, and most of the streets built on it were named after members of the family (Wilfrid Road, after himself, Ronald Road after his son, Barnadiston Road from the maiden name of his wife, Greenwood Road from his own family name) after family ancestors (all the names on the Littledale housing estate, including the name Littledale itself were from Staniforth ancestors), or from places in Yorkshire in which the family had some interest, (Swarcliffe, Cattal, Tockwith, Bramham, Ribston, Ouseburn, etc). Col Stanyforth, a noted agriculturist and stock raiser, died in 1939.

Stanley Lane, Street, 3
Stanley Street is shown on the 1823 map of Sheffield. I have a strong feeling (but no proof) that it was named after Richard Stanley, of Walker, Eyre and Stanley, bankers. Their business started in the eighteenth century and continued till 1836 when it was merged into the Sheffield and Rotherham Bank.

Stanley Place, 9
not known.

Stanley Road, 8
after Sir Henry Morton Stanley, journalist and explorer, who traced the source of the Nile. The parallel road was called Livingstone Road, after David Livingstone, the Scottish missionary and traveller, with whom Stanley's name is always remembered. But Livingstone Road was renamed Lismore Road in 1903.

Stannington Road, Stannington View Road, 6
from the village of Stannington which is mentioned in deeds of 1330 and 1331 as Stanyton and is believed to mean 'stone villa.

Stanton Crescent, 12
from the place called Stanton in the Peak, near Rowsley, one of a group of streets given Derbyshire names.

Stanwell Avenue, Close, Street, Walk, 9
Stanwell Street, built by the Meadowhall Freehold Land Society in the 1870s, was originally called Stanley Street, after Jabez Stanley, ironfounder, and one of the two trustees of the society. It was renamed in 1903 to avoid confusion with Stanley Street, 3, and the new name was an effort to stay as near as possible to the old one. Stanwell is a place in Surrey.

Stanwood Avenue, Crescent, Drive, Road, 6
an abbreviation of Stannington Wood.

Starling Mead, 2
a group name on the bird theme (see Curlew Ridge).

Station Lane, 9
the approach to Brightside railway station.

Staniforth Road, Darnall, in the days of horse transport and gas lamps.

There have been at least five Station Roads in Sheffield. Most were renamed. This one still exists, at Woodhouse.

Station Road, 9

the approach to Darnall railway station.

Station Road, 13

leads to Woodhouse railway station.

Station Road, 19

used to lead to two railway stations, Killamarsh West (closed 1954) and Killamarsh Central (closed 1963).

Staton Avenue, 19

after James Staton, magistrate, member of Beighton Parish council (and its chairman for several years), Chesterfield Rural Council, Derbyshire County Council, and North East Derbyshire Water Committee, Mr Staton, who lived in Orchard Lane, Beighton, died in 1947.

Staveley Road, 8

after General Sir Charles William Dunbar Staveley who fought in the Crimea, Abyssinia and China, one of a group of streets named after nineteenth century military men.

Steade Road, 7

after Thomas Steade (1821-1889) who started as an ironfounder, turned to building and became one of the town's leading builders. He built many of the houses in Sharrow, his business prospered and he lived for a time at Chipping House. But when he started to build outside the town his business collapsed.

Steadfast Street, 9

seems to be a variation on the name of Thomas Steade, the builder (see Steade Road, above). He bought the site, formerly common land, in 1867 and built on it in the 1870s.

Steelhouse Lane, 3

is shown on the 1771 map and the assumption is that there was some kind of small steel workshop nearby. But it could come from the old word for style – Style House.

Steel Road, 11

was one of five roads approved in 1897 for Messrs Neill and Hickmott (see Neill Road and Hickmott Road). There doesn't seem to have been anyone called Steel connected with the families of either man. A descendant of the Neill family suggested to me that Steel Road might have been named from the Steel family of Steel, Peach and Tozer.

Stemp Street 11

not known, built about 1880.

Stenton Road, 8

not known.

Stephen Drive, Hill, Stephen Hill Road, 10

from an old field name, Steven Field was mentioned in Harrison's survey of 1637. S.O. Addy thought it might have come from St Stephen being the patron saint of horses, but it might simply be from the name of a local person.

Stepney Row, Street, 2

Stepney Street was originally called New Street. It was renamed in 1886 because there was another street with the same name. There was no local reason for the new name. Stepney is an area of London. (Even in 1886, the street was by no means 'new'. It had certainly been in existence since the 1780s.)

Sterndale Road, 7

was built in 1875 as part of the Oakdale estate at Millhouses, and named after the Sheffield-born musician and composer Sir William Sterndale Bennett who died in February of that year. He was buried in Westminster Abbey and a bust of him was unveiled at the Cutlers' Hall around the same time.

Steade Road, Nether Edge, in the 1920s. It was named after a man who built many houses in the Sharrow-Nether Edge area, Thomas Steade.

Stevenson Road, Way, 9
After Philip Stevenson, part-owner of a steam corn mill at Attercliffe in the 1850s. The mill, which had three acres of land, burned down in 1863 and the road was built soon after through the mill land.

Stewart Road, 11
after Field Marshal Sir Donald Martin Stewart (1824-1900) who served in the Indian Mutiny and the Afghan War, one of a group of streets named after nineteenth century military men.

Stock Road, 2
from the village of Stock near Billericay, one of a group of streets given Essex place names.

Stocks Green Court, Drive, 17
in the early 1800s Totley village stocks stood in what is now Totley Hall Lane, but was then called Stocks Green.

Stockton Close, Place, 3
from the earlier Stockton Street, no longer listed, which was built on the Duke of Norfolk's land and named after the village of Stockton, near Bungay, Norfolk.

Stoke Street, 9
was originally called Blast Lane, from a nearby blast furnace. It was renamed in 1886. The new name seems to have been an arbitrary choice from the city of Stoke.

Stonecliffe Close, Place, Road, 2
as with many Manor estate street names, Stonecliffe comes from the ancient history of the parish of Eckington, where a field called Stoney Cliffe was recorded in 1570. At the time of the enclosures the name appears twice, as Great Stoney Cliffe and Little Stoney Cliffe, fields totalling thirteen acres which were awarded to John Porter.

Stonecroft Road, 17
see Marstone Crescent.

Stone Delf, 10
from an old field name. Harrison's survey of 1637 mentions a close called ye

Stone Delph measuring three roods nineteen perches, held by Hugh Beighton and his son William. Delph, or delf, is the old word for a quarry.

Stonegravels Croft, Way, 19
from the Chesterfield rugby ground at Stonegravels, one of a group of streets named after rugby grounds, although this one is in exalted company (see Arms Park Drive).

Stone Grove, 10
from a house nearby called Stone Grove, once the home of George Wragg, merchant.

Stone Lane, 13
descriptive name. There were fields nearby called Stoney Flatts (ten acres) and Stone Foare (two acres). It was sometimes known as Pit Lane.

Stoneley Close, Crescent, 12
from the nearby Stoneley Wood.

Stonesdale Close, 19
from the place in north Yorkshire called Stonesdale, one of a group of streets named on a dale theme.

Stone Street, 19
was originally known as Peat's Style. It was renamed in the early 1900s and the new name seems to have been from the fact that it was at that time a stony, unmade road.

Stonewood Court, Grove, 10
from the nearby Burnt Stones Wood.

Stony Walk, 6
descriptive name.

Stopes Road, 6
was first called Dungworth Road. Stopes comes from an old field name and is a corruption of stoops, meaning stakes. Three fields fronting the road were called Near, Far and Low Stoop Fields, collectively known as The Stoops.

Store Street, 2
was built on the Duke of Norfolk's land about 1911 and named after the warehouse alongside which it was built. The warehouse was used for storage by Samuel Hartley.

Storm Street, 8
was built by Sheffield Brick Company Ltd and named after William Storm, of Furnival Road, who was a shareholder in the company.

**Storrs Bridge Lane,
Storrs Carr, Green, Lane, 6**
Storrs, also the name of an area nearby, comes from the old word star, or storr, meaning bent or coarse grass, as in High Storrs.

Storrs Hall Road, 6
from the house called Storrs Hall, home of farmer Thomas Wragg in the 1850s. He was president of Loxley and Stannington Farmers' Club.

**Storth Avenue, Lane, Park,
Storthwood Court, 10**
Storth is thought to come from an old word meaning a young wood or plantation. It was a fairly common field name in the Sheffield area. There were also several houses called Storth House, Farm, or Lodge.

Stothard Road, 10
after Henry Stothard, builder and mason in Broomhall Street during the second half of the nineteenth century, who built houses at Crookes. He died in the 1890s.

Stour Lane, 6
was originally called School Lane, from Wadsley School. It was renamed in 1903. There seems to have been no local reason for the choice of Stour which is the name of five English rivers.

Stovin Drive, Gardens, Way, 9
from the earlier Stovin Road which was built in the 1880s by Edwin Scarth Bramwell, for many years vestry clerk at Attercliffe, and later vestry clerk to Sheffield township. It was named after his wife who was a daughter of Joseph Stovin, the builder. Their son, Edwin Stovin Bramwell, was also well-known in the town and was a keen student of Sheffield history.

Stowe Avenue, 7
not known, plans were approved for H.H. Andrews (along with those for Rex Avenue and Dewar Drive) in 1934.

Stradbroke Avenue, Close, Crescent, Drive, Place, Road, Walk, Way, 13
from the small town of Stradbroke, near Eye, East Suffolk. Stradbroke Road was originally called Stubbin Lane. It was changed in 1924.

Stumperlowe Hall on a picture postcard used in September 1916.

Stratford Road, 10
was approved in the 1870s for Thomas F. Cocker, of Cocker Brothers Ltd, who lived in Westbourne Road. It seems to have been named after Stratford-upon-Avon.

Strathtay Road, 11
is another link with the Murray family of Banner Cross Hall. One of the family's titles, granted in the eighteenth century, was the earldom of Strathtay and Strathardle (see Blair Athol Road).

Strawberry Avenue, 5
was built on or near the site of an old house called Strawberry Cottage, home of Mrs Hannah Brinnen in the 1850s.

Strawberry Lee Lane, 17
from Strawberry Lee Farm which is recorded in a document of the 1600s and was owned for more than 200 years by the Pegge family. Strawberry Lee means strawberry field.

Straw Lane, 6
was built in 1909 on land used by John L. Oliver, of Portland Street. It was named after Mr Oliver's business. He was a hay and straw dealer.

Streetfield Crescent, Lane; Streetfields, 19
from an old field name. Street fields, part of the Mosborough Hall land, were offered for sale in 1889 together with Blackberry Flat. Together they totalled just over eight acres. Streetfield Lane was the north-west boundary of the site.

Strelley Avenue, Road, 8
after the Strelley family who were lords of the manor of Ecclesall from the time of Sir Nicholas Strelley in 1517 up to the death of Gervase Strelley in 1609.

Stretton Road, 11
probably from the Derbyshire village of Stretton, although there are at least four other villages elsewhere with the same name. The name was approved in 1907.

Struan Road, 7
from the village of Struan, four miles west of Blair Castle, Scotland, a link with the Murray family of Banner Cross Hall (see Blair Athol Road).

Strutt Road, 3
was built on the Duke of Norfolk's land in 1938, and named after the Duchess of Norfolk. Before their marriage in 1937, she was the Hon Lavinia Mary Strutt, daughter of the third Baron Belper.

Stubbing House Lane, 6; Stubbin Lane, 5
stubbin, and stubbings, were words used to indicate an area of woodland which had been cleared for farming. It was therefore quite a common name. The name stubbing slasher, for a hook used to cut hedges, comes from the same source.

Studfield Crescent, Drive, Grove, Hill, Rise, Road, 6
from an old Loxley Valley field name. A document of 1574 recording the transfer of land from one owner to another mentions a 'close called Studfield.

Studley Court, 9
from the earlier Studley Road, no longer listed, which was built on Staniforth family land (see Staniforth Road) and named after Studley Park, near Ripon, former seat of the Marquis of Ripon. Col Stanyforth was agent for the Marquis of Ripon for a time.

Stumperlowe Avenue, Close, Croft, Lane, View, Stumperlowe Crescent Road, 10
the name Stumperlowe appears as Stumperlawe in a sixteenth century document. Experts are not sure of its meaning. They agree that lowe means hill but they are not sure about Stumper. S.O. Addy was pretty certain though. 'What else can it mean', he wrote, 'but a monolith, stone, or other erection, upon or near a barrow to mark the last resting place of some dead hero or chief?'

Stumperlowe Hall Chase, Road, 10
from the house called Stumperlowe Hall built in the seventeenth century. It changed hands many times, and in the nineteenth century was the home of Henry Isaac Dixon, of the well-known silver firm, and later of his son, James.

Stumperlowe Park Road, 10
from the area of land around Stumperlowe Grange. When the house was offered for sale in 1928 it had thirteen acres of land.

Stupton Road, 9
not known; it was built about 1910 for Mrs Alice Barry, of Oxted, Surrey. The name was probably her idea.

Sturge Croft, 2
from the earlier Sturge Street, no longer listed, which was probably named after Joseph Sturge, the Victorian philanthropist, Birmingham alderman, anti-slavery campaigner, anti-Corn Law League member, and – for a time – Chartist sympathiser. He visited Sheffield in 1842 in support of the Complete Suffrage Movement.

Sturton Road, 4
was approved in 1898 for the Duke of Norfolk and executors of William Wake, along with Blayton and Kirton Roads, all three named after places ending with the same three letters. There are five places called Sturton, two in Lincolnshire, two in Yorkshire, one in Nottinghamshire.

Sudbury Street, 3
was originally called Suffolk Street. It was changed in 1887 and renamed after the town in Suffolk where Gainsborough, the painter, was born.

Suffolk Lane, Road, 2
were built on the Duke of Norfolk's land and named from a title held by one of the Duke's ancestors, Lord Thomas Howard, first Baron Howard de Walden, and eldest son of the fourth Duke of Norfolk, who was created Earl of Suffolk in 1603.

Summerfield, 10
from an old field name which, like Sunny Bank, meant that it was in a sunny position.

Summerfield Street, 11
was built in 1884 for Bernard Wake and was originally called Dale Street. It was renamed in 1887, probably from an old field name.

Summer Lane, 17
not known.

Summer Street, 3
was built in 1861 and named by association with the parallel street, Winter Street (built ten years earlier and named after landowner John Winter).

Sunderland Street, 11
not known.

Sundown Place, Road, 13
seems to be a fanciful name perhaps suggested by the westward facing nature of the development.

Sunningdale Mount, 11
was built with Ranelagh Drive and Hurlingham Close, all three apparently named after places in the south of England with a sporting link. Sunningdale, Berkshire is the site of a well-known golf course.

Sunny Bank, 10
from the name of the field over which it was built. Fields in a sunny position were naturally prized.

Sunnyvale Avenue, Road, 17
is an adaptation of an old field name, Sun Fields, which were part of the land attached to Totley Hall.

Surrey Street in the 1930s. The building next to the Central Library was Surrey Street United Methodist Church which opened in December 1831, and was demolished in the 1960s to make way for redevelopment.

Surbiton Street, 9
was originally called Sorby Street after the Sorby family of Attercliffe. It was renamed to avoid confusion with Sorby Street near Spital Hill. The new name was chosen for its slight similarity to the old one. Surbiton is a place in Surrey.

Surrey Lane, Place, Street, 1
from a title held by one of the Duke of Norfolk's ancestors – Earl of Surrey. The part of Surrey Street alongside the Town Hall is an extension of the old Surrey Street and was known for a time as New Surrey Street.

Sussex Road, Street, 4
from a title held by the Duke of Norfolk's family. The second Duke's grandson, Thomas Radcliffe, was given the title Earl of Sussex in the sixteenth century.

Suthard Cross Road, 10
was originally called Cross Lane, because it crossed from Mulehouse Road to Lydgate Lane. It was renamed in 1912 and the new name was a variation on the old one, Suthard presumably meaning southward.

Sutherland Road, Street, 4
were built on the Duke of Norfolk's land and named from the marriage of Henry Charles, thirteenth Duke, to Sophia Granville, daughter of George Granville, first Duke of Sutherland.

Sutton Street, 3
after Dr Thomas Sutton, vicar of Sheffield for forty-five years. When he became vicar in 1805 Sheffield was a parish of 50,000 people with three churches. When he died in 1851 there were sixteen parish churches in the town. Philip Gell, who owned the land on which the street was built, was his patron.

Swaledale Road, 7
from Swaledale, Yorkshire; one of four neighbouring roads named after dales.

Swale Gardens, 9
from the earlier Swale Road, no longer listed, which was built on land owned by the Staniforth family (see Staniforth Road) and named after the River Swale which rises in north west Yorkshire and flows into the River Ure.

Swallow's Lane, 19
after Richard Swallow of Mosborough Hill and his sons, Richard junior and John, who were coal owners at Mosborough in the mid nineteenth century. They were descendants of the Richard Swallow after whom Swallow Street, 9, below, was named.

Swallow Street, 9
after Richard Swallow who lived at nearby New Hall in the early nineteenth century. Swallow, an associate of John Fell, of Attercliffe Forge, inherited the hall, the forge and a fortune of £100,000 from Fell's widow who is reputed to have said she would make him 'the richest Swallow that ever flew over Attercliffe'.

Swallow Wood Court, 13
from the Swallow Wood coal seam which was mined at a nearby pit.

Swamp Walk, 6
up to the 1850s the area near Capel Street was a field known as The Swamp. It was referred to in a 1906 court case when H. L. Coath, of the Town Clerk's department, said the area was previously known as 'The Dismal Swamp'. The walk was named after the field.

Swanbourne Place, Road, 5
from part of Arundel Park, Sussex, around the Duke of Norfolk's stately home, which was planned and improved by the eleventh Duke in the early nineteenth century. The Duke had the mill pond at Swanbourne enlarged to make an ornamental lake.

Swan Street, 9
not known. Originally Alma Street, it was changed in 1886.

Swarcliffe Road, 9
was originally called Lown Street after John Lown who built some of the houses. It was renamed in 1902 after the place called Swarcliffe, North Yorkshire. The Staniforth family, Darnall landowners, had a house at Swarcliffe.

Sweet Tree Lane, 13
from an old field name. When it was offered for sale in 1883 Sweet Tree Croft, south of another field called Lamb Croft, was just over two acres in size and was occupied by Thomas Swift.

Swift Way 2
group name on the birds theme (see Curlew Ridge).

Swinton Street, 3
was originally called Cross Chapel Street, but the name became meaningless when the Chapel Street that it crossed was renamed Chatham Street in 1886. The old name lingered on for four years. The street was then renamed after a place called Swinton. There are at least five Swintons, three in Yorkshire, the best known locally the one near Mexborough.

Sycamore House Road, 5
from the house called Sycamore House. In the 1870s and 1880s it was the home of Henry Mabson, Sheffield butcher.

Sycamore Street, 19
(Beighton): group name – trees.

Sycamore Street 19
(Mosborough): group name – trees.

Sydney Road, 6
probably after Algernon Sydney, son of the Earl of Leicester, who joined the Parliamentary forces and fought against the Royalists at Marston Moor. He spent seventeen years in exile, returned on a pardon, was accused of high treason and executed in 1683.

Sylvester Gardens, 1
was built over the filled-in dam of the Sylvester Wheel, one of Sheffield's old grinding wheels. Little is known of its early history, but it was run by John Wilson from the 1780s to about 1814.

Syvia Close, 13
after a member of the Watson family, builders (see David Close).

Symons Crescent, 5
after Arthur William Symons (1865-1945) poet, playwright and essayist; one of a group of streets named after literary figures.

Tadcaster Crescent, Road, Way, 8
after the Yorkshire town of Tadcaster; one of a group of streets at Woodseats all of which were given Yorkshire place names. One of them, Thurcroft Road, ceased to have its own name and became part of Tadcaster Road in 1931.

Talbot Crescent, Gardens, Place, Road, Street, 2
from the family name of the Earls of Shrewsbury who were lords of Hallamshire from the time of John Talbot, the first Earl, in the fourteenth century, to Gilbert, the seventh Earl, in the seventeenth century. The lordship then passed to the Duke of Norfolk.

Talmont Road, 11
plans for the road were approved for Mrs Martha Greaves Bagshawe in November 1922. Most of the streets built on Bagshawe land were given Scottish names (see Blair Athol) and Talmont has a Scottish sound to it, but I can't find a place called Talmont in the Gazetteer of Scotland, so it might be a family name of some kind.

Tanfield Road, 6
after Harry Corker Tanfield of the firm of Tanfield and Sayles, timber and slate merchants, Eclipse Sawmills. Both the sawmills and Mr Tanfield's home were in Tanfield Road.

Tannery Close, Street, 13
tanning was a traditional trade in the village of Woodhouse for many years. There were at least five tanneries in the village at one time, two of them on this street. Lionel Keyworth had a tanyard in the area in 1680.

Tansley Drive, Street, 9
Tansley Street, built first, was originally called Thomas Street, after an ancestor of the Duke of Norfolk. It was renamed in 1903 to avoid confusion with Thomas Street in the city centre, and the new name came from the village of Tansley, near Matlock.

Taplin Road, 6
was built in the 1890s by Hillsborough Freehold Land Society and almost certainly named after Charles Taplin, joiner and builder, who lived in Fielding Road at that time and may

have been involved with the land society.

Tapton Bank, Court, Hill, Walk; Tapton Crescent Road; Tapton Hill Road, 10

Tapton Hill is referred to in a will dated 1580 and is believed to have been named after Henry de Tapton (from Tapton in Derbyshire) who lived in the area in the fourteenth century.

Tapton House Road, 10

from the house called Tapton House, home in the nineteenth century of George Eadon, of George Eadon and Son, carvers, gilders, etc, Norfolk Street and New Church Street.

Tapton Park Road,10

from a house called Tapton Park, home of the Howson family, notably George Howson JP, partner in Harrison Brothers and Howson, and Master Cutler in 1893.

Taptonville Crescent, Road, 10

in the 1850s Taptonville was the name of a group of five houses. In later years it became the name of the area around them. The name was simply a Victorian variation on Tapton.

Tasker Road, 10

after John Tasker, pioneer of electricity and the telephone in Sheffield. Mr Tasker, who lived at Crookes House, died in 1895. He owned land and property on Mulehouse Lane (now Road), Salisbury Road, Crookes and Tasker Road, and farms at Dungworth and Ughill.

Taunton Avenue, Grove, 9

from the Vale of Taunton Deane, Somerset; one of a group of streets named after well-known English vales (see Aylesbury).

Tavistock Road, 7

was built in 1881 for the executors of Peter Spooner and named after the town of Tavistock, Devon.

Tay Street, 6

from the Scottish River Tay which rises in West Perthshire and flows into the Firth of Tay, near Perth.

Teesdale Road, 12

from the upper valley of the River Tees; one of a group of streets named after north country dales (see Camdale).

Behind the tram terminus at Millhouses in the 1950s is Terminus Road. The road remains, but trams and terminus have gone.

Tennyson Road, 6

after Alfred, Lord Tennyson (1809-1892), the English poet who succeeded Wordsworth as Poet Laureate in 1850. The road was built on land belonging to the Burgoyne family around the time of Tennyson's death.

Tenterden Road, 5

was originally called Tenter Road, which came (like Tenter Street in the city centre) from the old word *tainter*, meaning a dyer of woollen clothes. The name was changed in 1930, to avoid confusion with the city centre street, by adding three letters to make Tenterden, the name of a market town in Kent.

Tenter Street, 1

Tenter Croft appears as a field name in Sheffield area. There was one at Dore, another at Ecclesall. In towns, the name often appears as Tenter Yard. It comes from the old word *tainter*, meaning a dyer of woollen clothes. Tenter fields and Tenter yards were places where the dyed cloth was stretched on tenter hooks.

Terminus Road, 7

from the old Millhouses tram terminus nearby. The Millhouses tram route was extended from Millhouses Lane to the *Wagon and Horses* in 1926. The road was named in 1928.

The Terrace, 5

built across the hillside, terrace-style.

Terrace Walk, 11

a small pathway which rises up the hill from Junction Road to Hardwick Road in terraces.

Terrey Road, 17

after William Terrey who was general manager of Sheffield Water Department for thirty-four years and supervised several large schemes to improve the city's water supply. The road was built in 1930 at the time of his retirement. He died in 1935.

Terry Street, 9

after Stephen Terry who was a farmer at Attercliffe in the 1850s. He owned and lived at a large house called Belle Vue at the end of Terry Street. He also owned the nearby *Travellers Inn*.

Tetney Road, 10

from the village of Tetney, near Cleethorpes.

Teynham Drive, Road, 5

were built on the Duke of Norfolk's land and named from the fact that one of his family, Bernard Howard of Glossop, grandson of the Earl of Arundel, was married in 1710 to Anne Roper, daughter of Christopher, Lord Teynham.

Thirlmere Road, 8

after the lake called Thirlmere in the Lake District; one of a group of streets given Lake District names (see Arnside Road).

Thirlwell Road, 8

was built in the early 1860s. It appears in the 1863 directory but not the 1859 directory. It seems to have something to do with the firm of Chadwick and Thirlwell, contractors, who were involved in the 1860s with building the nearby Midland Railway and did some of the work on Heeley Station. I have not been able to find out anything about Mr Thirlwell, or to establish a link between him and the road, but his activity in the area at the time it was built (and the fact that there was no-one else of the same name in the area) make him the prime candidate for the road name.

Thirza Street, 6
after two women called Thirza. Joseph Stoven and John Wreaks bought the site of the old Sheffield barracks, Infirmary Road, for £2,850 in 1855. They built three streets on the site — Florence Street, Gertrude Street and Thirza Street. Mr Stovin's wife and daughter were both called Thirza.

Thomas Street, 1
was built on Earl Fitzwilliam's land and named after someone in his family tree, probably his celebrated ancestor Sir Thomas Wentworth, first Earl of Strafford (1593-1641), statesman and MP for Yorkshire, who became Baron and Viscount Wentworth in 1628, and Earl in 1639. He was accused of high treason and beheaded in 1641.

Thompson Road, 11
was first called Drayton Place. It was renamed in 1904 after Mrs Elizabeth A. Thompson, a member of the Wilson family, who owned land in the Ecclesall Road area. Mrs Thompson and her sister, Mrs Louisa E. Harland, gave a drinking fountain at Hunters Bar in memory of their father, Henry Wilson, and their brother, Alfred Wilson.

Thoresby Road, 6
was built with Manvers Road and named after the family seat of Earl Manvers at Thoresby, near Mansfield.

Thornborough Close, Place, Road, 2
were built on the Duke of Norfolk's land and named from the fact that Lord Henry Thomas Howard, brother of the twelfth Duke, and Deputy Earl Marshal of England, lived at Thornborough Castle, Gloucestershire.

Thornbridge Avenue, Close, Crescent, Drive, Grove, Place, Rise, Road, Way, 12
from Thornbridge Hall, near Ashford, Derbyshire, which was the home of Charles Boot, the man whose firm built much of the housing at Frecheville. Mr Boot suggested that the area should be called Frecheville. When it was offered for sale in 1930, Mr Boot's Derbyshire estate was 185 acres in size. There is also a Thornbridge Road near the famous Pinewood film studio, named for the same reason as the one at Frecheville. Most of the Pinewood housing was built by Mr Boot's firm.

Thorndon Road, 4
was built on the Duke of Norfolk's land and named after Thorndon, a village in east Suffolk. Lord Petre, a relative of the Duke (and the man after whom nearby Petre Street was named) lived at Thorndon.

Thorne Road, 7
not known; the name was approved in January 1925. It could be from the Yorkshire town of Thorne but it could just as easily be named after a person.

Thornsett Gardens, 17
from an old house called Thornsett. In the early 1900s it was the home of John William Cooper of Cooper Brothers and Son Ltd, silversmiths and electroplaters, Don Plate Works, Arundel Street.

Thornsett Road, 7
after a house called Thornsett, built on Priory Road, Sharrow, about 1860. In the 1870s it became a ladies' boarding school run by the Misses Ann and Ellen Maria Potts. In the 1890s, when Thornsett Road was built, Miss Sarah Jane Roberts lived at the house.

Thornville Road, 9
after the village of Thornville, North Yorkshire, which is near Cattal; one of a group of streets, most of them built on Staniforth family land, and given Yorkshire place names (see Staniforth Road).

Thorpe Drive, Green, 19
the original intention was to call them Waterthorpe Drive and Waterthorpe Green, but as there were already six streets on the Mosborough development with Waterthorpe names, these two were given shortened versions of the name.

Thorpe House Avenue, Rise, Road, 8
from Thorpe House which stood opposite the Bishop's House and was the home of the Hall Brothers, George and Joseph who were partners in an engineering firm in Hereford Street. Later it was owned by the Cockayne family. The house was demolished some years ago.

Threshfield Way, 12
from the village of Threshfield, one mile west of Grassington, North Yorkshire.

Thrush Street, 6
one of a pair of parallel streets, along with Lark Street, both named after birds.

Thurley Place, 9
not known.

Thurston Avenue, 8
after a man called Thurston Kirke, member of a well-known local family who lived at Greenhill Hall in the sixteenth Century.

Tideswell Road, 5
from the Derbyshire town of Tideswell; one of a group of streets given Derbyshire names.

Tilford Road, 13
was originally called Talbot Road. It was renamed in 1924, to avoid confusion with Talbot Road, 2. The new name was from the village of Tilford, Surrey. To several generations of Woodhouse residents its unofficial name was The Buck Croft, the name of the field on which it was built.

Tillotson Close, Rise, Road, 8
after John Tillotson who owned land at Heeley. In the 1850s he had a field called Lower Well Dole and two acres of Upper Well Dole.

Tinker Lane, 6 and 10
from a field name. Tinker Field was recorded in a document dated 1506. There was also a Tinker Brook and a Tinker Hill, and all three are believed to have come from a local surname.

Tinsley Park Close, Road, 9
from the wood called Tinsley Park which covered a large area of the old manor of Tinsley. In the sixteenth century it was forbidden to carry off wood, dry or green, from the park, and anyone who did was liable to a fine of 'twopence per bundle, when found'. Some of the old woodland remains in Tinsley Park golf course.

Tipton Street, 9
was originally called George Street. It was changed in 1886. The new name was from Tipton, a market town in Staffordshire.

Tithe Barn Avenue, Close, Lane, Way, 13
tithe barns were barns belonging to a lord or religious house in which the crops representing rents, or tithes, were stored. The old tithe barn at Woodhouse stood near these streets, on the site of what is now St James's Church.

Titterton Close, Street, 9
were built through a large area of gardens, mostly used for the growing of rhubarb, which were owned in the 1870s by Henry Titterton, grocer and newsagent in nearby Carlton Road. The Tittertons were an old Attercliffe family.

Tockwith Road, 9
was built on Staniforth family land (see Staniforth Road) and named after the small Yorkshire village of Tockworth which is near the scene of the battle of Marston Moor. During the battle Cromwell is said to have received attention to his wounds in one of the village's thatched cottages.

Todwick Road, 8
after the place called Todwick, between Sheffield and Worksop; one of a group of streets given South Yorkshire place names.

Tofts Lane, 6
from a group of fields called the Toft, the Toft Head, and The Toft Bottom, collectively known as The Tofts. Toft is an old Scandinavian word meaning a house, or homestead.

Toftwood Avenue, Road, 10
from a wood called Tofts. Harrison's survey of 1637 mentions 'a shroggwood called Tofts' at Crookes consisting of one acre one rood eighteen perches. The origin of the name is the same as in Tofts Lane, above.

Toll Bar Avenue, Close, Drive, Road, 12
from a toll bar which stood at Myrtle Springs on a private road from Heeley to Gleadless. It operated till the 1950s when the tolls were one penny for pedestrians and cyclists, twopence for motor cycles and threepence for cars.

Tom Lane, 10
either from a person's name or from the old celtic word *tom*, meaning a hillock. It is referred to – as Thom Lane – in a document of 1564.

Topham Drive, Road, Way, 8
from the name of an old Greenhill family, the Tophams, sometimes spelt Toppam. They appear in the Norton parish registers as far back as the 1580s, when George Topham was a cooper in the village.

Top Terrace, 10
one of two rows of old terraced houses off Parkers Lane. This was the upper, or top one.

Torbay Road, 4
from Torbay on the Devon coast. William of Orange landed at Torbay in 1688 and there are the remains of an abbey built in the twelfth century.

Torksey Road, 5
from the place in Lincolnshire called Torksey, between Gainsborough and Lincoln, at the junction of the Foss Dyke and the Trent.

Torry Court, 13
not known; there are two places called Torry, both in Scotland.

Torwood Drive, 8
not known; name approved 1938.

Totley Brook Close, Croft, Glen, Grove, Road, Way, 17
the origin of the name is obvious. It comes from the stream called the Totley Brook. The reasoning is less obvious. The development is much nearer to the Old Hay Brook than it is to Totley Brook. It isn't even in the same valley, or on the same side of the main road (Baslow Road) as Totley Brook.

Totley Grange Close, Drive, Road, 17
from the house called Totley Grange, one-time home of Thomas Earnshaw, fish, game and poultry dealer (of Thomas Earnshaw and Son Ltd). After his death in May 1893 Mrs Hannah Earnshaw lived at the Grange till the 1930s. It was nicknamed 'Fish Villa'.

Totley Hall Lane, 17
from the seventeenth century house, Totley Hall, built by George Newbold, later the home of the Barker and Coke families, and later still of W.A. Milner. It was bought by the Corporation in 1944 and with large extensions, became a training college.

Totley Lane, 17
from the area called Totley. Domesday Book recorded it as Totingelie. In later years it changed spelling several times. Most dialect experts say it means the clearing of Tota's people, from the old personal name Tota. But S.O. Addy had another theory. He said toting hills were mounds or hills used as defensive look-out places. To tote means to spy, or watch out, he said.

Tower Close, Drive, 2
from the house called Queen's Tower, built in the 1830s, home of Samuel Roberts, industrialist, Town Trustee, Town Councillor, and member of a well-known Sheffield family. It remained in the Roberts family for nearly 100 years.

Townend Street, 10
after John Townend, land agent and surveyor, whose office was in Paradise Square. He lived first at Holly House (which he built) in Bates Street, then in Mooroaks Road. He owned property in Townend Street and his son, Joseph Dobson Townend, lived for a time in the street. He was also involved in several freehold land societies.

Townhead Road, 17
from the area called Townhead – land at the top of the village.

Townhead Street, 1
marked the upper boundary – the town head – of the old town of Sheffield. Beyond it were fields which were not built on till the 1770s. The Townhead Cross stood at the junction of Townhead Street and Church Street.

Town Street, 9
old Tinsley village was in two parts, one called Top End, the other called The Bottom. Local people spoke of going 'up t'town' when they went to the Top End. The lane between the two areas was named Up Town Street, later shortened to Town Street.

Toyne Street, 10
after a former land owner, David Toyne, who owned a house, stable, other buildings, and five closes of land described as being 'in a high state of cultivation' and 'eligible sites for country residences' when he offered them for sale in 1840.

Trafalgar Road, 6; Trafalgar Street, 1
from the naval battle of 1805 when Nelson defeated the combined French and Spanish fleets. There was a plan to erect a 'naval pillar', a miniature Nelson's Column, at the gates of Sheffield Parish Church in honour of Nelson (who was killed in the battle) but the column was never built.

Trap Lane, 11
uncertain; the lane is shown on the 1841 Ordnance Survey map and the name may simply indicate use of the lane by horse and trap.

Travey Road, 2
not known; name approved April 1924.

Travis Place, 10
after George William Travis, joiner and builder, of Broomhall Road, who was involved in building work in this area when the Broom Hall estate was developed by John Watson in the 1830s.

Tree Root Walk, 10
from the tree roots that protruded into the walk at one time. Trees on the top side of the walk are well above the level of the road and their roots would still protrude if the bank had not been walled.

Trenton Close, Rise, 13
from the fact that Mahlon Stacye, of the Stacye family of Ballifield Hall and Handsworth Grange, emigrated to America with his family in 1666 and in 1680 founded the settlement of Trenton, now state capital of New Jersey.

Trent Street, 9
was originally called Bridge Street (from the nearby Washford Bridge). It was renamed in 1886 to avoid confusion with Bridge Street in the town centre. The new name was from the River Trent – possibly because of the association of ideas between Trent and Bridge.

Treswell Crescent, 6
from the Nottinghamshire village of Treswell, near Rampton.

Trickett Road, 6
probably after Thomas Trickett who owned land at Loxley and Hillsborough in the nineteenth century.

Trinity Street, 3
uncertain; building leases were granted in the street in the 1760s by the Church Burgesses, who owned the land. The name may have come about because the Parish Church, now the Anglican Cathedral, was known for a short time as the Church of the Holy Trinity.

Trippet Lane, 1
from the name of one of the oldest families in Sheffield, the Trippets, whose name has had various spellings over the years. There is evidence of a John Trypet in the town in 1379, and the name crops up in documentary records over the following 500 years. A John Trippet was Master Cutler in 1694. The street was first called Red Croft, but it has been Trippet Lane since about 1770.

Troutbeck Road, 7
from the village of Troutbeck, near Windermere; one of a group of streets given Lake District names.

Truswell Avenue, Road, 10
from an old Crookes field name, Truswell Field.

Tudor Place, Street, Way, 1
after Henry Tudor who was partner with Thomas Leader in a silver-plating business. He built a house called Tudor House which stood where the *Lyceum Theatre* is today.

Tuffolds Close, 2
not known; name approved (as Tuffolds Way) April 1924.

Tulip Tree Close, 19
after a tree which was left in place when the houses were built. The tulip tree, sometimes called the yellow poplar, has yellowish-green tulip-like blossoms.

Tullibardine Road, 11
from the Murray and Athol link with Banner Cross Hall (see Blair Athol Road). The Duke of Athol's eldest son has the title Marquis of Tullibardine, a small village near Blair Athol.

Tummon Road, 2
from the earlier Tummon's Row, named after Charles Tummon and Robert Tummon, both of whom were joiners and builders, and both of whom were councillors for the Park ward at various times between 1849 and 1863.

Tunwell Avenue, Drive, Greave, 5
from an old field name, Tunwell Field, a thirty-acre open field in Ecclesfield manor. There was a spring at one end of it and the name was probably a corruption of town well.

Turie Avenue, Crescent, 5
after the Rev Robert Turie, one of the chaplains of Sheffield Parish Church and curate of Ecclesall from 1695 to 1720. A Scot, he owned land and considerable property, all of which he left to various parishes in the Sheffield area, including a legacy to Parson Cross School.

Turin Street, 9
one of two streets named after Italian cities. The other, Florence Street, was later renamed Vine Street.

Turners Lane, 10
after John Turner, cabinet maker, and his wife, who lived on Whitham Road, alongside the lane, in the 1870s.

Turner Street, 2
from the firm of Thomas Turner and Co, merchants, and manufacturers of table, pen and pocket knives, cutlery, etc, whose works, Suffolk Works, were on Suffolk Road from the middle of the nineteenth century. Turner Street was built round the side and back of their premises.

Tuxford Road, 9
was originally called Wentworth Road. It was changed in 1906 because there was another Wentworth Road. The new name was from Tuxford, the Nottinghamshire village between Worksop and Newark.

Twentywell Drive, Lane, Rise, Road, View, 17
Twentywell Sick is the old name of the deep valley leading to the north end of Totley Tunnel. It is referred to in a twelfth-century document as *Quintinewelle*, from St Quentin's Well. Presumably there was a well of this name in the area.

Twickenham Close, Court, Crescent, Glade, Glen, Grove, 19

from the England rugby ground at Twickenham; one of a group of streets named after famous rugby venues (see Arms Park Drive).

Twitchill Drive, 13

twitchill, or twitchel, means a narrow footpath or passage. This street got its name from an old twitchill between Sheffield Road and Stradbroke Road. Some houses nearby were known as Twitchill Cottages.

Tyas Road, 5

after the Rev John Tyas, vicar of Ecclesfield from 1549 till his death in 1580. He left a legacy to be distributed among the needy of the parish and another legacy for the needy of Bradfield.

Tye Road, 19

after Thomas Tye who was a farmer nearby in the 1850s.

Tyler Street, Way, 9

not known; Tyler Street first appeared in directories in the early 1860s. There were several people called Tyler living in Sheffield around that time. The nearest one to the street was John Tyler, Britannia metal manufacturer, of Andover Street. The name may have something to do with him.

Tynker Avenue, 19

after the Rev John Tynker who was vicar of Beighton from 1456 till his death in 1480. His gravestone was set in the floor of Beighton parish church.

Tylney Road, 2

was built on the Duke of Norfolk's land and named after two ladies in the Duke's family history. Thomas, Earl of Surrey (who later became second Duke of Norfolk) married Elizabeth Tylney in 1472. Four months after her death in 1497 he married Agnes Tylney. Both women were heiresses in their own right.

Tyzack Road, 8

after Joshua Tyzack, of the well-known Sheffield family, who lived at Wood Lodge, in nearby Abbey Lane. After a spell in the family firm Mr Tyzack became a farmer. He was a Derbyshire County Councillor for eighteen years, Totley parish councillor and magistrate. He died in 1930.

The old Ecclesall Union later became part of Nether Edge Hospital, but the road in front of it retained the name of Union Road.

Ulley Crescent, 13

from the South Yorkshire village of Ulley, near Rotherham.

Ullswater Avenue, Close, 19

from the lake called Ullswater; one of a group of streets given Lake District names (see Ambleside Close).

Ulverston Road, 8

from the market town and seaport of Ulverston, on Morecambe Bay.

Undercliffe Road, 6

was originally called Union Road. The name was changed in 1904. Undercliffe, unlike Underbank, means a site on or under a hillside.

Underhill Lane, 6

from the area called Underhill, because of its position beneath Birley Edge.

Underwood Road, 8

was originally called Clarke Road, after Reuben Clarke who was a landowner in the Chesterfield Road-Scarsdale Road area. It was renamed in 1902 and the name Underwood was a descriptive name chosen because of the woodland, now gone, which used to stretch up to Derbyshire Lane.

Umpire Lane, 2

no longer listed; it was named after a public house, *The Umpire,* which opened in 1860 in what was then called New George Street and is now Boston Street. It closed in 1934.

Union Lane, Street, 1

in this sense union means a joining. When it was first built, Union Street joined Norfolk Street to the foot of Coalpit Lane (now called Cambridge Street) giving a more direct route to Moorhead. Pinstone Street did not become a through road till much later.

Union Road, 11

was named after the Guardians of the Poor Building – the old Ecclesall Union – which, much enlarged, later became part of Nether Edge Hospital. The first houses in the road were built in the 1860s.

Unstone Street, 2

from the place called Unstone, near Chesterfield.

Unwin Street, 9
after John Unwin, landowner, of Cross Villas, Brunswick Road, who sold seven acres of land 'between the Sheffield to Worksop turnpike and the Manchester, Sheffield and Lincolnshire Railway' for building purposes in 1866. This was one of the streets built.

Upper Albert Road, 8
see Albert Road, 8

Upper Allen Street, 3
see Allen Street, 3

Uppergate Road, 6
was originally Upper Gate, gate meaning road or cattle walk. It is mentioned in Langdale's *Topographical Dictionary of Yorkshire*, dated 1822, and it means the upper road.

Upper Hanover Street, 3
see Hanover Street.

Upperthorpe Glen, Road, 6
from the area called Upperthorpe, the meaning of which is uncertain. It looks as if it ought to mean upper farm or settlement, but in Harrison's survey of 1637 it is mentioned as Huppathorpe, and Hunter says that in 1594 it was called Hooperthorpe. S.O. Addy concluded from this that it came either from a personal name or from the old word *huopa*, meaning an enclosed or measured piece of ground.

Upper Valley Road, 8
see Valley Road.

Upwell Hill, Lane, Street, 4
Upwell Lane, which appeared first, was originally called Coldwell Lane, from a well called Cold Well, nearby. Why it was changed is not clear.

Upwood Road, 6
not known.

Uttley Close, Croft, Drive, 9
from the older Uttley Street, no longer listed, which was named after Fredrick Uttley Laycock, for whom it was built in 1898. Mr Laycock was a solicitor with offices in the Independent Buildings, Fargate. He owned a large number of houses at Attercliffe.

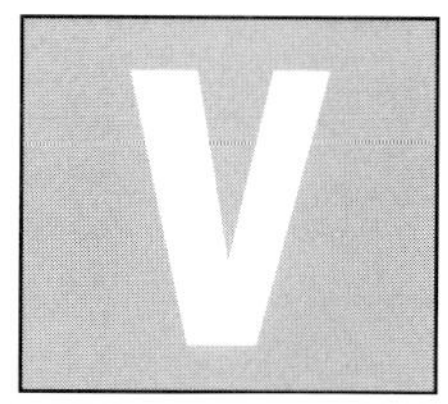

Vainor Road, 6
was originally called Vicarage Road, from the nearby vicarage. It was renamed in 1904. Reason for the new name not known.

Vale Grove, 6
not known.

Valentine Close, Crescent, Road, 5
uncertain; one suggestion I have heard is that the name came from St Valentine because Valentine Road, Close, and Crescent were built in the shape of a heart. With street names almost anything is possible, but this seems unlikely. The name was approved in August 1931.

Vale Road, 3
the area around used to be known as The Vale.

Valley Road, 8
runs down the valley of Meers Brook.

Valley Road, 12
from the valley of the Ochre Dyke.

Vauxhall Close, Road, 9
Vauxhall Road was originally called Victoria Road, after Queen Victoria. It was changed in 1903 to avoid confusion with other Victoria Roads and the new name was from the Vauxhall area of London.

Ventnor Place, 7
from the resort in the Isle of Wight.

Verdant Way, 5
not known; name, approved February 1920. It may simply mean that the area was well covered with grass and trees before it was built on.

Verdon Street, 3
was built on the Duke of Norfolk's land and named from a title held by the Duke's family, the Barony of Verdon. The title went into abeyance in 1777 when the ninth Duke died without leaving any children.

Vere Road, 6
not known

Vernon Delph, 10
not known; name approved February 1936. The word delph usually means a quarry or area where digging has taken place.

Vernon Road, 17
not known; first mentioned in the street directory of 1932.

Vernon Terrace, 10
after William Henry Vernon who was a grocer and beer retailer on Manchester Road in the 1870s. He owned land and property on Vernon Terrace and also had land in the Fern Road-Welbeck Road area. He left Sheffield in 1880 to live abroad.

Vicarage Lane, 17
from the Dore vicarage which is on the lane.

Vicarage Road, 9
from the old vicarage of Christ Church, Attercliffe.

Vicar Lane, 1; Vicar Lane, 13
vicars lived on both of them. The old vicarage of the parish church (now the Cathedral) stood in its own field, west of the churchyard. The old vicarage at Woodhouse was made from two converted houses about 1890. It was condemned in 1959. A new vicarage built on the Church Croft came into use in 1964. Vicar Lane, Woodhouse was formerly called Adland Lane.

Vickers Drive, Lane, 5
after Thomas Edward Vickers, JP, Master Cutler in 1872, head of Vickers, Sons and Co, who lived at nearby Bolsover Hill in the nineteenth century. He later moved to London.

Victoria Road, 10; Victoria Road, 19; Victoria Street, 3; Victoria Terrace, 10
after Queen Victoria, Queen of England from 1837 to 1901. Streets, roads, hotels, public houses, halls, railway stations and houses were named after her all over the country.

Victoria Station Road, 4
was the approach road to Sheffield Victoria railway station which opened in September 1851 and closed in 1970.

Victor Road, 17
after the Hon Victor Cavendish, MP for West Derbyshire 1891-1908, Mayor of Chesterfield in 1911, and later ninth Duke of Devonshire; one of several

streets named from the Devonshire family who owned land in the area.

Victor Street, 6
possibly after Prince Albert Victor, Duke of Clarence, son of King Edward VII. He visited Sheffield in 1885 soon after his twenty-first birthday and around the time this street was built. As the King's eldest son, he was in line for the throne but he died in 1892 at the age of twenty-eight, and his younger brother, who was next in line, became King George V.

View Road, 2
descriptive name; it commands a view up the Sheaf Valley to the Derbyshire moors.

Villiers Close, Drive, 2
were built on the Duke of Norfolk's land and named after Barbara Villiers who married James, third Earl of Suffolk, and third Baron Howard de Walden (a branch of the Duke's family) in 1650.

Vincent Road, 7
not known; built around 1888 and presumably named after a person called Vincent.

Vine Street, 9
was originally called Florence Street, from the Italian city of Florence (one of a pair along with Turin Street). It was renamed in 1906 probably after George Robert Vine, who was well-known in the area.

Violet Avenue, 19
group name – flowers (see Aster).

Violet Bank Road, 7
from a house called Violet Bank, built in the early nineteenth century and the home for many years of Charles Milner, Quaker, Guardian and owner of an ironmongery business in Fargate. Mr Milner died in 1887 and the house was demolished about 1907 for the making of Raven and Briar Roads.

Vivian Road, 5
not known; the name first appears in the directories in the late 1890s. The street was built on land formerly owned by the Firth family.

Vulcan Road, 9
was developed and named in the early 1900s by which time Vulcan, the Roman god of fire, was already well established in Sheffield mythology. His statue was on top of the Town Hall, he appeared with Thor on the city's coat of arms, and several offices and factories were named after him. It was inevitable that sooner or later a street would be named after him too.

For more than ten years after the tram service between Sheffield and Rotherham was replaced by buses, Sheffield carried on running trams on its half of the route, turning round at Vulcan Road, the nearest they could get to the City boundary. But in those days Vulcan Road was very convenient for Sheffield's steel workers

W

Wadbrough Road, 11
uncertain; plans for the road were approved in 1892 for A.J. Denton and Co, solicitors, and the first mention of it in the Town Council minutes has it as 'Wadborough' Road. There is a village called Wadborough near Worcester.

Wade Meadow, 6
from the ancient name of Wadsley – Wade's Leah, meaning the meadow belonging to someone called Wade.

Wade Street, 4
not known; it first appeared in the 1906 directory. Two people called Wade were listed as living in nearby Bell House Road at the time. It may have something to do with them.

Wadsley Lane, 6
from the area called Wadsley which appeared in Domesday book as Wadelei, and in later documents as Waddeslay. Language experts say it comes from the Old English personal name Wade and means Wade's meadow, or forest clearing.

Wadsley Park Crescent, 6
Wadsley Park was about ninety acres of land surrounding Wadsley Park House which was built about 1840 by Mark Maugham, linen and wool draper in Angel Street. He lived there till his death in 1848.

Wadsworth Avenue, Close, Drive, Road, 12
after S. Wadsworth who was involved in the setting up of a Methodist chapel at nearby Normanton Springs in the nineteenth century. The chapel started with Sunday evening meetings at a miner's cottage and a permanent building opened in 1878.

Waingate, 3
wain meaning wagon (as in hay wain), gate meaning road: the road where the wagons came in.

Wainwright Avenue, Crescent, 13
after John Wainwright (1723-1768) hymn writer. He wrote the melody called Yorkshire to the hymn *Christians awake! Salute the happy morn* (see also Widdop Close).

Wake Road, 7
after William Wake, well-known lawyer, Registrar of Sheffield County Court for nearly fifty years, and a trustee of the Spooner estate, which built the road.

Walden Road, 2
was built on the Duke of Norfolk's land and named from a title held by a branch of the Duke's family. The first Baron Howard de Walden was the eldest son of Thomas, fourth Duke of Norfolk. The title was created in 1597.

Walders Avenue, 6
not known; appeared first in the 1932 directory when only one house was listed.

Wales Place, 6
like Wales Road (now gone) was named after the place called Wales, near Kiveton Park. Both streets were built on land owned by B.P. Broomhead Colton-Fox, solicitor, who lived at Wales Lodge, Wales (see Fox Road).

Walker Street, 3
after John Walker who was tenant of a large area of land west of The Wicker, on the Duke of Norfolk's nursery gardens, around 1800.

Walkley Bank Close, Road, 6
from the area of common land called Walkley Bank which was enclosed in the eighteenth century. Much of it was developed for housing in the nineteenth century by Walkley Bank Freehold Land Society.

Walkley Crescent Road, Walkley Lane, Road, Street, Terrace, 6
from the area called Walkley, said to mean the forest clearing belonging to Walca, an Old English personal name.

Wallace Road, 3
was originally called Orchard Road, because there was an orchard nearby. It was changed in 1872 to avoid confusion with other Orchard Roads and the reason for the new name is not known.

Waller Road, 6
was built by Walkley Bank Freehold Land Society around 1868 and named after someone connected with the society, probably George Waller, fender manufacturer, who lived at Portmahon around that time.

Walling Close, Road, 9
from an area called Walling Fen on Humberside; one of several streets in the area given Yorkshire names.

Walter Street, 6
was built about 1880 on land belonging to the Burgoyne family and named after someone called Walter, but I don't know who he was.

Waltham Gardens, 19
from Waltham Forest, in Essex and Hertfordshire; one of a group of streets named after British forests (see Ashdown Gardens).

Waltheof Road, 2
after Waltheof, son of Earl Siwald of Northumbria, and lord of Hallamshire at the time of William the Conqueror. He married William's niece, Judith, unwisely took part in a plot against William and was beheaded.

Walton Road, 11
was built on land belonging to the Wilson family and seems to have been named after Walton-on-Thames, Surrey. Several of the streets built on Wilson land were named after places near Harefield, Middlesex (see Harefield Road), but Walton-on-Thames seems a bit too far south to be included with them. Perhaps it has some special significance to the family.

Wansfell Road, 4
from Wansfell Peak, near Ambleside; one of a group of streets given Lake District names.

Warburton Close, Gardens, Road, 2
not known; Warburton Road was the first one named, in October 1934.

Looking towards Waingate in the 1930s, with Exchange Street to the right.

Warburton Square, 1
no longer listed; it was named after Thomas Warburton, razor manufacturer in Charles Street in the early nineteenth century. He built houses in the area.

Warden Street, 9
probably after Thomas Warden who was a mason and builder around the time the street was built in the 1860s.

Wardlow Road, 12
from the village of Wardlow, near Tideswell; one of a group of streets given Derbyshire place names.

Ward Place, 7
after Fredrick Ward who was a trustee of the Mount Pleasant Land Society which developed the area for housing between 1867 and 1872. The name has long associations with the area. The Ward family lived at the house called Mount Pleasant for many years.

Wardsend Road, Wardsend Road North, 6
from the area called Wardsend, a name which dates back to the twelfth century and is said to be a corruption of World's End, signifying that it was on the boundary or outer limits of the old town.

Ward Street, 3
the earliest lease I have traced on the street is dated 1817. The name may come from an old land holder. Harrison's survey of 1637 mentions two Wards in the area, Robert and William.

Wareham Court, 19
from Wareham Forest, near Poole; one of a group of streets named after British forests (see Ashdown Gardens).

Warley Road, 2
from Great and Little Warley, Essex; one of a group (with Dovercourt, Stock and Harwich Roads) named after places in Essex.

Warminster Close, Crescent, Drive, Gardens, Place, Road, 8
the part of Warminster Road built first (between Mount View Road and Harvey Clough Road) was originally called Wilkinson Road. It was renamed in 1907 after the Wiltshire market town of Warminster.

Warner Road, 6
after Sir Pelham 'Plum' Warner (1873-1963) one-time England and Middlesex cricket captain, and later president of the MCC. The road was one of several built on land owned by the Dixon family. Two of the Dixons, Archibald Willis Dixon and Lennox Burton Dixon, were close friends of Warner at Rugby School.

Warren Street, 4
was built on the Duke of Norfolk's land and named from the Duke's ancestry. William de Warren, who succeeded his father in 1202 as Earl of Warren and Surrey, married Maud, widow of Hugh Bigod, Earl of Norfolk. The Warren estates passed to the Fitzalan family in 1347 when John de Warren died without children and his sister Alice, wife of Edmund Fitzalan, Earl of Arundel, inherited.

Warrington Road, 10
after Warrington Slater who lived in Crookesmoor Road in the 1890s and built houses in the area. He was a partner in Slater Brothers, cutlery manufacturers, of Beehive Works, Rockingham Street. He died in 1907. Another of his developments was named Beehive Road, after the works.

Warris Place, 2
after Councillor George Warris, silver plate manufacturer, who lived in Crescent Road, Nether Edge, and represented Park ward on the Town Council from November 1873 till November 1884.

Warwick Street, 10
was built in the 1890s for S.S Bower along with Leamington Street – both named after places in Warwickshire.

Wasdale Avenue, Close, 19
from the valley called Wasdale, near Wast Water in Cumbria; one of a group of streets given Lake District names (see Ambleside Close).

Washford Road, 9
from the nearby Washford Bridge over the River Don. The bridge was originally called Westforth Bridge. It is referred to as Westforth in a will dated 1535. It means the river crossing to the west (of Attercliffe).

Washington Road, 11
was built on land owned by George Wostenholm, the cutler, and named after Washington in the USA. He also named his works, in Wellington Street, Washington Works. Wostenholm visited Washington more than thirty times, did business there, and admired many of the things he saw there.

Watch Street, 13
seems to have been a bit of self indulgence on the part of the Watch Committee who used to have responsibility for the naming of streets. It was originally called Clarke Street. It was changed in 1924 to avoid confusion with another street name and the Watch Committee seem to have named it after themselves. Three months later responsibility for naming streets passed to the Council's Highways Committee.

Water Lane, 17
in the early days it was a steep bridleway well known for being very wet. It was shown on Sanderson's 1836 map of Derbyshire. G.H.B. Ward, writing about it in the 1930s, said: 'As in 1836, it is still aptly known as Water Lane'.

Waterloo Road, 3
from the Battle of Waterloo, 1815, between the British and the French.

Waterloo Walk, 6
from a group of houses called Waterloo Houses which stood in Cornish Street. The name came originally from the battle.

Water Slacks Close, Drive, Lane, Road, Walk, Way, 13
from a small colliery which stood nearby in the nineteenth century. It was said to produce coal of an inferior quality, mainly water and slack, hence Waterslacks.

Watersmeet Road, 6
because it was built where two streams, the Rivelin and the Loxley, meet.

Water Street, 3
from the nearby spring which provided an early water supply for the area.

Waterthorpe Crescent, Gardens, Glade, Glen, Greenway, Rise, 19
from the old Waterthorpe Farm, recorded in 1276 as Waltertorp, meaning Walter's outlying farmstead.

Watery Street, 3
from the earlier Watery Lane (no longer listed). It is a descriptive name. Up to the mid-1880s an open brook ran down the lane. According to one account it was famous for the watercress that grew in it. In 1851 there was a dispute between Sheffield Board of Highways and Nether Hallam Board of Highways about which of them owned the brook (which was part of the boundary between their respective areas). The magistrate ruled that it was jointly owned and ordered that the two boards should share the cost of having it covered.

Wath Road, 7
after the place called Wath in South Yorkshire; possibly a link with James Montgomery, who lived at Wath in his early days.

Watkinson Gardens, 19
after John Watkinson who was a sicklesmith in Queen Street, Mosborough, in the nineteenth century.

Watson Road, 10
was built about 1880 and named after somebody called Watson but I don't know who. There were several people called Watson living in the area at the time including one on Whitham Road and another on Newbould Lane.

Watsons Walk, 1
after John Watson of Watson, Pass and Co, silversmiths, who had workshops in the area in the early nineteenth century.

Watt Lane, 10
not known.

Waverley Lane, 13; Waverley Road, 9
from the old Waverley Coal Co Ltd. The company offices, Waverley House, were on Main Road, Darnall, alongside Waverley Road. Waverley Lane, some distance away led to the company's Waverley Colliery. The company became part of the Nunnery Colliery Co.

Wayland Road, 11
not known; plans were approved in 1893 for Harry Kitchin, of S. and J. Kitchin, cutlery manufacturers, who lived at Clifford, Psalter Lane. The name may simply have been a variation on the Vulcan theme. Wayland, or Weland, the smith, features in European mythology.

Weakland Close, Crescent, Drive, Way, 12
after John Weakland who is shown renting a wheelwright's shop in the area in the 1774 manor rental.

Webbs Avenue, 6
not known.

Webster Street, 9
after J. Webster, brick manufacturer in nearby Alfred Street, who was given planning permission to build in Webster Street in 1875.

Weedon Street, 9
was originally called Mill Lane because there was a mill nearby. It was renamed in 1886 after the village of Weedon, Northamptonshire.

Weetwood Drive, 11
from the house called Weetwood at the junction of Ecclesall Road and Knowle Lane. The home of Sir William Ellis, Master Cutler from 1914 to 1917, it later became Ecclesall branch library.

Weigh Lane, 2
from the old Park Weigh House which was built nearby in 1828 for the Surveyor of Highways and was demolished in 1913 for the building of the *Norfolk Cinema*.

Weir Head, 9
from the nearby weir on the River Don.

Welbeck Road, 6
was built in the 1860s by the Welbeck Freehold Land Society. The original intention was to call it Hinsby Road but this idea was dropped for some reason and it was named after the society instead.

Welbury Gardens, 19
from the village of Welbury, north Yorkshire.

Welby Place, 8
after Edward Montague Earle Welby, Sheffield's Stipendiary Magistrate for more than fifty years from 1874. He lived at Norton House and took an active part in village affairs. He was the first chairman of the Norton parish council and of Norton School Board, and was connected with Norton Agricultural Show.

Welland Close, 3
was built on Rutland Road and named after the River Welland which used to be the southern boundary of the old county of Rutland.

Wellcarr Road, 8
was built in 1906 and named after the field across which it was built – Well Carr. Other fields nearby were called East Carr and North Carr. Carr usually indicates wet ground.

Well Court, 12
there was an old well nearby.

Wellesley Road, 10
after the English statesman Richard Colley Wellesley (1760-1842), Governer General of India, Foreign Secretary from 1809 to 1812, and Lord Lietenant of Ireland from 1821 to 1828.

Wellfield Close, 12; Wellfield Road, 6
from old field names – fields with wells in them. When the field on which Wellfield Road was built was offered for sale as freehold building land in the nineteenth century it was said to contain 'a never-failing spring of excellent water'.

Well Green Road, 6
was built on land that was a green from medieval times. Harrison's Survey of 1637 refers to it as 'Stanington Greene', north of land called Hopwood Toft Head. Presumably there was a well in the area too.

Wellhead Road, 8
from a nearby well (see Well Road, 8).

Wellington Road, 6; Wellington Street, 1
after the Duke of Wellington (1769-1852), soldier and statesman. As a soldier he achieved fame for his victory at Waterloo. As a politician, he was Prime Minister from 1828 to 1830, Foreign Secretary under Peel, and Minister Without Portfolio from 1841 to 1846.

Well Lane, 6
from a nearby well.

Well Meadow Drive, Street, 3
from an old field name which is mentioned in Harrison's survey of 1637 as 'the Well Meadow'.

Well Road, 8
was originally called Townwell Street

from its nearness to the old Heeley town well. Nearby Wellhead Road got its name from the same source. Two nearby fields owned by the Duke of Norfolk, were called Upper Well Dole and Lower Well Dole.

Welney Place, 6
was originally called Ward Place. To avoid confusion with Ward Place, Highfield, it was renamed in 1924 from the village of Welney, Norfolk.

Welwyn Close, Road, 12
from the place called Welwyn, Hertfordshire. Neighbouring Elstree Drive and Road were also given a Hertfordshire name.

Wenlock Street, 13
was originally called Walker Street. It was renamed in 1924 to avoid confusion with Walker Street in the city centre. The new name was from the villages of Much Wenlock and Little Wenlock, Shropshire.

Wensley Close, Court, Croft, Drive, Gardens, Green, Street, 4
from the village of Wensley, near Masham, north Yorkshire.

Wentworth Avenue, 11
from Wentworth Woodhouse, stately home of the Earls Fitzwilliam for many years; one of a group of streets named after famous family seats.

Wesley Lane, 10
from the old Wesleyan Chapel opened in 1836 on School Road and later converted into a Sunday school.

Wessex Gardens, 17
from the area's historical association with King Ecgbert of Wessex. After defeating the Mercians and being accepted by the Northumbrians without a fight, he became King of all England at Dore in the year 829.

West Bank Lane, 1
descriptive name – the bank, or hillside to the west of the town. The lane follows the line of a seventeenth century footpath.

West Bar, 3; West Bar Green,1
bar in this sense means a gate, as in Hunter's Bar, and the gate in question was on one of the routes out of town to the west. It is referred to, as 'Weste Barre' in a document dated 1555. West Bar Green, thought to be a much later name, was an open area nearby.

Western Bank in 1957, with the University, Children's Hospital and old-fashioned students.

Westbourne Road, 10
from the house called Westbourne House. In the 1820s it was the home of Bernard John Wake, solicitor. After his death in 1872 it became the home of Edwin Cadman, merchant.

Westbrook Bank, 11
from a house built by Joseph Wilson (of the famous snuff firm) in 1795 and called Westbrook House. In 1831, a new mill built for the Wilson firm above the house was called Westbrook Mill.

Westbury Street, 9
after Richard Bethell, first Lord Westbury, Liberal MP, Solicitor Genaral in 1852, Attorney General 1856, and Lord Chancellor 1861; one of a group of streets named after famous lawyers (see Brett).

Westcroft Crescent, Drive, Gardens, Glen, Grove, 19
from a field called West Croft which was part of 152 acres of land at Mosborough awarded to Samuel Staniforth in the 1795 land enclosures.

West Don Street, 6
on the west bank of the River Don.

Western Bank, 10
S.O. Addy said it came from the ancient word *westen*, meaning waste land, but it seems just as likely to mean a hill on the western side of town. According to Hunter, John Hodgson, surgeon, built a house at Crookesmoor in which he was living in 1821, and which he named Western Bank.

Western Road, 10
the western boundary of a site on which several streets were built in the 1870s by the Springfield Freehold Land Society.

Westfield Avenue, Grove, 12
from a local field name – the West Field.

Westfield Crescent, Northway, Southway, 19
from the old Westfield Farm, nearby, which was owned up to 1912 by Earl Manvers.

Westfield Terrace, 1
from several old fields which were known as the West Fields. A house built in the area in the area in the early nineteenth century was also called West Field. In 1832 it was bought for conversion into a public dispensary which eventually became the Royal Hospital.

Westhill Lane, 3
from a farmstead called West Hill which is shown in this area on a Fairbank map made in 1795. The name is a straightfoward descriptive one.

Westland Close, Gardens, Grove, Road, 19
sounds as if it might be from a field name but I have not been able to find a field of this name in the area. It may simply be a variation on the 'west' theme of nearby streets – Westcroft and Westfield.

West Lane, 6
the lane to the west of Loxley Chase.

Westminster Avenue, Close, Crescent, 10
from Westminster Abbey; one of a group of streets named after English churches.

Westmoreland Street, 6
was approved in 1878 (along with Cleveland and Carnarvon Streets) for John Yeomans and apparently named after the county of Westmoreland.

Westnall Road, Terrace, 5
from the old *byrlaw*, or division, of Bradfield called Westnall. S.O. Addy says it was spelt Westmundhalch in 1403, and means west point rock.

Weston Street, 3
was originally called Bathfield Road. The new name, like that of Weston Park, was from Weston Hall, home of the Harrison family. When the Harrison sisters gave the hall to the city, the grounds became Weston Park and the house became a museum.

West Street in 1941, long before the Royal Hospital and the old tram lines disappeared. The lamp standards had white rings painted round them so they could be more easily seen in the blackout. The tram lines have since re-appeared.

Westover Road, 10
not known; the name first appeared in the 1927 directory.

West Quadrant, 5
descriptive name; a quadrant is a quarter of a circle.

West Street, West Street Lane, 1
West Street is a straightfoward directional name. Up to 1819 it was only a narrow lane which petered out into a footpath. When the Glossop turnpike road was completed in 1820, it made West Street a principal route out of town to the west.

West Street, 19
directional name.

West View Close, Lane, 17
from a cottage called West View, presumably because it faced west, which was the home of Fred Fox up to the 1920s.

Westwell Place, 19
from the West Well Farm which is mentioned in a document of 1487.

Westwick Crescent, Grove, Road, 8
Westwick Road was originally called Alison Road. It was changed in 1934 and the new name was taken from a nearby wood called Westwick Plantation. There is some doubt about the origin of the wood name. It might mean the wic, or dwelling, to the west of Greenhill, but the stronger possibility is that it is a corruption of west sick, meaning the stream to the west. A 1731 map shows a West Sick Lane in the area. Westwick Crescent was originally called Alison Crescent.

Westwood Road, 11
was approved in 1902 (with Frickley and Fulney Roads) and named after a place called Westwood but I am not sure which. There are several places with this name.

Wetherby Court, 9
from the earlier Wetherby Road, no longer listed. The road was named after the market town of Wetherby, twelve miles from Leeds.

Wharf Lane, 9
from the nearby canal wharf. A group of cottages nearby was called Wharf Row.

Wharf Street, 2
from the main wharf of the Sheffield Canal which opened in February, 1819.

Wharncliffe Road,10
after John Stuart Wortley, second Baron Wharncliffe, born 1801, MP for the West Riding from 1841 to 1845, and Colonel Commandant of the South West Regiment of Yorkshire Yeomanry Cavalry. The road was built around the time of his death in 1855.

Wheata Drive, Place, Road, 5
from an old field name meaning wheat enclosure. There was also a wood nearby called Wheata Wood.

Wheatfield Crescent, 5
from an old field name, Wheat Field, which is recorded on a list of local fields made in 1622.

Wheatley Grove, 13
uncertain; it may be from a field name, but there was a man called S.K. Wheatley for whom houses were built on nearby Richmond Road in the late 1920s and it may be something to do with him.

Wheats Lane, 1
after John James Wheat (1825-1915), solicitor, whose offices were in Paradise Square. He was clerk to the Church Burgesses (an office held by his family for more than 100 years), and lived at Norwood Hall.

Wheeldon Street, 1
not known; it was built in the 1790s on land belonging to the Church Burgesses.

Wheel Hill, 1
from the old Park Steam Works where the first steam grinding wheel in Sheffield was built in 1785. There was probably a water wheel on the site before then.

Wheldrake Road, 5
from the village of Wheldrake, near York.

Whinacre Close, Place, Walk, 8
from the old Whinacre Wood, near Jordanthorpe, which is shown on a Fairbank map of 1741 as Winny-Car Wood. There was also a field nearby called Whinacre Close. The word winny, or whinny, comes from the Old Norse *hvin*, meaning a place where lots of gorse grew.

Whinfell Court, 11
from the house called Whinfell, for thirty-one years home of Sir Frederick Neill, former Master Cutler, and the first man to be High Sheriff of Hallamshire. In the early 1900s, Samuel Doncaster, of Daniel Doncaster and Sons Ltd, lived there.

Whinmoor Road, 5
from the Whinmoor coal seam which runs under the north Sheffield area.

Whirlow Court Road, 11
from the house Whirlow Court, built in 1884 by Ernest D. Fawcett, executive (and later partner) in the firm of James Dixon and Sons. It was bought by the Corporation in 1954 for use as Judges' lodgings, and was also used as the official residence of the Lord Mayor.

Whirlowdale Close, Rise, 11; Whirlowdale Crescent, 7; Whirlowdale Road, 7 and 11,
a variation of Whirlow (see below). The building of Whirlowdale Road was approved by the City Council in May 1921 at a cost of £40,000 to provide work for the unemployed. It was opened on 12 January 1922.

Whirlow Farm Mount, 11
from a nearby farm.

Whirlow Grove, Lane; Whirlow Park Road, 11
from the area called Whirlow, sometimes spelt Hurlowe, or Whorelowe in ancient times, and thought to mean boundary mound.

Whitby Road, 9
was built in the 1870s by the Albert Freehold Land Society and named after an official of the society, Frederick Whitby.

White Croft, 1
from an old field name. White may be the name of a former tenant of the land, or it might refer to the light coloured nature of the soil.

Whitehouse Lane, 6
from an old house nearby called the White House which certainly dated back to the seventeenth century because the lane is mentioned several times in Harrison's Survey of 1637. It was a common house name in Sheffield. There was another White House on Bramall Lane, another at Pitsmoor, and one at Woodseats.

White Lane, 12
is shown on a map of Gleadless made in 1798 and mentioned in a document dated 1717; possibly named after George White who lived in the area in the early 1700s.

Whiteley Lane, 10
from an old field name, recorded in 1280 as Wyteley, meaning a light coloured soil.

Whiteley Wood Close, Road, 11
from the nearby wood, the name of which came about in the same way as Whiteley Lane, above. Whiteley Wood Road, originally called Meadow Lane, was renamed in 1912.

Whitelow Lane, 17
Whitelow, meaning white hill, or mound, was recorded in the 1822 Enclosures Act.

White's Lane, 2
from the White family who farmed Manor Farm, at the end of the lane, for many years. John White was farmer there in the 1850s, James White in the 1870s.

Whitethorns Close, Drive, View, 8
from the farm called White Thorns on Dyche Lane. Whitethorn is another name for hawthorn.

Whiteways Close, Drive, Grove, Road, 4
were built on the Duke of Norfolk's land and named after Whiteways, one of the Duke's Sussex estates.

Whitfield Road, 10
the origin is the same as Whiteley. It means white, or bright field.

Whitham Road, 10
was built and named in the early 1860s. It appears in the 1865 directory, but not in the 1863 directory. It was probably named after somebody called Whitham, but I don't know who. There were two Whithams, blacksmiths, at Lydgate around that time, but they seem a bit far away to have been the reason for this name.

Whiting Street, 8
after J.E. Whiting, one of the creditors of the Meersbrook Tannery Co when it went bankrupt in the early 1900s. Mr Whiting, with others, petitioned for the winding up of the company in 1906. The street was built shortly after this on land that had formerly belonged to the tannery.

Whitwell Street, 9
was originally called Victoria Street,

The Wicker, one of the best known of all Sheffield street names – and one of the trickiest to explain.

after Queen Victoria. It was renamed in 1903 from the Derbyshire village of Whitwell.

Whitworth Croft, Road, 10
after Ralph S. Whitworth, a well-known tailor in West Bar around 1900. He lived in Kenbourne Road and owned land and property in Ranmoor, Sandygate and elsewhere in the city.

Whitworth Lane, 9
was built on land farmed by the Whitworth family, one of whom, George Whitworth, is reputed to be the man who (on the squire's instructions) chopped down the Attercliffe gibbet which had been a gruesome feature of the area for many years. Whitworth's farm was opposite the old Attercliffe burial ground.

Whixley Road, 9
from the Yorkshire village of Whixley, six miles from Boroughbridge.

Wicker, Wicker Lane, 3
uncertain; there are three theories: from the old word *wick*, meaning the land near a castle; from another old word, *wic*, meaning a bend or angle in the river (Don); or from the Old Norse word *vikir*, meaning willow.

Wickfield Close, Drive, Grove, Place, Road, 12
from a field name. Upper Wick Field and Lower Wick Field, totalling nine acres, were awarded to Sarah Clark in the 1795 land enclosures.

Widdop Close, Croft, 13
after a man called Accepted Widdop (1750-1801), a Yorkshire hymn writer who wrote the hymn tunes called *Birstall* and *Ossett*.

Wigfull Road, 11
was built in the 1870s by Brocco Bank Freehold Land Society and named after the society's vice-president and co-trustee, Henry Wigfull.

Wilbury Drive, 12
not known; name approved 1939.

Wilcox Close, Road, 6
after Ella Wheeler Wilcox (1850-1919) who wrote her first novel at the age of nine, had her first essay published at fourteen and wrote more than forty volumes of verse. One of a group of streets named after famous literary figures.

Wilfrid Road, 9
after Lt-Col Edwin Wilfrid Stanyforth, of Kirk Hammerton Hall, York, who owned a large area of land at Darnall (see Staniforth Road).

Wilkinson Lane, Street, 10
was built for the Church Burgesses and named after the Rev James Wilkinson, vicar of Sheffield from 1754 to 1805, magistrate and landowner. When the vicar, already wealthy, was awarded nearly 300 acres of land under the enclosure acts of the late 1700s, a crowd attacked and damaged his home, Broom Hall.

Willey Street, 3
after William Willey, owner of the *Falstaff Inn* in the Wicker in the early nineteenth century and owner of property in the Wicker, Stanley Street, Scotland Street and elsewhere. He died in 1846.

William Close, Crescent, 19
after the builder.

Williamson Road, 11
was built on land owned by Henry Newbould, Church Burgess, and son of the founder of S. Newbould and Co, Bridgefield Works. He named the road after his wife. In 1817, Mr Newbould married Mary Williamson of Buntingford, Herts. Their elder son was called William Williamson Newbould. In the 1870s the family owned more than 250 acres of land.

William Street, 10
after William Watson, son of John Watson, of Shirecliffe Hall, who bought Broomhall Park in 1809 and twenty years later leased the land for the building of gentlemen's residences, some of which were built on this street. (see also Bangor Steet).

Willington Road, 5
from the south Derbyshire village of Willington; one of a group of streets named after Derbyshire villages.

Willis Road, 6
was built on land owned by the Dixon family of Hillsborough Hall and named after a member of the family, Archibald Willis Dixon. Willis was a recurring

name in the family. Mr Dixon's father and grandfather were both called James Willis Dixon.

Willoughby Street, 4
was approved in 1897 for the Firth family on land that had previously been part of their Page Hall estate. It was probably named after a member of the family, Edward Willoughby Firth.

Willow Drive, 9
group name – trees (see Alder Lane).

Wilson Place, 8
was built in 1870, with Wilson Road (no longer listed) by Heeley Central Land Society and named after someone connected with the society. I don't know who he was.

Wilson Road, 11
after the Wilson family of Sharrow who owned extensive land in the area in the nineteenth century, including land on which the Botanical Gardens were built.

Wilson Street, 3
after James Wilson who held land nearby in the mid-nineteenth century. He was granted a lease on two pieces of land 'at or near Harvest Lane', in March 1834.

Wilstrop Road, 9
was built on Staniforth land (see Staniforth Road) and named after the village of Wilstrop, west of York.

Wilthorpe Gardens, 19
from the place called Wilthorpe, near Barnsley.

Wilton Place, 10
not known. It was listed first in the 1856 directory, built on land formerly part of Broomhall Park.

Winchester Avenue, Crescent, Drive, Road 10
from Winchester Cathedral; one of a group of streets named after churches.

Wincobank Avenue, Close, Road, 5; Lane, 4
from the area called Wincobank, recorded as Winkley in a document on 1345, Winkleybank by the sixteenth century. It comes from the name of a man called Wineca, and it means Wineca's forest clearing or mound.

Winco Road, 4; Winco Wood Lane, 9
variations on the name of Wincobank.

Windermere Road, 8
from Lake Windermere; one of a group of streets given Lake District names (see Arnside).

Windmill Greenway, 19
the original intention was to call it Southland Greenway but local residents thought Windmill Greenway would be a better name because it was near the site of an old windmill. The City Council agreed. The council had earlier decided that all east-west grid roads on the Mosborough development should be called greenways and all north-south grid roads should be called ways.

Windmill Lane, 5
an old windmill stood nearby. In the 1856 directory Robert Thorpe is listed as miller.

Windmill Street, 9
from an old windmill that stood on Attercliffe Common. It was built about 1810 and pulled down in the 1870s. James Hill was miller there in the 1850s.

Windsor Road, 8
uncertain; presumably from the well-known Berkshire town.

Windsor Street, 4
was built on the Duke of Norfolk's land and named from the fact that Henry the seventh Duke, was Constable and Governor of Windsor Castle in the seventeenth century.

Windy House Lane, 2
from an old farm nearby called Windy House Farm (for obvious reasons). It was claimed that on a clear day the towers of Lincoln Cathedral could be seen from the farm.

Wingerworth Avenue, 8
from the place called Wingerworth in north Derbyshire.

Wingfield Crescent, 12
probably from a field name. At the time of the enclosures there were three fields in the area called Near, Middle, and Far Wing Field, totalling nine acres.

Winkley Terrace, 5
from Winkley, the fourteenth-century name of Wincobank (see Wincobank Avenue).

Winn Close, Drive, Gardens, Grove, 6
uncertain; it may be from somebody called Winn (there was a family of this name in the area in the early 1900s), or it could be from the Old English word, *Wyn*, meaning meadow. The name was approved in 1962.

Winsford Road, 6
was originally called Salisbury Road. It was changed in 1924 and the new name, a random choice, was from the place called Winsford, near Middlewich, Cheshire.

Winster Road, 6
was originally called Wilson Road. It was changed in 1903 and renamed after the village of Winster, near Matlock.

Winter Street, 3
after John Winter, eighteenth century landowner in the area. He had a windmill which stood on what is now part of Weston Park.

Winterton Gardens, 12
from the village of Winterton, five miles from Scunthorpe.

Wiseton Road, 11
from the village of Wiseton, near Bawtry (see Everton Road).

Wisewood Avenue, Lane, Place, Road, 6
from the area called Wisewood. According to one account, the name was thought up by the Enclosure Commissioners. S.O. Addy suggested that it might come from the old Anglo Saxon word *waes*, meaning pasture ground, or meadow.

Withens Avenue, 6
a mystery; when the name was first approved by the Town Council in 1904, it was approved as Withers Road, so the intention may have been to name it after J.B. Mitchell-Withers, architect and surveyor (who certainly acted for developers in this area). But Withers quickly became Withens. Just to add to the confusion, in old field names, Withers and Withens both mean the same thing, land on which willow trees grow. There is no clue as to which meaning was intended.

Witney Street, 8
from the place called Witney, Oxon. (see Batt Street).

Woburn Place, 11
from Woburn Abbey, seat of the Duke of Bedford; one of a group of streets named after stately homes.

Wolfe Drive, Road, 6
after Charles Wolfe (1791-1823) the Irish poet who was ordained as a priest in 1817, a year after he had written his stanzas on the burial of Sir John Moore, the work for which he is chiefly remembered. One of a group of streets named after famous literary figures.

Wollaton Avenue, Drive, Road, 17
from Wollaton Hall, Nottingham, home of the Middleton family who were lords of the manor of Totley from the early 1700s to the late 1800s. The hall is now the Nottingham Natural History Museum.

Wolseley Road, 8
after Viscount Wolseley (1833-1913) who commanded the Nile campaign for the relief of General Gordon, and was later Commander in Chief of the British Army. One of a group of streets named after famous military men.

Wolverley Road, 13
was named in 1922 after a place called Wolverley. There are two, a village near Kidderminster, Worcestershire, and the more likely one for this road, a village in Shropshire.

Woodbank Crescent, 8
from the old Smithy Wood which used to stretch up to Meersbrook Park.

Woodbank Road, 6
descriptive name, like Woodbank Crescent – meaning wooded hillside. The area is referred to as 'Wood Banke' in Harrison's survey of 1637.

Woodbine Road, 9
was originally called Forge Lane, from a nearby works. It was changed in the late nineteenth century. The new name is difficult to explain. Woodbine commonly means honeysuckle, but there could hardly have been honeysuckle in the area at that time. The 1865 directory lists only one address in Forge Lane, that of Curtis Brady, rope and twine maker. Possibly Mr Brady's ropery inspired the thought of twining honeysuckle. Or it may just have been a fanciful name.

Woodbourn Hill, Road, 9
from Woodbourn Hall (sometimes spelt Woodburn, sometimes Woodbourne) which stood nearby and was built, probably by Henry Hartopp, of Park Iron Works, in the early 1800s. Later, it was the home of his brother-in-law, Henry Sorby.

Woodbury Close, Road, 9
Woodbury Road, built first, was originally called Woodside Road because of its nearness to Woolley Wood. It was changed in 1903, and the new name was simply a minor variation on the old one.

Wood Cliffe, 10
from the steep hill near Whiteley Woods.

Woodcock Place, 2
after Thomas Woodcock, herbalist in Duke Street in the nineteenth century, and councillor for Park ward from 1861 to 1882.

Woodend Close, Drive, 6
from Stannington Wood.

Woodfarm Avenue, Close, Drive, Place, 6
were built on land that was once part of Stannington Wood Farm.

Woodfield Road, 10
from an old field name.

Wood Fold, 3
from the old Cook Wood, nearby.

Woodgrove Road, 9
from an old house nearby called Wood Grove (because it was near to Woolley Wood). In the 1835 directory William Denton, 'gentleman' is listed as living there.

Woodhead Road, 2
after George Woodhead and his wife Sarah, who lived in the house called Highfield, nearby. He was a partner in the firm of Greaves Woodhead and Co, merchants, of Norfolk Street. When Thomas Asline Ward wrote in his diaries: 'Who in Sheffield ever became rich by trade?' he made one exception: Mr Woodhead.

Woodholm Place, Road, 11
Woodholm Road was originally called Ecclesall Hall Road from a nearby farm called Ecclesall Hall. It was changed in 1917 and the first intention was to rename it Nesscliffe Road (from the village of Nesscliffe, Shropshire). Residents objected to the new name, were asked to suggest a name of their own, and Woodholm Road was a resident's suggestion. It may have been an effort to reflect the wooded nature of the surrounding area, a variation on the name of a nearby house, Holmewood, or simply a name with a pleasant sound. Woodholm Place, originally called Cross Road (because it crossed from one road to another) was renamed in 1925.

Woodhouse Avenue, Court, Crescent, Lane, 19
Woodhouse Lane, built first, was a directional name – the lane to Woodhouse from Beighton. The others followed later.

Woodhouse Gardens, 13
from the place called Woodhouse, which means just what it says, the house in the wood.

Woodhouse Road, 12
directional name – the road from Intake to Woodhouse.

Woodland Drive, View, 12
looks towards Stoneley Wood.

Woodland Place, 17
from the nearby Clay Wood.

Woodland Road, 8
was built alongside Ashes Wood. It was originally called Woodlands Road.

Woodlands Avenue, 19
a collective variation on all the nearby streets which are named after trees – Oak, Poplar, Chestnut, etc.

The Woodlands, 10
from the number of trees around the site.

Woodland View Road, 6
descriptive name; there are several bits of woodland to be viewed from the site.

When it was photographed in 1905 Ecclesall Hall Farm had a somewhat ramshackle look about it. The road alongside was first called Ecclesall Hall Road. In 1917 it was given a new name, the one by which it is better known today, Woodholm Road.

Wood Lane, 6
from the ancient Stannington Wood which at the time of Harrison's survey in 1637, covered 217 acres.

Wood Road, 6
was built, with Ball, Harrison and Rippon Roads, by Hillsborough Mount Freehold Land Society about 1880. Since the other roads were all named after people, the chances are that this one was too, probably after an official of the society but I don't know who he was.

Woodrove Avenue, Close, 13
after John Woodrove (sometimes spelt Woodruffe), owner of Woodthorpe Hall, who died about 1736.

Woodseats House Road, 8
from the house called Woodseats House, home of Mrs Elizabeth Bingham in the 1890s. When it was offered for sale in 1895, the house, standing in its own grounds on Chesterfield Road, had four bedrooms, a billiard room, three carriage houses and stabling for six horses.

Woodseats Road, 8
was originally called Firth Road, after John Firth who lived at Abbeydale House and owned land and property in the area. It was changed in 1903 and given a directional name from the place called Woodseats, recorded as *Wodesetes* in 1280, and meaning houses or folds in the wood.

Woodside Lane, 3
from the old Cook Wood nearby.

Woodstock Road, 6;
Woodstock Road, 7
from the place called Woodstock, Oxfordshire, a royal seat from ancient times. Edward, the Black Prince, was born there, Henry II did his courting there, and Elizabeth I was imprisoned there.

Wood Street, 6
was built in 1880 on land belonging to M.G. Burgoyne, along with Lime Street and Ash Street, a trio of arborial names.

Woodthorpe Close, 2;
Woodthorpe Crescent, Road, 13
from the area called Woodthorpe, recorded in ancient times as *Wodetorp*, meaning the outlying farmstead near a wood.

Woodvale Road, 10
overlooks the valley of Endcliffe Woods.

Woodview Road, 6
looks towards several woods.

Woodview Terrace, 11
looks across the Porter Valley to Trippet Wood.

Woofindin Avenue, 11; Road, 10
after George Woofindin, manufacturer and benefactor, who died in 1895, leaving money for the building of twenty almshouses for old people in Ecclesall Road, and for a convalescent home overlooking Whiteley Woods (which opened in 1901). Woofindin Road led to the convalescent home which later became a hospital annexe.

Wooldale Close, Drive, 19
from the area called Wooldale, near Holmfirth; one of a group of streets named on the 'dale' theme.

Woollen Lane, Walk, 6
after a former landowner, Robert Woollen, who owned the Gatefields estate which was split up and sold after his death in the 1860s.

Woolley Wood Road, 5
from the nearby wood, the name of which appears in manorial records of 1597, and means wolf clearing.

Worcester Close, Drive, Road, 10
from Worcester Cathedral; among a group of streets named after churches.

Worksop Road, Woodhouse Mill, as it was known when this photograph was taken. It later became Retford Road.

Wordsworth Avenue, Close, Crescent, Drive, 5

after William Wordsworth (1770-1850), Poet Laureate from 1843 till his death and one of the greatest English poets; among a group of streets named after famous literary figures.

Workhouse Lane, 3

at one time led to the old workhouse on West Bar. The workhouse moved to a former cotton mill in Kelham Street and then, in 1881, to Firvale.

Worksop Road, 9

was originally called Church Street. It was renamed in 1886 at a time when it was still part of the main road from Attercliffe to Worksop. (Staniforth Road, at that time a small lane called Pinfold Lane, was not developed as part of the main road to Worksop till 1888)

Worrall Road, 6

was originally called Church Lane, from the nearby Wadsley parish church. It was renamed and given a directional name in 1903. Worrall is thought to mean nook of land where myrtle grows.

Worthing Road, 9

was built in the 1890s on the Duke of Norfolk's land and named after the town of Worthing, Sussex, because of the Duke's links with the town.

Wostenholm Road, 7

after George Wostenholm (1800-1876) cutlery maker, Master Cutler in 1856, and magistrate, who built and lived in, the house called Kenwood, around which he owned a large area of land. He was responsible for much of the development of Sharrow and Nether Edge. In 1907 Sir Charles Skelton suggested that Wostenholm Road, Washington Road and Montgomery Road should all be known by the one name, Wostenholm Road, but the City Council turned down the idea.

Wragby Road, 11

was built for the Otter family and named after the location of the family home, Ranby Hall, Wragby, Lincs (see Louth Road).

Wragg Road, 2

after Thomas Wragg, grocer and provision dealer, who lived in Bernard Street and was councillor for Park ward in the 1880s and 1890s.

Wreakin Place, 9

I suspect that this is an incorrect spelling, that it ought to be *Wrekin*, from the well-known hill called The Wrekin, two miles from Wellington, Shropshire.

Wren Bank, 2

group name – birds (see Curlew Ridge).

Wright's Hill, 2

after William Wright, stay busk and legging spring manufacturer, whose works were at the foot of the hill in the 1870s when it was named. He lived first in Lansdowne Road, then in Hill Street.

Wulfric Close, Place, Road, 2

after Wulfric Spott, the last Saxon lord of the manor of Eckington, during the reign of Ethelred; one of a group of Manor Estate street names connected with the history of Eckington.

Wyatt Avenue, 11

was built on land that was once part of the Banner Cross Hall estate and named after Jeffry Wyatt, the architect who rebuilt Banner Cross Hall for General Murray in the nineteenth century. Wyatt designed, or restored, more than a hundred well-known buildings, including the north wing of Chatsworth House. In the 1820s he remodelled the royal apartments at Windsor Castle, after which, by sanction of King George IV, his name was changed to Wyattville. He was later knighted.

Wybourn House Road, 2

from the house called Wybourn House. In the 1860s it was spelt Wyburn and it was used by the Rev John Messenger as a boarding school.

Wybourn Terrace, 2

from the area called Wybourn, the name of which is something of a mystery. Bourn, or burn, usually means a stream, but the Wy element is more difficult. There are several possibilities, the likeliest of which seems to be the Old Norse word for willow – the stream with willow trees. An added complication is that in Harrison's survey of 1637 there is mention of Wybroomewell, which appears elsewhere as Mybroomewell. J.G. Ronkesley, in his transcription of the survey, suggests that both entries refer to Wybournewell.

Wychwood Croft, Glen, Grove, 19

from the Wychwood Forest, Oxfordshire; among a group of streets named after British forests (see Ashdown).

Wyedale Croft, 19

group name – dales. I suspect this ought to be Wydale, from the area of that name in north Yorkshire.

Wynyard Road, 6

was built on land owned by the Dixon family and named after Wynyard Dixon, son of J.W. Dixon, of the Sheffield cutlery and silver family, who lived at Hillsborough Hall. Mr Dixon was a well-known surveyor, and vice president of Yorkshire County Cricket Club for a time.

Wyvern Gardens, 17

from the wyvern, a dragon-like heraldic creature with two wings, two eagle's legs and a tapering body. It was the emblem of the ancient kingdom of Mercia. Dore was the northern boundary of the kingdom and the place where Mercia and Northumbria were united under one king – Ecgbert – in the ninth century. In modern times the Midland Railway also used the wyvern on its crest.

Yardley Street, 3
not known; built in the 1870s.

Yarmouth Street, 9
presumably from the Norfolk seaside resort; planning permission for the street was granted in 1867.

Yeomans Road, 6
after John Yeomans, solicitor in Bank Street, who lived in Woollen Lane, Upperthorpe. He was Town Clerk of Sheffield from 1859 till his death in 1887 and he owned the land on which this road was built.

Yew Greave Crescent, Yew Lane, 5; Yew Tree Drive, 9
there were yew trees in the area. They gave their name to fields, farms, and eventually, streets. Yew Tree Drive was built near the site of a farm called Yew Tree Farm, Greave, as in Yew Greave, means grove.

York Road, 9
from the *Duke of York* public house at Darnall which dates back to the early neneteenth century. Like most pubs of this name, it was named after the second son of King George III who died in 1827.

York Street, 1
uncertain; the street was built about 1770 and its name may come from the fact that some years earlier, during a visit to Sheffield, the Archbishop of York was entertained at an old inn called the *Crown* which stood at what is now the entrance to York Street.

Youlgreave Drive, 12
from the place called Youlgreave in Derbyshire; one of a group of streets given Derbyshire names.

Young Street, 3
after a former landowner. Under the Ecclesall Enclosure Act of 1788, John Trevor Young was allotted twenty-two perches of land on what was then called Little Sheffield Moor.

York Street, probably just before the buildings on the left were pulled down to make room for the new newspaper offices.

Zion Lane, Place, 9
from the Zion Chapel, formed by a congregation of dissenters from Attercliffe Hilltop Chapel in 1770. At first they met in a local schoolroom, then in 1805 they built their own chapel. The chapel became too small, was demolished and a new chapel was built in 1863.

Appendix 1

Streets that have changed their names

For all sorts of reasons, many Sheffield street names have been changed over the years.

Old name	*New name and date of change*	
A		
Abbeydale Road (part), 7 & 17	Abbeydale Road South	1894

Old name	New name	Date
Addey Street, 6	Addy Street	1915
Adland Lane, 13	Vicar Lane	1800s
Albert Road, 9	Armley Road	1886
Albert Road, 9	Asquith Road	1903
Albert Road, 12	Alnwick Road	1924
Albert Street, 10	Damer Street	1872
Albert Street, 9	Bawtry Road	1886
	and then to Bridport Road	*1907*
Alflat Street, 6	Bilston Street	1886
Alison Crescent, 8	Westwick Crescent	1934
Alison Road, 8	Westwick Road	1934
Allen's Lane, 3	Allen Street	1800s
Alma Street, 9	Dearne Street	1872
Alma Street, 9	Swan Street	1886
Alms Hill, 11	Broad Elms Lane (part)	1934
Alpine Road, 8	Skelton Road	1903
Alport Close, 13	Lathkill Close	1954
Andover Street West, 3	Andover Street (part)	1890
Andrew Lane, 11	Harrow Street	1886
Andrew Lane, 10	Andwell Lane	1903
Argyle Road, 6	Airedale Road	1904
Arthur Street, 3	Finlay Street	1872
Arthur Street, 9	Beighton Street	1903
Arthur Street, 7	Southcroft Gardens	1980s
Arundel Road, 13	Halesworth Road	1929
Arundel Street (part)	Tudor Way	1959
Ashgrove Road, 13	Ashwell Road	1924

Old name	New name	Date
Ashmore Road, 8	Charles Ashmore Road	1926
B		
Back Lane, 3	Alton Street	1886
Back Lane, 3	Shirley Road	1899
Back Lane, 5	Norwood Lane (part)	1903
Back Lane, 10	Gorse Lane	1903
Back Lane, 13	Hunters Lane	1900s
Back Lane, 6	Baxter Road	1924
Back Lane, 5	Beckford Lane	1924
Back Lane, 6	Borough Road	1900s
Back Lane, 9	Shirland Lane	1800s
Back Lane, 10 (part)	Stephen Hill	1936
Bagshaw Road, 8	Hemsworth Road (part)	1907
Ball Street North, 3	Ball Street (part)	1890
Bank Street, 6	Grouse Street	1872
Bardwell Road, 9	Barrow Road	1886
Bates Street, 9	Ardmore Street	1872
Bathfield Road, 3	Weston Street	1800s
Batley Street, 5	Crabtree Close	1967

Old name	New name	Date
Bawtry Road, 9	Bridport Road	1907
Belmoor Road, 13	Balmoral Road	1924
Belvoir Crescent, 10	Rutland Park	1800s
Berlin Street, 9	Arras Street	1919
Bernard Road 13	Hall Road	1925
Beverley Road, 6	Beulah Road	1903
Bingham Park Avenue, 11	Bingham Park Crescent	1926
Blagden Street, 1	Dene Lane	1872
Blast Lane, 9	Stoke Street	1886
Blucher Street, 9	Mons Street	1919
Bole Hill Lane, 10	Lodge Moor Road (part)	1903
Bole Hill Lane, 8	Cobnar Road	1903
Bow Street, 1	West Street (part)	1926
Bradford's Court, 9	Baltic Lane	1800s
Bradway Bank, 17	Prospect Road	1937
Bridge Street, 9	Cromer Street	1886
Bridge Street, 9	Trent Street	1886
Bright Street, 1	Fitzwilliam Street (part)	1872
Broad Oaks Lane, 11	Broad Elms Lane	1903
Broadfield Park Square, 8	Broadfield Park Avenue	1800s

Brooklands Place, 10	Brooklands Drive	1939
Brook Lane, 5	Batley Street	1886
Brook Lane, 5	Beck Lane	1924
Brook Street, 9	March Street	1886
Brook Street, 9	Luton Street	1886
Broomfield Road, 8	Bromwich Road	1903

Bull Stake, 1	Haymarket	1830s
Burlington Road, 10	Carsick Hill Drive	1967
Burlington Road, 17 (part)	Gilleyfield Avenue	1957
Burns Terrace, 9	Sheffield Road	1912
Burslem Street, 4	Holywell Road (part)	1931
Burton Street, 3	Haddon Street	1886
Bute Street, 10 (part)	Nairn Street	1909

C

Calvert Road, 13	John Calvert Road	1924
Canada Road East, 3	Blythe Street	1890
Carlton Road, 9	Attercliffe Road (part)	1887

Carr Lane, 10	Mayfield Road	1903
Carr Lane, 10	Blakeney Road (part)	1903
Carr Lane, 13	Beaver Hill Road	1924
Carr Lane, 5	Crowther Lane (part)	1924
	and then to Crowder Road	*1926*
Carr Place, 6	Alney Place	1924
Carr Road, 6	Carlby Road	1903
Carr Road, 6	Carrville Road	1924
Cartmell Place, 8	Cartmell Crescent	1930
Cemetery Road, 6	Livesey Street	1872
Cemetery Road, 4	Danville Street	1872
Cemetery Road, 9	Coventry Road	1886
Chantrey Road, 10	Fulwood Road (part)	1886
Chantrey Road, 3	Favell Road	1903
Chapel Lane, 10	Whiteley Lane	1903
Chapel Street, 6	Shipton Street	1872
Chapel Street, 6	Capel Street	1872
Chapel Street, 3	Chatham Street	1886
Chapel Street, 13	Carlin Street	1924
Chapel Street, 9	Colwall Street	1924
Chapel Street, 9	Chapman Street	1903
Chapel Walk, 1	Bethel Walk	1800s
Charles William Street, 6	Cannock Street	1908
Charlotte Street, 1	Mappin Street	1922
Cherry Tree Hill, 11	Cherry Tree Road	1800s
Cherry Tree Road, 8	Cherry Bank Road	1903
Chesterfield Road, 8, *(Abbey Lane to city boundary)*	Meadowhead	1909
Chorley Street, 10	Chorley Road	1907
Church Lane, 10	Chorley Street	1886
	and then to Chorley Road	*1907*
Church Lane, 1	Church Street	1800s
Church Lane, 6	Worrall Road	1903
Church Street, 9	Worksop Road	1886
Clarence Street, 3	Hunt Street	1872
Clark Grove, 10	Clarke Dell	1913
Clarke Road, 8	Underwood Road	1904

Clarke Street, 13	Watch Street	1924
Clay Lane, 9	Maltby Street	1886
Cliffe Street, 6	Otley Street	1886
Clifford Road, 11	Ashford Road	1886
Clifton Road 9	Clifton Street	1800s
Clifton Street, 9	Clevedon Street	1872
Clifton Street, 9	Ripon Street	1886
Clifton Street, 9 (part)	Lynn Place	1918
Clough Road, 13	Medlock Road	1924
Clyde Terrace, 8	Clyde Road	1890s
Coalpit Lane, 1	Cambridge Street	1850s
Coalpit Lane, 6	Aldene Road	1959
Cockshutt Lane, 5	Shirecliffe Road (part)	1935
Coldwell Lane, 1	Well Lane	1872
Coldwell Lane, 4	Upwell Lane	1800s
Common Lane, 11	Little Common Lane	1903
Common Road, 5	Bellhouse Road (part)	1930
Conway Street, 4	Kirk Street	1872
Cookes Lane, 9	Lock House Road	1913
Copse Avenue, 7	Hastings Mount	1934
Copster Road, 9	Coleford Road	1908
Crabtree Lane, 6	Laird Road	1903
Crescent Road, 6	Camborne Road	1924
Cromwell Street North, 6	Burnaby Street	1887
Cross Chapel Street, 3	Swinton Street	1890
Cross George Street, 2	Arley Street	1890
Cross Lane, 6	Morley Road	1887
Cross Lane, 10	Suthard Cross Road	1912
Cross Road, 11	Woodholm Place	1925
Cross Street, 6	Aysgarth Road	1926
Crowther Lane, 5	Crowder Road	1926

D

Dale Street, 11	Summerfield Street	1887
Dark Lane, 10	Northfield Road	1893
Dixon Lane, 5	Bolsover Road	1906
Drayton Place, 11	Thompson Road	1904
Doncaster Road, 9	Sheffield Road	1912
Don Road, 9	Brompton Road	1886
Duke Street, 1	Matilda Street	1872
Duke Street, 3	Dutch Street	1872
Duke Street, 9	Dara Street	1903
Dungworth Road, 6	Stopes Road	?
Dun Street, 9	Dunlop Street	1872
Dyson Lane, 11	Dyson Place	1924

E

East Spital Street, 3	Spital Street (part)	1890

Ebenezer Street, 9	Eben Street	1871
Ecclesall Hall Road, 11	Woodholm Road	1917
Edith Street, 9	Heath Street	1886
Edward Street, 6	Spring Vale Road (part)	1872
Edward Street, 3	Denholm Street	1872
Egerton Street West, 3	Exeter Street	1890
Elizabeth Street, 9	Eccles Street	1903
Ellen Road, 9	Helen Road	1800s
Ellis Street, 6	Elton Street	1872
Elm View, 9	Elm View Road	1900s
Endcliffe View Road, 10	Carsick View Road	1906
Essex Street, 2	Essex Road	1935
Evandale Road, 6	Cotswold Road	1926
Exchange Street, 6	Grammar Street	1872

F

Fairbank Road, 5 (part)	Bishopsholme Road	1921
Fargate, 1 (Leopold Street to Pool Square)	Barkers Pool	1963
Fern Road, 7	Belper Road	1886
Firbeck Road, 6	Farndale Road	1924
Firbeck Road, 8 (part)	Tadcaster Way	1966
Firth Road, 8	Woodseats Road	1903
Fisher Road, 8	Newsham Road	1917
Fitzwilliam Street, 9	Milford Street	1886
Florence Street, 6	Flora Street	1872
Florence Street, 9	Vine Street	1906
Folds Place, 8	Dale View Road	1927
Forge Lane, 1	Shude Lane	1872
Forge Lane, 9	Woodbine Road	1800s
Forres Street, 10	Forres Road	1934
Foster Road, 9	Howden Road	1886
Fowler Street, 6	Findon Street	1903
Fowler Street, 9	Fife Street	1903
Fox Lane, 10	Foxhall Lane	1903
Fox Lane, 6	Rural Lane	1903
Frederick George Street, 6	Cheadle Street	1908
Frederick Street, 9	Beverley Street	1886
Frederick Street, 11	Croydon Street	1886
Freedom Hill, 9	Basford Street	1886
Furnival Street, 1 (part)	Furnival Gate	1964

G

Garden Street, 11	Leverton Street	1872
Garth Road, 6	Garry Road	1903
George Street, 6	Gilpin Street	1872

George Street, 2	New George Street	1872
	Boston Street	1890
George Street, 9	Tipton Street	1886
George Street, 13	Rodman Street	1924
Gin Stables Lane, 2	Stafford Lane	1908
Gladstone Road, 12	Ridgeway Road (part)	1925
Grange Road, 7	Hastings Road	1886
Green Lane, 8	Scarsdale Road	1903

Green Street, 6	Greenhow Street	1872
Green Street, 6	Greenock Street	1903
Grove Street, 6	Grove Square	1872

H

Hagg Lane, 12	Hurlfield Road	1928
Hall Road West, 13	Dodson Drive	1961
Hammerton Street, 9	Ouseburn Street	1926
Hampton Street, 2	Manor Oaks Road (part)	1963
Handley Lane, 3	Handley Street	1889
Hands Lane, 10	Hands Road	1909
Havelock Square, 10	Holberry Close/Gardens	1982
Hawksley Road, 6	Oakland Road (part)	1903
Hawkwell Road, 13	Hannah Road	1964
Hawley Street, 9	Hayland Street	1903
Heeley Road, 2	Gleadless Road	1925

Henry Street, 10	Bangor Street	1886
Henry Street, 13	Hendon Street	1923
Henry Street, 2	Long Henry Street	1800s
High Lane, 11	Ringinglow Road (part)	1917
High Street, 2	Bard Street	1872
High Street, 6	Highton Street	1872
High Street, 4	Upwell Street	1872
High Street, 9	Attercliffe Road (part)	1887
High Street, 13	Haxby Street	1924
High Tinsley Road	Attercliffe Road (part)	1887
Hill Street, 6	Rivelin Street	1872
Hirst Road, 6	Midhurst Road	1924
Holly Lane, 10	Sandygate Road (part)	1903
Holly Lane, 12	Hollybank Road	1924
Hope Street, 13	Harbury Street	1924
Howard Road, 13	Hall Road West	1925
	Dodson Drive	1961
Hukin Lane, 5	Collinson Road	1938
Hurlfield Hill, 12	Gleadless Road (part)	1924
Hutchinson Lane, 10	Greenhouse Lane	1924

I

Intake Lane, 10	Lodge Moor Road (part)	1933
Intake Road, 2	City Road	1898

Ivy Road, 6	Ivanhoe Road	1906

J

James Street, 6	Hessle Road	1904
Jenkin Hill, 11	Hangingwater Road	1901
Jenkinson Street, 9	Jardine Street	1903
Johnson Lane, 9	Janson Street	1872
Johnson Street, 9	Jedburgh Street	1903
John Street, 6	Poplar Street	1886

K

Kidnapper Lane, 8	Lees Hall Avenue	1933
King Street, 6	Martin Street	1872
Kirkby View, 12 (part)	Gleadless Mount	1961
Kitchin Street, 8	Kitchen Street	1800s

L

Lamb Pool Lane, 9	Johnson Lane	1800s
	and then to Janson Street	*1872*
Leven Road, 10	Clarke Drive	1948
Limbrick Lane, 6	Limbrick Road	1898
Linacre Road, 8	Linburn Road	1903
Lister Road, 8	Cliffe Field Road (part)	1926

Little Pond Street, 1	Pond Street (part)	1890
Livingstone Road, 8	Lismore Road	1903
Longley Avenue, 5	Norwood Avenue	1952
Lord Street, 9	Leeds Road	1886
Lower Fawcett Street, 3	Fawcett Street (part)	1890
Lower Graham Road, 10	Graham Road (part)	1890
Lower Montgomery Terrace Road, 6	Montgomery Terrace Road (part)	1890

Lower Oakbrook Road, 11	Oakbrook Road (part)	1890
Lown Street, 9	Swarcliffe Road	1909
Ludlow Street, 4	Petre Street	1926

M

Mackenzie Walk, 11	Cemetery Road	1800s
Main Road, 9	Handsworth Road	1924
Main Road, 12	Mansfield Road (part)	1924
Malthouse Lane, 2	Lenton Street	1886
Malthouse Lane, 9	Merton Lane	1903
Malton Street, 3	Bury Street	1886
Marchwood Close, 6	Marchwood Avenue	1960
Market Place, 10	Marr Terrace	1903
Market Place, 13	Market Square	1924
Market Street, 19	Chapel Street	1800s
Marlborough Road, 6	Marlcliffe Road	1906
Masdin Lane, 3	Marsden Lane	1870s
Masefield Avenue, 13	Masefield Road	1934

Meadow Lane, 11	Whiteley Wood Road	1912
Meadow Street, 9	Mandeville Street	1870s
Meersbrook Bank Road, 8	Meersbrook Avenue	1927
Melbourne Road, 5	Mortlake Road	1903
Miller Road, 6	Milden Road	1904
Mill Lane, 11	Renton Street	1872
Mill Lane, 9	Weedon Street	1886
Milner Road, 8	Millmount Road	1903
Milner Road, 5	Monckton Road	1903
Milner Road, 6	Minto Road	1903
Milton Street, 9	Dundas Road	1912
Milton Street, 9	Jedburgh Drive	1962
Montgomery Road, 6	Burns Road	1872
Moorbrook Road, 10	Moorbank Road	1924
Mount Pleasant Road, 6	Maidstone Road	1924
Mount View Road, 10	Mulehouse Lane (part)	1903
Mulehouse Lane, 10	Mulehouse Road	1903

N

Nelson Road, 6	Farnley Avenue	1924
New Barnsley Road, 4 & 5	Barnsley Road	1800s
New Edward Street, 3	Edward Street (part)	1890
New Endcliffe Vale Road, 10	Riverdale Road	1890
New Fawcett Street, 3	Fawcett Street (part)	1890
New George Street, 2	Boston Street	1890
New Hereford Street, 1	Hereford Street (part)	1890
New Lane, 10	Newent Lane	?
New Machon Bank Road, 7	Moncrieffe Road	1890
New Meadow Street, 3	Meadow Street (part)	1890
New Porter Street, 10	Filey Street	1890
New Queen Street, 1	Queen Street	1890
New Queen Street, 6	Lock Street	1872
New Street, 2	Stepney Street	1886
New Surrey Street, 1	Surrey Street (part)	1890
New Thomas Street, 2	Denby Street	1890
Norfolk Avenue, 2	Norfolk Park Avenue	1930
Norfolk Road North, 2	Douglas Road	1872
North Street, 1	North Church Street	1872
Northumberland Street, 10	Northumberland Road	?
Norton Parkway, 8	Bochum Parkway	1982

Norwich Street West, 2	Norwich Street (part)	1890
Nursery Lane, 3	Gun Lane	1860s

O

Old Haymarket, 1	Haymarket (part)	1890
Olivant Road, 8	Olivet Road	1890s
Orchard Road, 3	Wallace Road	1872
Orchard Street, 3	Apple Street	1872
Orchard Street, 9	Bodmin Street	1886
Osborne Road, 8	Osmaston Road	1903
Owlergreave Road, 9	Prince of Wales Road (part)	1925

P

Palmer Road, 6	Leake Road	1924
Palmerston Road, 11	Chelsea Road	1886
Park Lane, 13	Finchwell Road	1924
Park Lane, 17	Sunnyvale Avenue	1938
Park Road, 6	Wadsley Park Crescent (part)	1937
Pass House Lane, 4	Passhouses Road	1908
Patmore Street, 5	Patmore Road	1926
Paythorne Road, 8	Warminster Road (part)	1935
Peacroft, 1	Solly Street (part)	1898
Pear Street, 3	Plum Lane	1872
Pear Street West, 11	Pear Street (part)	1890
Peats Style, 19	Stone Street	early 1900s
Peel Street, 6	Woodland Street	1872
Petre Street, 3	Bolton Street	1886
Pickering Road, 9	Pickering Street	?
Pinfold Lane, 9	Staniforth Road	1901
Pismire Hill, 5	Bellhouse Road	1902
Plain Street, 2	Donnington Road	1902
Plantation Road, 11	Jarrow Road	1886
Plum Street, 11	Plumpton Street	1872
Pothouse Lane, 9	Coleridge Road	1887
Pothouse Road, 9	Manningham Road	1904
Primrose Hill, 6	Arnold Street	1886
Princess Street, 10	Travis Place	1872

Princess Street, 9	Prestwich Street	1903
Prospect Road, 6	Fulton Road	1872
Prospect Road, 3	Pickering Road	1872
Prospect Road, 10	Redcar Road	1886
Providence Road, 6	Portsea Road	1903
Pudding Lane, 3	King Street	1700s

Q

Queen Anne Street, 6	Drill Square	1910
Queen Street, 9	Cardiff Street	1886
Queen Street, 6	Adelphi Street	1872

R

Railway Street, 13	Driver Street	1924
Richmond Avenue, 10	Antrim Avenue	1925
River Street, 1	River Lane	1872
Robert Street, 3	Robertshaw Street	1872
Roe Wood Lane, 3	Roe Lane	?
Rose Street, 6	Roselle Street	1903
Russell Street, 9	Ross Street	1903

S

St. James Street, 6	King James Street	1872
Sales Row, 9	Sheffield Road (part)	1912
Salisbury Road, 10	Severn Road	1886
Salisbury Road, 6	Winsford Road	1924
School Hill, 9	Bootle Street	1886
School Lane, 3	Scholey Street	1872
School Lane, 10	School Road	1872
School Lane, 3	Brandon Street	1886
School Lane, 11	Bagshot Street	1886
School Lane, 9	Naseby Street	1886
School Lane, 6	Stour Lane	1903
School Lane, 10	Canterbury Avenue	1903
School Lane, 5	Southey Green Road (part)	1924
School Street, 9	Robin Hood Road	1903
Scotter Road, 4	Ellesmere Road	1905
Segrave Road, 2	Seabrook Road	1924
Sharpe Street, 9	Margate Street	1886
Sheaf Street, 2	Shelf Street	1872
Sheaf Street, 2	Gleadless Road	1886
Sheffield Road, 6	Penistone Road North	1924
Sheffield Road, 13	part of Woodhouse Road	1924
Sheffield Road, 2	part of Heeley Road	1925
	and then to Gleadless Road	*1925*
Shelfanger Road, 9	Logan Road	1909
Smithy Road, 12	Main Street	?
Sorby Street, 9	Surbiton Street	1872
Southey Lane, 5	Southey Green Road	1924
South Parade, 1	St Paul's Parade	1901
South Street, 1	The Moor	1922
Speeton Road, 7	Raven Road	1905
Spring Street, 13	Hessey Street	1924
Stafford Street (part), 2	Glencoe Road	1900
Stanley Street, 9	Stanwell Street	1903
Stanhope Road, 8	Leyburn Road	1924
Stanwood Road, 11	Brentwood Road	1906
Station Road, 7	Archer Road (part)	1906
Station Road, 9	Standon Road	1903
Stephen Road, 10	Coppice View	1932
Storth Road, 6	Forbes Road	1924
Strafford Street, 9	Hatherley Road	1912
Stubbin Lane, 13	Stradbroke Road	1924
Suffolk Street, 3	Sudbury Street	1887
Summer Street, 3	Platt Street	1872
Sycamore Street, 6	Compton Street	1886

T

Talbot Road, 13	Tilford Road	1924
Tenter Road, 5	Tenterden Road	1930
Thirlwell Mount, 8	Barton Road	1890s
Thomas Street, 9	Lincoln Street	1886
Thomas Street, 9	Barking Street	1886
Thomas Street, 9	Tansley Street	1903
Thorpe Road, 12	Grassthorpe Road	1924
Thurcroft Road, 8	Tadcaster Road (part)	1931
Tinsley Road, 9	Attercliffe Road (part)	1887
Toad House Lane, 5	Southey Green Road (part)	1924
Tomcross Lane, 3	Brunswick Road	1860s
Townhead Road, 6	Prescott Road	1922
Townwell Street, 8	Well Road	1800s
Trippet's Yard, 1	Aldine Court	1800s
Tuckers Alley, 1	Chapel Walk	1700s
Tudor Street, 3	Thomas Street	1872
Tuxford Road, 6	Eskdale Road	1924

U

Under-the-Water, 3	Bridge Street	1800s
Union Road, 6	Undercliffe Road	1904
Union Street, 2	Ascot Street	1886
Upper Charles Street, 1	Charles Street (part)	1890
Upper Chippinghouse Road, 7	Chippinghouse Road (part)	1890

Old name	New name	Year
Upper Hoyle Street, 3	Hoyle Street (part)	1890
Upper Myrtle Road, 2	Derby Street	1890
Upper Oborne Street, 3	Oborne Street (part)	1890
Upper Ranmoor Road, 10	Ranmoor Road (part)	1890
Upper St. Philips Road, 3	St. Philips Road (part)	1929

V

Old name	New name	Year
Vicarage Road, 6	Vainor Road	1904
Victoria Road, 4	Furnival Road (part)	1872
Victoria Road, 8	Shirebrook Road	1887
Victoria Road, 8	Cavill Road	1900s
Victoria Road, 9	Vauxhall Road	1903
Victoria Road, 17	Queen Victoria Road	1935
Victoria Road, 12	Kirkby View	1953
Victoria Street, 9	Sleaford Street	1886
Victoria Street, 9	Whitwell Street	1903
Virgins Walk, 1	West Parade	?
	and then to St. James Row	?

W

Old name	New name	Year
Walker Lane, 6	Watkin Lane	1872
Walker Street, 6	Watkin Street	1872
Walker Street, 13	Wenlock Street	1924
Walker Street, 13	Bridby Street	1924
Ward Place, 6	Welney Place	1924
Ward Street, 13	John Ward Street	1924
Warner Street, 3	Horton Place	1906
Water Lane, 10	Storth Lane	1886
Water Lane, 6	Coalpit Lane	1904
Water Street, 9	Askern Street	1886
Wentworth Road, 9	Tuxford Road	1906
Wentworth Road, 9	Greasbrough Road	1912
West Bank Place, 10	Durham Road	1890
Westbourne Road East, 10	Southbourne Road	1886
West Grove Square, 3	Dart Square	1890
West John Lane, 1	Bala Street	1890
West John Street, 1	Abney Street	1890
Wharncliffe Road, 6	Matlock Road	1886
Wharncliffe View Road, 6	Overton Road	1906
White House Crescent, 8	Smithywood Crescent	1926
White House Lane, 2	Bramall Lane	1800s

Old name	New name	Year
Wilkinson Road, 8	Warminster Road (part)	1907
Wilson Road, 6	Gresham Road	1886
Wilson Road, 8	Hyde Road	1886
Wilson Road, 6	Winster Road	1903
Woodland Road, 6	Woodland View Road	1907
Wood Lane, 9	Winco Wood Lane	1907
Woodside Road, 9	Woodbury Road	1903
Woodside Road, 9	Ranskill Road	1912
Wood View Terrace, 7	Marriott Lane	1910
	and then to Marriott Road	?
Workhouse Lane, 17	Ash House Lane	1951
Worksop Road, 13	Retford Road	1924
Wostenholm Road, 13	Greengate Road	1927
Writtle Street, 4	Maxwell Way	?

Appendix 2

Books referred to in the text

Addy, S O, *A Glossary of words used in the neighbourhood of Sheffield*, 1891.

Addy, S O, *The Hall of Waltheof*, 1893.

Armitage, Harold, *Chantrey land*, 1910.

Atkin, Ernest, *History of Woodhouse*, unpublished manuscript in Sheffield Central Library Local History Department.

Eastwood, Jonathan, *History of the parish of Ecclesfield*, 1862.

Fairfield, S, *The Streets of London*, 1983.

Ferraby, Heneage, *Ground-work of the history of Handsworth*, 1963.

Hunter, Joseph, *Hallamshire*, revised edition, 1875.

Hunter, Joseph, *South Yorkshire*, 1828.

Jones, Melvyn and Joan, *Sheffield's historic woodlands past and present*, 1985.

Kirk-Smith, H, *A history of Wadsley*, 1957.

Leader, R E, *Reminiscences of old Sheffield, its streets and its people*, 1876.

Le Tall, W J, *Gathered fragments of the past and present history of Handsworth Woodhouse*, 1876.

Pegge, Samuel, *An historical account of Beauchief Abbey*, 1801.

Stainton, J H, *The making of Sheffield*, 1924.

Vine, G R, *The story of old Attercliffe*.

Walton, Mary, *Street names of central Sheffield*, 1977.

Walton, Mary and Mettam, Gerald R, *History of the Parish of St. Peter, Abbeydale*, 1972.

Walton, Mary, *A History of the Parish of Sharrow*, 1968.

Ward, Thomas Asline, *Peeps into the Past*, 1909.

Woodriff, Brian, *Forkmaking and farming at Shiregreen*, 1980.

Woolhouse, Joseph, *Sheffield 150 years ago*, 1926.